PROGRAMMING IN
3 DIMENSIONS

PROGRAMMING IN 3 DIMENSIONS

3-D Graphics, Ray Tracing, and Animation

Christopher D. Watkins and Larry Sharp

Edited by Mark Finlay

M&T Books
A Division of M&T Publishing, Inc.
411 Borel Avenue
San Mateo, CA 94402

© 1992 by M&T Publishing, Inc.

Printed in the United States of America

Limits of Liability and Disclaimer of Warranty
The Author and Publisher of this book have used their best efforts in preparing the book and the programs contained in it. These efforts include the development, research, and testing of the theories and programs to determine their effectiveness.

The Author and Publisher make no warranty of any kind, expressed or implied, with regard to these programs or the documentation contained in this book. The Author and Publisher shall not be liable in any event for incidental or consequential damages in connection with, or arising out of, the furnishing, performance, or use of these programs.

Library of Congress Cataloging-in-Publication Data

Watkins, Christopher.
Programming in 3 dimensions 3-D graphics, ray tracing, and animation / Christopher Watkins and Larry Sharp.
    p.   cm.
Includes bibliographical references and index.
ISBN 1-55851-220-9
1. Computer graphics. 2. C (Computer program language) I. Sharp, Larry. II. Title. III. Title: Programming in three dimensions 3-D graphics, ray tracing, and animation
T385.W377   1992
006.6- -dc20   92-8550
                                                   CIP

Project Editor: Christine de Chutkowski

Trademarks:
All products, names, and services are trademarks or registered trademarks of their respective companies.

Cover Design: Lauren Smith Design

95 94 93 92   4 3 2 1

Contents

VIII

PART III: RAY TRACING

X

PART IV: ANIMATION

PART V: COLOR PROCESSING

CHAPTER 16: REDUCING COLORS

PART VI: APPENDICES

APPENDIX A: MATHEMATICS

Acknowledgements

The outline of this book and the original Turbo Pascal source code were written by Christopher Watkins. Larry Sharp converted the programs to Borland C, and wrote the C animator. The text was written by Christopher Watkins and Larry Sharp, and edited by Christopher Watkins and Mark Finlay.

All of the software in this book was written in C using Borland C++ version 2.0. The software was furnished by Borland International, 1800 Green Hills Road, Scotts Valley, CA 95066.

Computer graphics displays, including the high-resolution 1024x768 pixel and 256-color displays were produced on Powergraph ERGO-VGA boards with 1 megabyte of memory. The boards were funished by Scott Montgomery and Gary Keller of STB Systems, Inc., 1651 N. Glenville, Suite 210, Richardson, Texas 75081.

Some displays were generated on the Ilon VGA. The boards were furnished by Robert Neville of Ilon USA, Inc., 31238 Via Colinas, Suite D, Westlake Village, CA 91362.

Thanks goes to Mark Terrence VandeWettering for the conic-section intersection test routines found in his public domain MTV ray tracer. Thanks also to Stephen Coy for some corrections to the MTV ray tracer intersection test.

And special thanks goes to our families and friends, whose understanding and patience was essential to the writing of this book.

Why This Book is For You

If you watch movies or television, you've probably seen three-dimensional, computer-generated imagery. This book is for people who wish to produce similar images on an inexpensive PC but have been frustrated by a lack of basic programming tools. The programs and libraries in this book will enable you to produce high-quality computer renderings and animation using both common (VGA), and more advanced (SVGA) graphics hardware. The software is modular enough that you should be able to adapt it to a variety of other environments.

- Part I covers the tools needed to handle the vector mathematics and matrix algebra required for computer graphics. The use of these tools is illustrated through sample programs.

- Part II reviews the production of a three-dimensional modeling tool. The creation of animation using this modeling tool is explained.

- Part III discusses the use of a ray tracer, with explanations illustrated with C code in the text. Included is a discussion of conceptual theory on ray tracing for animation and illumination models. Scenes for animation sequences are generated via programs that model physical reality, creating scripts for the ray-tracer to animate objects in a file.

- Part IV covers the animation program. This program takes the animation file created by either the three-dimensional modeler or the ray tracer and animates the scenes stored in it.

- Part V describes the color compression method for a 256 color VGA.

One 1.2Meg 5-1/4" floppy disk contains all of the graphics software referenced in the book. Included on the disk is all of the ray tracing and animation software. Also included on the disk are animation files, as well as some single-frame high-resolution images.

Introduction

Rendering complex, three-dimensional scenes is analogous to producing a movie. As director, you must coordinate the various components: the actors (objects in the environment); the script (defining what the objects will do during an animation); art direction (specifying how the scene will be lit and the look of the various elements); the cameraperson (controlling camera motion, focus, depth of field, and so on); and the assorted supporting roles. All these elements go toward placing the final image on the screen. Using the software in this book, you'll be able to create scenes that depict both startling realism and environments that could exist only in a computer-generated world.

Organization of the Book

The book is divided into five parts, each of which addresses a particular aspect of computer image generation. Each chapter is comprehensive, building on the information in previous chapters to produce more complex imagery.

Part I presents the tools that handle the vector mathematics and matrix algebra required for three-dimensional computer graphics. All the elements that make up a scene are defined in a three-dimensional context. The routines allow manipulation—rotation, scaling, and translation—of those objects. Most of the graphics routines are written to be as device- and compiler-independent as possible. The device-specific calls (to draw a line or plot a point on the screen, for example) are grouped together. Any compiler dependencies are also pointed out.

Part II discusses the three-dimensional modeling tool for creating the objects that populate the computer environment. Objects are built from collections of three-dimensional polygonal facets. For example, a cube can be defined by the six polygons (squares) describing each face. These objects can be grouped together to make a more complex object, similar to constructing a building from building blocks. Several objects may then be placed into a scene to define the whole environment, as buildings of differing sizes and shapes can be combined to form a city. The modeling

program renders these scenes using a simplified lighting model. Its speed gives it an advantage over the ray-tracing rendering approach described in Part III. The modeling program provides an animation script generator utility that defines a fly-over camera path to produce a file-based animation sequence (like those found in commercial animation software). In addition to scripted camera motion, the utility lets you translate, scale, or rotate any of the objects during the fly-over to allow for additional motion in the scene. The animator program (presented in Part V) can load this file to play the final animation sequence.

Part III discusses the photorealistic scene-rendering program. This program uses a technique known as *ray tracing* to model the interaction of light with the objects in the scene. Unlike other rendering techniques, ray tracing provides a straightforward way of handling reflective surfaces (including refraction), surface textures, and inter/intra-object reflections. Conceptual theory on ray tracing for animation and on illumination models is provided. Explanations are enhanced by C code in the text. Scenes for animation sequences are generated via programs that model physical reality, creating scripts for the ray tracer. Animation of the ray-traced scenes is similar to the modeled scenes in that it is file-based.

Part IV covers the animation program, which takes an animation file created by either the three-dimensional modeler or the ray tracer and animates (plays back) the scenes stored in it. The program controls the rate and direction of animation and allows smooth, repeated motion by continually cycling a sequence.

Part V describes a histogram (an array that stores counts of occurences of a certain color in an image) method for reducing the 32,768 colors computed by the modeler and ray tracer to the 256 available VGA colors. You'll find specific information on the graphics cards in this section.

The following are more detailed descriptions of each chapter.

The Mathematics Module

Chapter 1 describes the header files for the mathematics and graphics modules discussed in Chapters 2 and 3. These files and modules are the foundation for all the software in this book. Variable types and global data used by the mathematics and graphics modules are found here.

Chapter 2 describes the mathematical functions commonly required for computer graphics. These functions, which are at the heart of most of the programs in this book, provide for straightforward manipulation of three-dimensional objects and their environment. All mathematical operations on three-dimensional vectors and matrices are handled here. Transformations—including translation (moving a point in space), scaling (changing the length of a vector), and rotation (rotating a point around a coordinate axis)—are represented as matrix operations. One of the nicest features of these types of transformations is that any combination of them may be expressed as a single transformation. This is a compact, efficient way to express the motion of an object or camera and model light sources.

The Graphics Interface Module

Chapter 3 contains a number of useful graphics routines required for the software in this book. Basic plotting, color-palette manipulation, circle and line generation, and graphics-mode selection are all included here. This chapter describes three-dimensional theory, orthographic versus perspective projection of three-dimensional points onto the two-dimensional screen, and coordinate system conversions.

How To Use the Modules

Chapter 4 is where the fun begins. Here you'll learn how to use the tools developed in the first three chapters. The first eight color plates in the center of this book will give you an idea of the types of images you can create: fractal iterated function systems, such as the familiar Sierpinski triangle (Plate 1), a tetrahedron (Plate 2), and a very abstract IFS in which you can see landscapes and firelike images; puffy white clouds moving across a deep blue sky (Plate 4), eerie fluorescent plasmas crawling around your screen, and wicked electrical discharges, all generated by a recursive cloud and plasma generator; a simulation of three particles orbiting in three-dimensional space (Plate 5); plantlike objects output from a recursive plant- and tree-generator program; and the computer world of cellular automata that lives by certain "rules" from one generation to the next.

Modeling Theory and Database Structure

Chapter 5 takes us into Part II, where the three-dimensional modeling tool is discussed. A method for faster computation (real numbers are converted to integers) is given. At the end of the chapter, you'll manually enter the data for an object to get a feel for how an actual database is constructed.

Adding Objects to a Scene

Chapter 6 explains how objects are added to the environment to create a scene. Objects are defined by their size, orientation, and position in three-dimensional space. They are also given material characteristics and parameters that indicate their surface and whether they are reflected (drawn as if mirror-image objects were positioned off-screen).

Sorting and Displaying Objects

Chapter 7 brings us to the topic of sorting objects for a particular view. The renderer must decide which objects are nearer to the camera and hence obscure objects that are further away. Hidden surface removal, in which parts of an object that are off-screen or facing away from the camera need not be drawn, is discussed, as is the problem of reflected objects. Display routines that sort the objects and then render them in solid format are included; these routines handle both actual objects and their reflections.

Creating Animation with the Modeling Program

Chapter 8 brings together everything discussed so far by describing the main three-dimensional modeling program. The program loads a file that defines how the scene should look, including object location, orientation, and size; light source; and camera position. A simple illumination model determines how each object facet should be colored based on its orientation with respect to a single light source. The direction each facet is facing is computed and used in the illumination calculation and a facet visibility test. Once designated as visible, the facet is projected onto the screen and a polygon facet-fill routine called to draw the polygon and any of its reflections.

The final computed image is written to a temporary file of screens using a full 32,768-color palette. The display of individual images and animated sequences is controlled by the animation program presented in Part IV.

Creating Object Databases

Chapter 9 shows how to create objects for the modeling program to load and display. These objects are constructed using polygonal facets (planar surfaces such as those found on a cut gemstone), which are in turn defined by vertices (points defining the corners of the facet). Programs are supplied that use trigonometry and geometry to generate cones, pyramids, cylinders, spheres, tori, grids, and solids of revolution. This chapter also describes how collections of these objects may be assembled to produce more complex objects.

Creating Scenes and Animation Sequences with the 3-D Modeler

Chapter 10 describes an animation script file generator that defines the motions of all the objects in the scene as well as camera motion. This chapter also describes how to generate single images.

Ray-Tracing Theory and Database Structure

Chapter 11 takes us into Part III, where ray tracing and animation of ray-traced images are discussed. Ray-tracing theory and the basic ray-tracing algorithm are discussed here, along with shadows, light sources, recursion for reflection and refraction of rays, perspective, and texturing. You'll learn how single- and multiframe animation is produced and the VGA issues involved. The final conversion of the file of screens into a suitable animation sequence is described here.

Creating Animation with the Ray-Tracing Program

The theory from Chapter 11 is implemented in Chapter 12, which discusses the actual ray-tracing program. We'll trace a ray from the camera through the environment to see how the object and lighting interact.

Creating Scenes and Animation Sequences with the Ray Tracer

In Chapter 13 we produce programs that generate the .RT files, which the ray tracer uses to create animation and single-frame, high-resolution renderings. Some examples are shown in the color plates: bouncing orbs (Plates 13 and 14), a spinning DNA molecule (Plate 15), a four-cylinder engine and cam (Plate 16), Newton's cradle (Plate 17), planetary orbits (Plate 18), a walking robot (Plate 19), a spinning mechanical part (Plate 20), and a windswept ocean (Plate 21).

All the single-frame renderings can be seen in the plates as well: dice and an ace of spades (Plate 22), a cannon (Plate 23), a moon-illuminated desert pyramid scene (Plate 24), the M&T Publishing logo (Plate 25), a fractal mountain scene (Plate 26), an office desk scene (Plate 27), a wooden piano on a marble floor (Plate 28), a pool-table scene (Plate 29), a "tetrahedron of tetrahedrons" scene (Plate 30), a tetrahedron of spheres (Plate 31), and partially transparent objects (Plate 32).

Animation Theory

Chapter 14 takes us into Part IV, where animation is the focus. The animator takes a finished sequence of frames and, like a movie projector, displays them in a repetitive, timed manner. This chapter presents general animation techniques, such as color cycling and page flipping, to accomplish this with the PC. Techniques such as motion blur and image filtering are presented to combat this problem.

Operation of the Animator

Chapter 15 walks you through the *ANIMATE.C* animation program, explaining how an animation file of screens is loaded. Special features like frame rate control, animation direction control, and vertical image flip are presented.

Histogram Least-Squares Color Reduction

Chapter 16 bring us into Part V and color processing. This is where the 32,768 colors calculated by the rendering programs are reduced to the 256 VGA/SVGA-displayable colors. A color histogram of the colors is created; the most commonly used colors are kept, while the least used are discarded. This chapter also presents information about the STB ERGO PowerGraph VGA and Ilon VGA graphics cards.

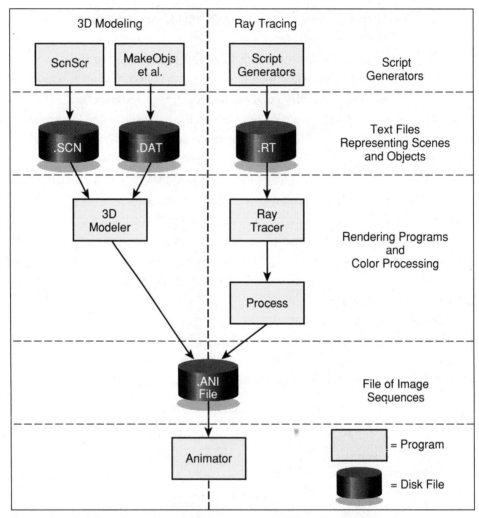

Figure I-1. An Overview of How the Programs and Files Work Together

Hardware and Software Required

This book assumes a basic working knowledge of the C programming language, particularly the use of defined types (*TypeDefs*), structures, and pointers.

The software for this book was developed using the C compiler in Borland C++ 2.0 using standard C conventions so that it can be ported easily to other compilers

and machines. With minor modifications, you should be able to compile it with Microsoft C or the Turbo C++ compiler.

If you're using an earlier version of C, consider switching to Borland C++. Borland International's upgrade policy lets you get the latest version at a reduced price. This compiler is especially good for beginning C programmers.

All the software on the program disks and in the book should run on any IBM PC or compatible that has a VGA card and monitor or better. Graphics modes 19 (320x200x256) and 56 (1024x768x256) are used here. This book uses the STB System PowerGraph ERGO VGA and the Ilon VGA, both of which can handle the super VGA 1024x768, 256-color mode and use the Tseng 4000 chip. Since techniques for driving SVGA cards have not been standardized, the drivers in this book are guaranteed to drive these graphics cards (and probably most other graphics cards using the Tseng 4000 chip). If you can obtain the necessary addressing and port information from your graphics card manufacturer, you can easily adapt the drivers in this book to your card.

The software will run on any IBM PC or compatible, but the faster the machine the better. These programs are compute-intensive; a 286 or 386 with a math coprocessor or a 486 is suggested to generate the animations and single-frame renderings in a reasonable amount of time.

UNIVERSAL ROUTINES

Introduction to the Modules

We begin our discussion of computer graphics and animation with a review of the basic software tools required. These tools include routines that perform common mathematical functions and provide the interface between the graphics software, like the ray tracer and three-dimensional modeler, and your computer's graphics hardware. This chapter describes the header files required for proper operation of these mathematical and graphical units. The header files contain variable types and global variables used by the mathematics and graphics modules in Chapters 2 and 3. There, you'll learn how the various functions in the modules work and why they're important to computer graphics. Chapter 4 will tie it all together by taking you through sample programs that use many of the functions found in the modules.

Now let's examine the header files.

The Header Files

The header files—*Defs.H*, *Globals.H*, *MathB.H*, and *GraphB.H*—contain a variety of variable types and global data used by the mathematics and graphics interface modules. None of the other modules in this book will compile correctly without these files; though short, they contain crucial data that allows the modules to be compiled and linked in separately.

Defs.H

The *Defs.H* header file (Listing 1-1) contains constant definitions (#defines) and redeclared variable types.

```
/*

┌─────────────────────────────────────────────────────────┐
│                                                           │
│                   Defs.H Header File                      │
│             Written by Christopher D. Watkins             │
│              'C' Conversion by Larry Sharp                │
│                                                           │
└─────────────────────────────────────────────────────────┘

*/


typedef unsigned char          Byte;

typedef unsigned int           Word;

typedef unsigned long          DWord;

typedef enum {false, true}     Boolean;


typedef struct
{
      Byte Red;
      Byte Grn;
      Byte Blu;
}     RGB;

typedef RGB      Palette_Register[256];

typedef float    TDA[3];

typedef int      TDIA[3];

typedef float    FDA[4];

typedef float    Matx4x4[4][4];


#define MaxCol 7
#define MaxInten 35

#define Ln10            2.30258509299405E+000
```

```
#define OneOverLn10    0.43429448190325E+000
#define Pi             3.1415927
#define PiOver180      1.74532925199433E-002
#define PiUnder180     5.72957795130823E+001
```

Listing 1-1. *Defs.H* **Header File.**

Several variable types have been redefined to make them easier to recognize and understand. For instance, an *unsigned char* is now called a *Byte*, and an *unsigned int* is now a *Word* (these are the most commonly used names for each variable type). The # defined constants are used by the mathematics and graphics interface modules; an example is the irrational number *pi* (π).

Globals.H

The *Globals.H* header file (Listing 1-2) defines the global variables for the mathematics and graphics interface modules. These variables, which are accessed by the modules and main program code, pertain primarily to image resolution and the three-dimensional graphics routines.

```
/*

            Globals.H Header File
        Written by Christopher D. Watkins
          'C' Conversion by Larry Sharp

*/

int       XRes, YRes;
Word      MaxXRes, MaxYRes;
Word      MaxX, MaxY;
float     Asp;
Boolean   PerspectivePlot;
float     Mx, My, Mz, ds;
Boolean   Draw_Axis_And_Palette;
int       Angl, Tilt;
```

Listing 1-2. *Globals.H* **Header File.**

MathB.H

The *MathB.H* header file (Listing 1-3) contains all of the function prototypes for the mathematical functions defined in the mathematics module. Function prototypes are a feature of ANSI standard C that specify the names of the functions found in the mathematics module, along with their arguments. These prototypes make a great table of commands because all the functions in the module are listed.

```
/*

            MathB.H Header File
            Prototypes for MathB.C
       Written by Christopher D. Watkins
        'C' Conversion by Larry Sharp

*/


extern int      Round(double x);
extern float    Frac(double x);
extern int      Trunc(double x);
extern float    SqrFP(float x);
extern int      Sqr(int x);
extern float    Radians(float Angle);
extern float    Degrees(float Angle);
extern float    CosD(float Angle);
extern float    SinD(float Angle);
extern float    Power(float Base, int Exponent);
extern float    Log(float x);
extern float    Exp10(float x);
extern float    Sign(float x);
extern int      IntSign(int x);
extern int      IntSqrt(int x);
extern int      IntPower(int Base, int Exponent);
extern float    MIN(float a, float b);
extern float    MAX(float a, float b);
extern float    MIN3(float a, float b, float c);
extern float    MAX3(float a, float b, float c);
```

```
extern float    MIN4(float a, float b, float c, float d);
extern float    MAX4(float a, float b, float c, float d);
extern void     Vec(float r, float s, float t, TDA A);
extern void     VecInt(int r, int s, int t, TDIA A);
extern void     UnVec(TDA A, float *r, float *s, float *t);
extern void     UnVecInt(TDIA A, int *r, int *s, int *t);
extern float    VecDot(TDA A, TDA B);
extern void     VecCross(TDA A, TDA B, TDA C);
extern float    VecLen(TDA A);
extern void     VecNormalize(TDA A);
extern void     VecMatxMult(FDA A, Matx4x4 Matrix, FDA B);
extern void     VecSub(TDA A, TDA B, TDA C);
extern void     VecSubInt(TDIA A, TDIA B, TDA C);
extern void     VecAdd(TDA A, TDA B, TDA C);
extern void     VecAdd3(TDA A, TDA B, TDA C, TDA D);
extern void     VecCopy(TDA A, TDA B);
extern void     VecCopyInt(TDIA A, TDIA B);
extern void     VecLinComb(float r, TDA A, float s, TDA B, TDA C);
extern void     VecScalMult(float r, TDA A, TDA B);
extern void     VecScalMultI(float r, TDIA A, TDA B);
extern void     VecScalMultInt(float r, TDA A, TDIA B);
extern void     VecAddScalMult(float r, TDA A, TDA B, TDA C);
extern void     VecNull(TDA A);
extern void     VecNullInt(TDIA A);
extern void     VecElemMult(float r, TDA A, TDA B, TDA C);
extern void     VecNegate(TDA A);
extern void     VecMin(TDA a, TDA b, TDA c);
extern void     VecMax(TDA a, TDA b, TDA c);
extern void     VecNegate(TDA A);
extern void     ZeroMatrix(Matx4x4 A);
extern void     Translate3D(float tx, float ty, float tz,
                    Matx4x4 A);
extern void     Scale3D(float sx, float sy, float sz, Matx4x4 A);
extern void     Rotate3D(int m, float Theta, Matx4x4 A);
extern void     Multiply3DMatrices(Matx4x4 A, Matx4x4 B,
                    Matx4x4 C);
extern void     MatCopy(Matx4x4 a, Matx4x4 b);
extern void     PrepareMatrix(float Tx, float Ty, float Tz,
                              float Sx, float Sy, float Sz,
                              float Rx, float Ry, float Rz,
```

```
                             Matx4x4 XForm);
extern void     PrepareInvMatrix(float Tx, float Ty, float Tz,
                             float Sx, float Sy, float Sz,
                             float Rx, float Ry, float Rz,
                             Matx4x4 XForm);
extern void     Transform(TDA A, Matx4x4 M, TDA B);
extern void     InitRand(float Seed);
extern int      RandInt(Word Range);
extern float    Rand();
```

Listing 1-3. *MathB.H* Header File.

GraphB.H

The *GraphB.H* header file (Listing 1-4) contains prototypes of the functions found in the graphics interface module. As in *MathB.H*, these prototypes specify the functions found in that module and the arguments they require.

Compiling the Modules

Now that we've looked briefly at the header files for the modules, let's see how the modules are compiled using those files. Header files allow you to compile and link the modules separately. You link your other graphics software with the already compiled mathematics and graphics modules, thereby reducing the total compilation time.

```
/*

        GraphB.H Header File
        Prototypes for GraphB.C
     Written by Christopher D. Watkins
      'C' Conversion by Larry Sharp

*/

extern int      XRes, YRes;
extern Word     MaxXRes, MaxYRes;
extern Word     MaxX, MaxY;
extern float    Asp;
```

```
extern Boolean    PerspectivePlot;
extern float      Mx, My, Mz, ds;
extern int        Angl, Tilt;
extern Boolean    Draw_Axis_And_Palette;

extern void       Set_Mode(int Mode);
extern void       Pre_Calc();
extern void       Plot(Word x, Word y, Byte color);
extern void       Set_Palette(Palette_Register Hue);
extern void       Init_Palette(Palette_Register Color);
extern void       Init_Palette_2(Palette_Register Color);
extern void       Cycle_Palette(Palette_Register Hue);
extern void       Swap(int *first, int *second);
extern void       Circle(Word x, Word y, Word radius, Byte color);
extern void       Draw(int xx1, int yy1, int xx2, int yy2, Byte color);
extern void       Init_Graphics();
extern void       Set_Graphics_Mode(Word xRes, Word yRes);
extern void       Wait_For_Key();
extern void       Exit_Graphics();
extern void       Title();
extern void       Init_Plotting(int Ang, int Tlt);
extern void       Init_Perspective(Boolean Perspective, float x,
                      float y, float z, float m);
extern void       Map_Coordinates(float X, float Y, float Z,
                      int *Xp, int *Yp);
extern void       Cartesian_Plot_3D(float X, float Y, float Z,
                      Byte Color);
extern void       Cylindrical_Plot_3D(float Rho, float Theta, float Z,
                      Byte Color);
extern void       Spherical_Plot_3D(float R, float Theta,
                      float Phi, Byte Color);
extern void       Draw_Line_3D(TDA Pnt1, TDA Pnt2, Byte Color);
extern void       Put_Pixel(int x, int y, Byte Color, Byte Intensity);
extern Byte       Get_Pixel(Word x, Word y);
extern Byte       Get_Pixel_2(Word x, Word y);
extern void       Put_Axis_And_Palette(Boolean PlaceOnScreen);
```

```
extern void    Display_Axis();
extern void    Display_Palette();
extern void    Axis_And_Palette();
```

Listing 1-4. *GraphB.H* **Header File.**

For these modules to compile, all the header files must be present in your working directory. If any are missing, an error will occur during compilation. The best way to use this software is to set up Turbo C/C++ project files (or *make* files, if you're using a different compiler).

The first step is to compile first the modules, then your graphics program (or one of the programs presented later in this book). You then simply link in the produced object file (one with an .OBJ extension, for most compilers) with the program-specific code. To compile the modules using a Borland compiler, you load each module into the editor separately and press **Alt-C C** for each. Next, press **Alt-P** in the Borland editor. When you're asked for the name of the project file, type in the program name (like "EXAMPLE"). Now press **Alt-A** and add the appropriate .OBJ files (the ones you just compiled) to the project list. When they're all entered, you can link the .OBJ files together by typing **Alt-C L**. Remember, all this software must be compiled using the large memory model.

CHAPTER 2

The Mathematics Module

Before we dive into the production of images and animation, we must familiarize ourselves with the various program support modules. These modules form the basis for most of the graphics programs in this book. This chapter describes the mathematics module in the file *Math.C* (Listing 2-1). Most of the functions in this module are used to manipulate two- and three-dimensional vectors using the basic techniques of linear algebra. (Vectors describe the geometry of the three-dimensional world, including the position and orientation of the objects, viewer, and light sources.) The routines described here provide an efficient, eloquent means of manipulating vectors to perform operations such as rotation, scaling, and translation of objects and light-intensity calculations.

```
/*

  ┌─────────────────────────────────────────────────┐
  │                    MathB.C                       │
  │            Mathematical Functions                │
  │        Written by Christopher D. Watkins         │
  │          'C' Conversion by Larry Sharp           │
  └─────────────────────────────────────────────────┘


  Radians    - convert degrees to radians
  Degrees    - convert radians to degrees
  CosD       - cosine in degrees
  SinD       - sine in degrees
  Power      - power a^n
  Log        - log base 10
  Exp10      - exp base 10
  Sign       - negative=-1 positive=1 null=0
  IntSign    - negative=-1 positive=1 null=0
```

```
     IntSqrt    - integer square root
     IntPower   - integer power a^n
*/

#include "stdio.h"
#include "math.h"
#include "defs.h"
#include "mathb.h"

int Round(float x)
{
   return((int)(x+0.5));
}

int Trunc(float x)
{
   return((int)(x));
}

float Frac(float x)
{
   int y;

   y=((int)(x));
   return(x-(float)y);
}

float SqrFP(float x)
{
   return(x*x);
}

int Sqr(int x)
{
   return(x*x);
}

float Radians(float Angle)
{
   return(Angle*PiOver180);
```

```
}

float Degrees(float Angle)
{
   return(Angle*PiUnder180);
}

float CosD(float Angle)
{
   return(cos(Radians(Angle)));
}

float SinD(float Angle)
{
   return(sin(Radians(Angle)));
}

float Power(float Base, int Exponent)
{
   float BPower;
   int t;

   if(Exponent==0)
        return(1);
   else
   {
     BPower=1.0;
     for(t=1; t<=Exponent; t++)
     {
        BPower*=Base;
     }
     return(BPower);
   }
}

float Log(float x)
{
   return(log(x)*OneOverLn10);
}

float Exp10(float x)
{
```

```
   return(exp(x*Ln10));
}

float Sign(float x)
{
   if(x<0)
      return(-1);
   else
   {
      if(x>0)
         return(1);
      else
      {
         return(0);
      }
   }
}

int IntSign(int x)
{
   if(x<0)
      return(-1);
   else
   {
      if(x>0)
         return(1);
      else
      {
         return(0);
      }
   }
}

int IntSqrt(int x)
{
   int OddInt, OldArg, FirstSqrt;

   OddInt=1;
   OldArg=x;
   while(x>=0)
```

```
    {
      x-=OddInt;
      OddInt+=2;
    }
    FirstSqrt=OddInt >> 1;
    if(Sqr(FirstSqrt)-FirstSqrt+1 > OldArg)
      return(FirstSqrt-1);
    else
      return(FirstSqrt);
}

int IntPower(int Base, int Exponent)
{
    if(Exponent==0)
      return(1);
    else
      return(Base*IntPower(Base, Exponent-1));
}

float MIN(float a, float b)
{
    if(a<b)
      return(a);
    else
      return(b);
}

float MAX(float a, float b)
{
    if(a>b)
      return(a);
    else
      return(b);
}

float MIN3(float a, float b, float c)
{
    float t;

    t=MIN(a, b);
    return(MIN(t, c));
```

```
}

float MAX3(float a, float b, float c)
{
   float t;

   t=MAX(a, b);
   return(MAX(t, c));
}

float MIN4(float a, float b, float c, float d)
{
   float t;

   t=MIN3(a, b, c);
   return(MIN(t, d));
}

float MAX4(float a, float b, float c, float d)
{
   float t;

   t=MAX3(a, b, c);
   return(MAX(t, d));
}


/*
```

┌───┐
│   │
│   Vector and Matrix Routines   │
│   │
└───┘

```
     Vec            - Make Vector
     VecInt         - Make Integer Vector
     UnVec          - Get Components of Vector
     UnVecInt       - Get Components of Integer Vector
     VecDot         - Vector Dot Product
     VecCross       - Vector Cross-Product
     VecLen         - Vector Length
     VecNormalize   - Vector Normalize
```

```
       VecMatxMult      - Vector Matrix Multiply
       VecSub           - Vector Subtraction
       VecSub           - Vector Subtraction Integer
       VecAdd           - Vector Addition
       VecAdd3          - Vector Addition
       VecCopy          - Vector Copy
       VecLinComb       - Vector Linear Combination
       VecScalMult      - Vector Scalar Multiple
       VecScalMultI     - Vector Scalar Multiple
       VecScalMultInt   - Vector Scalar Multiple and Rounding
       VecAddScalMult   - Vector Add Scalar Multiple
       VecNull          - Vector Null
       VecNullInt       - Vector Null Integer
       VecElemMult      - Vector Element Multiply
*/

void Vec(float r, float s, float t, TDA A)
{
  A[0]=r;
  A[1]=s;
  A[2]=t;
}

void VecInt(int r, int s, int t, TDIA A)
{
  A[0]=r;
  A[1]=s;
  A[2]=t;
}

void UnVec(TDA A, float *r, float *s, float *t)
{
  *r=A[0];
  *s=A[1];
  *t=A[2];
}

void UnVecInt(TDIA A, int *r, int *s, int *t)
{
  *r=A[0];
  *s=A[1];
```

```
  *t=A[2];
}

float VecDot(TDA A, TDA B)
{
   return(A[0]*B[0] + A[1]*B[1] + A[2]*B[2]);
}

void VecCross(TDA A, TDA B, TDA C)
{
  C[0]=A[1]*B[2] - A[2]*B[1];
  C[1]=A[2]*B[0] - A[0]*B[2];
  C[2]=A[0]*B[1] - A[1]*B[0];
}

float VecLen(TDA A)
{
   return(sqrt(SqrFP(A[0])+SqrFP(A[1])+SqrFP(A[2])));
}

void VecNormalize(TDA A)
{
   float dist,invdist;

   dist=VecLen(A);
   if(!(dist==0.0))
   {
     invdist=1.0/dist;
     A[0]*=invdist;
     A[1]*=invdist;
     A[2]*=invdist;
   }
   else
   {
     puts("Zero-Length Vectors cannot be Normalized");
     exit(1);
   }
}

void VecMatxMult(FDA A, Matx4x4 Matrix, FDA B)
{
```

```
    int mRow, mCol;

    for(mCol=0; mCol<4; mCol++)
    {
      B[mCol]=0;
      for(mRow=0; mRow<4; mRow++)
        B[mCol]+=A[mRow]*Matrix[mRow][mCol];
    }
}

void VecSub(TDA A, TDA B, TDA C)
{
  C[0]=A[0]-B[0];
  C[1]=A[1]-B[1];
  C[2]=A[2]-B[2];
}

void VecSubInt(TDIA A, TDIA B, TDA C)
{
  C[0]=(float)(A[0]-B[0]);
  C[1]=(float)(A[1]-B[1]);
  C[2]=(float)(A[2]-B[2]);
}

void VecAdd(TDA A, TDA B, TDA C)
{
  C[0]=A[0]+B[0];
  C[1]=A[1]+B[1];
  C[2]=A[2]+B[2];
}

void VecAdd3(TDA A, TDA B, TDA C, TDA D)
{
  D[0]=A[0]+B[0]+C[0];
  D[1]=A[1]+B[1]+C[1];
  D[2]=A[2]+B[2]+C[2];
}

void VecCopy(TDA A, TDA B)
{
  B[0]=0.0+A[0];
```

```
    B[1]=0.0+A[1];
    B[2]=0.0+A[2];
}


void VecCopyInt(TDIA A, TDIA B)
{
   B[0]=A[0];
   B[1]=A[1];
   B[2]=A[2];
}


void VecLinComb(float r, TDA A, float s, TDA B, TDA C)
{
   C[0]=r*A[0]+s*B[0];
   C[1]=r*A[1]+s*B[1];
   C[2]=r*A[2]+s*B[2];
}


void VecScalMult(float r, TDA A, TDA B)
{
   B[0]=r*A[0];
   B[1]=r*A[1];
   B[2]=r*A[2];
}


void VecScalMultI(float r, TDIA A, TDA B)
{
   B[0]=r*(float)A[0];
   B[1]=r*(float)A[1];
   B[2]=r*(float)A[2];
}


void VecScalMultInt(float r, TDA A, TDIA B)
{
   B[0]=Round(r*A[0]);
   B[1]=Round(r*A[1]);
   B[2]=Round(r*A[2]);
}


void VecAddScalMult(float r, TDA A, TDA B, TDA C)
```

```
{
  C[0]=r*A[0]+B[0];
  C[1]=r*A[1]+B[1];
  C[2]=r*A[2]+B[2];
}

void VecNull(TDA A)
{
  A[0]=0.0;
  A[1]=0.0;
  A[2]=0.0;
}

void VecNullInt(TDIA A)
{
  A[0]=0;
  A[1]=0;
  A[2]=0;
}

void VecElemMult(float r, TDA A, TDA B, TDA C)
{
  C[0]=r*A[0]*B[0];
  C[1]=r*A[1]*B[1];
  C[2]=r*A[2]*B[2];
}

void VecMin(TDA a, TDA b, TDA c)
{
    if(a[0]<b[0])
      c[0]=a[0];
    else
      c[0]=b[0];
    if(a[1]<b[1])
      c[1]=a[1];
    else
      c[1]=b[1];
    if(a[2]<b[2])
      c[2]=a[2];
    else
```

```
        c[2]=b[2];
}

void VecMax(TDA a, TDA b, TDA c)
{
    if(a[0]>b[0])
      c[0]=a[0];
    else
      c[0]=b[0];
    if(a[1]>b[1])
      c[1]=a[1];
    else
      c[1]=b[1];
    if(a[2]>b[2])
      c[2]=a[2];
    else
      c[2]=b[2];
}

void VecNegate(TDA A)
{
  A[0]=-A[0];
  A[1]=-A[1];
  A[2]=-A[2];
}

/*
```

```
┌────────────────────────────────────────────────────────┐
│ ┌──────────────────────────────────────────────────────┐ │
│ │          Affine Transformation Routines              │ │
│ └──────────────────────────────────────────────────────┘ │
└────────────────────────────────────────────────────────┘
```

```
    ZeroMatrix           - zero the elements of a 4x4 matrix
    Translate3D          - make translation matrix
    Scale3D              - make scaling matrix
    Rotate3D             - make rotation matrix
    ZeroAllMatrices      - zero all matrices used in
                           transformation
    Multiply3DMatrices   - multiply two 4x4 matrices
    PrepareMatrix        - prepare the transformation matrix
      (Tm=S*R*T)
```

```
    PrepareInvMatrix      - prepare the inverse transformation
                            matrix
    Transform             - multipy a vertex by the transformation
                            matrix
*/

void ZeroMatrix(Matx4x4 A)
{
   int i, j;

   for(i=0; i<4; i++)
   {
     for(j=0; j<4; j++)
       A[i][j]=0.0;
   }
}

void Translate3D(float tx, float ty, float tz, Matx4x4 A)   {
   int i;

   ZeroMatrix(A);
   for(i=0; i<4; i++)
     A[i][i]=1.0;
   A[0][3]=-tx;
   A[1][3]=-ty;
   A[2][3]=-tz;
}

void Scale3D(float sx, float sy, float sz, Matx4x4 A)
{
   ZeroMatrix(A);
   A[0][0]=sx;
   A[1][1]=sy;
   A[2][2]=sz;
   A[3][3]=1.0;
}

void Rotate3D(int m, float Theta, Matx4x4 A)
{
   int m1, m2;
   float c, s;
```

```
    ZeroMatrix(A);
    A[m-1][m-1]=1.0;
    A[3][3]=1.0;
    m1=(m % 3)+1;
    m2=(m1 % 3);
    m1-=1;
    c=CosD(Theta);
    s=SinD(Theta);
    A[m1][m1]=c;
    A[m1][m2]=s;
    A[m2][m2]=c;
    A[m2][m1]=-s;
}

void Multiply3DMatrices(Matx4x4 A, Matx4x4 B, Matx4x4 C)
{

    int i, j, k;
    float ab;

    for(i=0; i<4; i++)
    {
      for(j=0; j<4; j++)
      {
        ab=0;
        for(k=0; k<4; k++) ab=A[i][k]*B[k][j];
        C[i][j]=ab;
      }
    }
}

void MatCopy(Matx4x4 a, Matx4x4 b)
{
  Byte i, j;

  for(i=0; i<4; i++)
  {
    for(j=0; j<4; j++)
      b[i][j]=a[i][j];
  }
}
```

```
void PrepareMatrix(float Tx, float Ty, float Tz,
          float Sx, float Sy, float Sz,
          float Rx, float Ry, float Rz,
          Matx4x4 XForm)
{
   Matx4x4 M1, M2, M3, M4, M5, M6, M7, M8, M9;

   Scale3D(Sx, Sy, Sz, M1);
   Rotate3D(1, Rx, M2);
   Rotate3D(2, Ry, M3);
   Rotate3D(3, Rz, M4);
   Translate3D(Tx, Ty, Tz, M5);
   Multiply3DMatrices(M2, M1, M6);
   Multiply3DMatrices(M3, M6, M7);
   Multiply3DMatrices(M4, M7, M8);
   Multiply3DMatrices(M5, M8, M9);
   MatCopy(M9, XForm);
}

void PrepareInvMatrix(float Tx, float Ty, float Tz,
        float Sx, float Sy, float Sz,
        float Rx, float Ry, float Rz,
        Matx4x4 XForm)
{
   Matx4x4 M1, M2, M3, M4, M5, M6, M7, M8, M9;

   Scale3D(Sx, Sy, Sz, M1);
   Rotate3D(1, Rx, M2);
   Rotate3D(2, Ry, M3);
   Rotate3D(3, Rz, M4);
   Translate3D(Tx, Ty, Tz, M5);
   Multiply3DMatrices(M4, M5, M6);
   Multiply3DMatrices(M3, M6, M7);
   Multiply3DMatrices(M2, M7, M8);
   Multiply3DMatrices(M1, M8, M9);
   MatCopy(M9, XForm);
}

void Transform(TDA A, Matx4x4 M, TDA B)
{
```

```
   B[0]=M[0][0]*A[0]+M[0][1]*A[1]+M[0][2]*A[2]+M[0][3];
   B[1]=M[1][0]*A[0]+M[1][1]*A[1]+M[1][2]*A[2]+M[1][3];
   B[2]=M[2][0]*A[0]+M[2][1]*A[1]+M[2][2]*A[2]+M[2][3];
}


/*
┌─────────────────────────────────────────────────────────┐
│                                                         │
│             Pseudorandom Number Generator               │
│                                                         │
└─────────────────────────────────────────────────────────┘
*/

float OldRand;

void InitRand(float Seed)
{
   OldRand=Seed;
}

int RandInt(Word Range)
{
   float sigma=423.1966;

   OldRand=Frac(sigma * OldRand);
   return(Trunc(OldRand * (float)Range));
}

float Rand()
{
   float sigma=423.1966;

   OldRand=Frac(sigma * OldRand);
   return(OldRand);
}
```

Listing 2-1. *MathB.C.*

In the last chapter, we examined the header files required by the mathematics and graphics modules. These header files contain type declarations and global data definitions used by the modules. *Math.C* should be compiled separately and linked with the programs that require it, as described in Chapter 1.

The mathematics module contains three kinds of routines: numerical, vector and matrix, and affine transformation. The numerical routines are single-valued functions that take a single number as input and compute a function of that number. The sine and cosine functions fall into this category. This module also defines common mathematical constants, such as *pi* and *e*.

The vector and matrix functions create and manipulate vectors. For our purposes, a vector is a collection of numbers—normally two or three—representing a point either on the plane (*X,Y*) or in three-dimensional space (*X,Y,Z*). Vectors are also used to define directions, such as the direction a surface is facing. Since we will often need to transform vectors (such as when rotating an object), several transformation routines are provided here. We transform vectors by multiplying their coordinates by a single four-by-four-element matrix. One of the most convenient aspects of vector transformation is that each type of transformation can be represented by one four-by-four matrix. Individual matrices can be combined together to produce a single matrix that represents all the desired transformation operations: rotation, scaling, and translation. Such transformations allow us to create complex objects from primitive objects like triangles and parallelograms and place them in our virtual world.

So let's take a look at the functions in the mathematics interface module and examine some of their uses. This chapter can be used as a reference guide to the more complicated graphics routines presented later.

Numerical Functions

The mathematics module contains some useful numerical conversion functions:

Function	Description
Round(x)	Returns the nearest integer to x.
	If x > 0, Round(x) = Trunc(x + 0.5).
	If x < 0, Round(x) = Trunc(x - 0.5).

35

Trunc(x)	Returns the integer part of x, truncating the fractional part.
Frac(x)	Returns the fractional part of x.
	If x > 0, Frac(x) = x - Trunc(x).
Sqr(i)	Returns i*i.
SqrFP(x)	Returns x*x.

These routines could also be expressed easily in C code (*N*=N* is the same as *N=Sqr(N)*, for example); they are provided for you here because they're more portable for converting the software to other languages.

Radians and *Degrees*

The *Radians* and *Degrees* functions are useful when manipulating data based on angles. Much of the software in this book requires them to calculate lighting and viewing vectors correctly. Most of the time, we need to manipulate angles represented as radians (2*pi radians = 360 degrees). However, we often need to enter and express angles as degrees. Using these routines, we can easily convert between the two. As shown in the following table, these routines use the *PiOver180* and *PiUnder180* constants.

Function	**Description**
Radians(x)	Returns x expressed in radians.
	Radians(x) = x * PiOver180
Degrees(x)	Returns x expressed in degrees.
	Degrees(x) = x * PiUnder180

CosD and *SinD*

CosD and *SinD* use the C math library trigonometric functions *cos* (cosine) and *sin* (sine) as well as our own *Radians*. They perform the same function except that they take as their argument an angle expressed in degrees. These functions are particularly useful for generating the animation sequences that require repeated motion. We'll see more on animation and repeating loops in Chapter 13.

Function	Description
CosD(x)	CosD(x) = cos(Radians(x))
SinD(x)	SinD(x) = sin(Radians(x))

Power

This function has two arguments: a base value and an integer exponent. It returns the value of the base raised to the exponent (base $\wedge$ ^{exponent}). Essentially, *base* is multiplied by itself *exponent* number of times. If the exponent is 0, the function returns a value of 1.0 (any number raised to the power of 0 is 1). Otherwise, the variable *BPower* is initialized to 1.0, and a loop from 1 to the value of *exponent* begins. *BPower* is multiplied by *base* on each iteration of the loop. When the loop ends, the value in *BPower* is returned.

Function	Description
Power(x,i)	Raises x to the power i.
	Power(x,i) = x^i

Log

This function finds the base 10 logarithm of a number. Using the C *log* function, it finds the natural logarithm of the number and divides this value by the constant *Ln10* (the natural logarithm of 10). The real-valued result is then returned.

Function	Description
Log(x)	Compute the base 10 logarithm of x.
	Log(x) = log(x) / Ln10

Exp10

This function finds the value of 10.0 raised to the power of a floating-point number. First, the value passed to the function is multiplied by the constant *Ln10*. Then, using the C *exp* function, the natural logarithm of the new value is calculated. The result of this operation is returned.

Function	Description
Exp10(x)	Raises 10 to the power x.
	Exp10(x) = exp(x*Ln10)

Sign and IntSign

These functions are used to find the sign of a floating-point number and of an integer number, respectively. Both return a -1 if the number is less than 0, 0 if the number is equal to 0, and 1 if the number is greater than 0.

Function	Description
Sign(x)	Sign(x) = 1, x > 0
	=-1, x < 0
	= 0, x == 0
IntSign(i)	Same as for Sign, except integer argument.

IntSqrt

IntSqrt computes the nearest integer to the square root of its integer argument. It may be somewhat difficult to follow at first, but if you try a few simple examples such as 4, 9, and 16 you'll see that it's not all that complex.

First, a value is passed to x, *OddInt* is initialized to 1, and *OldArg* is set to x. With these values set, a *while* loop begins. On each iteration, *OddInt* is subtracted from x and 2 is added to *OddInt*. This continues until x is less than 0. When the loop terminates, *OddInt* is divided by 2 and the value is stored in the variable *FirstSqrt*. At this point, *FirstSqrt* contains either the integer square root or the integer square root plus one. An *if...else* statement then checks to see if the value in *FirstSqrt* needs to be decremented. The appropriate action is taken, and the value in *FirstSqrt* is returned. This routine is included because, for simple square-root calculations, it's faster than the square-root function built into some compilers.

Function	Description
IntSqrt(i)	Finds the integer nearest the square root of its argument.
	IntSqrt(i) = Round(sqrt((float)i)))

IntPower

IntPower is a recursive function that raises an integer value to an integer power. Recursion implies that a function calls itself. As in the *Power* function, if the exponent is 0, a 1 is returned. Otherwise, the exponent is decremented and the function calls itself. When the exponent reaches 0 through successive calls, the 1 is returned to the previous call. That number is then multiplied by *base* and returned to the next previous call and so on until the highest level is reached. The power of the integer is returned.

Function	Description
IntPower(i,j)	Same as Power, but for integer arguments only.
	IntPower(i,j) = i^j

MIN and MAX

These functions return the minimum and maximum values of two floating-point numbers, respectively.

The minimum and maximum routines are useful for finding the boundaries of an object (often referred to as the *extent* of the object). By running through the list of points that make up an object (such as the vertices of its sides) and computing the maximum and minimum found so far, you can determine the maximum and minimum values for each dimension. For example, a three-dimensional object requires three tests for each point (usually a vertex). A bounding box can then be defined by two points: the minimum value in each X, Y, and Z and the maximum value. We'll see more of this in the ray-tracing section, where we'll use this technique to increase our ray-tracing program's efficiency.

Function	Description
MIN(x,y)	Minimum of (x,y).
MAX(x,y)	Maximum of (x,y).
MIN3(x,y,z)	Minimum of (x,y,z).
MAX3(x,y,z)	Maximum of (x,y,z).
MIN4(x,y,z,a)	Minimum of (x,y,z,a).
MAX4(x,y,z,a)	Maximum of (x,y,z,a).

39

MIN3 and *MAX3*

These functions return the minimum and maximum values of three floating-point numbers, respectively.

MIN4 and *MAX4*

These functions return the minimum and maximum values of four floating-point numbers, respectively.

Vector and Matrix Routines

So far, we've only seen relatively simple mathematical functions that perform uninteresting, though necessary, feats. In this section, we'll be looking at the vector and matrix types used extensively in most computer graphics applications. This set of modules will allow us to move objects around in space, prepare their projection onto a two-dimensional display, and perform most standard vector operations.

To do this, we need to define several new datatypes. The first is *TDA*, an array of three floating-point numbers representing the components of a three-dimensional vector. These numbers represent the coordinate in the X, Y, and Z directions. In accordance with normal mathematical notation, we'll refer to the three standard unit vectors (those of length 1) as i, j, and k. These are simply vectors that point along the positive X, Y, and Z axes. They are defined as:

```
i (1, 0, 0)
j (0, 1, 0)
k (0, 0, 1)
```

and can be manipulated like any other vectors. Any vector V *(X,Y,Z)* may be represented as the sum of vectors i, j, and k:

```
V = Xi + Yj + Zk                              (Equation 2-1)
```

This equation may help you understand some of the other vector operations, such as rotation and scaling.

For computational efficiency, we also need to define the *TDIA* variable type. This is the same as the *TDA* type except that it uses three integer values rather than floating-point values. We also need the *FDA* type, a four-dimensional vector of floating-point numbers. We use four-dimensional vectors to express the translation operation compactly. For our purposes, the fourth element is almost always 0.0 or 1.0.

Finally, the *Matx4x4* type represents a four-by-four-element matrix of floating-point values. We'll use this type to express our vector transformation functions.

Vec and *VecInt*

These are the functions that actually create the vectors. The *Vec* function takes three floating-point numbers and stores them in a *TDA* type that it creates. The *VecInt* function does the same except that it stores three integers in a *TDIA*. This is a very efficient way of working with vectors. The code will now pass a pointer to the *TDA* structure representing our vector, rather than passing all three values as separate arguments.

UnVec and *UnVecInt*

These functions do exactly the opposite of the *Vec* and *VecInt* functions. *UnVec* extracts the three values stored in *TDA* and places them in three separate floating-point variables. *UnVecInt* extracts them and places them in integer variables.

VecDot

This routine computes one of the most useful geometric functions of two vectors: their dot product. The dot product of vectors *A* and *B* is defined as:

```
VecDot(A,B) = VecLen(A) * VecLen(B) * cos(theta)
```

where *VecLen* computes the magnitude, or length, of the vector and *theta* is the angle between the two vectors. This is the same as simply multiplying each element of *A* by the corresponding elements in *B* and summing all the products. The value of the dot product is as follows.

```
A•B = ab cos x                                    (Equation 2-2)
```

VecDot is the floating-point number this equation returns; *a* and *b* are the magnitude of vectors *A* and *B*; and *x* is the angle between the two vectors.

This function has three interesting properties:

- If *VecDot* = 0, the vectors are perpendicular.
- If *VecDot* = *VecLen(A)* * *VecLen(B)*, the vectors lie in exactly the same direction.
- If *VecDot* = -*(VecLen(A)* * *VecLen(B))*, the vectors point in exactly opposite directions.

One important use of this function in computer graphics is in determining whether or not we're facing a particular facet of an object. If the surface normal of the facet—which defines the direction the surface is facing—is dotted with the viewing direction and the resulting number is negative, we can see the facet because the vectors are pointing in opposite directions (the face is pointing in our general direction). If the resulting number is positive, the vectors are pointing in the same general direction and we can't see the face (it's turned away from us).

VecCross

This routine finds the cross-product of two vectors, which is defined as a third vector that is perpendicular to the plane defined by the first two vectors. The vector cross-product has a length of:

```
| a x b | = AB sin x                              (Equation 2-3)
```

where a and b are vectors, *A* and *B* are the magnitudes of the two vectors, and *x* is the angle between them. *VecCross* is the resulting vector. The two argument vectors (if they aren't the same vector) define a plane. *VecCross* is therefore very useful in determining the surface normal for an object facet. For example, we can take two of the edges of a facet as vectors and compute their cross-product, resulting in a vector representing the direction the surface faces (the surface normal). This surface normal

is then used to shade the facet lying in that plane. (This is discussed in more detail in the modeling and ray-tracing chapters.)

The vector cross-product is computed as follows:

```
A x B = |A_y B_z - A_z B_y, A_z B_x - A_x B_z, A_x B_y - A_y B_x|   (Equation 2-4)
```

Note that the directions *i*, *j*, and *k* refer to the *x*, *y*, and *z* axes. As a simple example, *k* is the cross-product of *i* and *j*. Note that the order of the two vectors is important. *VecCross(v2, v1)* is a vector pointing in the exact opposite direction of *VecCross(v1, v2)*.

VecLen

This function finds the magnitude of a vector. It's essentially a three-dimensional extension of the Pythagorean theorem. The length is the square root of the sum of the squares of the component values:

```
VecLen(v) = sqrt(x*x + y*y + z*z)                   (Equation 2-5)
```

This function can also be used to find the distance between two points in three-dimensional space. The vector would then contain the differences between each component of the two desired points.

VecNormalize

A normalized vector is one that has the same direction as another but has a magnitude of 1. You'll need to use this kind of vector quite often—for example, in the computation of the surface normal for a facet. The *VecCross* function computes a vector pointing in the right direction, but the lighting model needs a vector of unit length (length 1). *VecNormalize* solves this problem by normalizing the vector, thus giving it a unit length.

The first thing this routine does is find the length of the vector passed to it. Next, it checks to see if the length is 0; if it is, it prints an error message and exits. This is because a vector with a length of 0 has no direction and therefore cannot be normalized.

Once we've determined that our vector is usable, we find the inverse distance by dividing 1.0 by the length. Next, we multiply each element in the vector by the inverse distance, giving us our normalized vector.

Note that this function (and several others in this module) performs its operations in place; in other words, it modifies the vector passed to it. Therefore, if you need to save your original vector, you pass a temporary vector to this function and use *VecCopy* to store the new values in the destination vector.

VecMatxMult

VecMatxMult is our fundamental vector transformation function. It multiplies a four-element *FDA* by a 16-element *Matx4x4* matrix using the standard mathematical definition (as illustrated in Equation 2-9). As stated earlier, this function lets us transform a vector by rotating, scaling, and translating it in one operation.

The operation is accomplished using two *for* loops ranging from 0 to 3. This allows us to cover all 16 elements of the matrix as well as the four elements of the *FDA*. The results are stored in a separate *FDA*.

VecSub and VecSubInt

These functions subtract vector *B* from vector *A* and place the result in a third vector, *C*. They are provided for both the *TDA* and *TDIA* types.

VecAdd

This function performs the same operation as *VecSub* except that it adds rather than subtracts the vector components.

VecAdd3

VecAdd3 is similar to *VecAdd* except that it passes four vectors. The elements of the first three vectors are added together and the results stored in the fourth.

VecCopy and VecCopyInt

These functions simply copy the elements of one vector into another vector. *VecCopy* and *VecCopyInt* are for floating-point and integer numbers, respectively.

VecLinComb

This function computes the linear combination of two vectors, A and B, and places the result in a third vector, C.

Five variables are passed: two floating-point numbers and three vectors (r, s, A, B, and C, respectively). The elements of A are multiplied by r, and the elements of B are multiplied by s. The results are added and stored in vector C. The operation is:

```
C = rA + sB
```
(Equation 2-6)

Note that *VecAdd* is equivalent to *VecLinComb(1.0, A, 1.0, B, C)* and *VecSub* is equivalent to *VecLinComb(1.0, A, -1.0, B, C)*.

VecScalMult, VecScalMultI, and VecScalMultInt

These functions scale a vector by multiplying each element of the passed vector by a given floating-point number and storing the result in a new vector. This operation keeps the vector's direction the same but changes its length. *VecScalMultI* uses the C typecasting facility, which converts one data type to another, to convert the integers in the passed *TDIA* to floating point before multiplying. *VecScalMult* and *VecScalMultI* return floating-point *TDA* vectors, while the *VecScalMultInt* function returns an integer *TDIA* vector.

VecAddScalMult

VecAddScalMult is a convenient function that combines several operations into one call. It performs a *VecAdd* on input vectors A and B, followed by a *VecScalMult* using the argument r. The result is stored in C. The operation is:

```
C = rA + B
```
(Equation 2-7)

VecNull and VecNullInt

The *VecNull* function simply sets all elements in a *TDA* to 0. Similarly, the *VecNullInt* function sets all elements in a *TDIA* to 0.

VecElemMult

This function accepts a floating-point number and three *TDAs* as input (r, A, B, and C). The elements of vector A are multiplied by the elements of vector B, and the resulting vector is multiplied by r. The results are stored in vector C.

$$C = |rA_xB_x, \quad rA_yB_y, \quad rA_zB_z|$$

(Equation 2-8)

VecMin and VecMax

These functions find the minimum and maximum components of a vector. For example, if we're using *VecMin* and the x component of the vector being passed to the function is the least of the x, y, and z components of the vector, the function returns the x component.

VecNegate

This function reverses the direction of a vector by changing the sign of each element.

Affine Transformation Routines

The affine transformation is the core of all geometric manipulations of vectors. It allows concise expression of the graphics transformations we need to perform on objects (translation, scaling, and rotation).

You may be wondering why we use a four-by-four matrix when our vectors are all three-dimensional. The answer is that we wish to incorporate translation into our single matrix transformation. We therefore take our *TDA* (or *TDIA*) types and convert them to the *FDA* type by setting the first element to 1.0. The first column of the four-by-four matrix then represents the translation of the vector using standard matrix multiplication:

$$\begin{bmatrix} b_0 \\ b_1 \\ b_2 \\ b_3 \end{bmatrix} = \begin{bmatrix} m_{00} & m_{01} & m_{02} & m_{03} \\ m_{10} & m_{11} & m_{12} & m_{13} \\ m_{20} & m_{21} & m_{22} & m_{23} \\ m_{30} & m_{31} & m_{32} & m_{33} \end{bmatrix} \times \begin{bmatrix} a_0 \\ a_1 \\ a_2 \\ a_3 \end{bmatrix}$$

(Equation 2-9)

where $a0 = 1.0$ and (a_1, a_2, a_3) represents our three-dimensional input vector. In addition, $m_{00} = 1.0$ and $m_{01} = m_{02} = m_{03} = 0.0$ for most matrices, so b_0 will also be equal to 1.0 after the transformation.

The routines in this section create matrices for scaling, rotation, and translation, combine them into a single transformation matrix, and use them to perform various mathematical operations. All the matrix operations use the *Matx4x4* type.

ZeroMatrix

This function zeros out the elements in a given matrix.

Translate3D

This function creates a linear translation matrix to translate a vector to a new location in space. (Technically, only points can be manipulated in this manner since a vector is always assumed to refer to the origin; for our purposes, however, points and vectors are interchangeable.) This matrix consists of a diagonal of ones and is referred to as the *identity matrix* because it leaves a vector unchanged when applied as a transformation. The first elements of the last three rows are set to the negative of the three translation parameters passed to the function. The result is the following matrix:

$$T = \begin{bmatrix} 1 & 0 & 0 & 0 \\ -t_x & 1 & 0 & 0 \\ -t_y & 0 & 1 & 0 \\ -t_z & 0 & 0 & 1 \end{bmatrix}$$

(Equation 2-10)

Scale3D

This function creates a matrix to scale each component of a vector. The diagonal consists of the three scaling parameters passed to the procedure and a 1.0 in the first position. Only the scale of a three-dimensional vector, not its origin, will be changed by this transformation. If all three scale factors are the same, the result will be the same as using *VecScaleMult*, which leaves the direction unchanged. If the factors are different, both the direction and the length of the vector may change. The scaling matrix is as follows.

47

$$S \quad = \quad \begin{bmatrix} s_x & 0 & 0 & 0 \\ 0 & s_y & 0 & 0 \\ 0 & 0 & 0s_z & 0 \\ 0 & 0 & 0 & 1 \end{bmatrix}$$

(Equation 2-11)

Rotate3D

This function creates a matrix to rotate a vector in space about the *x*, *y*, or *z* axis. It requires an integer indicating the axis about which to rotate (1 for the *x* axis, 2 for *y*, and 3 for *z*) and a real number representing the rotation angle in degrees. The function first sets the matrix to the identity matrix, then places the cosine and sine of the angle in certain matrix elements depending on the axis.

The matrix for rotation about *x* is:

$$R_x \quad = \quad \begin{bmatrix} 1 & 0 & 0 & 0 \\ 0 & \cos\theta & \sin\theta & 0 \\ 0 & -\sin\theta & -\cos\theta & 0 \\ 0 & 0 & 0 & 1 \end{bmatrix}$$

(Equation 2-12)

The matrix for rotation about *y* is:

$$R_y \quad = \quad \begin{bmatrix} \cos\theta & 0 & -\sin\theta & 0 \\ 0 & 1 & 0 & 0 \\ -\sin\theta & 0 & \cos\theta & 0 \\ 0 & 0 & 0 & 1 \end{bmatrix}$$

(Equation 2-13)

The matrix for rotation about *z* is:

$$R_z \quad = \quad \begin{bmatrix} \cos\theta & \sin\theta & 0 & 0 \\ -\sin\theta & \cos\theta & 0 & 0 \\ 0 & 0 & 1 & 0 \\ 0 & 0 & 0 & 1 \end{bmatrix}$$

(Equation 2-14)

Multiply3DMatrices

This function multiplies two four-by-four, real-number matrices, effectively combining two separate transformations into one. By chaining our transformations together, we produce a single transformation that represents the rotation, scaling, and translation for each axis.

We generate this composite transformation by first setting it equal to the identity matrix (the diagonal elements are all 1.0; everything else is 0.0). We then compute each transformation we need (rotation, scaling, and translation) separately and combine it with the composite matrix using *Multiply3DMatrices* as we go along. The result is a matrix that represents all the transformation operations and may be applied to our points and vectors as needed. Note that the order of matrix composition is crucial; a different multiplication order can produce entirely different and unexpected results.

Because each object in a scene can be moved separately, we may need different composite matrices for each object. As you'll see, these are all generated using the same procedure.

MatCopy

This function simply copies a matrix into another matrix.

PrepareMatrix

This function generates a complete affine transformation matrix that translates, scales, and rotates a point in space. The function calls *Scale3D* to create the scaling matrix, *Rotate3D* for each of the three axes (*x*, *y*, and *z*) to create the rotation matrices, and *Translate3D* to create the translation matrix. *Multiply3DMatrices* is then called several times to build the final transformation matrix, a composite of the translation, scaling, and rotation matrices. The resulting composite matrix is then returned.

PrepareInvMatrix

This function creates the inverse matrix to the one generated by *PrepareMatrix*. An inverse matrix undoes the transformations of its complementary matrix; if you transform a point, you can apply the inverse matrix to get the original point. This

routine computes the inverse matrix for each operation by using the negative values of the translation coefficients, the negative rotation angles, and the inverse (1.0 /) scaling coefficients. The final inverse matrix is then computed by combining the component matrices in the reverse order of *PrepareMatrix*. The reverse order is necessary so that each component will precisely cancel its corresponding transformation in *PrepareMatrix*.

Transform

This function multiplies a real-number, three-dimensional vector (*TDA*) by a real-number, four-by-four matrix (*Matx4x4*). The resulting vector corresponds to the various transformations represented by the passed matrix.

Pseudorandom Number Generation

These routines create pseudorandom numbers using a technique known as the power residue sequence approach to generate positive pseudorandom numbers. *Pseudorandom* means that the sequence only appears to be random; we can regenerate it by passing the same "seed" value to the routine on initialization. In addition, the sequence is uniformly distributed only approximately in the interval 0.0 through 1.0.

The pseudorandom number generator starts by initializing with an arbitrary floating-point number, referred to as a *seed value*. We generate new numbers by multiplying a constant (*sigma*) by the seed value and returning the fractional part, thus guaranteeing that the result is between 0 and 1. Every time the routine is called, a new number in the sequence is generated based on the previous value and, indirectly, the seed. Therefore, any sequence can be regenerated if you know the seed; if your program generates an image you like and the program uses a random number generator, you can regenerate the image just by knowing the seed value.

InitRand

This function initializes the random number generator with a real number. The variable *OldSeed,* the current value, is set to the passed seed value. *InitRand* must be called before the *Rand* and *RandInt* functions can be used. Any time *InitRand* is

called with the same seed value, the same sequence is generated by *Rand* and *RandInt*.

Rand

This function returns a positive, float random number between 0.0 and 1.0. *OldRand* takes on the fractional part of *OldRand* times the constant *sigma* and is the returned value.

RandInt

This function returns a positive, integer random number from a word-type range argument—in other words, a value from 0 to (*Range*-1). We simply get the next value from *Rand( )*, which is always in the range 0.0 through 1.0, multiply it by *Range*, and return *Trunc( )* of the result.

CHAPTER 3

The Graphics Interface Module

In the last chapter, we discussed the functions found in the mathematics module and some of their possible uses. In this chapter, we'll look at several graphics functions found in the *Graph.C* graphics interface module (Listing 3-1).Throughout this book, we will use the term *module* to refer to a group of logically-related functions found in a single source file. They cover a wide variety of operations, from setting a graphics mode on a VGA graphics card, to three-dimensional plotting and coordinate axis display. These routines are easy to use; try exploring them with your own software.

The graphics routines were written for use primarily with an STB ERGO PowerGraph SVGA graphics card. They'll also work on the Ilon SGVA card with no modification. With the proper programming information (normally included with your graphics card), you should be able to make these routines work with your graphics card. Only 256-color SVGA modes are supported by these graphics drivers; the images they produce would look atrocious in 16-color EGA, and worse still in four-color CGA.

Basic Graphics Functions

Set_Mode

The *Set_Mode* function determines the graphics mode in which we wish to run. Since most SVGA boards can emulate normal VGA as well as other display resolutions, we use this function to set the number of colors (always 256) and the desired screen resolution. Here, the passed mode number is stored in the AL half of the AX register. *Set_Mode* then calls a ROM BIOS routine, via the *int86* function,

to set the desired graphics mode. Essentially, *Set.Mode* asks the operating system to put the display card into the desired mode. The ROM BIOS and Int86 routines effectively tell the PC what graphics mode we are currently running.

Calc_Offsets

This function sets up two offset variables for a viewing window. If you use the *Set_Graphics_Mode* function (discussed later) and your window is smaller than the actual graphics-mode window, this function sets the variables *X_Off* and *Y_Off* to the appropriate values to keep points from being plotted outside the window. It also ensures that the window is in the middle of the screen.

Pre_Calc

This function initializes two global arrays, *Pre_Calc_Y1* and *Pre_Calc_Y2*. These arrays are used in the plotting functions to avoid having to multiply every time we wish to write to graphics memory. If we want to write to a location (*X,Y*) on the screen, we determine its memory address using the equation:

```
ADDRESS = X + (Y*X_RES)                        (Equation 3-1)
```

where *X_RES* is the number of columns on the screen. Using these arrays makes the multiply unnecessary; instead, we use indexing and one addition to compute the memory address at which to plot the pixel. Reducing the number of multiplies during plotting makes the plotting function much more efficient and dramatically increases the speed at which pixels are placed on the screen.

The arrays are the sizes of the vertical resolutions of the middle-resolution (800x600) and high-resolution (1024x768) graphics modes. The values stored in these arrays are the horizontal resolutions multiplied by each row number. The *Pre_Calc_Y1* array is used for high- and low-resolution modes; *Pre_Calc_Y2* is used by all other graphics modes. We need two separate arrays because in medium resolution mode, we use a double-word to store each pre-computed values whereas the other modes do not need this much storage per value.

Plot

The primary function of this routine is to plot a pixel of a given color to the specified (X,Y) location on the screen. It first checks to see if the point to be plotted is within the boundaries of the screen. If not, we return without plotting the point. Next, it checks to see which resolution we're using (high, medium, or low) and goes to the appropriate plotting routine. If necessary, it then adds the *X_Off* and *Y_Off* values to the *x* and *y* coordinates. These offsets guarantee that the image is placed in the center of the screen.

If we're using high or medium resolution, the routine checks to see if we need to flip the graphics writing page. The memory on the graphics card is set up in twelve 64K pages for high-resolution mode; to access different parts of the screen, we must select the page this particular screen location is on. Lower resolution modes use fewer pages as appropriate. The current page (what we see on the screen) is mapped to memory address A0000000H.

Flipping the page for every plot would be so time-consuming as to be extremely impractical. To sidestep this problem, we compare the stored previous page (*OldPage*) with the newer page each time we want to plot, changing the page number and *OldPage* only when the newer page and *OldPage* differ. A difference indicates that we must flip the pages to access the desired part of the screen. Finally, we place the point on the screen by storing the value of the color directly into the graphics card's display memory, which begins at the already-computed address.

Clear_Palette

This function takes a predefined variable type called *Palette_Register* and zeros it out. The *Palette_Register* variables contain the red, green, and blue components of the colors, one for each color. The palette determines how each color value (0 through 255) is displayed on the screen.

Set_Palette

This function sets the palette using the passed *Palette_Register* array address. First, we store the appropriate BIOS function number in the AX register. The function tells the BIOS that we need to pass data to the graphics card—the data being our palette—and we give it the address of our data. Now we call the BIOS via the *int86x* function to perform the task, and our palette is set.

Init_Palette

This function sets up a standard palette containing 64 levels of gray, red, green, and blue. We first calculate the gray by making the first 64 r, g, and b (red, green, and blue) components of the palette equal. (Equal shades of red, green, and blue result in gray.) For the next 64 components, we set only the red values and zero out the green and blue components. Doing the same for green and blue completes our palette.

Init_Palette_2

This palette will consist of seven colors—blue, green, cyan, red, magenta, brown, and gray—each having 35 intensities. We need seven *for* loops, each ranging from 0 to 35:

- The first loop sets up the blue colors by setting red and green to 0 and calculating 35 shades of blue (be sure to scale out the levels of blue so that the brightest blue has an intensity of 63).

- Next, we set up green by setting red and blue to 0 and calculating 35 shades of green.

- For cyan, we zero out the red component and make the 35 green and blue components equal.

- We then set up the red colors by setting the green and blue values to 0 and calculating 35 shades of red.

- Now we calculate magenta by setting green to 0 and giving equal values to the 35 red and blue components.

- Next, we calculate the 35 brown colors by making the blue values zero and giving equal values to the red and green components.

- Finally, we set the 35 gray shades by giving equal values to the red, green, and blue components. The remaining palette entries are left at zero.

Cycle_Palette

This simple animation technique can be used many different ways. It performs a circular rotate of the current palette, moving the first entry (for pixel value 0) to the last (for pixel value 255). We save our first palette entry in a temporary variable, shift the remaining 255 entries down by one, replace the last entry with the one stored in our temporary variable, and finally call *Set_Palette* to set up the new palette of colors.

Swap

This function simply swaps two integer values. The first is stored in a temporary variable; the second is placed in the first and the temporary placed in the second, swapping the two integers.

Circle

This function draws a circle on the screen with the correct aspect ratio for the given resolution. It requires an (x, y) position, a radius, and a color number. Because a circle is symmetrical, eight points are plotted at once. The only difference in the eight points is the sign of their x and y components; therefore, we only need to span one-eighth of the circle to draw the entire circle.

Note that the routine also handles aspect correction. The aspect ratio comes into play because in certain resolutions a pixel may not be square (i.e. equal size in both horizontal and vertical dimensions when shown on the monitor). If the pixels are not square, then a circle drawn with an equal number of pixels vertically and horizontally will appear elliptical rather than circular, due to the distortion. For the ERGO PowerGraph and Ilon SVGA cards, the 1024x768 and 640x480 modes have square pixels and thus an aspect ratio of 1. The 320x200 VGA mode has an aspect ratio of 1.2 $(1.0/(1024/768) * (YRes/XRes))$. To correct the aspect, *Circle* multiplies the x or y components by this ratio for the graphics card being used.

Computations for the circle are as follows. One offset starts with the value of the radius; the second offset is 0. The target value is also set to 0. We loop until the second offset is less than the first, indicating that one-eighth of the circle has been traversed. Within this loop, the function computes the value of the second offset (using the equation for a circle) and swaps it with the target value.

We then enter a new loop that iterates until the value of the second offset is greater than or equal to the target value. For each iteration, the *x* offsets are computed (including computation for aspect ratio) and eight symmetric points are plotted. The second offset is then incremented by 1. This second loop guarantees that pixels are filled in where there is little change in the second offset. When the loop finishes, the first offset is decremented by 1 and the first loop is reiterated. This process yields a circle with just enough points for the specified resolution.

Draw

The *Draw* routine draws a line from one point to another using a specified color number. The line-generation algorithm is based on Bresenham's line-drawing algorithm and is the generally accepted method for generating a line. This method is desirable because it requires only integer arithmetic with no multiplies. It starts by calculating *LgDelta*, the distance between the beginning and ending points in the *x* direction, and *ShDelta*, the distance between the beginning and ending points in the *y* direction. *LgDelta* and *ShDelta* have the step parameters *LgStep* and *ShStep*, respectively. If either distance parameter is less than 0, the sign is changed and the step parameter for that distance is -1; otherwise, the step parameter is 1.

If the *y* line distance is less than the *x* line distance, we compute the parameter *Cycle* as half the longer *x* line distance (*LgDelta*). We loop until the *x* pixel coordinate (*xx1*) is equal to the ending *x* line coordinate. First, a pixel is plotted at the *x* and *y* coordinates in the given color. *Cycle* is then incremented by the shorter distance. If this process makes *Cycle* larger than the longer distance, we reduce it by the longer distance and alter the *y* coordinate with *ShStep*. The *x* coordinate is then altered with *LgStep*. This loop terminates with all but the final point plotted, so our last step is to plot it.

If the *y* line distance is greater than the *x* line distance, we compute the parameter *Cycle* as half of *ShDelta*. *LgDelta* and *ShDelta* are swapped, as are *LgStep* and *ShStep*. The remainder of the routine is similar to that described in the preceding paragraph except that loop termination is based on *y* rather than *x* and the order in which the *x* and *y* pixels are changed is reversed.

Init_Graphics

This function must be called before any other graphics routines. It performs basic initialization for all graphics operations and sets the graphics mode using the passed argument.

First, *Init_Graphics* checks to see which graphics mode is being requested. If the mode is illegal, an error message is printed and the program tells us to press a key to exit. Otherwise, the appropriate variables are initialized. The first is *Res*, which the plotting function uses to determine which pixel placement routine to use; The others are bounding variables used in clipping operations. These clipping operations allow you to only plot pixels to the display screen. Next, we check to see if *XRes* and *YRes* have been set. If not, we give them the maximum values for the resolution. We call *Calc_Offsets* to calculate the window offsets, then *Pre_Calc* to set the *Pre_Calc_Y** buffers. An aspect variable is set to ensure the proper aspect ratio of all the graphics modes. *CentreX* and *CentreY* are calculated, defining the center pixel of the display. Next we call *Set_Mode* to set up the requested graphics mode, then initialize our palette with a call to *Init_Palette_2*. Finally, we call *Set_Palette* to load the graphics card with that palette.

Set_Graphics_Mode

This function lets us set up a graphics window of any size (up to 1024x768). We pass the *X* and *Y* resolutions to this function, and it calculates the best possible graphics mode for the window. It also calls *Init_Graphics* to set up variables required for proper operation in a particular graphics mode (determine the appropriate offsets to center the window on the screen, for example).

Wait_For_Key

This function allows the program to wait for any keystroke before continuing.

Exit_Graphics

This function is called when the program has finished using the graphics display. *Exit_Graphics* starts by sounding a beep and calling *Wait_For_Key*. It then frees up the *Pre_Calc_Y** buffers (which are stored in far memory) and calls *Set_Mode* to return the screen to normal DOS text mode.

Title

This routine sets the screen colors to a blue background with yellow text and clears the screen. This is useful for initial display screens and data display screens.

Three-Dimensional Plotting Routines

Now that we have examined some of the low-level graphics functions, let's look at some of the more advanced three-dimensional plotting concepts. The following routines are useful for creating three-dimensional computer displays. They initialize the perspective routines, map three-dimensional space onto a two-dimensional surface (the computer screen), display an axis and a palette, and provide general graphics support.

Init_Plotting

This routine initializes variables that are used in three-dimensional plotting and depend on the rotation and tilt angles *Angl* and *Tilt*. *Angl* specifies the *Z* rotation angle (the location of the viewer with respect to the origin of the three-dimensional world coordinate system), and *Tilt* specifies the pitch (the angle above the x-y plane) of the viewer. These angles are passed to the routine. Various precalculations are performed for the trigonometric concerns of the *Map_Coordinates* function to make the mapping calculations more efficient.

Init_Perspective

This routine sets the perspective flag so the program knows whether or not to perform perspective projection in the *Map_Coordinates* routine. It also initializes the observer-position coordinates (*Mx*, *My*, and *Mz*) as well as the distance of the viewer's viewpoint from the plane of the screen.

Map_Coordinates

This routine transforms points from a three-dimensional space (X, Y, Z) to a two-dimensional screen (Xp, Yp). Both orthographic and perspective projections may be specified. In an orthographic projection there is no correction for the distance of objects from the viewer. All objects appear the same size regardless of how near or far away they are. A perspective projection scales objects for distance, just as you see objects in the real world. The origin of the three-dimensional space is at the center of the display screen. *Mx* and *My* offsets can be used to move the viewer relative to the screen, thus moving the origin about the screen, if perspective projection is chosen. We can make *Mz* less than *ds* (say *Mz* = 350 and *ds* = 500) to move closer to the origin if perspective projection is active. Equations 3-2 and 3-3 represent the orthographic projection of three-space coordinates (*X*, *Y*) to screen coordinates (*Xp*, *Yp*). Equation 3-3 is used when perspective calculation is desired.

$$x_t = m_x + x\cos\theta - y\sin\theta \qquad \text{(Equation 3-2)}$$

$$y_t = m_y + x\sin\theta\sin\phi + y\cos\theta\sin\phi + z\cos\phi \qquad \text{(Equation 3-3)}$$

$$z_t = m_z + x\sin\theta\cos\phi + y\cos\theta\cos\phi - z\sin\phi \qquad \text{(Equation 3-4)}$$

The values of *X* and *Y* are divided by *Z* and modified by *ds* to create perspective. These equations are derived through matrix multiplications for translation and rotation about two axes. They are similar to the affine transformation routines but are hard-coded here in the interest of speed.

Cartesian_Plot_3D

This function plots a point described by rectangular or Cartesian coordinates (*X*, *Y*, *Z*). It calls *Map_Coordinates* to project the point onto the screen and makes it the appropriate color. Figure 3-1 displays the Cartesian coordinates.

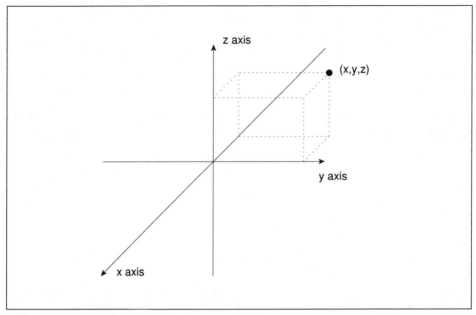

Figure 3-1. Cartesian coordinates.

Cylindrical_Plot_3D

This function plots a point described by cylindrical coordinates (*rho*, *theta*, and *z*). Here, *rho* is the radius of the cylinder and *theta* the angle around the *z* axis. Trigonometric relations transform the cylindrical coordinates into Cartesian coordinates. *Cylindrical_Plot_3D* calls *Map_Coordinates* to project the point onto the screen and makes it the appropriate color. See Figure 3-2 for a display of the cylindrical coordinates.

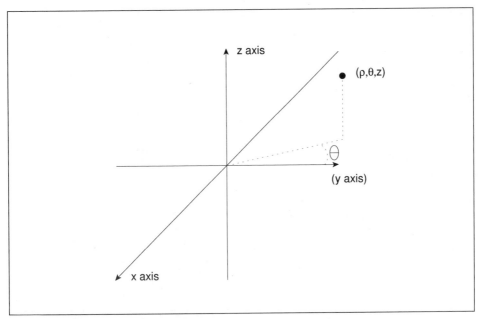

Figure 3-2. Cylindrical coordinates.

Spherical_Plot_3D

This function plots a point described by spherical coordinates (*r*, *theta*, and *phi*). Here, *r* is the radius of the sphere, *theta* is the angle around the *z* axis from the *x* axis in the *xy* plane, and *phi* is the angle off the *z* axis. Trigonometric relations transform the spherical coordinates into Cartesian coordinates. The function calls *Map_Coordinates* to project the point onto the screen and colors it the appropriate color. Figure 3-3 displays the spherical coordinates.

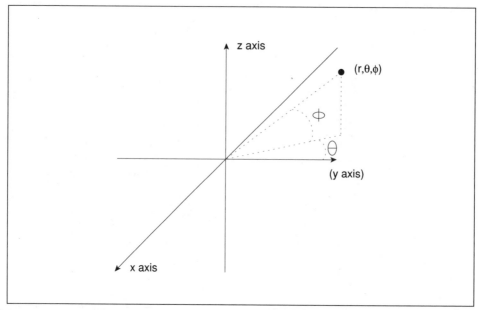

Figure 3-3. Spherical coordinates.

Draw_Line_3D

This function draws a line of a certain color number from one point in three-dimensional space to another. Two Cartesian three-dimensional points are passed to the routine in *TDA*-type format, and *Map_Coordinates* is called to project the points onto the two-dimensional display. A line is then drawn between the two projected screen coordinates.

Pixel Routines

The pixel routines put and get pixels (either singly or in blocks). They map pixels specified by a color and an intensity to the appropriate color value for the seven-color palette created by *Init_Palette_2*.

Put_Pixel

This function plots a pixel given a shade and an intensity. It begins by making sure the given shade and intensity don't exceed the values stored in the constants

MaxCol (7) and *MaxIntens* (35). If one does exceed its constant, the routine exits. Otherwise, the color is calculated and *Plot* is called to place the pixel on the screen at the given *x* and *y* coordinates.

Get_Pixel

This function returns the value of a pixel stored at the given *x* and *y* coordinates. It performs the inverse operation from the *Plot* function: It retrieves the color value directly from the graphics card's display, accounting for any necessary page flipping.

Setup of Coordinate Axes and Palette Routines

These routines display the color palette and Cartesian axes on the screen. The *x* axis is represented as a blue line, the *y* axis as green, and the *z* axis as cyan. White dots at the ends indicate the most endpoints of the lines. The palette display best shows the seven-color, 35-intensity palette created by the function *Init_Palette_2*.

Put_Axis_And_Palette

This function simply sets a flag to tell the programs whether or not we want the axis and palette to be displayed. This flag must be set before we call *Axis_And_Palette*, described later.

Display_Axis

Display_Axis draws the three coordinate axes using the *Cartesian_Plot_3D* routine. The white points indicate the most positive parts of the axes.

Display_Palette

This routine displays all the colors in the palette in the form of colored squares running down the left side of the screen. After setting up scaling factors for the size of the squares, it initializes four loops: *Color*, ranging from 1 to *MaxCol*; *Intensity*, ranging from 0 to *MaxInten*; *X*, ranging from 0 to four times our scaling factor (*sx*); and *Y*, ranging from 0 to four times our scaling factor (*sy*). The first two loops determine the color of the square to be placed on the screen, while the last two determine its size. Each pixel is placed on the screen via a call to *Put_Pixel*. *Display_Palette* shows the seven-color, 35-intensity palette created by the function *Init_Palette_2*.

Axis_And_Palette

This function tests to see if the *Draw_Axis_And_Palette* flag is set. If it is, *Display_Axis* and *Display_Palette* are called to place the axis and palette on the screen. Because *Axis_And_Palette* uses these flags, you may include it in your program and simply set the flags to determine whether or not the axes and palette are actually drawn.

We have now examined both the mathematics and graphics interface modules; in Chapter 4, we'll actually use the modules in various graphics programs.

```
/*

    ┌──────────────────────────────────────────────────────────────┐
    │          SVGA Graphics Driver - Tseng 4000 Chip Set           │
    │    for STB Systems ERGO PowerGraph VGA and Ilon USA VGA       │
    │        © 1990, 1991 Christopher D. Watkins and Larry Sharp     │
    └──────────────────────────────────────────────────────────────┘


    Plot              - place pixel to screen
    Set_Palette       - set palette register
    Init_Palette      - 64 levels of gray, red, green, and blue
    Init_Palette2     - 7 colors with 35 intensities each - use with
                        Pixel
    Cycle_Palette     - cycle through palette
    Circle            - circle-draw routine
    Draw              - line-draw routine
    Init_Graphics     - initialize graphics
    Wait_For_Key      - wait for key press
    Exit_Graphics     - sound and wait for keypress before exiting
                        graphics
    Title             - set up text-screen colors
*/
```

```
#include "stdio.h"
#include "dos.h"
#include "conio.h"
#include "math.h"
#include "malloc.h"
#include "defs.h"
#include "mathb.h"
#include "graphb.h"

union   REGS reg;
struct  SREGS inreg;

void Set_Mode(int Mode)

{
        reg.h.ah=0;
        reg.h.al=Mode;
        int86(0x10,&reg,&reg);
}

Word    X_Off, Y_Off;
static  Word far *Pre_Calc_Y1;
static  DWord far *Pre_Calc_Y2;
static  Byte Res;
float   Asp;

#define Low_Res        1
#define Medium_Res     2
#define High_Res       3

void Calc_Offsets()
{
        Word tmp, tmp2;

        if(XRes<MaxXRes)
        {
                tmp=MaxXRes>>1;
                tmp2=XRes>>1;
                X_Off=tmp-tmp2;
        }
```

```
        else
                X_Off=0;
        if(YRes<MaxYRes)
        {
                tmp=MaxYRes>>1;
                tmp2=YRes>>1;
                Y_Off=tmp-tmp2;
        }
        else
                Y_Off=0;
}

void Pre_Calc()
{
        Word j;

        for(j=0; j<=MaxYRes; j++)
        {
                if(Res==Medium_Res)
                        Pre_Calc_Y2[j]=(DWord)MaxXRes*(DWord)j;
                else
                        Pre_Calc_Y1[j]=MaxXRes*j;
        }
}
static Word Old_Page;

void Plot(Word x, Word y, Byte color)
{
        long L_Offset;
        Word Offset, Page;
        char far *address;

        if((x<XRes) && (y<YRes))
        {
                switch(Res)
                {
                        case High_Res :
Offset=Pre_Calc_Y1[y+Y_Off]+x+X_Off;
                        Page=y>>6;
                        if(Page!=Old_Page)
```

```
                              {
                                      outpw(0x3CD, Page|64);
                                      Old_Page=Page;
                              }
                              address=(char far*)
              (0xA0000000L+Offset);
                              *address=color;
                              break;
                       case Medium_Res :    x+=X_Off;
                              y+=Y_Off;
                              L_Offset=Pre_Calc_Y2[y]+x;
                              Page=L_Offset>>16;
                              Offset=L_Offset&65535;
                              if(Page!=Old_Page)
                              {
                                      outpw(0x3CD, Page|64);
                                      Old_Page=Page;
                              }
                              address=(char far*)
              (0xA0000000L+Offset);
                              *address=color;
                              break;
                       case Low_Res :
Offset=Pre_Calc_Y1[y+Y_Off]+x+X_Off;
                              address=(char far*)
              (0xA0000000L+Offset);
                              *address=color;
                              break;
              }
       }
}

static Palette_Register Color;

void Set_Palette(Palette_Register Hue)
{
       reg.x.ax=0x1012;
       segread(&inreg);
       inreg.es=inreg.ds;
       reg.x.bx=0;
```

```
        reg.x.cx=256;
        reg.x.dx=(int)&Hue[0];
        int86x(0x10,&reg,&reg,&inreg);
}

void Init_Palette(Palette_Register Color)
{
        Word i;

        for(i=0; i<64; i++)
        {
                Color[i].Red=i;
                Color[i].Grn=i;
                Color[i].Blu=i;
        }
        for(i=64; i<128; i++)
        {
                Color[i].Red=i-64;
                Color[i].Grn=0;
                Color[i].Blu=0;
        }
        for(i=128; i<192; i++)
        {
                Color[i].Red=0;
                Color[i].Grn=i-128;
                Color[i].Blu=0;
        }
        for(i=192; i<=255; i++)
        {
                Color[i].Red=0;
                Color[i].Grn=0;
                Color[i].Blu=i-192;
        }
}

void Init_Palette_2(Palette_Register Color)
{
        Word i;

        for(i=0; i<36; i++)
        {
```

```
        Color[i].Red=0;
        Color[i].Grn=0;
        Color[i].Blu=Round(1.8*i);
}
for(i=36; i<72; i++)
{
        Color[i].Red=0;
        Color[i].Grn=Round(1.8*(i-36));
        Color[i].Blu=0;
}
for(i=72; i<108; i++)
{
        Color[i].Red=0;
        Color[i].Grn=Round(1.8*(i-72));
        Color[i].Blu=Round(1.8*(i-72));
}
for(i=108; i<144; i++)
{
        Color[i].Red=Round(1.8*(i-108));
        Color[i].Grn=0;
        Color[i].Blu=0;
}
for(i=144; i<180; i++)
{
        Color[i].Red=Round(1.8*(i-144));
        Color[i].Grn=0;
        Color[i].Blu=Round(1.8*(i-144));
}
for(i=180; i<216; i++)
{
        Color[i].Red=Round(1.8*(i-180));
        Color[i].Grn=Round(1.8*(i-180));
        Color[i].Blu=0;
}
for(i=216; i<252; i++)
{
        Color[i].Red=Round(1.8*(i-216));
        Color[i].Grn=Round(1.8*(i-216));
        Color[i].Blu=Round(1.8*(i-216));
}
```

```
}

void Cycle_Palette(Palette_Register Hue)
{
      Word   i;
      RGB    tmp;

      tmp=Hue[0];
      memcpy(&Hue[0], &Hue[1], 765);
      Hue[255]=tmp;
      Set_Palette(Hue);
}

void Swap(int *first, int *second)
{
      int temp;

      temp=*first;
      *first=*second;
      *second=temp;
}

void Circle(Word x, Word y, Word radius, Byte color)
{
      int a, af, b, bf, target, r2, asp;

      if(Res==High_Res)
            asp=100;
      else
            asp=120;
      target=0;
      a=radius;
      b=0;
      r2=Sqr(radius);
      while(a>=b)
      {
            b=Round(sqrt(r2-Sqr(a)));
            Swap(&target,&b);
            while(b<target)
            {
```

```
                        af=(asp*a)/100;
                        bf=(asp*b)/100;
                        Plot(x+af, y+b, color);
                        Plot(x+bf, y+a, color);
                        Plot(x-af, y+b, color);
                        Plot(x-bf, y+a, color);
                        Plot(x-af, y-b, color);
                        Plot(x-bf, y-a, color);
                        Plot(x+af, y-b, color);
                        Plot(x+bf, y-a, color);
                        ++b;
                }
                -a;
        }
}


void Draw(int xx1, int yy1, int xx2, int yy2, Byte color)
{
        int LgDelta, ShDelta, Cycle, LgStep, ShStep, dtotal;

        LgDelta=xx2-xx1;
        ShDelta=yy2-yy1;
        if(LgDelta<0)
        {
                LgDelta=-LgDelta;
                LgStep=-1;
        }
        else
                LgStep=1;
        if(ShDelta<0)
        {
                ShDelta=-ShDelta;
                ShStep=-1;
        }
        else
                ShStep=1;
        if(ShDelta<LgDelta)
        {
                Cycle=LgDelta>>1;
                while(xx1!=xx2)
```

```
                {
                        Plot(xx1, yy1, color);
                        Cycle+=ShDelta;
                        if(Cycle>LgDelta)
                        {
                Cycle-=LgDelta;
                yy1+=ShStep;
                        }
                        xx1+=LgStep;
                }
                Plot(xx1, yy1, color);
        }
        else
        {
                Cycle=ShDelta >> 1;
                Swap(&LgDelta, &ShDelta);
                Swap(&LgStep, &ShStep);
                while(yy1 != yy2)
                {
                        Plot(xx1, yy1, color);
                        Cycle+=ShDelta;
                        if(Cycle>LgDelta)
                        {
                Cycle-=LgDelta;
                xx1+=ShStep;
                        }
                        yy1+=LgStep;
                }
                Plot(xx1, yy1, color);
        }
}

int     CentreX, CentreY;

void Init_Graphics(Byte Mode)
{
        switch(Mode)
        {
                case 19     : Res=Low_Res;
                              MaxXRes=320;
```

```
                            MaxYRes=200;
                            break;
          case 45    : Res=Medium_Res;
                            MaxXRes=640;
                            MaxYRes=350;
                            break;
          case 120 :   Res=Medium_Res;
                            MaxXRes=640;
                            MaxYRes=400;
                            break;
          case 46    : Res=Medium_Res;
                            MaxXRes=640;
                            MaxYRes=480;
                            break;
          case 48    : Res=Medium_Res;
                            MaxXRes=800;
                            MaxYRes=600;
                            break;
          case 56    : Res=High_Res;
                            MaxXRes=1024;
                            MaxYRes=768;
                            break;
          default    : printf("Mode %d is not a valid graphics
                            mode\n\n",Mode);
                            puts("Hit any key to exit");
                            getch();
                            exit(1);
                            break;
}
MaxX=MaxXRes-1;
MaxY=MaxYRes-1;
if(XRes==0)
      XRes=MaxXRes;
if(YRes==0)
      YRes=MaxYRes;
Calc_Offsets();
if(Res==Medium_Res)
      Pre_Calc_Y2=farcalloc(768, sizeof(DWord));
else
      Pre_Calc_Y1=farcalloc(768, sizeof(Word));
```

```
        CentreX=XRes/2;
        CentreY=YRes/2;
        Asp=(1024.0/768.0)*((float)YRes/(float)XRes);
        Pre_Calc();
        Set_Mode(Mode);
        Init_Palette_2(Color);
        Set_Palette(Color);
}

void Set_Graphics_Mode(Word xRes, Word yRes)
{
        XRes=xRes;
        YRes=yRes;
        if((XRes<321) && (YRes<201))
                Init_Graphics(19);
        else if((XRes<641) && (YRes<351))
                Init_Graphics(45);
        else if((XRes<641) && (YRes<401))
                Init_Graphics(120);
        else if((XRes<641) && (YRes<481))
                Init_Graphics(46);
        else if((XRes<801) && (YRes<601))
                Init_Graphics(48);
        else
                Init_Graphics(56);
}

void Wait_For_Key()
{
        char k;

        while(!(k=getch()));
}

void Exit_Graphics()
{
        sound(1000);
        delay(500);
        nosound();
        if(Pre_Calc_Y1>0)
```

```
        Set_Mode(3);
}

void Title()
{
        textcolor(YELLOW);
        textbackground(BLUE);
        clrscr();
}
```

```
/*
```

```
        Three-Dimensional Plotting Routines
```

```
    InitPlotting         - rotation and tilt angles
    InitPerspective      - observer location and distances
    MapCoordinates       - map 3D space onto the 2D screen
    CartesianPlot        - plot a cartesian system point
    CylindricalPlot3D    - plot a cylindrical system point
    SphericalPlot3D      - plot a spherical system point
    DrawLine3D           - plot a line from 3D coordinates
*/

float CosA, SinA;
float CosB, SinB;
float CosACosB, SinASinB;
float CosASinB, SinACosB;

void Init_Plotting(int Ang, int Tlt)
{
        CentreX=XRes/2;
        CentreY=YRes/2;
        Angl=Ang;
        Tilt=Tlt;
        CosA=CosD(Angl);
        SinA=SinD(Angl);
        CosB=CosD(Tilt);
```

```
        SinB=SinD(Tilt);
        CosACosB=CosA*CosB;
        SinASinB=SinA*SinB;
        CosASinB=CosA*SinB;
        SinACosB=SinA*CosB;
}


void Init_Perspective(Boolean Perspective, float x, float y,  float z,
                                                            float m)
{
        PerspectivePlot=Perspective;
        Mx=x;
        My=y;
        Mz=z;
        ds=m;
}


void Map_Coordinates(float X, float Y, float Z, int *Xp, int *Yp)
{
        float Xt, Yt, Zt;
        float OneOverZt;

        Xt=(Mx+X*CosA-Y*SinA);
        Yt=(My+X*SinASinB+Y*CosASinB+Z*CosB);
        if(PerspectivePlot)
        {
                Zt=Mz+X*SinACosB+Y*CosACosB-Z*SinB;
                OneOverZt=1.0/Zt;
                *Xp=CentreX+Round(ds*Xt*OneOverZt);
                if(Res!=Low_Res)
                        *Yp=CentreY-Round(ds*Yt*OneOverZt);
                else
                        *Yp=CentreY-Round(ds*Yt*OneOverZt*Asp);
        }
        else
        {
                *Xp=CentreX+Round(Xt);
                if(Res!=Low_Res)
                        *Yp=CentreY-Round(Yt);
```

```
            else
                    *Yp=CentreY-Round(Yt*Asp);
        }
}

void Cartesian_Plot_3D(float X, float Y, float Z, Byte Color)
{
        int Xp, Yp;

        Map_Coordinates(X, Y, Z, &Xp, &Yp);
        Plot(Xp, Yp, Color);
}

void Cylindrical_Plot_3D(float Rho, float Theta, float Z, Byte
                                                        Color)
{
        float X, Y;

        Theta=Radians(Theta);
        X=Rho*cos(Theta);
        Y=Rho*sin(Theta);
        Cartesian_Plot_3D(X, Y, Z, Color);
}

void Spherical_Plot_3D(float R, float Theta, float Phi, Byte
                                                        Color)
{
        float X, Y, Z;

        Theta=Radians(Theta);
        Phi=Radians(Phi);
        X=R*sin(Theta)*cos(Phi);
        Y=R*sin(Theta)*sin(Phi);
        Z=R*cos(Theta);
        Cartesian_Plot_3D(X, Y, Z, Color);
}

void Draw_Line_3D(TDA Pnt1, TDA Pnt2, Byte Color)
{
        int    Xp1, Yp1;
```

```
int    Xp2, Yp2;
float  x1, y1, z1;
float  x2, y2, z2;

UnVec(Pnt1, &x1, &y1, &z1);
UnVec(Pnt2, &x2, &y2, &z2);
Map_Coordinates(x1, y1, z1, &Xp1, &Yp1);
Map_Coordinates(x2, y2, z2, &Xp2, &Yp2);
Draw(Xp1, Yp1, Xp2, Yp2, Color);
}
```

```
/*
```

┌───┐
│ ┌───┐ │
│ │   │ │
│ │   Pixel Routines   │ │
│ │   │ │
│ └───┘ │
└───┘

```
PutPixel  - plot pixel
GetPixel  - get pixel

Color1    - blue
     2    - green
     3    - cyan
     4    - red
     5    - magenta
     6    - brown/yellow
     7    - gray-scale

     Intensity levels (0..35) for each color
*/

void Put_Pixel(int x, int y, Byte Color, Byte Intensity)
{
     Byte Col;

     if(Intensity>MaxInten)
          exit(1);
     Col=((MaxInten+1)*(Color-1)+Intensity) & 255;
     Plot(x, y, Col);
}
```

```
static Word Old_Page_2;

Byte Get_Pixel(Word x, Word y)
{
      long L_Offset;
      Word Offset, Page;
      char far *address;
      Byte color;

      if((x<XRes) && (y<YRes))
      {
            switch(Res)
            {
              case High_Res : Offset=Pre_Calc_Y1[y+Y_Off]+x+X_Off;
                        Page=(y>>6)&15;
                        if(Page!=Old_Page_2)
                        {
                                outpw(0x3CD, (Page>>4)|Old_Page);
                                Old_Page_2=Page;
                        }
                        address=(char far*)
                  (0xA0000000L+Offset);
                        color=*address;
                        break;
                    case Medium_Res :   x+=X_Off;
                        y+=Y_Off;
                        L_Offset=Pre_Calc_Y2[y]+x;
                        Page=L_Offset>>16;
                        Offset=L_Offset&65535;
                        if(Page!=Old_Page_2)
                        {
                                outpw(0x3CD, (Page>>4)|Old_Page);
                                Old_Page_2=Page;
                        }
                        address=(char far*)
                  (0xA0000000L+Offset); color=*address;
                        break;
                    case Low_Res :
Offset=Pre_Calc_Y1[y+Y_Off]+x+X_Off; address=(char far*)
                                (0xA0000000L+Offset);
```

```
                                    color=*address;
                                    break;
                       }
            }
        return(color);
}


Byte Get_Pixel_2(Word x, Word y)
{
        x+=X_Off;
        y+=Y_Off;
        reg.x.ax=3328;
        reg.x.dx=y;
        reg.x.cx=x;
        int86(0x10,&reg,&reg);
        return(reg.x.ax&255);
}


/*
```

```
                  Set Up Coordinate Axes and Color Palette
```

```
    PutAxisAndPalette      - toggle for axis and palette
    AxisAndPalette         - place axis and color palette on screen
*/


void Put_Axis_And_Palette(Boolean PlaceOnScreen)
{
        if(PlaceOnScreen)
                Draw_Axis_And_Palette=true;
        else
                Draw_Axis_And_Palette=false;
}


void Display_Axis()
{
        int x, y, z, sx, sy;

        sx=XRes/320;
        sy=YRes/200;
```

```
        for(x=-100*sx; x<101*sx; x++)
        {
                Cartesian_Plot_3D(x, 0, 0, 35);
                Cartesian_Plot_3D(100*sx, 0, 0, 251);
        }
        for(y=-100*sy; y<101*sy; y++)
        {
                Cartesian_Plot_3D(0, y, 0, 71);
                Cartesian_Plot_3D(0, 100*sy, 0,251);
        }
        for(z=-100*sx; z<101*sx; z++)
        {
                Cartesian_Plot_3D(0, 0, z, 107);
                Cartesian_Plot_3D(0, 0, 100*sx, 251);
        }
}


void Display_Palette()
{
        int    X, Y, sx, sy;
        Byte Color;
        Byte Intensity;

        sx=XRes/320;
        sy=YRes/200;
        for(Color=1; Color<=MaxCol; Color++)
        {
                for(Intensity=0; Intensity<=MaxInten; Intensity++)
                {
                        for(X=0; X<4*sx; X++)
                        {
                        for(Y=0; Y<4*sy; Y++)
                                Put_Pixel(X+(5*sx)*Color,
                                        (190*sy)-Y-(5*sy)*Intensity,
                                        Color,
                                        Intensity);
                        }
                }
        }
}
```

```
void Axis_And_Palette()
{
      if(Draw_Axis_And_Palette)
      {
            Display_Axis();
            Display_Palette();
      }
}
```

Listing 3-1. *Graph.C.*

CHAPTER 4

Using the Modules

Having examined the mathematics and graphics modules found in Chapters 1, 2, and 3, we now can explore some of their more practical uses. The fastest and easiest way to familiarize yourself with the modules is to use and study them with sample programs. You can then use them to produce your own graphics programs and perhaps modify them to suit your particular needs. In this chapter, the modules are used in interesting, easy-to-understand sample programs ranging from those that simulate physical reality and life processes to some that generate bizarre fractal objects.

Three-Dimensional Iterated Function System Programs

The first few programs we'll look at use a class of functions known as *procedural*: instead of defining and storing a large data set of points to describe a shape, we define a procedure for computing the value (color, intensity, and shape) at any point, given previously computed values for surrounding points. For instance, in one dimension, given values of a function at 0.0 and 1.0 and a function for generating the value at the halfway point, 0.5, we can calculate all the other points. We do this by computing the value at the midpoint and then recursively calling the procedure for each of the two new segments, from 0.0 to 0.5 and from 0.5 to 1.0. This gives us the values at 0.25 and 0.75, respectively. We can then reevaluate the function using the four smaller segments, and so forth.

A procedural function is one that takes as input the values at the "corners" of a region (*corners* here means the points along the boundary of the region, such as the corners of a square in two dimensions) and generates new values for a point or points inside the region. Most procedural functions simply generate new midpoint values. The region is then divided into smaller copies of the original region, and the function is called again. This process can continue indefinitely. For graphics purposes, the regions are subdivided until the subregions are less than one screen pixel in size. This is the essence of a fractal process: no matter how small a region gets, you can still generate more detail simply by evaluating the procedure on the new, smaller region.

A fractal process is a special case of a procedural process in that a fractal object is generally required to be *self-similar*; in other words, as you generate finer and finer object detail, that detail begins to look like the object itself. A leaf is a good example. The branching patterns in a leaf look very similar to the shape of the leaf itself. Examination with a magnifying glass reveals that the branches have finer branches, which in turn have finer branches, and so on. Each of these structures looks similar to the leaf, and even to the branch from which the leaf was taken. The shapes we'll see in this section—including clouds, plasmas, and mathematical shapes—also demonstrate this property.

The *3D-Avr.C IFS* Program

For our first example, let's start with a common fractal graphics program. Plates 1 and 2 depict the familiar Sierpinski triangle and its three-dimensional counterpart, the Sierpinski tetrahedron. Both images are generated by successively averaging randomly selected three-dimensional points from a given set of starting points in three-dimensional space (in this case, triangles and tetrahedrons). This technique is a subset of the iterated function system (IFS) process—another class of procedural functions in which the program iterates an equation by inserting the previously generated values into the equation. Since only translation of points into three-dimensional space is taken into account, this example is considered a subset of the IFS process which normally translates, scales and rotates points. Let's look at how this is done.

The program begins by initializing first the graphics mode, using Mode 56 (1024x768, 256 colors), then the three-dimensional plotting routines. *InitPerspective* is called and orthographic projection is chosen. To make the view more interesting, *InitPlotting* places the viewer 10 degrees around the z axis and tilts the xy plane toward the viewer 20 degrees. Finally, *PutAxisAndPalette* is set to true so that coordinate axes and a palette will be placed on the screen when *AxisAndPalette* is called.

3D-Avr.C (Listing 4-1) can generate nine fractal shapes, called *Line*, *Triangle*, *Pentagon*, *Tetrahedron2D*, *MengerSponge2D*, *Tetrahedron3D*, *MengerSponge3D*, *MengerSpongeSlice3D*, and *Diamond3D*. Each shape is defined by a number of points, or *maps*, representing the corners of the object in three-dimensional space. The program is seeded with one of the maps and is allowed to iterate using the following equation:

$$
\begin{aligned}
x_n &= (x + H[m]) / 2.0 \\
y_n &= (y + K[m]) / 2.0 \\
z_n &= (z + L[m]) / 2.0 \\
x &= x_n \\
y &= y_n \\
z &= z_n
\end{aligned}
$$

(Equation 4-1)

H, *K*, and *L* represent the *X*, *Y*, and *Z* elements of the point. The variable *m* represents the transformation map number corresponding to the transformation to be used (in this case, translation). *m* is randomly changed on each iteration to vary the map used for the point transformation. Successively averaging these randomly chosen points for each iteration creates the three-dimensional fractal shape. This program projects the point to the screen coordinates (by the *Cartesian_Plot_3D* routine using *Map_Coordinates*) and plots it on each iteration.

Next, we'll examine a program that uses rotation and scaling as well as translation.

```
/*

        Three-Dimensional Iterated Function Systems
                 By Christopher D. Watkins


*/
#include "stdio.h"
#include "stdlib.h"
#include "defs.h"
#include "globals.h"
#include "mathb.h"
```

```c
#include "graphb.h"
char mapping[80];
float h[8], k[8], l[8];
Byte maxmap;
float r, scale;
void Line()
{
    strcpy(mapping, "Line");
    h[0]=-1.00;   h[1]=1.00;
    k[0]=-1.00;   k[1]=1.00;
    l[0]=-1.00;   l[1]=1.00;
    maxmap=2;
    r=0.5;
    scale=500.0;
}
void Triangle()
{
    strcpy(mapping, "Triangle");
    h[0]=-0.71;   h[1]=0.00;   h[2]=0.71;
    k[0]=-0.71;   k[1]=1.00;   k[2]=-0.71;
    l[0]=0.00;   l[1]=0.00;   l[2]=0.00;
    maxmap=3;
    r=0.5;
    scale=500.0;
}
void Pentagon()
{
    strcpy(mapping, "2D Pentagon");
    h[0]=0.50;   h[1]=1.00;   h[2]=0.0;   h[3]=0.84;
h[4]=0.16;
    k[0]=0.00;   k[1]=0.30;   k[2]=0.30;   k[3]=1.00;
k[4]=1.00;
    l[0]=0.00;   l[1]=0.00;   l[2]=0.00;   l[3]=0.00;
l[4]=0.00;
    maxmap=5;
    r=0.5;
    scale=400.0;
}
void Tetrahedron2D()
{
```

```
    strcpy(mapping, "2D Tetrahedron");
    h[0]=0.56;   h[1]=0.00;   h[2]=0.67;   h[3]=1.00;
    k[0]=0.00;   k[1]=0.88;   k[2]=1.00;   k[3]=0.90;
    l[0]=0.00;   l[1]=0.00;   l[2]=0.00;   l[3]=0.00;
    maxmap=4;
    r=0.5;
    scale=600.0;
}

void MengerSponge2D()
{
    strcpy(mapping, "2D Menger Sponge");
    h[0]=0.00;   h[1]=0.50;   h[2]=1.00;   h[3]=1.00;
    h[4]=0.50;   h[5]=0.00;   h[6]=0.50;   h[7]=0.50;
    k[0]=0.14;   k[1]=0.00;   k[2]=0.14;   k[3]=0.64;
    k[4]=1.00;   k[5]=0.64;   k[6]=0.27;   k[7]=0.31;
    l[0]=0.00;   l[1]=0.00;   l[2]=0.00;   l[3]=0.00;
    l[4]=0.00;   l[5]=0.00;   l[6]=0.00;   l[7]=0.00;
    maxmap=8;
    r=0.3333333333;
    scale=700.0;
}
void Tetrahedron3D()
{
    strcpy(mapping, "3D Tetrahedron");
    h[0]=0.00;   h[1]=0.00;   h[2]=-0.71;   h[3]= 0.71;
    k[0]=0.00;   k[1]=1.00;   k[2]=-0.71;   k[3]=-0.71;
    l[0]=1.00;   l[1]=0.00;   l[2]= 0.00;   l[3]= 0.00;
    maxmap=4;
    r=0.5;
    scale=250.0;
}
void MengerSponge3D()
{
    strcpy(mapping, "3D Menger Sponge");
    h[0]=0.00;   h[1]=1.00;   h[2]=0.00;   h[3]=1.00;
    h[4]=0.00;   h[5]=1.00;   h[6]=0.00;   h[7]=1.00;
    k[0]=0.00;   k[1]=0.00;   k[2]=1.00;   k[3]=1.00;
    k[4]=0.00;   k[5]=0.00;   k[6]=1.00;   k[7]=1.00;
    l[0]=0.00;   l[1]=0.00;   l[2]=0.00;   l[3]=0.00;
```

```
    l[4]=1.00;  l[5]=1.00;  l[6]=1.00;  l[7]=1.00;
    maxmap=8;
    r=0.3333333333;
    scale=400.0;
}
void MengerSpongeSlice3D()
{
strcpy(mapping, "3D Menger Sponge Slice"); h[0]=0.00;
h[1]=1.00;  h[2]=0.00;  h[3]=1.00;
    h[4]=0.00;  h[5]=1.00;  h[6]=0.00;
    k[0]=0.00;  k[1]=0.00;  k[2]=1.00;  k[3]=1.00;
    k[4]=0.00;  k[5]=0.00;
    l[0]=0.00;  l[1]=0.00;  l[2]=0.00;  l[3]=0.00;
    l[4]=1.00;  l[5]=1.00;
    maxmap=6;
    r=0.3333333333;
    scale=400.0;
}
void Diamond3D()
{
    strcpy(mapping, "3D Diamond");
    h[0]= 0.00;  h[1]= 0.71;  h[2]=-0.71;  h[3]=0.71;  h[4]=-
0.71;  h[5]= 0.00;
k[0]= 0.00;  k[1]= 0.71;  k[2]=-0.71;  k[3]=-0.71;  k[4]= 0.71;
k[5]= 0.00; l[0]= 1.00;  l[1]= 0.00;  l[2]= 0.00;  l[3]=0.00;
l[4]= 0.00;  l[5]=-1.00;
    maxmap=6;
    r=0.3333333333;
    scale=600.0;
}
float x, y, z;

void Iterate()
{
    int m;
    float xn, yn, zn;
    Byte col;
    m=random(maxmap);
    xn=(x+h[m])*r;
    yn=(y+k[m])*r;
```

```
    zn=(z+l[m])*r;
    if(m==7)
        col=35;
    else
        col=(m+1)*36-1;
Cartesian_Plot_3D(Round(xn), Round(yn), Round(zn), col);
    x=xn;
    y=yn;
    z=zn;
}
Byte q;
int sel;
int Get_Selection()
{
    char c[4];
    clrscr();
    puts("0 : Line");
    puts("1 : Triangle");
    puts("2 : Pentagon");
    puts("3 : 2D Tetrahedron");
    puts("4 : 2D Menger Sponge");
    puts("5 : 3D Tetrahedrom");
    puts("6 : 3D Menger Sponge");
    puts("7 : Menger Sponge Slice");
    puts("8 : Diamond");
    puts("9 : Exit");
    while(!isdigit(c[0]))
    {
        while(!kbhit());
        c[0]=getch();
    }
    return(atoi(c));
}
void main()
{
    Title();
    while((sel=Get_Selection())<9)
```

```
    {
        for(q=0; q<8; q++)
        {
            h[q]=0.0;
            k[q]=0.0;
            l[q]=0.0;
        }
        Init_Graphics(56);
        switch(sel)
        {
case 0 : Init_Perspective(false, 0, 0, 500, 500);
Init_Plotting(205, 15); Put_Axis_And_Palette(true);
Axis_And_Palette();
                Line();
                break;
case 1 : Init_Perspective(false, 0, 0, 500, 500);
Init_Plotting(205, 45); Put_Axis_And_Palette(true);
Axis_And_Palette();
                Triangle();
                break;
case 2 : Init_Perspective(false, 0, 0, 500, 500);
Init_Plotting(205, 15); Put_Axis_And_Palette(true);
Axis_And_Palette();
                Pentagon();
                break;
case 3 : Init_Perspective(false, 0, 0, 500, 500);
Init_Plotting(205, 15); Put_Axis_And_Palette(true);
Axis_And_Palette();
                Tetrahedron2D();
                break;
case 4 : Init_Perspective(false, 0, 0, 500, 500);
Init_Plotting(205, 15); Put_Axis_And_Palette(true);
Axis_And_Palette();
                MengerSponge2D();
                break;
case 5 : Init_Perspective(false, 0, 0, 500, 500);
Init_Plotting(205, 15); Put_Axis_And_Palette(true);
Axis_And_Palette();
                Tetrahedron3D();
                break;
```

```
case 6 : Init_Perspective(false, 0, 0, 500, 500);
Init_Plotting(205, 15); Put_Axis_And_Palette(true);
Axis_And_Palette();
                MengerSponge3D();
                break;
case 7 : Init_Perspective(false, 0, 0, 500, 500);
Init_Plotting(205, 15); Put_Axis_And_Palette(true);
Axis_And_Palette(); MengerSpongeSlice3D();
                break;
case 8 : Init_Perspective(false, 0, 0, 500, 500);
Init_Plotting(205, 15); Put_Axis_And_Palette(true);
Axis_And_Palette();
                Diamond3D();
                break;
    }
    for(q=0; q<maxmap; q++)
    {
        h[q]*=scale;
        k[q]*=scale;
        l[q]*=scale;
    }
    x=h[0];
    y=k[0];
    z=l[0];
    while(!(kbhit()))
        Iterate();
    Exit_Graphics();
}
Set_Mode(3);
```

Listing 4-1. *3D-Avr.C.*

The *3D-Ifs.C* IFS Program

The other IFS sample program, *3D-Ifs.C*, (Listing 4-2) uses a similar technique to create images (the fractal image in Plate 3 is an example). However, the transformation equations aren't limited to translation: maps hold information describing each point, and each point is described by how it is translated (H,K,L), rotated (*Th* rotation about the z axis; *Ph* tilt of *xy* plane), and scaled (R,S,T).

The program proceeds much the same way as *3D-Avr.C* except that it uses perspective, rather than orthographic, projection. We must therefore set a desired observer position—in this case, at (*Mx* = 50, *My* = -20, *Mz* = 350)—and rotate the scene so that we're looking toward the origin from this position. *InitPlotting* sets the viewer -115 degrees around the *z* axis and tilts the *xy* plane toward the viewer 25 degrees.

This program can generate an infinite number of interesting fractal shapes. It contains two sets of object data; one is commented out, so to access it you must comment out the active set and "un-comment out" the other set. (You comment out code when you add /* and */ around the sections that you do not want to compile.) The program must be recompiled and linked each time a change is made. (As an exercise, you might try modifying the program to interactively ask which model to use.)

By putting a little time and thought into the map definitions, you can easily create objects that simulate trees, ferns, and other plantlike structures. Try clearing the maps and playing with various combinations and selected transformations. You can produce a range of diverse images by varying the transformations and their combinations.

Now let's move on to a program that generates cloud- and plasmalike structures.

```
/*

        Three-Dimensional Iterated Function Systems
               By Christopher D. Watkins

*/
#include "stdio.h"
#include "stdlib.h"
#include "defs.h"
#include "globals.h"
#include "mathb.h"
#include "graphb.h"
char mapping[80];
float h[8], k[8], l[8];
```

```
Byte maxmap;
float r, scale;
void Line()
{
    strcpy(mapping, "Line");
    h[0]=-1.00;   h[1]=1.00;
    k[0]=-1.00;   k[1]=1.00;
    l[0]=-1.00;   l[1]=1.00;
    maxmap=2;
    r=0.5;
    scale=500.0;
}
void Triangle()
{
    strcpy(mapping, "Triangle");
    h[0]=-0.71;   h[1]=0.00;   h[2]=0.71;
    k[0]=-0.71;   k[1]=1.00;   k[2]=-0.71;
    l[0]=0.00;   l[1]=0.00;   l[2]=0.00;
    maxmap=3;
    r=0.5;
    scale=500.0;
}
void Pentagon()
{
    strcpy(mapping, "2D Pentagon");
    h[0]=0.50;   h[1]=1.00;   h[2]=0.0;   h[3]=0.84;
h[4]=0.16;
    k[0]=0.00;   k[1]=0.30;   k[2]=0.30;   k[3]=1.00;
k[4]=1.00;
    l[0]=0.00;   l[1]=0.00;   l[2]=0.00;   l[3]=0.00;
l[4]=0.00;
    maxmap=5;
    r=0.5;
    scale=400.0;
}
void Tetrahedron2D()
{
    strcpy(mapping, "2D Tetrahedron");
    h[0]=0.56;   h[1]=0.00;   h[2]=0.67;   h[3]=1.00;
```

```
    k[0]=0.00;  k[1]=0.88;   k[2]=1.00;   k[3]=0.90;
    l[0]=0.00;  l[1]=0.00;   l[2]=0.00;   l[3]=0.00;
    maxmap=4;
    r=0.5;
    scale=600.0;
}

void MengerSponge2D()
{
    strcpy(mapping, "2D Menger Sponge");
    h[0]=0.00;  h[1]=0.50;  h[2]=1.00;  h[3]=1.00;
    h[4]=0.50;  h[5]=0.00;  h[6]=0.50;  h[7]=0.50;
    k[0]=0.14;  k[1]=0.00;  k[2]=0.14;  k[3]=0.64;
    k[4]=1.00;  k[5]=0.64;  k[6]=0.27;  k[7]=0.31;
    l[0]=0.00;  l[1]=0.00;  l[2]=0.00;  l[3]=0.00;
    l[4]=0.00;  l[5]=0.00;  l[6]=0.00;  l[7]=0.00;
    maxmap=8;
    r=0.3333333333;
    scale=700.0;
}
void Tetrahedron3D()
{
    strcpy(mapping, "3D Tetrahedron");
    h[0]=0.00;  h[1]=0.00;  h[2]=-0.71;  h[3]= 0.71;
    k[0]=0.00;  k[1]=1.00;  k[2]=-0.71;  k[3]=-0.71;
    l[0]=1.00;  l[1]=0.00;  l[2]= 0.00;  l[3]= 0.00;
    maxmap=4;
    r=0.5;
    scale=250.0;
}
void MengerSponge3D()
{
    strcpy(mapping, "3D Menger Sponge");
    h[0]=0.00;  h[1]=1.00;  h[2]=0.00;  h[3]=1.00;
    h[4]=0.00;  h[5]=1.00;  h[6]=0.00;  h[7]=1.00;
    k[0]=0.00;  k[1]=0.00;  k[2]=1.00;  k[3]=1.00;
    k[4]=0.00;  k[5]=0.00;  k[6]=1.00;  k[7]=1.00;
    l[0]=0.00;  l[1]=0.00;  l[2]=0.00;  l[3]=0.00;
    l[4]=1.00;  l[5]=1.00;  l[6]=1.00;  l[7]=1.00;
```

```
        maxmap=8;
        r=0.3333333333;
        scale=400.0;
}
void MengerSpongeSlice3D()
{
strcpy(mapping, "3D Menger Sponge Slice"); h[0]=0.00;
h[1]=1.00;   h[2]=0.00;   h[3]=1.00;
        h[4]=0.00;   h[5]=1.00;   h[6]=0.00;
        k[0]=0.00;   k[1]=0.00;   k[2]=1.00;   k[3]=1.00;
        k[4]=0.00;   k[5]=0.00;
        l[0]=0.00;   l[1]=0.00;   l[2]=0.00;   l[3]=0.00;
        l[4]=1.00;   l[5]=1.00;
        maxmap=6;
        r=0.3333333333;
        scale=400.0;
}
void Diamond3D()
{
        strcpy(mapping, "3D Diamond");
        h[0]= 0.00;  h[1]= 0.71;  h[2]=-0.71;  h[3]=0.71;  h[4]=-
0.71;  h[5]= 0.00;
k[0]= 0.00;  k[1]= 0.71;  k[2]=-0.71;  k[3]=-0.71;  k[4]= 0.71;
k[5]= 0.00; l[0]= 1.00;  l[1]= 0.00;  l[2]= 0.00;  l[3]=0.00;
l[4]= 0.00;  l[5]=-1.00;
        maxmap=6;
        r=0.3333333333;
        scale=600.0;
}
float x, y, z;

void Iterate()
{
        int m;
        float xn, yn, zn;
        Byte col;
        m=random(maxmap);
        xn=(x+h[m])*r;
        yn=(y+k[m])*r;
```

```
            zn=(z+l[m])*r;
            if(m==7)
                col=35;
            else
                col=(m+1)*36-1;
    Cartesian_Plot_3D(Round(xn), Round(yn), Round(zn), col);
            x=xn;
            y=yn;
            z=zn;
    }
    Byte q;
    int sel;
    int Get_Selection()
    {
        char c[4];
        clrscr();
        puts("0 : Line");
        puts("1 : Triangle");
        puts("2 : Pentagon");
        puts("3 : 2D Tetrahedron");
        puts("4 : 2D Menger Sponge");
        puts("5 : 3D Tetrahedrom");
        puts("6 : 3D Menger Sponge");
        puts("7 : Menger Sponge Slice");
        puts("8 : Diamond");
        puts("9 : Exit");
        while(!isdigit(c[0]))
        {
            while(!kbhit());
            c[0]=getch();
        }
        return(atoi(c));
    }
    void main()
    {
        Title();
        while((sel=Get_Selection())<9)
        {
            for(q=0; q<8; q++)
```

```
                {
                    h[q]=0.0;
                    k[q]=0.0;
                    l[q]=0.0;
                }
                Init_Graphics(56);
                switch(sel)
                {
case 0 : Init_Perspective(false, 0, 0, 500, 500);
Init_Plotting(205, 15); Put_Axis_And_Palette(true);
Axis_And_Palette();
                    Line();
                    break;
case 1 : Init_Perspective(false, 0, 0, 500, 500);
Init_Plotting(205, 45); Put_Axis_And_Palette(true);
Axis_And_Palette();
                    Triangle();
                    break;
case 2 : Init_Perspective(false, 0, 0, 500, 500);
Init_Plotting(205, 15); Put_Axis_And_Palette(true);
Axis_And_Palette();
                    Pentagon();
                    break;
case 3 : Init_Perspective(false, 0, 0, 500, 500);
Init_Plotting(205, 15); Put_Axis_And_Palette(true);
Axis_And_Palette();
                    Tetrahedron2D();
                    break;
case 4 : Init_Perspective(false, 0, 0, 500, 500);
Init_Plotting(205, 15); Put_Axis_And_Palette(true);
Axis_And_Palette();
                    MengerSponge2D();
                    break;
case 5 : Init_Perspective(false, 0, 0, 500, 500);
Init_Plotting(205, 15); Put_Axis_And_Palette(true);
Axis_And_Palette();
                    Tetrahedron3D();
                    break;
case 6 : Init_Perspective(false, 0, 0, 500, 500);
```

```
Init_Plotting(205, 15); Put_Axis_And_Palette(true);
Axis_And_Palette();
                MengerSponge3D();
                break;
case 7 : Init_Perspective(false, 0, 0, 500, 500);
Init_Plotting(205, 15); Put_Axis_And_Palette(true);
Axis_And_Palette(); MengerSpongeSlice3D();
                break;
case 8 : Init_Perspective(false, 0, 0, 500, 500);
Init_Plotting(205, 15); Put_Axis_And_Palette(true);
Axis_And_Palette();
                Diamond3D();
                break;
    }
    for(q=0; q<maxmap; q++)
    {
        h[q]*=scale;
        k[q]*=scale;
        l[q]*=scale;
    }
    x=h[0];
    y=k[0];
    z=l[0];
    while(!(kbhit()))
        Iterate();
    Exit_Graphics();
}
Set_Mode(3);
```

Listing 4-2. *3D-ifs.C.*

A Cloud and Plasma Generator

Plate 4's depiction of puffy white clouds against a deep-blue sky is one of the three types of plasmalike images that *Clouds.C* (Listing 4-3) can generate. Adjusting the colors in the palette will result in different images. First, let's back up and examine the fractal procedural generator.

The method described here has been used by many researchers to generate models of mountain ranges, forests, oceans, plants, and other natural phenomena.

(This technique is also discussed later in Part 3, the ray-tracing section, where a mountain database generator is described.) Our procedure is based on the four corners of a rectangle. To start the program, we generate four randomly colored points placed at the corners of a blank screen. We then compute a color for the midpoint of each pair of points and for the centerpoint of the screen. This color is based on the average of the two points in the surrounding pair and then offset slightly in a random manner. We recursively call the procedure using the four smaller squares defined by the newly computed points. The subdivision process continues until the entire screen is filled with color. The resulting display looks more chaotic than truly random because each pixel's color was computed relative to the surrounding pixels. If each pixel's value was not affected by surrounding pixels, or previously calculated values, it would look random.

Note that the program starts off by initializing a random seed for the pseudorandom number generator. By changing this seed, you can create entire new varieties of patterns. If you find a plasma structure you really like, you can regenerate the image using the seed value.

Next, we initialize a color palette that determines which of the three images (clouds or plasmas) is generated. The first palette (*InitPalette3*) generates an eerie, fluorescent-looking plasma display, the second (*InitPalette4*) generates the clouds shown in Plate 4, and the third (*InitPalette5*) generates something that looks like a high-frequency, high-voltage electrical discharge.

Try your hand at generating other palettes that yield bizarre images. One rule of thumb: the best images are produced when a section of the palette has one color that increases in intensity while another color has decreasing intensity. This allows for smooth motion when the palette is cycled (shifted one color at a time), as it is in this program. Palette cycling (discussed in detail in Chapter 14) is a simple, effective animation technique that can, for instance, create puffy shapes that fade away and reappear against a deep-blue sky. Animation of fluorescent plasmas creates an eerie scene as they crawl across your screen, while animation of electrical discharges makes them resemble sizzling sparks between the points of a high-voltage spark gap.

Now let's turn away from the ethereal and model something in the real world.

```
/*
┌─────────────────────────────────────────────────────────┐
│                                                         │
│                  Clouds Generator                       │
│               by Christopher D. Watkins                 │
│                                                         │
└─────────────────────────────────────────────────────────┘
*/

    #include "stdio.h"
    #include "dos.h"
    #include "string.h"
    #include "math.h"
    #include "defs.h"
    #include "globals.h"
    #include "mathb.h"
    #include "graphb.h"

    void InitPalette3(Palette_Register color)  /*  plasmas  */
    {
      #define mcol 63

      Byte i;

      color[0].Red=0;
      color[0].Grn=Round(mcol/85.0);
      color[0].Blu=mcol;
      for(i=1; i<=85; i++)
      {
        color[i].Red=0;
        color[i].Grn=Round((float)(i*mcol)/85.0);
        color[i].Blu=Round((float)((86-i)*mcol)/85.0);
        color[i+85].Red=Round((float)(i*mcol)/85.0);
        color[i+85].Grn=Round((float)((86-i)*mcol)/85.0);
        color[i+85].Blu=0;
        color[i+170].Red=Round((float)((86-i)*mcol)/85.0);
        color[i+170].Grn=0;
        color[i+170].Blu=Round((float)(i*mcol)/85.0);
      }
    }

    void InitPalette4(Palette_Register color)  /*  clouds  */
    {
```

```
  #define mcol 63

  Word i;

  for(i=0; i<=255; i++)
  {
    color[i].Red=Round((float)(abs(i-127)*mcol)/127.0);
    color[i].Grn=Round((float)(abs(i-127)*mcol)/127.0);
    color[i].Blu=mcol;
  }
}

void InitPalette5(Palette_Register color)  /*  e-discharge  */
{
  #define mcol2 63.0

  Word i;

  for(i=0; i<=255; i++)
  {
    if(i<13)
    {
      color[i].Red=Round((float)(abs(i-12)/12.0)*mcol2);
      color[i].Grn=Round((float)(abs(i-12)/12.0)*mcol2/3.0);
      color[i].Blu=Round(mcol2/2.0);
    }
    else
    {
      color[i].Red=0;
      color[i].Grn=0;
      color[i].Blu=0;
    }
  }
}

void New_Col(int xa, int ya, int x, int y, int xb, int yb)
{
  long color;

  color=abs(xa-xb)+abs(ya-yb);
  color=RandInt(color<<1)-color;
```

```
    color=color+(Get_Pixel_2(xa, ya)+Get_Pixel_2(xb, yb)+1)>>1;
    if((color<1))
      color=1;
    else if ((color>255))
      color=255;
    if((Get_Pixel_2(x, y)==0))
        Plot(x, y, color);
  }

void Sub_Divide(int x1, int y1, int x2, int y2)
{
  int x, y, color;

  if(!(((x2-x1<2)&&(y2-y1<2)))
  {
    x=(x1+x2)>>1;
    y=(y1+y2)>>1;
    New_Col(x1, y1, x, y1, x2, y1);
    New_Col(x2, y1, x2, y, x2, y2);
    New_Col(x1, y2, x, y2, x2, y2);
    New_Col(x1, y1, x1, y, x1, y2);
    color=(Get_Pixel_2(x1, y1)+Get_Pixel_2(x2, y1)+
        Get_Pixel_2(x2, y2)+Get_Pixel_2(x1, y2)+2)>>2;
    Plot(x, y, color);
    Sub_Divide(x1, y1, x, y);
    Sub_Divide(x, y1, x2, y);
    Sub_Divide(x, y, x2, y2);
    Sub_Divide(x1, y, x, y2);
  }
}
```

```
/*
```

```
                            Main Program
```

```
*/
```

```
  Palette_Register Pal_Array;

  void main()
```

```
{
  InitRand(0.4231967);
  Init_Graphics(19);

/* plasmas */
/* InitPalette3(Pal_Array); */

/* clouds  */
 InitPalette4(Pal_Array);

/* electrical discharge */
/* InitPalette5(Pal_Array); */


  Set_Palette(Pal_Array);
  Plot(0, 0, RandInt(254)+1);
  Plot(XRes-1, 0, RandInt(254)+1);
  Plot(XRes-1, YRes-1, RandInt(254)+1);
  Plot(0, YRes-1, RandInt(254)+1);
  Sub_Divide(0, 0, XRes-1, YRes-1);
  do
  {
    Cycle_Palette(Pal_Array);
  }
  while (!kbhit());
  Exit_Graphics();
}
```

Listing 4-3. *Clouds.C.*

A Three-Dimensional Orbit Simulator

In this program, we're going to simulate particle motion in three-dimensional space. The particles (in this case, three) are given initial positions, velocities, and accelerations and are allowed to interact with one another over time. The basic procedure for simulating motion is to erase the current position of the particles, compute their new positions, and then redraw them. If the code that erases the old positions of the particles is removed or commented out, the resulting display will show the trails, or *paths*, of the particles. This can produce some interesting patterns, as Plate 5 illustrates.

```
/*

    ┌─────────────────────────────────────────────────────┐
    │                                                     │
    │            Three Particle Orbit Simulator            │
    │         Program by:Christopher D. Watkins            │
    │          'C' conversion by: Larry Sharp              │
    │                                                     │
    └─────────────────────────────────────────────────────┘

      increase time step "dt" to greater than zero to increase
   speed
*/

   #include "stdio.h"
   #include "conio.h"
   #include "math.h"
   #include "defs.h"
   #include "globals.h"
   #include "mathb.h"
   #include "graphb.h"


   float X1, Y1, Z1, Vx1, Vy1, Vz1, Ax1, Ay1, Az1;
   float X2, Y2, Z2, Vx2, Vy2, Vz2, Ax2, Ay2, Az2;
   float X3, Y3, Z3, Vx3, Vy3, Vz3, Ax3, Ay3, Az3;
   float D12, D23, D31, dt;
   float Dx12, Dx23, Dx31;
   float Dy12, Dy23, Dy31;
   float Dz12, Dz23, Dz31;
   float Tx12, Tx23, Tx31;
   float Ty12, Ty23, Ty31;
   float Tz12, Tz23, Tz31;
   int   Xp1, Yp1, Zp1, Xp2, Yp2, Zp2, Xp3, Yp3, Zp3;
   int   M1, M2, M3;
   float s;


   void main()
   {
     Init_Graphics(19);
     Init_Perspective(false, 0, 0, 500, 500);
     Init_Plotting(245, 25);
     Put_Axis_And_Palette(true);
```

```
    Axis_And_Palette();


/* stable orbit */

  M1=12;
  M2=1;
  M3=1;
  X1=0.0;    Y1=0.0;       Z1=  0.0;
  X2=0.0;    Y2=0.0;       Z2=-40.0;
  X3=0.0;    Y3=0.0;       Z3= 40.0;
  Vx1= 0.0000;  Vy1= 0.0000;    Vz1= 0.0000;
  Vx2=-0.1000;  Vy2=-0.1000;    Vz2=-0.1000;
  Vx3= 0.1000;  Vy3= 0.1000;    Vz3= 0.1000;
  dt=0.2;
  s=1.0;


/*
  M1=1;
  M2=10;
  M3=3;
  X1=-40.0; Y1=0.0;       Z1=0.0;
  X2= 00.0; Y2=0.0;       Z2=0.0;
  X3= 90.0; Y3=0.0;       Z3=0.0;
  Vx1= 0.1010;  Vy1= 0.2500;    Vz1=-0.0240;
  Vx2= 0.0010;  Vy2= 0.0010;    Vz2= 0.0240;
  Vx3=-0.0200;  Vy3=-0.1010;    Vz3= 0.1540;
  dt=0.4;
  s=1.0;
*/

/*
  M1=5;
  M2=1;
  M3=10;
  X1=-10.0; Y1=-90.0;    Z1= 10.0;
  X2=  0.0; Y2=-70.0;    Z2=-40.0;
  X3= 15.0; Y3=-90.0;    Z3= 40.0;
  Vx1= 0.2000;  Vy1= 0.0300;    Vz1= 0.0070;
  Vx2=-0.1000;  Vy2=-0.1020;    Vz2=-0.1000;
```

```
      Vx3= 0.1000;   Vy3= 0.0991;    Vz3= 0.1000;
      dt=0.3;
      s=1.0;
*/

/*
   M1=1;
   M2=6;
   M3=4;
   X1=-40.0; Y1=  0.0;   Z1=  0.0;
   X2=  0.0; Y2=  0.0;   Z2=  0.0;
   X3= 90.0; Y3=  0.0;   Z3=  0.0;
   Vx1= 0.1010;  Vy1= 0.2500;   Vz1=-0.0240;
   Vx2= 0.0010;  Vy2= 0.0010;   Vz2=-0.0440;
   Vx3=-0.0200;  Vy3=-0.1010;   Vz3= 0.1240;
   dt=0.1;
   s=1.0;
*/

/*
   M1=5;
   M2=7;
   M3=12;
   X1=-40.0; Y1= 16.0;   Z1=-20.0;
   X2=  0.0; Y2= 64.0;   Z2=  2.0;
   X3=-10.0; Y3=-20.0;   Z3= 52.0;
   Vx1= 0.2010;  Vy1= 0.2600;   Vz1=-0.1240;
   Vx2= 0.2600;  Vy2= 0.2010;   Vz2=-0.1623;
   Vx3=-0.0200;  Vy3=-0.1010;   Vz3= 0.3140;
   dt=0.15;
   s=0.5;
*/

/*
   M1=6;
   M2=1;
   M3=16;
   X1=-20.0; Y1=-16.0;   Z1=-25.0;
   X2= 20.0; Y2= 14.0;   Z2= -2.0;
   X3= 10.0; Y3= 20.0;   Z3= 12.0;
   Vx1= 0.2010;  Vy1= 0.2200;   Vz1=-0.1240;
```

```
      Vx2= 0.1600;   Vy2= 0.3010;     Vz2=-0.2623;
      Vx3=-0.1200;   Vy3=-0.3910;     Vz3=-0.1140;
      dt=0.30;
      s=0.25;
*/

/*
    M1=35;
    M2=2;
    M3=4;
    X1=  0.0; Y1=  0.0;    Z1=  0.0;
    X2=  0.0; Y2= 40.0;    Z2=  0.0;
    X3=  0.0; Y3= 80.0;    Z3=  0.0;
    Vx1= 0.0000;   Vy1= 0.0000;     Vz1= 0.0000;
    Vx2= 0.0000;   Vy2= 0.0000;     Vz2= 1.0000;
    Vx3= 0.0000;   Vy3= 0.0000;     Vz3=-0.6500;
    dt=0.10;
    s=1.0;
*/

/*
    M1=35;
    M2=2;
    M3=4;
    X1=  0.0; Y1=  0.0;    Z1=  0.0;
    X2=  0.0; Y2= 40.0;    Z2=  0.0;
    X3=  0.0; Y3=100.0;    Z3=  0.0;
    Vx1= 0.0000;   Vy1= 0.0000;     Vz1= 0.0000;
    Vx2= 0.0010;   Vy2= 0.0000;     Vz2= 1.0000;
    Vx3=-0.0010;   Vy3= 0.0000;     Vz3=-0.5000;
    dt=0.10;
    s=1.0;
*/

/*
    M1=35;
    M2=2;
    M3=4;
    X1=  0.0; Y1=  0.0;    Z1=  0.0;
    X2=  0.0; Y2= 40.0;    Z2=  0.0;
    X3=  0.0; Y3=100.0;    Z3=  0.0;
```

109

```
      Vx1= 0.0000;  Vy1= 0.0000;   Vz1= 0.0000;
      Vx2= 0.0000;  Vy2= 0.0000;   Vz2= 1.0000;
      Vx3= 0.6500;  Vy3= 0.4000;   Vz3=-0.0400;
      dt=0.10;
      s=1.0;
  */

      do
      {
        Cartesian_Plot_3D(X1*s, Y1*s, Z1*s, 0);
        Cartesian_Plot_3D(X2*s, Y2*s, Z2*s, 0);
        Cartesian_Plot_3D(X3*s, Y3*s, Z3*s, 0);
        X1+=Vx1*dt;
        Y1+=Vy1*dt;
        Z1+=Vz1*dt;
        X2+=Vx2*dt;
        Y2+=Vy2*dt;
        Z2+=Vz2*dt;
        X3+=Vx3*dt;
        Y3+=Vy3*dt;
        Z3+=Vz3*dt;
        Cartesian_Plot_3D(X1*s, Y1*s, Z1*s, 143);
        Cartesian_Plot_3D(X2*s, Y2*s, Z2*s, 169);
        Cartesian_Plot_3D(X3*s, Y3*s, Z3*s, 205);
        Dx12=X1-X2;
        Dy12=Y1-Y2;
        Dz12=Z1-Z2;
        Dx23=X2-X3;
        Dy23=Y2-Y3;
        Dz23=Z2-Z3;
        Dx31=X3-X1;
        Dy31=Y3-Y1;
        Dz31=Z3-Z1;
        D12=sqrt(SqrFP(Dx12)+SqrFP(Dy12)+SqrFP(Dz12));
        D12=1.0/(D12*D12*D12);
        D23=sqrt(SqrFP(Dx23)+SqrFP(Dy23)+SqrFP(Dz23));
        D23=1.0/(D23*D23*D23);
        D31=sqrt(SqrFP(Dx31)+SqrFP(Dy31)+SqrFP(Dz31));
        D31=1.0/(D31*D31*D31);
        Tx31=Dx31*D31;
        Ty31=Dy31*D31;
```

```
    Tz31=Dz31*D31;
    Tx12=Dx12*D12;
    Ty12=Dy12*D12;
    Tz12=Dz12*D12;
    Tx23=Dx23*D23;
    Ty23=Dy23*D23;
    Tz23=Dz23*D23;
    Ax1=(M3*Tx31-M2*Tx12);
    Ay1=(M3*Ty31-M2*Ty12);
    Az1=(M3*Tz31-M2*Tz12);
    Ax2=(M1*Tx12-M3*Tx23);
    Ay2=(M1*Ty12-M3*Ty23);
    Az2=(M1*Tz12-M3*Tz23);
    Ax3=(M2*Tx23-M1*Tx31);
    Ay3=(M2*Ty23-M1*Ty31);
    Az3=(M2*Tz23-M1*Tz31);
    Vx1+=Ax1*dt;
    Vy1+=Ay1*dt;
    Vz1+=Az1*dt;
    Vx2+=Ax2*dt;
    Vy2+=Ay2*dt;
    Vz2+=Az2*dt;
    Vx3+=Ax3*dt;
    Vy3+=Ay3*dt;
    Vz3+=Az3*dt;
  }
  while(!(kbhit()));
  Exit_Graphics();
}
```

Listing 4-4.*Orb3D-3p.C.*

Orb3D-3p.C (Listing 4-4) uses a simple physical model of particle motion and mutual interaction. Theoretically, a particle that is in motion will continue to move in the same direction until a force is applied in some other direction. If, instead, the particle is moving along a circular path at a constant velocity, then the velocity is changing toward the center of the path (a force is required to keep the particle moving in a circle). Changing velocity is referred to as *acceleration*. Acceleration for circular motion is given by the following equation.

$$a = \frac{v^2}{r}$$

(Equation 4-2)

where a is acceleration, v is velocity, and r is the radius of the circular orbit. By Newton's second law of motion, force equals mass times acceleration. Therefore:

$$F = ma = \frac{mv^2}{r}$$

(Equation 4-3)

Known as *centripetal force*, this is the force that is necessary to keep an object moving in a circular path, and that is directed inward toward the center of rotation. In terms of our program, it's what keeps the particle orbiting about another particle. In effect, this force is the same as gravity.

Let's consider a three-dimensional scenario. Each object in the system is given a position (x_n, y_n, z_n) and a mass (m_n), where n is the number of the object. Object positions and the distances between them are measured in meters, and the masses are in kilograms. The distance between the two objects is the length of the line connecting them. Using the (X,Y,Z) Cartesian coordinate system, the distances are:

$$d_x = \left| x_2 - x_1 \right|$$
$$d_y = \left| y_2 - y_1 \right|$$
$$d_z = \left| z_2 - z_1 \right|$$

(Equation 4-4)

The magnitude of the distance vector (d_x, d_y, d_z) is:

$$d = \sqrt{d_x^2 + d_y^2 + d_z^2}$$

(Equation 4-5)

Now we can calculate the gravitational force between the particles using the Law of Universal Gravitation. This law states that the force due to gravity, Fg, is directly proportional to the product of the masses $(m1 * m2)$ and inversely proportional to the square of the distance (d) between them. The Gravitational Constant of Proportionality (g) has the value 6.67E-11 (Nm/kg). The resulting equation is:

$$F_g = g = \frac{m_1 m_2}{d^2}$$

(Equation 4-6)

This attractive force is along the direction of the line connecting the two objects. The force here is a vector quantity having both magnitude and direction, and its components are Fx, Fy, and Fz.

Now let's examine a system of particles. Few orbiting patterns generated by $Orb3D$-$3p$ will remain in equilibrium for a long time; sooner or later, a particle will pick up enough momentum to escape the orbiting pattern or will be pulled in by another mass.

Combining the equations for acceleration and gravitational force yields:

$$a_{x1} = \frac{gm_2}{d^2} * \frac{d_x}{d}$$

$$a_{y1} = \frac{gm_2}{d^2} * \frac{d_y}{d}$$

(Equation 4-7)

$$a_{z1} = \frac{gm_2}{d^2} * \frac{d_z}{d}$$

Since acceleration is the change in velocity with respect to the change in time, we have the following equation:

$$dv_x = a_x t$$
$$dv_y = a_y t$$
$$dv_z = a_z t$$

(Equation 4-8)

Given the initial velocity v_0, and traveling through time to time t, we get a new vector velocity:

$$v_x = v_{x0} + a_x t$$

$$v_y = v_{y0} + a_y t$$

$$v_z = v_{z0} + a_y t$$

(Equation 4-9)

Thus, the velocity at the end of the time interval is $v_0 + at$. We can approximate the average velocity throughout the time interval using:

$$V_{avg} = \frac{v_0 + v_0 + at}{2} = v0 + at$$

(Equation 4-10)

We want the orbit simulator to show the positions of the particles as the time changes. Therefore, we need a set of equations that relate position to time. Since the velocity is the rate of change of the position with respect to time, over any time interval the change in position is the average velocity multiplied by the time:

$$d_x = v_{x0} t + \frac{a_x t^2}{2}$$

$$d_y = v_{y0} t + \frac{a_y t^2}{2}$$

$$d_z = v_{z0} t + \frac{a_z t^2}{2}$$

(Equation 4-11)

Because we know the initial position $(x(0), y(0))$, the position for any time is:

$$x = x_0 + v_{x0} t + \frac{a_x t^2}{2}$$

$$y = y_0 + v_{y0} t + \frac{a_y t^2}{2}$$

$$z = z_0 + v_{z0} t + \frac{a_z t^2}{2}$$

(Equation 4-12)

114

Having looked at the dynamics of two particles in three-dimensional space, let's look again at *Orb3D-3p*, which handles three particles in three-dimensional space. If you compare the preceding discussion with the code, you'll find only slight differences: in the denominator's exponent when (*d*) is calculated and in that all possible combinations of one particle's effect on another are handled (each particle interacts with every other particle).

The program begins by establishing initial conditions (masses, positions, velocities, and accelerations) for each particle. The time step is set to a constant (any real number greater than zero—in other words, moving forward in time). A larger step will cause particles to move faster, but the program will lose accuracy in position. The program then enters a loop that is terminated with a keystroke. Within the loop, the particle positions are converted to display coordinates and points are plotted at each particle position. Conversion of these particle positions to display coordinates is nothing more than the mapping (or projection) of that point onto the screen by *Map_Coordinates*. Next, the new position coordinates for each particle after a step in time are computed. The new distance between each set of particles is computed and used in the gravity equation to obtain the effective force on the particle, which in turn generates the new accelerations and velocities. The program loops continuously, plotting positions and erasing old positions, until a key is pressed. You may want to remove the erasures of the old positions' plot particle trails. (This will give you the type of display found in Plate 5.) A few sets of initial conditions are stored in the program itself; some of these are commented out, so to access them you must comment out the active set and un-comment out the desired set. The program must be recompiled and linked each time a new set of initial conditions is desired.

A Recursive Plant and Tree Generator

Plate 6 shows a plant structure created using a recursive tree-branching technique (another fractal process) originally developed by Aono and Kunii to generate botanical geometrical model tree images, that is, trees built from basic geometric shapes like cyclinders. In *Plant.C*, (Listing4-5) we use this technique to control the *angle* (trunk angle with respect to ground normal), *branchfan* (maximum spread of a branch grouping), *height* (height of the trunk), *heightfactor* (height multiplier to shorten

115

branches as we increase our branching depth—in other words, go further out on a limb), *anglefactor* (change in angle from the last depth level), *branchdensity* (number of branches per generation), and *depth* (recursive level of branching).

As with all random-process programs, this one starts by seeding the pseudoran-dom number generator (described in Chapter 2). It also initializes the graphics mode and calculates *invbranchdensity*. This is done here because multiplication by the inverse is faster than division when it must be done many times. We then call the main procedure, *Tree*, to start the process. Green branches are drawn based on the parameters and random seed, using the recursive routine *Tree*, until the recursion level is zero. Now we draw small magenta crosses that represent leaves. When the branchings are finished, the resulting image is a flowering, plantlike structure. Again, the basic principle is the same as in any procedural process: we define a procedure that describes how to generate new branches based on the current branch, then call the routine recursively to do the same to the newly created, smaller branches.

```
/*
```

```
                            Plant.C
                    Christopher D. Watkins
```

```
*/
```

```
#include "stdio.h"
#include "dos.h"
#include "string.h"
#include "defs.h"
#include "globals.h"
#include "mathb.h"
#include "graphb.h"

Word x=512;      /*  coordinate for base of trunk  */
Word y=767;
float Angle=0.0;      /*  trunk Angle with respect to ground
                                              normal  */
float BranchFan=45.0;    /*  maximum 'fan' of branch grouping
*/
```

```
float Height=120.0;      /*  Height of trunk  */
float HeightFactor=0.75;
float AngleFactor=0.75;
float BranchDensity=2.0;
Byte Depth=10;

#define TreeColor (2*36-1)-10
#define LeafColor (5*36-1)

float InvBranchDensity;

void Tree(Word y, Word x,
      float Angle, float BranchFan,
      float Height, float HeightFactor,
      Byte Depth)

{
  Byte i;
  Word xinc, yinc;
  float Start, Theta;
  Word NewHeight;

  if(Depth==0)
  {
    Draw(x-3, y, x+3, y, LeafColor);
    Draw(x, y-3, x, y+3, LeafColor);
  }
  else
  {
    Start=Angle-BranchFan*0.5;
    Theta=BranchFan*InvBranchDensity;
    if(Depth<3)
      HeightFactor=HeightFactor*0.5;
    xinc=Round(Height*SinD(Angle))&0xFFFF;
    yinc=Round(Height*CosD(Angle))&0xFFFF;
    Draw(x, y, x+xinc, y-yinc, TreeColor);
    for(i=0; i<=BranchDensity; i++)
    {
      NewHeight=Round(Height*HeightFactor)&0xFFFF;
      Tree(y-yinc, x+xinc,
        Start*0.5+Sign(Start)*RandInt(abs(Round(Start))+1),
```

```
      BranchFan*AngleFactor,
      NewHeight*0.5+RandInt(NewHeight+1),
      HeightFactor,
      Depth-1);
     Start=Start+Theta;
   }
  }
}

void main()
{
  InitRand(3.9);
  Init_Graphics(56);
  InvBranchDensity=1.0/BranchDensity;
  Tree(y, x, Angle, BranchFan, Height, HeightFactor, Depth);
  Exit_Graphics();
}
```

Listing 4-5. *Plant.C.*

A Linear Cellular Automaton Program

The study of linear cellular automata is a very active area of research that's based on a simple game, developed in the 1960s by John Conway, called Life. In effect, a "world" is created in which computer creatures live, die, move, and reproduce based on rules that we create. This class of programs is fascinating to experiment with by creating new rules and variations.

The basic idea behind linear cellular automata is that a world is composed of discrete cells (one per screen pixel). Each cell can exist in any of a number of discrete states. The world is closed because the left side wraps around to the right side, making something of an imaginary ring. It's also linear, because each generation of like in the world occurs in one (linear-space) dimension. Each world, and thus the generation of each world, can be represented by a horizontal line on the computer display. Each line has as many as 1,024 cells (the number of columns in high-resolution mode). The screen can hold as many as 768 generations because there are 768 rows in high-resolution mode.

The life of a cell is regulated by a rule, which must take into account the number of states any cell can have. In this case, our cells have 36 distinct, individual states. For display purposes, each cell's color is based on its state. The rule must also examine the states of neighboring cells and modify the tested cell's state accordingly. For a single dimension, this means testing the cells to the left and right of the cell.

Here's an example of a rule for our linear cellular automaton. If the cell being tested is in state 0 and the cells to its left and right are greater than 10, then the cell being tested takes on a value of 5. If the cell being tested is greater than 30 and the surrounding cells are greater than 25, the tested cell takes on the value 2. We apply this rule to all the members in the world to create the next generation of that world, thus filling the screen with generations after the 768th generation reaches the bottom of the screen. Notice that the rule can be related to the idea of birth and death. If the cell is dead, it can be born if there are life cells (and food) on both sides. If the cell is alive and fat and there are fat cells on both sides, it runs out of food and dies.

Plates 7 and 8 are two examples of cellular automata. Plate 7 is reminiscent of Sierpinski's triangle, where many growths share the basic triangular pattern. Plate 8 looks like an integrated circuit pattern or an aerial view of a city with streets and parks.

Our 36-state closed linear cellular automaton program is called *Cell1D.C* (Listing 4-6). It has three supporting programs: a world file maker (*World1D.C*) and two rule file makers. *Sier1D.C* (Listing 4-8) generates the rule for Plate 7, and *Rule1D.C* generates the rule for Plate 8.

World1D.C generates a random world. (Notice that these routines use the pseudorandom number generator; therefore, since the random number generator is seeded, all you need to know are the seeds for the rule, world, and automaton programs to generate the same images over and over again.) It creates the random-world file by setting some of the 1,024 cells to a randomly chosen number up to 36.

Rule1D.C (Listing 4-7) generates a rule file that contains the logic for all combinations of occurrences of logical states of being, while *Sier1D.C* generates three types of triangle patterns. Some of these code sets are commented out; to access them, simply comment out the active set and un-comment out the desired set, then recompile and link the program. *Sier1D.C* also has a density control hard-coded near the beginning of the program. The possible values are 2 for the least dense, and 1 for the most dense.

You can also set up a random world within the cellular automaton program simply by setting the hard-coded *RandWorld* flag in the main procedure to true. The cell arrangement for the automaton is:

```
I    J    K
```

showing that the cells are aligned side-by-side in a row. Now let's extend this cellular world to two dimensions. The two programs that follow differ only in the number of states in which tested cells can exist and in how many neighboring cells affect a tested cell.

A Planar Cellular Automaton Program

This program is very similar to *Cell1D.C* but is extended to two dimensions. (No plates were made of this automaton because you would need to see it interactively to appreciate it.) Where all life (cells) previously existed on a line, they now exist in a plane. This plane is represented as a block of pixels on the screen (100 x 100 for our purposes). Again, the program is closed because the top loops to the bottom and the left side to the right side, creating a spherical world of sorts. We have only eight states per cell, as opposed to the previous 36 states per cell, due to memory constraints. This time, each cell has four neighbors rather than two. These extra cells cause many new things to happen: oscillatory actions take place, causing the screen to pulsate with color patterns, and animated Sierpinski-like triangles grow and disappear.

```
/*
```

```
       36 State Finite Closed Linear Cellular Automation
              (c) 1991 Christopher D. Watkins
```

```
*/
```

```
#include "stdio.h"
```

```
#include "dos.h"
#include "conio.h"
#include "alloc.h"
#include "string.h"
#include "defs.h"
#include "globals.h"
#include "mathb.h"
#include "graphb.h"
#define MaxColumn 1024
#define MaxRow 768
#define States 36
#define MaxState (States-1)
#define WorldTop (MaxColumn-1)
typedef Byte State[36];
typedef Byte WorldArray[1024];
typedef State RuleI;
typedef RuleI Rule[36];
WorldArray NewWorld;
WorldArray OldWorld;
WorldArray TempWorld;
Word row;
Word i;
static Rule far *Rules;
void Pix()
{
    Plot(i, row, (NewWorld[i]<<4));
}
void DoWorld()
{
/*  Mod operations can be used here -  */
/*   but logical operations are faster  */
i=0;
NewWorld[i]=Rules[OldWorld[WorldTop]][OldWorld[i]][OldWorld[i+1]];
Pix();
    for(i=1; i<=WorldTop-1; i++)
    {
NewWorld[i]=Rules[OldWorld[i-1]][OldWorld[i]][OldWorld[i+1]];
        Pix();
    }
i=WorldTop;
NewWorld[i]=Rules[OldWorld[i1]][OldWorld[i]][OldWorld[0]];
```

121

```
Pix();
_fmemcpy(TempWorld, NewWorld, sizeof(WorldArray));
_fmemcpy(NewWorld, OldWorld, sizeof(WorldArray));
_fmemcpy(OldWorld, TempWorld, sizeof(WorldArray));
row=(row+1)%MaxRow;
}
typedef char Name[33];

Boolean RandWorld;
Name WorldFileName;
FILE *WorldFile;
void LoadWorld()
{
    Word i;
    row=0;
    if(RandWorld)
    {
        for(i=0; i<=WorldTop; i++)
        OldWorld[i]=RandInt(States);        /*  Make up a Random
                                                    World  */
    }
    else
    {
        if((WorldFile=fopen(WorldFileName, "rb"))==NULL)
        {
            ungetch(32);
            Exit_Graphics();
            printf("Can't open world file.\n");
            exit(1);
        }
fread(OldWorld, sizeof(OldWorld), 1, WorldFile);
fclose(WorldFile);
    }
}
Name Rulefilename;
FILE *Rulefile;
void LoadRules()
{
    if((Rulefile=fopen(Rulefilename, "rb"))==NULL)
    {
        ungetch(32);
```

```
        Exit_Graphics();
        printf("Can't open Rule file.\n");
        exit(1);
    }
    fread(Rules, sizeof(Rule), 36, Rulefile);
    fclose(Rulefile);
}
void ClearMemory()
{
    Word i, j, k;
    for(i=0; i<=WorldTop; i++)
    {
        NewWorld[i]=0;
        OldWorld[i]=0;
        TempWorld[i]=0;
    }
    for(i=0; i<=MaxState; i++)
    {
        for(j=0; j<=MaxState; j++)
        {
            for(k=0; k<=MaxState; k++)
                Rules[i][j][k]=0;
        }
    }
}
Palette_Register palarray;

void main()
{
    Rules=farcalloc(36, sizeof(Rule));
    if(Rules==NULL)
    {
        printf("can't get the mem!\n");
        exit(1);
    }
    ClearMemory();
    strcpy(WorldFileName,"WORLD1D.CA");
    strcpy(Rulefilename,"RULE1D.CA");
    RandWorld=false;   /*  when true -> WorldFileName := ''  */
    InitRand(0.4231966);
```

```
    LoadRules();
    LoadWorld();
    Init_Graphics(56);
    Init_Palette(palarray);
    Set_Palette(palarray);
    do
    {
        DoWorld();
    }
    while(!kbhit());
    Exit_Graphics();
    farfree(Rules);
```

Listing 4-6. *Cell1D.C.*

```
/*

    36 State Finite Closed Linear Cellular Automation
                    Rule File Maker
            (c) 1991 Christopher D. Watkins

*/

    #include "stdio.h"
    #include "dos.h"
    #include "alloc.h"
    #include "string.h"
    #include "defs.h"
    #include "globals.h"
    #include "mathb.h"

    #define States 36
    #define MaxState States-1

    typedef Byte State[36];
    typedef State Rulei;
    typedef Rulei Rule[36];
    typedef char Name[33];
```

```
Name RuleFileName;
FILE *RuleFile;
Rule far *Rules;
Word i, j, k;
int x;
Byte o;
Byte r;

void WriteRuleFile()
{
  fwrite(Rules, sizeof(Rule), 36, RuleFile);
  fclose(RuleFile);
}

void main()
{
  strcpy(RuleFileName, "RULE1D.CA");
  if((RuleFile=fopen(RuleFileName, "wb"))==NULL)
  {
    printf("can't open file.\n");
    exit(1);
  }
  Rules=farcalloc(36, sizeof(Rule));
  if(Rules==NULL)
  {
    printf("can't get the mem!\n");
    exit(1);
  }
  clrscr();
  printf("Generating Rule\n");
  InitRand(14.4166);
  for(i=0; i<=35; i++)
  {
    for(j=0; j<=35; j++)
    {
      for(k=0; k<=35; k++)
      {
    if(i==k)
      x=RandInt(States);
    else
      {
```

```
        r=j%2;
        switch(r)
        {
          case 0: x=i;
               break;
          case 1: x=k;
               break;
        }
      }
      o=(x%States)&0xFF;
      Rules[i][j][k]=o;
        }
      }
    }
  WriteRuleFile();
  farfree(Rules);
}
```

Listing 4-7. *Rule1D.C.*

```
/*
```

```
┌──────────────────────────────────────────────────────────┐
│ ┌────────────────────────────────────────────────────────┐ │
│ │                                                        │ │
│ │   36 State Finite Closed Linear Cellular Automation    │ │
│ │             Sierpinski Rule File Maker                 │ │
│ │            (c) 1991 Christopher D. Watkins             │ │
│ │                                                        │ │
│ └────────────────────────────────────────────────────────┘ │
└──────────────────────────────────────────────────────────┘
```

```
*/
```

```
  #include "stdio.h"
  #include "dos.h"
  #include "alloc.h"
  #include "string.h"
  #include "defs.h"
  #include "globals.h"
  #include "mathb.h"

  #define States 36
  #define MaxState States-1
  #define density 1    /* 1 - most dense  Or  2 - least dense */
```

```
typedef Byte State[36];
typedef State Rulei;
typedef Rulei Rule[36];
typedef char name[33];

name RuleFileName;
FILE *RuleFile;
Rule far *Rules;
Word i, j, k;
int x;
Byte o;
Byte r;

void WriteRuleFile()
{
  fwrite(Rules, sizeof(Rule), 36, RuleFile);
  fclose(RuleFile);
}

void main()
{
  strcpy(RuleFileName, "RULE1D.CA");
  if((RuleFile=fopen(RuleFileName, "wb"))==NULL)
  {
    printf("can't open file.\n");
    exit(1);
  }
  Rules=farcalloc(36, sizeof(Rule));
  if(Rules==NULL)
  {
    printf("can't get the mem!\n");
    exit(1);
  }
  clrscr();
  printf("Generating Rule\n");
  strcpy(RuleFileName,"RULE.CA");
  InitRand(0.4231966);
  for(i=0; i<=MaxState; i++)
  {
    for(j=0; j<=MaxState; j++)
```

```
{
  for(k=0; k<=MaxState; k++)
  {
if(i == 0)
  x = k;
else
{
  if(j < k)
  {
    if(k == 0)
      x = i;
    else
      x = 0;
  }
  else
  {
    if(i == k)
      x = RandInt(States);
    else
    {
      r=j%density;
      switch(r)
      {
    case 0: x=i;
        break;
    case 1: x=k;
        break;
      }
    }
  }
}
/*
    x=i+j+k;
*/
/*
    x=i+j;
*/
    o=(x%States)&0xFF;
    Rules[i][j][k]=o;
      }
```

```
      }
    }
    WriteRuleFile();
    farfree(Rules);
}
```

Listing 4-8.*Sier1D.C.*

A program called *World2D.C* generates the world, while *Rule2D.C* and *Sier2D.C* generate rules for the world to follow. A number of rules are commented out in both programs, so use the same method of selection as described for *Cell1D.C*.

The following is the cell arrangement for the automaton:

```
    I
J   K   L
    M
```

showing that the cells are aligned side-by-side in two directions.

A Life Cellular Automaton Program

The *LifeWrld.C* program is similar to *Cell2D.C* in that it is planar and dissimilar in that it examines the Boolean (born or dead) states of all eight neighboring cells to process the rule. With even more neighbors being processed from one generation to the next, more fantastic automata occur.

LifeWrld.C generates one of three types of worlds. One is random, another is full of walking creatures, and the last has a number of blooming growths. You select one of the worlds by changing the hard-coded Boolean states at the beginning of the program for *RandomWorld*, *WalkerWorld*, and *BloomerWorld*. The rule selected for the world that resulted in the most interesting automaton is as follows: if an empty cell has exactly three neighbors, it will be born; if an occupied cell has fewer than two or more than three neighbors it will die. *LifeRule.C* generates the rule file.

The cell arrangement for the automaton is:

```
I    J    K
L    M    N
P    Q    R
```

showing that the cells are aligned aside the center cell. A dizzying amount of variation is possible with cellular automata programs. Three examples are to extend the simulation to three dimensions, investigate which types of rules cause stable (cell population roughly constant over time) and unstable (population eventually dies out) results, and allow for different types of rules for different types of cells. (This last possibility is the same as dividing the states into classes, such as using 0 through 10 to indicate a food cell, 11 through 20 for predator cells, 21 through 30 for omnivorous cells, and so forth.)

In the next chapter, we plunge into the heart of three-dimensional graphics. To take that plunge, you'll need a thorough understanding of the modules in this chapter; they're the foundation for a three-dimensional modeling tool that lets you display complex objects built from surfaces.

PART II

THREE-DIMENSIONAL MODELING

CHAPTER 5

Modeling Theory and Database Structure

In the previous chapters, we developed a library of mathematical and graphical tools that allowed us to produce useful and entertaining programs. Now we'll use these tools to meet our primary objective: rendering complex three-dimensional scenes. We'll develop a modeling tool that will allow you to render complex scenes consisting of a virtually unlimited set of objects that you design.

The modeler developed here renders objects using the *direct projection* method. This technique is used by most three-dimensional rendering packages on the PC, such as AutoCad 3D and RenderMan. The basic approach is to perform a perspective projection of an object's elements—typically polygonal facets—onto the screen. A program using this projection takes a three-dimensional object and creates the two-dimensional polygon to be drawn on the screen. This polygon is then filled with the appropriate color depending on the light source, its direction, and the position of the viewer. This technique is the opposite of the ray-tracing method. Its principal advantage is computational speed—it can be many times faster than the equivalent ray-tracing technique—while its principal disadvantage is that it doesn't produce very realistic scenes. That's because it doesn't accurately model the interaction of light between objects, such as those that are translucent or reflective.

Because the modeler allows rapid scene generation, we'll use it extensively to position objects and produce the correct scene content (for instance, the position and size of the objects) before taking the extra time to ray-trace the image. This will substantially reduce the time needed to orient and position the objects correctly. We'll also preview our animation sequences before producing the ray-traced animation sequences.

How To Construct Objects

A scene consists of a collection of three-dimensional objects positioned within our computer-defined world. An example is a model city in which the buildings are defined as objects, each of which is placed separately. A building might be defined by a collection of simpler objects, such as rectangular blocks, that are combined to form a new, more complex object. In effect, we have an infinite set of building blocks with which to create our scene.

The modeler developed here uses objects that are defined by a collection of polygonal facets. For instance, a cube is described by 6 four-sided facets, one for each of its faces. Each facet is defined by the three-dimensional coordinates of each vertex. The vertices must be specified in counterclockwise order around the polygon, starting at any convenient vertex. Defining the object is essentially a game of connect-the-dots with the vertices. The counterclockwise order defines which way the facet faces (it lies in a plane, which could be said to face in one of two opposite directions). This direction is represented in the *ModelSup.H* program (Listing 5-1) using a vector called the *surface normal*, as discussed in Chapter 2. The surface normal is used for both visibility computations (deciding whether or not the facet is facing the viewer) and the lighting calculation (how the facet faces the light source and the viewer). The modeler automatically computes the surface normal based on your facet definition as well as the *VecCross* function described in Chapter 2. Also associated with each facet are attributes that determine such things as color and material characteristics.

The modeler imposes three restrictions on facets:

1. Each facet can have only three or four vertices.

2. All vertices of a single facet must lie within a single plane.

3. The facet must be convex (it can't have any *dips*, as shown in Figure 5-1).

```
/*
```

```
        Variable Declarations

  Original Material by Christopher D. Watkins

            'C' conversion by
            Larry Sharp
```

```
*/
#define NumVerticiesInFacet 4
#define MaxVertexNumInFacet 4
#define ScaleData 23000
#define ScaleImage 100
/*
#define MaxFacet 1678    independant : MaxFacet  = n
#define MaxVertex 6712   verticies   MaxVertex = 4 * n
*/
#define MaxFacet 3600
#define MaxVertex 3721
int LastVertex, LastFacet;
int LastVertexNumInFacet;
int VertexNum, FacetNum;
int VertexNumInFacet;
TDIA Vertex[MaxVertex+1];
static int far *Facet;
/*
```

```
        Routines to Load and Save Vertex and Facet Data
```

```
InitVertexBuffer - clear memory for facet and vertex data
LoadData         - load facet and vertex data
SaveData         - save facet and vertex data

*/
```

```
float InvScaleData, InvScaleImage;
void InitVertexBuffer()
{
InvScaleData=1.0/ScaleData; InvScaleImage=1.0/ScaleImage;
for(VertexNum=0; VertexNum<=MaxVertex; VertexNum++)
            VecNullInt(Vertex[VertexNum]);
    for(FacetNum=0; FacetNum<=MaxFacet; FacetNum++)
    {
for(VertexNumInFacet=0; VertexNumInFacet<=MaxVertexNumInFacet;
VertexNumInFacet++) Facet[(FacetNum*5)+VertexNumInFacet]=0;
    }
}
typedef char Name[20];
FILE *DiskFile;
Name FileName;
void LoadData(Name FileName)
{
    TDIA temp;
    int x, y, z;
    DiskFile=fopen(FileName, "r+b");
    LastVertex=getw(DiskFile);
    LastFacet=getw(DiskFile);
    LastVertexNumInFacet=getw(DiskFile);
    for(VertexNum=1; VertexNum<=LastVertex; VertexNum++)
    {
        x=getw(DiskFile);
        y=getw(DiskFile);
        z=getw(DiskFile);
        if((abs(x)>ScaleData) || (abs(y)>ScaleData) ||
(abs(z)>ScaleData))
        {
            printf("Error : data out of range - Vertex #%d\n",
VertexNum);
            exit(1);
        }
        else
            VecInt(x, y, z, Vertex[VertexNum]);
    }
    for(FacetNum=1; FacetNum<=LastFacet; FacetNum++)
    {
```

```
    for(VertexNumInFacet=1; VertexNumInFacet<=LastVertexNumInFacet;
                                              VertexNumInFacet++)
    Facet[(FacetNum*5)+VertexNumInFacet]=getw(DiskFile);
        }
        fclose(DiskFile);
    }
    void SaveData(Name FileName)
    {
        int x, y, z;
        DiskFile=fopen(FileName, "w+b");
        putw(LastVertex, DiskFile);
        putw(LastFacet, DiskFile);
        putw(LastVertexNumInFacet, DiskFile);
        for(VertexNum=1; VertexNum<=LastVertex; VertexNum++)
        {
            UnVecInt(Vertex[VertexNum], &x, &y, &z);
            putw(x, DiskFile);
            putw(y, DiskFile);
            putw(z, DiskFile);
        }
        for(FacetNum=1; FacetNum<=LastFacet; FacetNum++)
        {
    for(VertexNumInFacet=1; VertexNumInFacet<=LastVertexNumInFacet;
    VertexNumInFacet++) putw(Facet[(FacetNum*5)+VertexNumInFacet],
                                              DiskFile);
        }
        fclose(DiskFile);
    }
    typedef struct{
        int x;
        int y;
    }   PixelVector;
    typedef PixelVector PixelArray[NumVerticiesInFacet+2];
```

Listing 5-1. Listing of *ModelSup.H.*

Any three-sided facet automatically meets conditions 2 and 3 (three points are needed to define a plane, and a triangle is always convex). Note that a more complex shape (one with more vertices) can always be broken down into facets of the type used here.

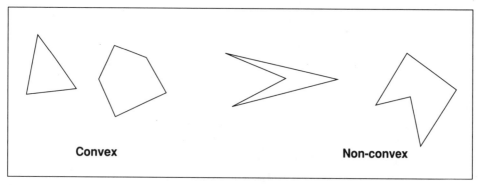

Figure 5-1. Examples of convex versus non-convex facets.

A Note on Coordinate Systems

A scene is built using a global world coordinate system in three-dimensional space (X,Y,Z). Each object, however, is always defined within its own independent three-dimensional space (with certain restrictions, as described in a moment). If this were not the case, it would be exceedingly difficult to build a scene from objects because we would have to recreate each object just to move it. Here we will create the object once, and then manipulate its size, shape, and position. Similarly, creating a complex object from simpler ones would require creating new definitions of the latter each time we wanted to make a simple change.

One solution is to create an instance of an object. An object instance is a local copy of an object that is manipulated before being placed in a scene or added to a more complex object. This process is analogous to using the C function *malloc* to allocate memory for a structure.

Once we have defined an object instance, we use the affine transformations defined in Chapter 2 to transform the object from its local coordinate system to that of the world coordinate system. This transformation allows us to reposition, resize, and reorient the object with very simple changes. This means, for instance, that we need only define a cube object once and can then rescale it to create any rectangular block we like. This feature is described in more detail in the next chapter, where we discuss the *.SCN* scene-definition file.

Floating-Point vs. Integer Coordinates

On most PCs, integer arithmetic is generally much faster than the equivalent floating-point operations. Floating-point coprocessors greatly increase the speed of these operations; however, the software in this book was designed to run on the widest possible variety of platforms and thus does not assume that a fast floating-point processor is available. The most compute-intensive operations are therefore converted to integer operations wherever possible.

Because we're constantly transforming object coordinates to project them into a scene, we need to make the affine transformation as efficient as possible. To do this, we'll adopt the convention of representing object coordinates within the modeler using 16-bit integer values. This provides a dynamic range of -32,768 to +32,767. An interactive utility program, *MakeObjs.C*, is provided on the disk to let you create objects graphically on the screen. The actual facet data stored in the files is written as integers, approximately in the range -23,000 to +23,000. This range is smaller to allow for rotations up to the worst case of 45 degrees. If we rotate a square whose corners are at ±23,000, the new corners will be at about ±32,768 (23,000 * *sind(45)*).

Creating an Object

Now let's look at how an object is created. *ModelSup.H* (Listing 5-1) is a header file containing functions, definitions, and variables needed by the modeling program. The functions defined in this file allow us to initialize, load, and save the vertex and facet data in an object database file used by the modeler.

The first definition in this file is *ScaleData*, the range factor of 23,000. All the facet data must be in the range from -*ScaleData* to +*ScaleData*. The next definition is *ScaleImage*. This conversion factor, described in Chapter 6, converts projected screen coordinates to physical screen coordinates. At this point, we're simply initializing the value for later use.

Declaring the *Vertex* and *Facet* Arrays

The *Vertex* and *Facet* arrays are buffers used by the modeler to hold the data describing each object in our scene. When it's time for an object to be placed on the screen, the data for the object is loaded from its associated *.DAT* file and stored in these buffers. The *Vertex* array lists the unique vertices that form an object. For example, the cube has only eight unique vertices even though there are six facets with four sides each, for a total of 24 vertices.

To save storage space, we use the *Facet* array to store an index (a single integer) to the *Vertex* array entry containing the actual vertex data for this facet. For the cube, using *Facet* results in a 3:1 space savings over storing a separate vertex for each vertex of each facet. The savings are even greater for generated objects, such as spheres and cylinders, in which many vertices are shared by even more facets. As described above, each vertex has three integers that define the point's three-dimensional spatial coordinates (X, Y, Z).

Loading and Saving Array Data

The *InitVertexBuffer* function initializes the vertex and facet buffers by setting their entries to 0. It also computes *InvScaleData* and *InvScaleImage* as 1.0/ *ScaleData* and 1.0/*ScaleImage*, respectively. These values are used to scale the resulting data that's read into the vertex buffers; they're generated here for later use because multiplication is generally faster than division and because we need to perform this scaling operation many times.

The *LoadData* function loads the vertex and facet data from a disk file into the buffers prepared by *InitVertexBuffer*. The file name of the object is passed to this function, which first tries to open the file. If the open is successful, the function reads the first three values, stored in the variables *LastVertex*, *LastFacet*, and *LastVertexNumInFacet*. *LastVertex* represents the number of unique vertices stored in the file, *LastFacet* is the number of facets, and *LastVertexNumInFacet* is the number of vertices per facet (either three or four). Once these values are read in, the function reads and stores the object's vertices. To do this, we set a loop ranging from 1 to *LastVertex*. On each iteration, we read the x, y, and z components that make up the coordinates of the vertex and check to see if they're within the legal range set by *ScaleData*. If the absolute value of the x, y, or z component is greater than *ScaleData*, we print an out-of-range error message and exit from the program. Otherwise, we convert the three values to our *TDIA* integer vector structure (described in Chapter 2) using *VecInt* and store it in the *Vertex* array.

When the loop terminates, we proceed to load in the facet data. We read in *LastVertexNumInFacet* integer values for each facet and store them directly in the *Facet* array. Note that although only *LastVertexNumInFacet* vertices are read and stored, the *Facet* array is always structured as if four values were read in. This is simply a structural convenience that can be changed if desired. After all the facets have been read in, we close the file and return. At this point, all the vertex and facet information has been stored for the object being loaded.

The *SaveData* function does the opposite of the *LoadData* function—it writes the *Vertex* and *Facet* arrays out to a disk file. First, we write the values of *LastVertex*, *LastFacet*, and *LastVertexNumInFacet* to our file (represented by the file name passed to the function). Next, we extract the three components of our vectors, which make up the vertices, and write these to the output file. We then write the facets (four integer values per facet, representing an index to the *Vertex* array) out to the file and close the file. We now have all the vertex and facet information for the object stored in a *.DAT* file. Notice that both the *LoadData* and *SaveData* functions use binary-format files, so you can't edit them with a text editor; instead, you use the utilities described in the following paragraphs.

Manually Generating a Data File

This book contains an interactive utility, preceded by the source-code file *MakeObjs.C*, that allows you to create simple objects manually. The best way to understand how to use it is to try several examples; one is presented below. This program lets you enter coordinates by typing them in and seeing how they look using a simple line drawing. The program is described in more detail in Chapter 9.

We'll create an object called *Plane.DAT*, which will consist of a single square, and see exactly what data is written to the *.DAT* file for the object. The program will ask you to input the number of facets for the object. Enter the number 1. The data file now contains:

    4   1   4

These numbers mean that our object has four vertices and one facet and that each facet has four vertices (*MakeObjs* assumes that all entered facets are four-sided). The program now enters graphics mode and displays an axis. (You may want to turn up the brightness on your monitor so you can see the data as you enter it.) Now you enter four sets of three variables (x, y, and z), where each set defines one vertex (corner) of the facet. Each vertex should be entered on its own line, and the x, y, and z variables must be separated by one or more spaces. After typing a set of three variables, press *Enter* and begin the next set. As you enter each set, a point will be plotted on the screen to show you your position in three-dimensional space. The four sets of coordinates for this plane are:

```
-1   -1    0
 1   -1    0
 1    1    0
-1    1    0
```

This is a square with sides of length 2, centered at the origin and lying in the *X-Y* plane. These coordinates indicate that we started at a -x and -y position and were in the $z=0$ plane; next, we moved in the positive x direction and remained in the same y and z positions. We then moved in a positive y direction, remaining in the same x and z positions. Finally, we moved in a -x direction and stayed the same in the y and z positions. Looking from the top (the positive *Z* axis) down onto the *X-Y* plane, we moved around the square counterclockwise. This means the facet is facing up (toward us), with the surface normal pointing along the positive *Z* axis. If we had gone around the other way, the surface normal would point toward the negative *Z* axis, and thus the facet would be facing away from us. Also note that we could have started with any of the vertices; as long as we proceeded in a counterclockwise fashion, we would generate exactly the same facet.

The data written to the file looks like this:

```
-23000   -23000   0
 23000   -23000   0
 23000    23000   0
-23000    23000   0
```

The data looks like this instead of consisting of ones and negative ones because it has been scaled by *ScaleData* for faster integer manipulation. This means that the data, when written to the *.DAT* file, is already scaled appropriately for integer manipulation.

Finally, we write out the data that tells us which vertex makes up each side of the facet. This set of data looks like this:

```
1    2    3    4
```

Note that these numbers represent the indices for the *Vertex* array; for example, *1* refers to vertex number one (-23000, -23000, 0) and *3* refers to vertex number three (23000, 23000, 0). Note once again that the vertices are called in an order that yields a counterclockwise set of vertices.

Our data file is now closed and complete. We have successfully generated a plane *(Plane.DAT)* to use as an object in our three-dimensionally modeled scenes.

You can use the *MakeObjs* program to enter more complex objects by entering additional facets. It will always scale the facet data to the dynamic range of the internal integer coordinate system. This program is not terribly convenient for an object with many facets, so several other utilities are provided in later chapters. These utilities will allow you to generate more complex shapes (such as spheres, toroids, and cylinders) quickly and use the *.SCN* file to combine the objects into still more complex shapes.

In the next chapter, you'll see how these objects are built into scenes via the scene file and how the modeler handles the list of objects in its database.

CHAPTER 6

Adding Objects to a Scene

In the last chapter, we looked at how the object database structure could be used to create individual objects. In this chapter, we'll look at how to build a scene by adding objects to the environment. We'll do this with *.SCN* files, which allow us to create *object instances*—copies of our objects—and place them wherever we wish in the scene. We can scale, rotate, and translate these object instances and alter their material characteristics. We can use the same object over and over, applying different characteristics for each instance. Using this approach, we can create complex objects by using instances of simpler objects, much like creating models from an infinite box of Legos.

The Object Database Structure

The principal structure in the *.SCN* file is *ObjL*, one for each object instance. The collection of all object instances is stored in *ObjList*, an array of pointers to the *ObjL* structures. The first element in the object list structure (*ObjL*) is the string *ObjectName*, which contains the name of the data disk file of a particular object. Next are three *TDA* vector variables that define the translation (offset in *X,Y,Z*), rotation, and scale to be applied to this instance of the object. We have complete control of scaling, so objects can be stretched and distorted along the *x*, *y*, and *z* dimensions independently.

An example is conversion of a sphere to an ellipsoid (egg shape) by scaling the *z* dimension twice as much as the *x* and *y* dimensions. Another example is a cube scaled in the *z* dimension twice as much as the *x* and *y* dimensions, yielding a parallelopiped (rectangular prism or box). Similarly, we may orient the object any way we desire using the three rotation variables.

It's important to note the order in which rotations are applied. The object is always rotated about the *Z* axis first, followed by the *Y* axis and finally the *X* axis.

When multiple orientations are specified, it's often hard to see why an object ends up looking the way it does; some experimentation will help you see how the various rotations work.

Finally, we place the object in the world by specifying the translation. The object coordinate *(0, 0, 0)* will be set to the point specified by the translation offset. For example, the *plane* object from Chapter 5 would be centered over the point *(X, Y, Z)* specified as the offset.

As discussed in Chapter 5, each object has its own internal coordinate system. The parameters specified above *(X, Y, Z)* for translation, axis rotations, and scaling are used to position the object in our scene's world coordinate system. We must also specify the viewer's position and orientation in this system using a similar type of specification—namely, an offset and viewing angle (orientation in the *X-Y* plane and tilt angle). We normally want the viewer to face the origin of the coordinate system, but that's not a requirement.

We can create more complex objects simply by using object instances and the aforementioned transformations to place objects next to each other. For example, we can stack cubes by specifying different offsets for each cube instance. (You'll see many examples of this throughout the book.)

The next *ObjL* element is the Boolean variable *Reflection*, which indicates whether or not the object can be reflected in mirrors. Most objects are capable of being reflected in mirrors, so this variable is usually set to true. You may, however, want to set *Reflection* to false so that not all reflections need to be processed, thereby simplifying the rendering of a scene.

Next, we have three *TDA*s: *AmbColor*, *DifColor*, and *SpcColor*. These specify the ambient, diffuse, and specular components of the object's color. Each is a vector representing the red, green, and blue components of each lighting factor.

- The *ambient* light contribution represents the amount of background light (light that pervades the environment rather than emanating directly from a light source, such as the sun) and therefore the color of the object in shadow (no light shining directly on the object).

- The *diffuse* light contribution is light that falls on the object and whose observed intensity is the same regardless of the observer position. This component represents the inherent color of the object surface. A red object is that color because the surface reflects the red wavelengths of visible light. This factor is independent of your position when you view the object. A good example is the sun's light, which illuminates half the Earth and distinguishes night from day.

- The *specular* component represents the light reflected directly off the object surface and back at the observer (in other words, how much the object surface acts as a mirror). This component represents the color of the light source and is further controlled by the next byte, *Gloss*. This quantity determines how mirrorlike the object is by controlling the size of the specular dot on the object. This dot represents the image of the light source reflected back at the observer. The larger the value of *Gloss*, the more mirrorlike the object surfaces become. (The lighting model is discussed in more detail in Chapter 8, where the mathematics of the modeler algorithms is described.)

Next is the Boolean variable *Sortable*. This tells us if the object should be sorted before being placed on the screen. We would normally set this variable to true, indicating that the object must be sorted (as described in Chapter 7) for proper scene placement. Sometimes this variable must be manipulated for objects in certain scenes so they appear on the screen in the correct order. *Sortable* is important because ordering of objects can become a problem with certain observer scene-viewing angles and object combinations. In some instances, you know ahead of time what the object ordering should be for a scene viewed from a certain direction; objects can then be entered in the order in which they should be drawn, and all sorting can be disabled.

Finally, we have the Boolean variable *Mirror*. This tells us if the object is a mirror—in other words, that the other objects should be reflected off the facets of this object. Mirrors must have a gray diffuse color. There is also a provision for automatic mirrors, called *edge reflectors* (these are discussed in more detail later).

Now let's look at the object buffer.

Initializing and Loading the Object Buffer

InitObjectBuffer clears and initializes the elements of the *ObjList* array. To use this function, we start a loop ranging from 0 to the number of objects in the scene. On each iteration, we nullify (set to 0 or false) each element of each structure pointed to by our loop variable within the array.

We'll use a series of functions to take the data read in from the scene file and store it in the *ObjList* array. *ObjectNum* points to the *ObjL* structure of the object instance being read from the .*SCN* file. This pointer is incremented once for each object instance in the scene.

Several functions read the various components from the .*SCN* file and add them to the *ObjL* structure. The first is *AddObject*, which simply takes the name of the object (a .*DAT* data-file name) and stores it in the *ObjectName* element of the structure pointed to by *ObjectNum*. Next, *Scale*, *Rotate*, and *Translate* are called. These functions each read their *x*, *y*, and *z* components, turn them into a *TDA* vector structure, and store them in their respective *TDA* elements in the structure. Next is the function *ReflectedObject*, which stores a Boolean value in its respective element in the structure.

Next are *ObjAmbColor*, *ObjDifColor*, and *ObjSpcColor*, which take the red, green, and blue components passed to them and store them in the *AmbColor*, *DifColor*, and *SpcColor* elements in the structure, respectively. Next is *ObjGloss*, which takes the byte passed to it and stores it in the *Gloss* element in the structure, followed by *AllowSort*, which stores the Boolean value passed to it in the *Sortable* element. The last variable is *Mirrored*, which, like *AllowSort*, takes the Boolean value passed to it and stores it in the *Mirror* element in the structure. This process continues until we have read the entire .*SCN* file and stored the corresponding *ObjL* structures in memory for every object in the scene.

Adding Edge Reflectors to a Scene

Edge reflectors are essentially mirrors added to the floor and both sides of a scene. They're implemented using two functions: *AddEdgeReflectors* and *AddEdgeReflectorsAtZero*. The first places the floor near the bottom of the screen, with two back walls. The *z* location of the plane is -50. *AddEdgeReflectorsAtZero* places the floor near the center of the screen, with two back walls. The *z* location of the floor plane is 0. The floor and walls are created by a database generator program, *Grid.C*.

The mirror colors are set so that the color components—ambient, diffuse, and specular—are all set to gray. The *Gloss* factor is set to 20, making the object very shiny. The Boolean variable *Sortable* is set to false, meaning that these objects should not be sorted. We do this because these objects, since they will be mirrors, have to be drawn first; if we sort them by position relative to the viewer, that may no longer be the case. Next, we set *Mirror* to true, making this object a mirror or a highly reflective surface.

Adding Objects from a Disk File

The function *AddObjectsToScene* reads in the information stored in the scene file. First, it reads in some global parameters that affect all the objects in the scene. To start, let's read in two lines from the file: a comment describing the scene and a blank line. Next, we read in five parameters—one Boolean and four integers—to set up the perspective of the scene. These parameters are passed to the *Init_Perspective* function in the graphics module (described in Chapter 3), which then sets up the perspective viewing geometry. We then read two integer values representing the viewing angle and tilt and pass them to the *Init_Plotting* function. We call *GetViewVector* to get the vector defining the position of the viewer in the world coordinate system, then read two integer values that specify the heading and tilt angle for our global light source (the sun). These angles are passed to *InitLighting* to set up the scene lighting geometry. Now we call *GetLightVector* to get a vector representing the direction of the light source; we then read in a Boolean parameter to be passed to *VertSort*. This value will determine whether or not sorting is to be turned on. Next, we read in two Boolean values that control whether and which edge reflectors are used. If the first value is true, we call *AddEdgeReflectors*; if the second value is true, we call *AddEdgeReflectorsAtZero*.

Next, we read in floating-point values for *Mix* and *Darken*. These variables determine the color of a reflected object (reflected either in a mirrored object or in the edge reflector mirrors). *Mix* blends the color of the object with the color of the reflective surface, while *Darken* darkens the color so that the reflection isn't as brilliant as the actual object. This often produces a more realistic reflection.

Finally, we read in a value that tells us how many objects are in the scene. At this point, we begin to load information concerning the objects themselves. To do this, we start a loop ranging from 0 to the number of objects in the scene. On each iteration, the information concerning one object is loaded and stored. Once all the data has been read in, we close the *.SCN* file and return from the function. We now have all the data defining the scene and material characteristics for each object. You'll soon see how this data is used to create a perspective view.

Now that we have examined the production of objects and the construction of a scene of those objects, let's move on to a discussion of how to determine the order in which objects are drawn.

CHAPTER 7

Sorting and Displaying Objects

The last chapter described how to create a scene by combining objects. In this chapter, we'll explore two additional aspects of drawing such a scene: determining the order in which objects are drawn, and converting their three-dimensional facet descriptions into two-dimensional sets of polygons. We'll also discuss how to draw reflections of objects in mirrors.

The modeler draws a scene much the same way a painter does, drawing the far away objects first, proceeding to the nearer ones. Any part of a closer object that overlaps a previously drawn object will simply overwrite that area. (The closer object is said to *occlude* the more distant object.) Using this painter's algorithm, the modeler can simply draw each object methodically without worrying about previously drawn objects. This means we must sort the objects in a back-to-front order (furthest from the viewer to nearest to the viewer). Because the viewpoint and the objects can move for any particular frame, we must sort the objects each time a frame is drawn.

An alternative approach is to draw the objects from front to back; in other words, the program draws the closest objects first. When a more distant object is drawn, it isn't allowed to overwrite any previously drawn areas of the screen. Although we don't use this technique in *3DModel.C*, many rendering programs do use it to implement advanced graphic effects.

Once the sorting order is determined, we can actually draw, or *render*, the objects onto the screen. We perform the following algorithm for each object in the scene, proceeding from back to front. First, we convert our object's three-dimensional facet data into two-dimensional screen coordinates using the viewer position and viewing geometry. Next, we determine whether or not the facet faces the viewer. If not, the facet is not visible to the viewer and we can proceed to the next facet. If it is visible, we determine its color, taking into account the position of the light source; the ambient, diffuse, and specular color attributes of the object; the position of the observer; and the facet's surface-normal vector (the direction the facet is facing). In addition, any object reflections will use the values contained in the variables *Mix* and *Darken*, described in Chapter 5, to modify the facet color.

After we have found the correct color, if necessary, we can draw the facet (now a two-dimensional polygon) onto the screen using the scan-conversion technique described under "Drawing Objects on the Screen." This process is repeated for all facets of the current object, and we proceed to the next nearest object in the scene.

Let's examine the sorting algorithm in more detail.

Sorting Objects

Given a scene as a collection of objects, we must determine the furthest-to-nearest order in which the objects are to be drawn. The basic method for doing this is to compute the distance of each object from the viewpoint and list the objects from furthest to nearest. To simplify this computation, we look at the view vector, which defines the position of the viewer with respect to the origin of the world coordinate system. We then examine the X, Y, and Z components and compare the largest of them to the corresponding component (X, Y, or Z) of each *object center* (the translation offset specified for the object in the *.SCN* file).

The objects are sorted based on the appropriate component, relative to the value at the viewer position. For instance, if the viewer is at $(100, 0, 0)$, looking toward the origin, we sort using the X component of each object. For each object with translation offset (X, Y, Z), we compute $100 - X$. If this value is negative, the object is behind the viewpoint and we need not draw the object at all since it cannot be seen. Otherwise, we find the largest value of all the visible objects and draw that object first. We then proceed to the next most distant object and continue until all the objects have been drawn.

This discussion assumes the scene contains no mirror objects. These objects (almost always single planar facets) are drawn first. If the mirror is visible—that is, facing the viewer—we'll draw it first and the reflections of the various objects later. Therefore, the modeler doesn't sort the mirror objects with the non-mirror objects.

The sorting routines set a number of variables when processing *ObjList*:

- *First* stores the first sortable (non-mirror) object in the list, while *FirstObject* stores its object number.

- *Last* stores the last object in the list and *LastObject* the corresponding object number.

  If *First* and *Last* are equal, the list contains only one non-mirror object. No sorting is needed, and the *Sorting* flag is set to false. Otherwise, sorting is necessary and the *Sorting* flag is set to true.

- *ReflSurface* is true if the scene contains mirror objects and false if not. We'll use it as a simple test later to decide whether any reflection processing is necessary.

- *NumMirrors*, which is equal to *FirstObject - 1*, tells us how many mirror objects exist.

To sort the objects, we use a doubly nested loop in which every object is compared against every other sortable object to see if it's in the correct order in the list. The outer loop runs from the *FirstObject* to the *LastObject*; the inner loop runs from the current object number set by the outer loop to the *LastObject*. The function *SortObjectBackToFront* compares the appropriate coordinates of the two objects being evaluated using the function *Order_X*, *Order_Y*, or *Order_Z*, depending on which coordinate of the viewer position was largest. If the first argument is further away than the second object, nothing needs to be done. If, however, the first object is nearer, then the two objects are swapped.

The components of the *Object* structures are switched using the following swap routines:

- *SwapStrings*   - Swaps two strings.
- *SwapRealNums* - Swaps two floating-point values.

151

- *SwapTDANums* - Swaps two *TDA* variables (all components).
- *SwapByte*   - Swaps two bytes (*unsigned char*).
- *SwapBoolean*   - Swaps two Boolean values.

These routines perform the same basic function—namely, switching the contents of their two arguments.

Once the current outer-loop object has been compared against all other objects, we iterate the outer loop and again compare this object with the other objects. After running through all the objects in the outer loop, we're assured that they're in the correct order.

Now that we've established the correct drawing order for our list of objects, let's look at how each object is rendered on the screen.

Drawing Objects on the Screen

The primary object-drawing function is *PlaceObjectOnScreen*. This function loops from 1 to the number of facets of the specified object. For each facet, we check to see if any of the *ReflectedObject* flags (*X*, *Y*, and *Z*) have been set. If so, we're drawing a reflected object; if not, we're processing the object itself. In either case, *PlaceFacet* is called to draw the current facet.

PlaceFacet begins with a loop ranging from 1 to the last vertex in the current facet. Using the previously computed scale factor, *InvScaleImage*, we scale each of the facet's vertices (multiply each component by *InvScaleImage*) and check to see if the facet is potentially visible. The facet is potentially visible if it's facing the viewer (the surface normal is pointing in the opposite direction of our view vector).

If the facet satisfies this condition, we calculate an intensity for it and check to see if any of the three intensity components (ambient, diffuse, and specular) are greater than 0. If so, we call *GetProjectedCoords* to project the three-dimensional facet vertices onto the two-dimensional screen. Finally, we call *PutFacet* (described in the next chapter) to take the two-dimensional, polygonal facet and draw it on the screen with the computed color.

Displaying Objects and Their Reflections

The modeler provides a rudimentary capability to display not only objects but also reflected images of the objects. An object may be reflected in any of the following two-dimensional planes in the world coordinate system:

- xy plane $z = 0$
- xy plane $z = -50$
- xz plane $y = 0$
- yz plane $x = 0$

We generate the reflected object from the original object simply by changing the sign of the corresponding coordinate for every vertex of the object. For example, an object is reflected in the xy plane when the sign of all the z coordinates is changed. Similarly, we reflect an object in the xz plane by negating the y coordinates and in the yz plane by negating the x coordinates.

As previously mentioned, the modeler can also process mirror objects. These are planar facets that lie in the xy plane at $z=0$ and for which the object mirror flag is set. Mirror objects allow you to place mirrors on the floor of the image in any desired arrangement. They are rendered not directly onto the screen, but into a *reflection buffer*. This buffer defines all the pixels that mirror objects occupy in the image. The reflection of an object is only drawn to the screen wherever a mirror object has been drawn. The program *3DModel.C* lets you create mirror objects explicitly, or you may simply treat the entire floor ($z=0$ plane) as a mirror.

We actually have several lists of objects to draw: mirror objects, reflections of objects, and the objects themselves. The modeler always processes objects in this order. First, any mirror facets are rendered into the reflection buffer. *ObjList* is then sorted into back-to-front order using *SortObjectsBackToFront*. Next, the reflections in the various planes, if enabled, are processed. Since the sorting order is different for reflections, three other sort functions are provided here: *SortTopToBottom*, for reflections in the xy plane; *SortObjectsFrontToBackInX*, for reflections in the yz plane; and *SortObjectsFrontToBackInY*, for reflections in the xz plane. These functions use the Z, X, and Y coordinates, respectively, to sort the objects into the opposite order from the actual object list. That's because objects closest to the mirror will appear to be nearest the viewer.

The *DisplayObjectsInScene* function implements the same procedure to render the scene. It uses the functions *DisplayReflectiveSurfaces*, *DisplayReflections*, and *DisplayActualImages* to render the mirror objects, reflections in the mirror objects, and the actual objects, respectively. It begins by calling *PrepareSort* to initialize the sorting routines and variables. Next, *DefineReflection* is called to set all the reflection variables to false since we won't initially process object reflections. If the *Sorting* flag is true, we call *SortObjectsBackToFront* to put *ObjList* in the proper order for drawing the actual objects.

Next, we call *DisplayReflectiveSurfaces* to draw any mirror objects. We then begin processing any reflected objects by examining the *ReflSurface* flag. If it's set to true, we call *DefineReflection* to make the z (reflect in the xy plane) reflection variable true. If the sorting variables are true, we call the function *SortTopToBottom* to sort the objects by their z values independent of the viewer position, then *DisplayReflections* to draw any objects reflected in the xy plane. Reflections in the xz and yz planes are processed the same way.

Once all reflections have been processed, we use *DefineReflection* to set the reflection flags to false and call *SortObjectBackToFront* again to order the objects. If the *VerticalSort* flag is set, we use *SortBottomToTop* to sort the objects into bottom-to-top order. *DisplayActualImages* is then called to draw the final set of objects (without reflections), and our scene is complete.

The main rendering functions work in a similar manner. Because the list has already been sorted, each object in *ObjList* is independently processed in order. As each object is processed, we check to see if its vertex data has been loaded. If not, the vertex buffer is reinitialized and the object's data loaded from the appropriate disk file. The *AffineTransformation* routine transforms the object from its local coordinate system to that of the world coordinate system. *PlaceObjectOnScreen* then actually draws the object by processing the object facets. *InvAffineTransformation* converts the object back to its original coordinate system so the other drawing routines can process it as necessary.

DisplayReflectiveSurfaces displays any mirror objects by processing objects 1 through FirstObject - 1. This routine first sets the flags *Reflect* and *ReflectedObjects* to false because the mirror objects are actual objects (in other words, not reflected by any of the planes or by other mirror objects). If we have any mirror objects, the *ReflectedObjects* and *Mirroring* flags are set to true to indicate that the actual objects must be reflected in the mirror objects. Once all the mirror objects have been drawn, we draw any object reflections.

The *DisplayReflections* function draws the object reflections in any of the three planes depending on how the reflection flags are set. It processes the object list starting at *FirstObject* through *LastObject*, drawing each reflected object with facet colors modified by the values of *Mix* and *Darken*.

DisplayActualImages draws the non-reflected objects onto the screen. As with *DisplayReflections*, we process all objects from *FirstObject* to *LastObject*. The *Reflect* flag is now false since these are actual objects.

What's Ahead

Chapter 5 described how to construct objects using three-dimensional facets, while Chapter 6 showed how to take those objects and create a complex, three-dimensional environment by combining primitive models using affine transformations. In this chapter, we discussed how the modeling program reads in the objects and sorts them into the proper order for display. We also saw how the three-dimensional facets that make up an object are converted into two-dimensional screen polygons that can then be scan-converted to produce displayed images. In the next chapter, you'll learn how to apply these techniques to the rest of the modeling program and how these pieces work together to produce scenes for the animation sequences.

CHAPTER 8

The Modeling Program and Creating Animation

In previous chapters, we saw how our facet data is loaded in and saved, how to add objects to a scene, and how to sort objects so they can be drawn in the proper order. This chapter describes in more detail how the viewer, light source, and surface normal vectors are calculated. We'll see how to determine whether or not a facet is visible and how reflections in mirror objects are handled. We'll also examine how the two-dimensional facets we produced by projecting three-dimensional facets are drawn on the screen. Finally, we'll see how the image data for the scene is written to temporary files for later color reduction playback and review. Let's begin our discussion by reviewing how scene description data is loaded.

The first thing the modeler must do is load the scene data for the first animation frame to be generated. The modeler reads a *.SCN* file containing data for each frame of an animation sequence. As you may recall from Chapter 6, this data is stored in the array *ObjList*, which holds the scene description data for the current frame. This data tells the modeler which objects are in the scene, their orientation and color, and whether or not the scene contains mirrors. It also determines whether or not we need to sort the objects before placing them on the screen. The data is read for one frame at a time. Once all the data for a frame has been read and stored in the *ObjList* array, we're ready to begin rendering the objects in the scene.

Affine Transformations

As discussed in Chapter 6, an object is defined by a collection of planar facets with three-dimensional vertex coordinates. To be able to place objects anywhere in our environment, we must have a way of mathematically transforming them from their local coordinate system to the desired location, size, and orientation within the world coordinate system. To do this, we use the *AffineTransformation* function specified as a four-by-four matrix.

This function begins by calling *PrepareMatrix* (in the *Math.C* module), which uses the current scaling, rotation, and translation values to prepare the transformation matrix. It then processes all the vertex data to place the object in the desired location. We loop through all the vertices in the facet, then call *VecScalMultI* to perform a scalar multiplication of the vertex data. This function converts our integer number, ranging from -23,000 to 23,000, to a real number suitable for transformation. Next, the *Transform* function is called to multiply the vertex coordinates (X, Y, Z) by the transformation matrix already prepared. Finally, we *project* the three-dimensional coordinates onto the two-dimensional screen by calling *VecScalMultInt*. Thus, each facet is converted from a three-dimensional polygon to a two-dimensional polygon that can be drawn on the screen. We also need to convert the transformed coordinates back to the original object coordinates; this is done by *InvAffineTransformation*.

Viewer and Light Source Vectors

The viewer's position determines how the objects are oriented and how the scene looks on the screen. We specify this position using two angles: *ViewPhi,* which represents the angle of the viewer around the z axis, and *ViewTheta,* representing the tilt, or *pitch*, of the viewer relative to the z axis. Both are specified in degrees. A *ViewTheta* of 0^0 puts the viewer on the negative y axis. (Increasing the z axis points upward.) Increasing values up to 90^0 moves us towards the positive z axis. *ViewPhi* is used to move us around the z axis in a counter-clockwise direction. We start on the negative y axis, and move along to the positive x axis with increasing *ViewPhi*.

These angles are passed to the *GetViewVector* function, which converts them to radians. It uses these angles to calculate the x, y, and z coordinates of a unit vector (of length 1) pointing from the origin of the three-dimensional space to the position of the viewer. This type of specification assumes we're looking directly at the origin. Thus, the point (0, 0, 0) will always be in the center of the screen.

The light direction is handled the same way as the viewing direction. We use *LightPhi* and *LightTheta* to store the angles. After setting these variables via a call to *InitLightDirection*, which reads the angles from the file, we call *GetLightVector*. This function converts the angles to radians and determines the *x, y,* and *z* coordinates of a vector pointing from the origin of the three-dimensional space to the position of the light source. The light direction is used to determine how our objects are shaded—in other words, which parts are light and which are dark.

The Surface Normal Vector

Each facet faces a particular direction, as described by the *surface normal vector*. This vector is of length 1 and is perpendicular to the plane the facet lies in. We use the surface normal to determine whether the facet is facing away from or toward the viewer and its angle relative to the light source.

The *GetSurfaceNormalVector* function finds the surface normal from the facet vertex description. As you may recall from Chapter 3, the *VecCross* function takes two vectors as arguments and generates a third vector that's perpendicular to both. The vertex description of a facet can be used to generate the necessary vectors. The first vector goes from the second vertex of the facet to the first, and the second vector goes from the last vertex of the facet to the first.

We then compute the cross-product. If it's nonzero, the computed vector is in the direction of the surface normal (though its length is not necessarily 1); otherwise, the two vectors were collinear (in a straight line), and we must try another pair of facet points. The next time, we repeat the process using the last three vertices of the facet. Once we have found a nonzero cross-product, we generate the surface normal by normalizing it. To normalize this surface normal vector, we must find the length of the vector and divide each of the components of the vector by this length. We now have a normalized unit vector that defines the facet's surface normal.

The Illumination Model

The illumination model is a mathematical description of how to color a facet based on its material properties, the direction of the viewer, and the direction of the light source. The primary routine in this model is *IntensityCalc*, which determines the shade of each facet drawn onto the screen. *IntensityCalc* returns color values ranging from 0 to 63 for red, green, and blue in the *TDIA* variable *Intensity*. The color is based on three separate intensity calculations.

The first is the ambient intensity, which is simply a constant and comes from background illumination. Any facet facing away from the light source or in shadow is drawn with a color at this intensity.

Next, we compute the diffuse component, which depends only on the facet and light source direction. Diffuse light is the light that you would see half-reflecting from a planet's surface on the side of its' sun. Using the *VecDot* function, we find the dot product of the surface normal vector and the light vector and store this value in the variable *CosTheta*. We can do this because both vectors have a length of 1. If *CosTheta* is less than 0.0, the facet is facing away from the light source and has no diffuse or specular component.

Otherwise, we continue and calculate another vector for the specular component, which represents how shiny the object is. Depending on the facet's material type, this component has the visual effect of adding specular highlights (the light source reflects off the surface and directly at the viewer). First, we multiply *CosTheta* by 2 and store this value in the variable *TwoCosTheta*. Next, we multiply the surface normal vector by *TwoCosTheta*, normalize the resulting vector, subtract the light vector from it, and normalize this vector as well. This is the *reflection vector*—in other words, the direction in which the light source is reflected from the surface of the facet. The light source is reflected at the viewer if the viewing vector lies close to the reflection vector.

We again use the dot product to get *CosAlph,* which is 0 when the viewer is at right angles to the reflection vector and 1 when the viewer is directly along the reflection vector (the light bounces right into the viewer's eyes).

To finish computing the diffuse factor, we multiply that component by *CosTheta* and store it in variable *Diffuse*. Next, we obtain the specular factor by multiplying the specular component by *CosAlpha* and raising the result to the power of our gloss factor, usually referred to as the *Phong exponent*. The larger the exponent, the sharper the highlight. We then multiply the specular color (or the color of the light source) by this factor.

We now have three separate color components—ambient, diffuse, and specular— each having red, green, and blue components. We now add these components together and check to see if any are greater than 63. If so, they're set to 63, the maximum color value. The values are then stored in the output *TDIA Intensity* variable to be used by the scan-conversion routine described later in this chapter.

The Facet Visibility Test

The speed at which a scene is rendered depends on the number of facets that must be drawn. The fewer facets to be drawn, the less time it will take to complete the scene. Therefore, anything we can do to eliminate facets that aren't visible on the screen will speed up the process. The method described here is a straightforward visibility test. If a facet is facing away from the viewer, it cannot be seen (it will be covered up by a facet that faces the viewer). Therefore, we don't have to convert this facet to two dimensions, compute a color for it, or write it to the screen.

The *Visible* function tests a facet's visibility by obtaining its surface normal, which is passed to *Visible* in the form of an array. Next, the *View* vector is copied into a temporary vector so we can manipulate it without destroying the original. (We'll need to manipulate this temporary view vector to properly compute the visibility of reflected objects.) *Visible* proceeds by multiplying the surface normal vector by the temporary view vector and storing the result in a variable called *Temp*. This variable is then broken down into its *X*, *Y*, and *Z* components, which are stored in the variables *nvx*, *nvy*, and *nvz*. These variables are used to calculate a variable called *CosBeta*, which determines the facet's visibility. *CosBeta* is the dot product of the *View* vector and *Temp* variable. If it's less than 0, the facet is facing away from the viewer and is therefore not visible, so *Visible* returns a value of false. Otherwise, the facet is facing the viewer and *Visible* returns a value of true.

Reflected objects are handled slightly differently because, just as we change the sign of the vertex component, we must also change the sign of the corresponding surface normal component. A series of *if* statements checks to see which mirror plane is active (if any), changes the appropriate sign of *nvx*, *nvy*, or *nvz*, and computes *CosBeta* as described earlier. For a typical scene, this test eliminates roughly half the facets being drawn (half the facets normally face the viewer, while the other half face away).

The Reflection Screen Buffer

To use a mirror of limited size (rather than the entire $z=0$ plane), we need a *reflection buffer* to store the extra information used in rendering other (non-mirror) facets. The buffer is the same size as the screen. Since the modeler uses a screen size of 160 by 100 pixels, our reflection buffer is 16,000 bytes.

We use three functions to manipulate the reflection buffer: *InitReflectionBuffer*, *Reflected*, and *MakeReflected*.

> *InitReflectionBuffer* simply zeros out the entire buffer using a set of nested *for* loops. This is done for each new frame so we don't have reflections left over from previous frames.

> *Reflected* reads the buffer and tells the calling function whether or not a pixel is reflective. If the bit representing our pixel is set (true), the pixel is reflective; otherwise, we return false to the calling function.

> *MakeReflected* sets a bit in the buffer to indicate that the corresponding screen pixel is reflective.

The scan-conversion routine (described later) uses the reflection buffer to decide whether or not to draw a reflected object to the screen.

The Polygonal Facet Fill Routine

Once a three-dimensional facet has been projected onto the screen and its color determined, we use *PutFacet* to fill the pixels with the specified color in a shape corresponding to that of the facet. This function begins by calculating the minimum and maximum values for the x and y screen coordinates of the facet, then loops from the minimum y value to the maximum y value. The goal is to determine where the facet intersects the horizontal line specified by the current y. A horizontal line on a screen is called a *scan line* (a term borrowed from television parlance); hence, the process of rendering a polygon is called *scan conversion*.

We now loop through each vertex in the facet and find which facet edges intersect the scan line. These will be the edges where the y coordinate for one vertex is less than or equal to the scan-line value, and the other vertex y coordinate is greater than or equal to the scan-line value. For these edges, we calculate the slope of the edge and, from this value, the x coordinate of the point at which the facet edge intersects the scan line. We must make sure the calculated values are valid (within the minimum and maximum x values). If not, we truncate them to the legal limit—the boundary of the screen.

Now we begin filling the scan line by looping from the minimum x coordinate to the maximum x coordinate. First, we check to see if we're processing a mirror object. If so, we call *MakeReflected* to turn on the corresponding bit in the reflection buffer. Next, we copy the integer color array *Intensity* into a floating-point array called *Intens*. For the rest of the process, we'll use the integer representation of facet color.

Finally, we call *Put_Gray_Pixel* to put a pixel both on the screen and in our internal image pixel buffer for later processing. The pixels on the screen are shades of gray while the image is being generated. Until we have color-processed the image, we cannot map the 16-bit color values we have generated to the eight-bit values of our screen. Therefore, during actual image rendering, we simply display the intensity level (referred to as the *gray level*) until final color processing is completed. This is why we save the colors in an internal pixel buffer: so that the colors may be processed later to determine the corresponding colors on an eight-bit, 256-color screen.

The scan conversion writes pixels differently for reflected and nonreflected objects. For an actual (non-reflected) object, we copy the *Intensity* array into the *Intens* array as described earlier. Next, we call *Put_Gray_Pixel* to display a gray-scale representation of the pixel color data. (We don't need to call *MakeReflected* because this object isn't a mirror and therefore won't have anything reflected in it.) If we're dealing with a reflected object, we calculate the values for the *Intens* array using *Intensity*, *Mix*, and *Darken*. *Mix* and *Darken* are used to blend the color of the reflected facet with the color of the reflective surface and darken it respectively, making the reflection more realistic.

Reflections generally have some light loss (because of scattering of light) compared to the actual object, so we calculate this loss for red, green, and blue. After these have been calculated, we call *Put_Gray_Pixel* once again to initialize the pixel data and display a gray-scale representation of the color data to the screen. However, we use the *Reflected* function to see if the corresponding bit in the reflection buffer has been set. If so, the pixel is drawn; if not, the reflection is not on a mirror object and the pixel is not drawn to the screen.

The scan-line algorithm is repeated for every scan line in the facet. We then process the next facet and so forth until we've processed each object in the scene.

Writing to a Temporary File

After the objects in our scene have all been drawn onto the screen, the final image of the scene is stored in the internal pixel buffers and then written to a temporary file. The internal pixel buffers such as, *Red_Plane*, *Green_Plane*, and *Blue_Plane* are allocated in the main program section of the modeler, and defined in the *Put_Gray_Pixel* routine. To write the *.TMP* temporary file, we scan these buffers using two nested *for* loops that represent the image resolution, which for these images is 160 by 100. On each iteration, we take one value from each of the planes, form a 16-bit word (five bits each for red, green, and blue), and store it in a new temporary buffer. Once we've processed a complete line of the image, the buffer is written to a *.TMP* file.

At this point, the scan-conversion routine has generated a pixel buffer representing 15 bits of color information. We must convert this to a form displayable on our eight-bit, 256-color monitor. (This process is described in detail in Chapter 16, which discusses how the *.TMP* file is converted to the displayed *.ANI* file.) The process is complicated by the fact that we want to generate animation and therefore must ensure that all the images in the *.ANI* file can use the same palette. We want the objects to use the same palette for two reasons.

First, display flicker may result otherwise. If an object's color computation is between two colors, we may oscillate back and forth between them every other frame or so (this is known as *temporal color aliasing*). Suffice to say that it can be a very annoying and distracting side effect of switching color palettes.

Second, speed of display is very important to our animation. If we had to update the palette every time we drew a new frame on the screen, we would end up with a slow, choppy animation display due to the time needed to transfer the palette to the graphics super VGA card and initialize it. Thus, this color-processing step is necessary if we want smooth animation playback.

After all the data is written to the *.TMP* file, the file is closed. Now we're ready for the final color-processing step: converting the *.TMP* file to an *.ANI* file. (Further discussion of color reduction processing is presented in Chapter 16.)

The *3DModel.C* Program

Now that we've studied the major functions used by the modeler, let's take a quick run through the program (Listing 8-1). First, we clear out the reflection, object, and vertex buffers. Next, we initialize the graphics screen and set up our screen palette. We call *AddObjectsToScene* to fill in the *ObjList* array describing the scene (or scenes) to be generated. *DisplayObjectsInScene* is then called to draw the objects and their reflections into the internal pixel buffers. Next, *WriteTMPFile* is called to write the temporary file used by the color-processing routines for the final (color) screen display. Finally, the files are closed and the next frame is processed. This continues until each frame has been processed and written to the *.TMP* file.

```
/*




              Modeling and Shading Routines for
                 Objects Constructed of Facets


                        Program by
                  Christopher D. Watkins


                    'C' conversion by
                       Larry Sharp




*/
#include "stdio.h"
#include "dos.h"
#include "conio.h"
#include "math.h"
#include "string.h"
#include "malloc.h"
#include "defs.h"
#include "globals.h"
#include "mathb.h"
```

```
#include "graphb.h"
#include "modelsup.h"
static Byte far *Red_Plane;
static Byte far *Green_Plane;
static Byte far *Blue_Plane;
#define xcyc (yc*160)+xc
#define xy (y*160)+x
void Allocate_Memory()
{
Facet=farcalloc(((MaxFacet+1)*(MaxVertexNumInFacet+1)),
sizeof(int)); Red_Plane=farmalloc(16000);
    Green_Plane=farmalloc(16000);
    Blue_Plane=farmalloc(16000);
if((Facet==NULL) || (Red_Plane==NULL) || (Green_Plane==NULL) ||
(Blue_Plane==NULL))
    {
            printf("Not enough memory!\n");
            printf("%p\n%p\n%p\n%p\n", Facet, Red_Plane,
Green_Plane, Blue_Plane);
            getch();
            exit(1);
    }
}
void Free_Memory()
{
    farfree(Facet);
    farfree(Red_Plane);
    farfree(Green_Plane);
    farfree(Blue_Plane);
}
void Put_Grey_Pixel(int xc, int yc, TDIA Intens)
{
    Byte col;
    Red_Plane[xcyc]=Intens[0]&255;
    Green_Plane[xcyc]=Intens[1]&255;
    Blue_Plane[xcyc]=Intens[2]&255;
    col=((Intens[0]+Intens[1]+Intens[2])/3);
    Plot(xc, yc, col);
}

void Clear_Planes()
```

```
{
_fmemset(Red_Plane, 0, 16000); _fmemset(Green_Plane, 0, 16000);
_fmemset(Blue_Plane, 0, 16000);
}
/*
```

```
┌─────────────────────────────────────────────────────┐
│ ┌─────────────────────────────────────────────────┐ │
│ │                  Toggle Switches                │ │
│ └─────────────────────────────────────────────────┘ │
└─────────────────────────────────────────────────────┘
```

```
        VertSort          - vertically sort objects
*/
   Boolean VerticalSort;
   void VertSort(Boolean Sort)
   {
       VerticalSort=Sort;
   }
/*
```

```
┌─────────────────────────────────────────────────────┐
│ ┌─────────────────────────────────────────────────┐ │
│ │                Affine Transformations           │ │
│ │                                                 │ │
│ └─────────────────────────────────────────────────┘ │
└─────────────────────────────────────────────────────┘
```

```
   AffineTransformation    - translate, rotate and scale verticies
                                                    for viewing
   InvAffineTransformation - return verticies to original value
*/
   void DoTransform(Matx4x4 XForm)
   {
       TDA temp, temp2;
       for(VertexNum=1; VertexNum<=LastVertex; VertexNum++)
       {
   VecScalMultI(InvScaleData, Vertex[VertexNum], temp2);
   Transform(temp2, XForm, temp);
   VecScalMultInt(ScaleImage, temp, Vertex[VertexNum]);
       }
   }
   void DoInvTransform(Matx4x4 XForm)
   {
       TDA temp, temp2;
   for(VertexNum=1; VertexNum<=LastVertex; VertexNum++)
```

```
    {
VecScalMultI(InvScaleImage, Vertex[VertexNum], temp2);
Transform(temp2, XForm, temp); VecScalMultInt(ScaleData, temp,
Vertex[VertexNum]);
    }
}
void AffineTransformation(TDA T, TDA S, TDA R)
{
    Matx4x4 XForm;
    PrepareMatrix(T[0],      T[1],      T[2],
                S[0],      S[1],      S[2],
                R[0],      R[1],      R[2], XForm);
    DoTransform(XForm);
}
void InvAffineTransformation(TDA T, TDA S, TDA R) {
    Matx4x4 XForm;
    PrepareInvMatrix(-T[0],     -T[1],     -T[2],
            1.0/S[0], 1.0/S[1], 1.0/S[2],
-R[0],     -R[1],     -R[2], XForm);
    DoInvTransform(XForm);
}
/*
```

```
┌─────────────────────────────────────────────────────┐
│  ┌───────────────────────────────────────────────┐  │
│  │                                               │  │
│  │         Viewer and Light Source Vectors       │  │
│  │                                               │  │
│  └───────────────────────────────────────────────┘  │
└─────────────────────────────────────────────────────┘
```

```
    GetViewVector        - unit vector in direction of viewer
    InitLightDirection   - get direction for light source
    GetLightVector       - unit vector in direction of light source
*/
    #define ViewPhi 270
    #define ViewTheta 90
    TDA View;
    void GetViewVector()
    {
        float Phi, Theta;
        float x, y, z;
    Phi=Radians((float)ViewPhi-(float)Angl);
```

```
Theta=Radians((float)ViewTheta-(float)Tilt);
    x=sin(Theta)*cos(Phi);
    y=sin(Theta)*sin(Phi);
    z=cos(Theta);
    Vec(x, y, z, View);
}
float LightPhi;
float LightTheta;
void InitLightDirection(int LgtPhi, int LgtTheta) {
LightPhi=(float)LgtPhi; LightTheta=(float)LgtTheta;
}
TDA Light;
void GetLightVector()
{
    float Phi, Theta;
    float x, y, z;
Phi=Radians(LightPhi); Theta=Radians(LightTheta);
x=sin(Theta)*cos(Phi);
    y=sin(Theta)*sin(Phi);
    z=cos(Theta);
    Vec(x, y, z, Light);
}
/*
```

```
┌─────────────────────────────────────────────────┐
│                                                   │
│              Surface Normal Vector                │
│                                                   │
└─────────────────────────────────────────────────┘
```

```
        GetSurfaceNormalVector - unit vector normal to surface
*/
    TDA SrfNorm;
    void GetSurfaceNormalVector(VoxelArray Face3d)
    {
        float Length, Length2;
        TDA Dir1;
        TDA Dir2;
        TDA Temp1;
        TDA Temp2;
        TDA Temp3;
        TDA SrfNorm2;
```

```
   VecCopy(Face3d[2], Temp1);
   VecCopy(Face3d[1], Temp2);
   VecCopy(Face3d[LastVertexNumInFacet], Temp3);
   VecSub(Temp1, Temp2, Dir1);
   VecSub(Temp3, Temp2, Dir2);
   VecCross(Dir1, Dir2, SrfNorm); Length=VecLen(SrfNorm);
   VecCopy(Face3d[LastVertexNumInFacet], Temp1);
   VecCopy(Face3d[LastVertexNumInFacet-1], Temp2);
   VecCopy(Face3d[LastVertexNumInFacet-2], Temp3); VecSub(Temp1,
   Temp2, Dir1);
       VecSub(Temp3, Temp2, Dir2);
   VecCross(Dir1, Dir2, SrfNorm2); Length2=VecLen(SrfNorm2);
       if(Length==0.0)
   VecScalMult(1.0/Length2, SrfNorm2, SrfNorm);
       else
       {
               if(Length2==0.0)
       VecScalMult(1.0/Length, SrfNorm, SrfNorm); else
               {
       VecScalMult(1.0/Length, SrfNorm, SrfNorm); VecScalMult(1.0/
       Length2, SrfNorm2, SrfNorm2); VecAdd(SrfNorm, SrfNorm2,
       SrfNorm); VecScalMult(0.5, SrfNorm, SrfNorm);
               }
       }
   }
/*
```

```
+------------------------------------------------+
|                                                |
|                                                |
|              Facet Visibility Test             |
|                                                |
|                                                |
+------------------------------------------------+
```

```
        Visible - determine if facet is visible
*/
   Boolean Reflect;
   Boolean MirrorX;
   Boolean MirrorY;
   Boolean MirrorZ;
   Boolean Visible(VoxelArray Face3d)
   {
```

```
      float CosBeta;
      float nvx, nvy, nvz;
      TDA temp, v;
      Boolean vt;
   GetSurfaceNormalVector(Face3d); VecCopy(View, v);
      if(Reflect && MirrorZ)
            v[2]=-v[2];
   VecElemMult(1.0, SrfNorm, v, temp); UnVec(temp, &nvx, &nvy,
   &nvz); vt=true;
      CosBeta=nvx+nvy+nvz;
      if((MirrorZ || (!(MirrorX || MirrorY))) && (CosBeta<0.0))
            vt=false;
      else
      {
            CosBeta=-nvx+nvy+nvz;
            if(MirrorX && (CosBeta<0.0))
                vt=false;
            else
            {
                CosBeta=nvx-nvy+nvz;
                if(MirrorY && (CosBeta<0.0))
                    vt=false;
            }
      }
      return(vt);
   }
/*

┌─────────────────────────────────────────────────────────┐
│ ┌─────────────────────────────────────────────────────┐ │
│ │                                                       │ │
│ │               Reflection Screen Buffer                │ │
│ │                                                       │ │
│ └─────────────────────────────────────────────────────┘ │
└─────────────────────────────────────────────────────────┘

         Stores the reflective states of all screen pixel
                                              locations
   InitReflectionBuffer     - clear reflective states
   Reflected                - indicates whether or not reflective
   MakeReflected            - makes a screen location reflective
*/
   #define XBytes 39
```

```
Byte Refl[XBytes+1][101];
void InitReflectionBuffer()
{
    int i, j;
    for(i=0; i<=XBytes; i++)
    {
            for(j=0; j<YRes; j++)
                Refl[i][j]=0;
    }
}
Boolean Reflected(int x, int y)
{
    Byte tmp;
    tmp=Refl[x/8][y]&(128>>(x%8));
    if(tmp==0)
            return(false);
    else
            return(true);
}
void MakeReflected(int x, int y)
{
    Refl[x/8][y]=Refl[x/8][y]|(128>>(x%8));
}
/*
```

```
┌─────────────────────────────────────────────────┐
│ ┌─────────────────────────────────────────────┐ │
│ │                                             │ │
│ │      Add Objects to the Objects List Database│ │
│ │                                             │ │
│ └─────────────────────────────────────────────┘ │
└─────────────────────────────────────────────────┘
```

```
        InitObjectBuffer    - initialize object buffer
        AddObject           - add object of certain name
        Scale               - scale the object
        Rotate              - rotate the object
        Translate           - translate the object
        ReflectObject       - will this object reflect on a
                              reflective object
        ObjectColor         - color of object
        AllowSort           - is this object sorted
        Mirrored            - is this object reflective
*/
```

```
#define NumObjects 20
int ObjectNum;
int LastObject;
typedef struct{
    Name ObjectName;
    TDA Translate;
    TDA Rotate;
    TDA Scale;
    Boolean Reflection;
    TDA AmbColor;
    TDA DifColor;
    TDA SpcColor;
    Byte Gloss;
    Boolean Sortable;
    Boolean Mirror;
}ObjL;
ObjL ObjList[NumObjects+1];
void InitObjectBuffer()
{
for(ObjectNum=0; ObjectNum<=NumObjects; ObjectNum++)
    {
strset(ObjList[ObjectNum].ObjectName, 0);
VecNull(ObjList[ObjectNum].Translate);
VecNull(ObjList[ObjectNum].Rotate);
VecNull(ObjList[ObjectNum].Scale);
ObjList[ObjectNum].Reflection=false;
VecNull(ObjList[ObjectNum].AmbColor);
VecNull(ObjList[ObjectNum].DifColor);
VecNull(ObjList[ObjectNum].SpcColor);
ObjList[ObjectNum].Gloss=0; ObjList[ObjectNum].Sortable=false;
ObjList[ObjectNum].Mirror=false;
    }
    ObjectNum=0;
}
void AddObject(Name FileName)
{
    ++ObjectNum;
    strcpy(ObjList[ObjectNum].ObjectName, FileName);
    LastObject=ObjectNum;
}
```

```
void Scale(float x, float y, float z)
{
    Vec(x, y, z, ObjList[ObjectNum].Scale);
}
void Rotate(float x, float y, float z)
{
    Vec(-x, -y, -z, ObjList[ObjectNum].Rotate);
}
void Translate(float x, float y, float z)
{
    Vec(-x, -y, -z, ObjList[ObjectNum].Translate);
}
void ReflectObject(Boolean State)
{
    ObjList[ObjectNum].Reflection=State;
}
void ObjAmbColor(float r, float g, float b)
{
    Vec(r, g, b, ObjList[ObjectNum].AmbColor);
}
void ObjDifColor(float r, float g, float b)
{
    Vec(r, g, b, ObjList[ObjectNum].DifColor);
}
void ObjSpcColor(float r, float g, float b)
{
    Vec(r, g, b, ObjList[ObjectNum].SpcColor);
}
void ObjGloss(Byte Col)
{
    ObjList[ObjectNum].Gloss=Col;
}
void AllowSort(Boolean State)
{
    ObjList[ObjectNum].Sortable=State;
}
void Mirrored(Boolean State)
{
    ObjList[ObjectNum].Mirror=State;
}
```

```
/*
```

```
┌──────────────────────────────────────────────────────────┐
│  ┌────────────────────────────────────────────────────┐  │
│  │                                                    │  │
│  │              The Illumination Model                │  │
│  │                                                    │  │
│  └────────────────────────────────────────────────────┘  │
└──────────────────────────────────────────────────────────┘
```

```
        Intensity - calculated intensity of point on screen
*/
    TDIA Intensity;

    void IntensityCalc()
    {
        TDA Diffuse;
        TDA Specular;
        TDA Color;
        float CosTheta;
        float CosAlpha;
        TDA Ref;
        float TwoCosTheta;
        TDA temp;
        CosTheta=VecDot(SrfNorm, Light);
        if(CosTheta<=0.0)
            VecScalMultInt(63.0, ObjList[ObjectNum].AmbColor,
Intensity); else
        {
                TwoCosTheta=2.0*CosTheta;
VecScalMult(TwoCosTheta, SrfNorm, temp); VecNormalize(temp);
                VecSub(temp, Light, Ref);
                VecNormalize(Ref);
                CosAlpha=VecDot(View, Ref);
                VecScalMult(CosTheta, ObjList[ObjectNum].DifColor,
Diffuse);
VecScalMult(Power(CosAlpha, ObjList[ObjectNum].Gloss),
ObjList[ObjectNum].SpcColor, Specular);
VecAdd3(ObjList[ObjectNum].AmbColor, Diffuse, Specular, Color);
                VecScalMultInt(63.0, Color, Intensity);
                if(Intensity[0]>63)
                    Intensity[0]=63;
                if(Intensity[1]>63)
```

```
                    Intensity[1]=63;
            if(Intensity[2]>63)
                    Intensity[2]=63;
        }
    }
/*
```

┌───┐
│ ┌──┐ │
│ │   │ │
│ │   Routines to Add Edge Reflectors to a Scene   │ │
│ │   │ │
│ └──┘ │
└───┘

```
    AddReflectorAtZero - adds edge reflectors at x=-50, y=-50 and
    z=0
    AddReflectors       - adds edge reflectors at x=-50, y=-50 and
    z=-50
*/
    Boolean EdgeReflectorAtZero;
    Boolean EdgeReflector;
    void AddEdgeReflectorsAtZero()
    {
        EdgeReflectorAtZero=true;
        AddObject("GRID.DAT");
        Scale(50.0, 50.0, 50.0);
        Rotate(0.0, 0.0, 0.0);
        Translate(0.0, 0.0, 0.0);
        ReflectObject(false);
        ObjAmbColor(0.300, 0.300, 0.300);
        ObjDifColor(0.500, 0.500, 0.500);
        ObjSpcColor(0.200, 0.200, 0.200);
        ObjGloss(20);
        AllowSort(false);
        Mirrored(true);
        AddObject("GRID.DAT");
        Scale(25.0, 25.0,   25.0);
        Rotate(0.0, 90.0, 0.0); Translate(-50.0, 0.0, 25.0);
        ReflectObject(false); ObjAmbColor(0.300,    0.300,  0.300);
        ObjDifColor(0.500,  0.500,  0.500);
        ObjSpcColor(0.200,  0.200,  0.200);
        ObjGloss(20);
```

```
    AllowSort(false);
    Mirrored(true);
    AddObject("GRID.DAT");
    Scale(50.0, 25.0,   25.0);
    Rotate(-90.0, 0.0,  0.0);
    Translate(0.0, -50.0, 25.0); ReflectObject(false);
    ObjAmbColor(0.300,  0.300,  0.300);
    ObjDifColor(0.500,  0.500,  0.500);
    ObjSpcColor(0.200,  0.200,  0.200);
    ObjGloss(20);
    AllowSort(false);
    Mirrored(true);
}
void AddEdgeReflectors()
{
    EdgeReflector=true;
    AddObject("GRID.DAT");
    Scale(50.0, 50.0,   50.0);
    Rotate(0.0, 0.0, 0.0);
    Translate(0.0, 0.0, -50.0); ReflectObject(false);
    ObjAmbColor(0.300,  0.300,  0.300);
    ObjDifColor(0.500,  0.500,  0.500);
    ObjSpcColor(0.200,  0.200,  0.200);
    ObjGloss(20);
    AllowSort(false);
    Mirrored(true);
    AddObject("GRID.DAT");
    Scale(50.0, 50.0,   50.0);
    Rotate(0.0, 90.0, 0.0); Translate(-50.0, 0.0, 0.0);
    ReflectObject(false); ObjAmbColor(0.300,    0.300,  0.300);
    ObjDifColor(0.500,  0.500,  0.500);
    ObjSpcColor(0.200,  0.200,  0.200);
    ObjGloss(20);
    AllowSort(false);
    Mirrored(true);
    AddObject("GRID.DAT");
    Scale(50.0, 50.0,   50.0);
    Rotate(-90.0, 0.0,  0.0);
    Translate(0.0, -50.0, 0.0); ReflectObject(false);
    ObjAmbColor(0.300,  0.300,  0.300);
```

```
            ObjDifColor(0.500,  0.500,  0.500);
            ObjSpcColor(0.200,  0.200,  0.200);
            ObjGloss(20);
            AllowSort(false);
            Mirrored(true);
        }
/*
```

```
┌─────────────────────────────────────────────────────────────┐
│ ┌─────────────────────────────────────────────────────────┐ │
│ │                                                         │ │
│ │         Add Objects To Scene From .SCN Disk File        │ │
│ │                                                         │ │
│ └─────────────────────────────────────────────────────────┘ │
└─────────────────────────────────────────────────────────────┘
```

```
    AddObjectsToScene - add objects to database from .SCN disk file
*/
    typedef char Strg[6];
    Boolean Bool(Strg B)
    {
        if((B[0]=='F') || (B[0]=='f'))
                return(false);
        else
                return(true);
    }
    FILE *In_File;
    float Mix, Darken;
    Byte Last_Object_Num;
    void AddObjectsToScene()
    {
        int i1, i2, i3, i4;
        float f1, f2, f3;
        Name ObjectFileName;
        Byte ObjN;
        char blank[81];
        Strg B;
        fgets(blank, 80, In_File);
    fscanf(In_File, "%s %d %d %d %d", B, &i1, &i2, &i3, &i4);
    Init_Perspective(Bool(B), (float)i1, (float)i2, (float)i3,
    (float)i4); fscanf(In_File, "%d %d", &i1, &i2);
        Init_Plotting(i1, i2);
        GetViewVector();
```

```
    fscanf(In_File, "%d %d", &i1, &i2);
    InitLightDirection(i1, i2);
    GetLightVector();
    fscanf(In_File, "%s", B);
    VertSort(Bool(B));
    fscanf(In_File, "%s", B);
    if(Bool(B))
            AddEdgeReflectors();
    fscanf(In_File, "%s", B);
    if(Bool(B))
            AddEdgeReflectorsAtZero();
    fscanf(In_File, "%f", &f1);
    Mix=f1;
    fscanf(In_File, "%f", &f1);
    Darken=f1;
    fgets(blank, 80, In_File);
    fscanf(In_File, "%d", &i1);
    Last_Object_Num=i1;
for(ObjN=0; ObjN<Last_Object_Num; ObjN++)
    {
fgets(blank, 80, In_File); fgets(blank, 80, In_File);
strset(ObjectFileName, 0); fscanf(In_File, "%s",
ObjectFileName); AddObject(ObjectFileName);
fscanf(In_File, "%f %f %f", &f1, &f2, &f3); ObjAmbColor(f1, f2, f3);
fscanf(In_File, "%f %f %f", &f1, &f2, &f3); ObjDifColor(f1, f2, f3);
fscanf(In_File, "%f %f %f", &f1, &f2, &f3); ObjSpcColor(f1, f2, f3);
            fscanf(In_File, "%d", &i1);
            ObjGloss(i1);
fscanf(In_File, "%f %f %f", &f1, &f2, &f3); Scale(f1, f2, f3);
fscanf(In_File, "%f %f %f", &f1, &f2, &f3); Rotate(f1, f2, f3);
fscanf(In_File, "%f %f %f", &f1, &f2, &f3); Translate(f1, f2, f3);
fscanf(In_File, "%s", B); ReflectObject(Bool(B));
fscanf(In_File, "%s", B); AllowSort(Bool(B));
fscanf(In_File, "%s", B); Mirrored(Bool(B));
    }
}
```

```
/*
┌──────────────────────────────────────────────────────────┐
│ ┌──────────────────────────────────────────────────────┐ │
│ │                                                      │ │
│ │               Polygonal Facet Fill Routine           │ │
│ │                                                      │ │
│ └──────────────────────────────────────────────────────┘ │
└──────────────────────────────────────────────────────────┘

        GetProjectedCoords - 3D point mapped onto 2D screen
        PutFacet           - fills a facet
*/
void GetProjectedCoords(VoxelArray Face3d, PixelArray Face2d)
{
    float xt, yt, zt;
for(VertexNumInFacet=1; VertexNumInFacet<=LastVertexNumInFacet;
VertexNumInFacet++)
    {
            UnVec(Face3d[VertexNumInFacet], &xt, &yt, &zt);
            if(Reflect)
            {
                if(MirrorZ)
                {
                    zt=-zt;
                    if(EdgeReflector && (!(EdgeReflectorAtZero)))
                        zt-=100.0;
                }
                else
                {
                    if(MirrorY)
                    {
                        yt=-yt;
                        yt-=100.0;  /* Normally would have Edge
                                        Reflector Checking       */
                    }               /* but with these models, we
                                        make our own Reflectors */
                    else
                    {
                        if(MirrorX)
                        {
                            xt=-xt;
```

```
                            xt-=100.0;
                        }
                    }
                }
            }
        Map_Coordinates(xt, yt, zt,
&Face2d[VertexNumInFacet].x, &Face2d[VertexNumInFacet].y); }
    Face2d[LastVertexNumInFacet+1]=Face2d[1];
}
Boolean Mirroring;
void PutFacet(PixelArray Face2d)
{
    int xc, yc;
    int i, x;
    int OldVertNum;
    int VertNum;
    int mnx, mxx;
    int mny, mxy;
    float slope;
    TDIA Intens;
    mny=Face2d[1].y;
    mxy=Face2d[1].y;
    for(i=2; i<=LastVertexNumInFacet; i++)
    {
        if(Face2d[i].y>mxy)
            mxy=Face2d[i].y;
        if(Face2d[i].y<mny)
            mny=Face2d[i].y;
    }
    if(mny<0)
        mny=0;
    if(mxy>=YRes)
        mxy=YRes-1;
    for(yc=mny; yc<=mxy; yc++)
    {
        mnx=XRes+1;
        mxx=-1;
        OldVertNum=LastVertexNumInFacet;
for(VertNum=1; VertNum<=LastVertexNumInFacet; VertNum++)
        {
```

```
if((Face2d[OldVertNum].y>=yc) || (Face2d[VertNum].y>=yc))
            {
if((Face2d[OldVertNum].y<=yc) || (Face2d[VertNum].y<=yc)) {
if(Face2d[OldVertNum].y != Face2d[VertNum].y)
{    slope=(float)(Face2d[VertNum].x-Face2d[OldVertNum].x)/
(float)(Face2d[VertNum].y-Face2d[OldVertNum].y);
x=Round(slope*(float)((yc-Face2d[OldVertNum].y))+
Face2d[OldVertNum].x);
                        if(x<mnx)
                            mnx=x;
                        if(x>mxx)
                            mxx=x;
                    }
                }
            }
            OldVertNum=VertNum;
        }
        if(mnx<0)
            mnx=0;
        if(mxx>=XRes)
            mxx=XRes-1;
        if(mnx<=mxx)
        {
            for(xc=mnx; xc<=mxx; xc++)
            {
                if(Mirroring)
                {
                    MakeReflected(xc, yc);
                    VecCopyInt(Intensity, Intens);
                    Put_Grey_Pixel(xc, yc, Intens);
                }
                else
                {
                    if(!(Reflect))
                    {
                        VecCopyInt(Intensity, Intens);
                        Put_Grey_Pixel(xc, yc, Intens);
                    }
                    else
                    {
```

```
                                        if(Reflected(xc, yc))
                                        {
Intens[0]=(int)((Intensity[0]*Mix+Red_Plane[xcyc]*(1.0-
Mix))*Darken);
Intens[1]=(int)((Intensity[1]*Mix+Green_Plane[xcyc]*(1.0-
Mix))*Darken);
Intens[2]=(int)((Intensity[2]*Mix+Blue_Plane[xcyc]*(1.0-
Mix))*Darken); Put_Grey_Pixel(xc, yc, Intens);
                                        }
                                    }
                                }
                            }
                        }
                    }
                }
/*
```

```
+------------------------------------------------------------+
|                                                            |
|  +------------------------------------------------------+  |
|  |                                                      |  |
|  |           Routines for Sorting Objects for           |  |
|  |           Order of Placement on the Screen           |  |
|  |                                                      |  |
|  +------------------------------------------------------+  |
|                                                            |
+------------------------------------------------------------+
```

```
    PrepareSort                 - setup for sorting routines
    SortObjectsBackToFront      - sort for actual objects
    SortTopToBottom             - sort for reflections in Z
    SortBottomToTop             - sort for actual objects
    SortObjectsFrontToBackInY   - sort for reflections in Y
    SortObjectsFrontToBackInX   - sort for reflections in X
*/
    int First;
    int Last;
    int FirstObject;
    Boolean Sorting;
    Boolean ReflSurface;
    int NumMirrors;
    void PrepareSort()
    {
        ReflSurface=false;
        Last=LastObject;
```

```
    if(LastObject==1)
    {
            First=Last;
            FirstObject=LastObject;
    }
    else
    {
            First=1;
            while((ObjList[First].Sortable==false) &&
(First<Last))
                    ++First;
            FirstObject=1;
while((ObjList[FirstObject].Mirror==true) &&
(FirstObject<LastObject)) {
                    ++FirstObject;
                    ReflSurface=true;
            }
    }
    NumMirrors=FirstObject-1;
    if(First==Last)
        Sorting=false;
    else
        Sorting=true;
}
int Index;
void SwapStrings(Name A, Name B)
{
    Name T;
    strcpy(T, A);
    strcpy(A, B);
    strcpy(B, T);
}
void SwapRealNum(float *A, float *B)
{
    float T;
    T=*A;
    *A=*B;
    *B=T;
}
void SwapTDANums(TDA A, TDA B)
```

```
{
    TDA T;
    VecCopy(A, T);
    VecCopy(B, A);
    VecCopy(T, B);
}
void SwapByteNum(Byte *A, Byte *B)
{
    Byte T;
    T=*A;
    *A=*B;
    *B=T;
}
void SwapBoolean(Boolean *A, Boolean *B)
{
    Boolean T;
    T=*A;
    *A=*B;
    *B=T;
}
void SwapData()
{
SwapStrings(ObjList[Index].ObjectName,
ObjList[Index+1].ObjectName);
SwapTDANums(ObjList[Index].Translate,
ObjList[Index+1].Translate);
SwapTDANums(ObjList[Index].Rotate, ObjList[Index+1].Rotate);
SwapTDANums(ObjList[Index].Scale, ObjList[Index+1].Scale);
SwapBoolean(&ObjList[Index].Reflection,
&ObjList[Index+1].Reflection);
SwapTDANums(ObjList[Index].AmbColor,
ObjList[Index+1].AmbColor);
SwapTDANums(ObjList[Index].DifColor,
ObjList[Index+1].DifColor);
SwapTDANums(ObjList[Index].SpcColor,
ObjList[Index+1].SpcColor); SwapByteNum(&ObjList[Index].Gloss,
&ObjList[Index+1].Gloss); SwapBoolean(&ObjList[Index].Sortable,
&ObjList[Index+1].Sortable);
SwapBoolean(&ObjList[Index].Mirror, &ObjList[Index+1].Mirror);
}
```

```
int i;
void CheckForSwap(float v, float a, float b)
{
    if(v>=0.0)
    {
        if(a<b)
            SwapData();
    }
    else
    {
        if(a>b)
            SwapData();
    }
}
void OrderX()
{
    for(i=First; i<Last; i++)
    {
for(Index=First; Index<Last; Index++) CheckForSwap(View[0],
ObjList[Index].Translate[0],
ObjList[Index+1].Translate[0]);
    }
}
void OrderY()
{
    for(i=First; i<Last; i++)
    {
for(Index=First; Index<Last; Index++) CheckForSwap(View[1],
ObjList[Index].Translate[1],
ObjList[Index+1].Translate[1]);
    }
}
void OrderZ()
{
    for(i=First; i<Last; i++)
    {
for(Index=First; Index<Last; Index++) CheckForSwap(View[2],
ObjList[Index].Translate[2],
ObjList[Index+1].Translate[2]);
    }
```

```
}
void SortObjectsBackToFront()
{
    float x, y, z;
    x=fabs(View[0]);
    y=fabs(View[1]);
    z=fabs(View[2]);
    if((x>y) && (x>z))
        OrderX();
    else
    {
        if((y>x) && (y>z))
            OrderY();
        else
            OrderZ();
    }
}
void SwapDown(float a, float b)
{
    if(a>b)
        SwapData();
}
void SortTopToBottom()
{
    for(i=First; i<Last; i++)
    {
for(Index=First; Index<Last; Index++)
SwapDown(ObjList[Index].Translate[2],
ObjList[Index+1].Translate[2]);
    }
}
void SwapUp(float a, float b)
{
    if(a<b)
        SwapData();
}
void SortBottomToTop()
{
    for(i=First; i<Last; i++)
    {
```

```
    for(Index=First; Index<Last; Index++)
SwapUp(ObjList[Index].Translate[2],
ObjList[Index+1].Translate[2]);
        }
    }
    void CheckForSwap2(float v, float a, float b)
    {
        if(v>=0.0)
        {
            if(a>b)
                SwapData();
        }
        else
        {
            if(a<b)
                SwapData();
        }
    }
    void Order_Y()
    {
        for(i=First; i<Last; i++)
        {
            for(Index=First; Index<Last; Index++)
CheckForSwap2(View[1], ObjList[Index].Translate[1],
            ObjList[Index+1].Translate[1]); }
    }
    void SortObjectsFrontToBackInY()
    {
        Order_Y();
    }
    void Order_X()
    {
        for(i=First; i<Last; i++)
        {
for(Index=First; Index<Last; Index++) CheckForSwap2(View[0],
ObjList[Index].Translate[0],
ObjList[Index+1].Translate[0]);
        }
    }
    void SortObjectsFrontToBackInX()
```

```
    {
        Order_X();
    }
/*
```

```
                    Place an Object on to the Screen
```

```
PlaceObjectOnScreen - place an object on to the screen in
Vertex Format, Wire Frame Format or Solid Model Format
*/
    Boolean XReflectedObject;
    Boolean YReflectedObject;
    Boolean ZReflectedObject;
    void PlaceFacet(Boolean MirX, Boolean MirY, Boolean MirZ)
    {
        VoxelArray Face3d;
        PixelArray Face2d;
        MirrorX=MirX;
        MirrorY=MirY;
        MirrorZ=MirZ;
    for(VertexNumInFacet=1; VertexNumInFacet<=LastVertexNumInFacet;
    VertexNumInFacet++)
        {
                VertexNum=Facet[(FacetNum*5)+VertexNumInFacet];
    VecScalMultI(InvScaleImage, Vertex[VertexNum],
    Face3d[VertexNumInFacet]);
                Face2d[VertexNumInFacet].x = 0.0;
                Face2d[VertexNumInFacet].y = 0.0;
        }
        if(Visible(Face3d))
        {
                IntensityCalc();
                if((Intensity[0]>0) || (Intensity[1]>0) || (Inten-
    sity[2]>0))
                {
                    GetProjectedCoords(Face3d, Face2d);
                    PutFacet(Face2d);
```

```
                     }
          }
}
void PlaceObjectOnScreen()
{
     for(FacetNum=1; FacetNum<=LastFacet; FacetNum++)
     {
if(((!(Reflect)) && (!(ZReflectedObject)) &&
(!(YReflectedObject)) && (!(XReflectedObject)))
PlaceFacet(false, false, false);
          else
          {
               if(ZReflectedObject)
                    PlaceFacet(false, false, true);
               else
               {
                    if(YReflectedObject)
                         PlaceFacet(false, true, false);
                    else
                    {
                         if(XReflectedObject)
                              PlaceFacet(true, false, false);
                    }
               }
          }
     }
}
Name LastObjectName;
Boolean ReflectedObjects;
void DisplayReflectiveSurfaces()
{
     strset(LastObjectName, 0);
     ReflectedObjects=false;
     Reflect=false;
     for(ObjectNum=1; ObjectNum<FirstObject; ObjectNum++)
     {
if(strcmp(ObjList[ObjectNum].ObjectName, LastObjectName)!=0) {
InitVertexBuffer(); LoadData(ObjList[ObjectNum].ObjectName);
          }
          if(ObjList[ObjectNum].Mirror)
```

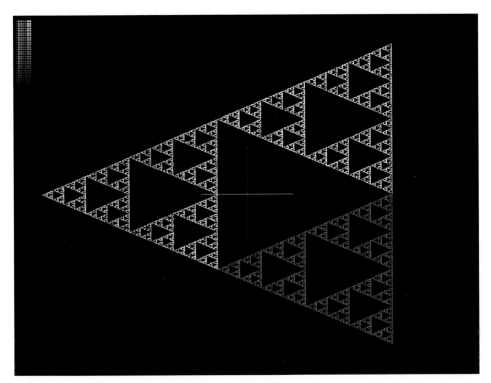

Plate 1. Three-dimensional IFS Sierpinski Triangle

Plate 2. Three-dimensional IFS Sierpinski Tetrahedron

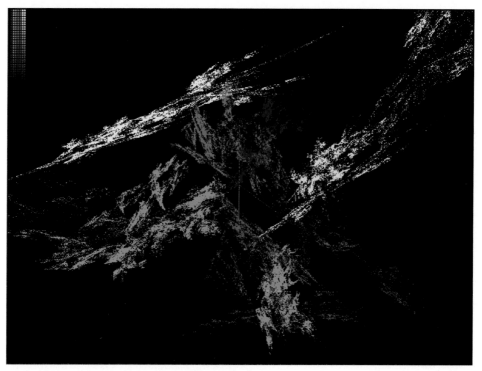

Plate 3. An Abstract Three-dimensional IFS

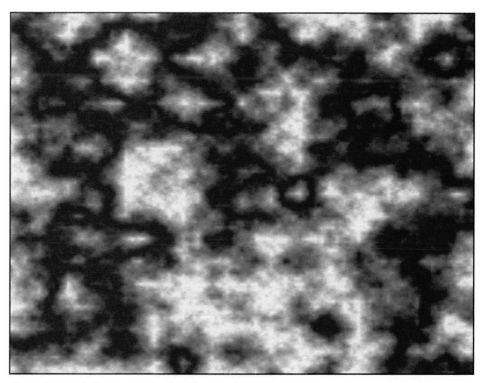

Plate 4. Cloud Generated by the Plasma Generator

Plate 23. Ray-traced Image of Cannon and Stack of Cannon Balls

Plate 24. Ray-traced Night Desert Scene

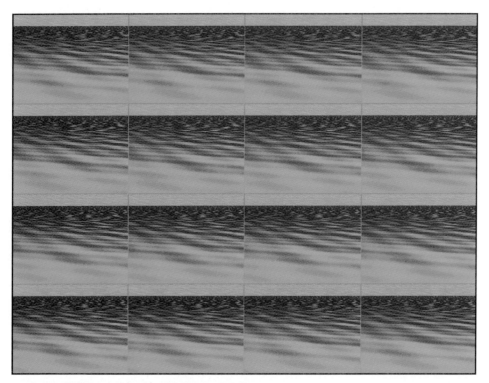

Plate 21. Ray-traced Ocean Waves in the Breeze

Plate 22. Ray-traced Dice and Ace of Spades

Plate 19. Animation of a Ray-traced Walking Robot

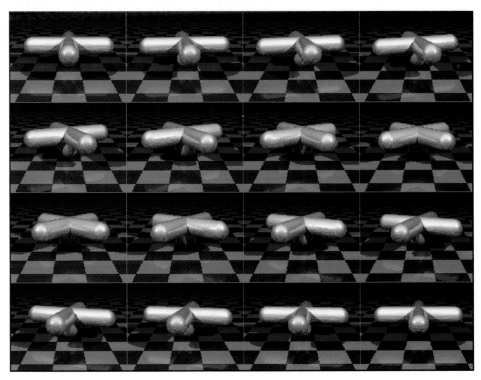

Plate 20. Spinning Ray-traced Mechanical Part

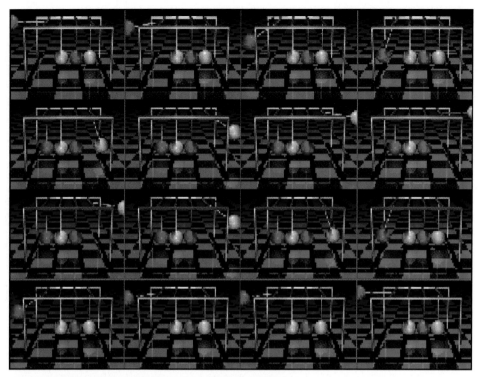

Plate 17. Ray-traced Animation of Newton's Cradle

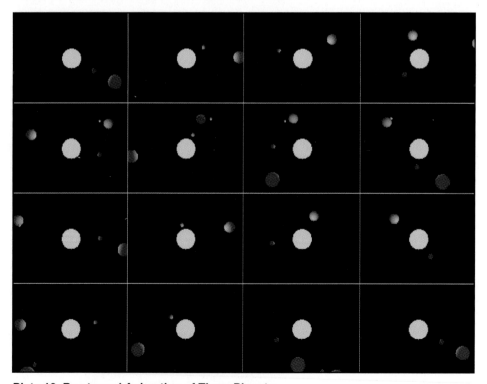

Plate 18. Ray-traced Animation of Three Planets

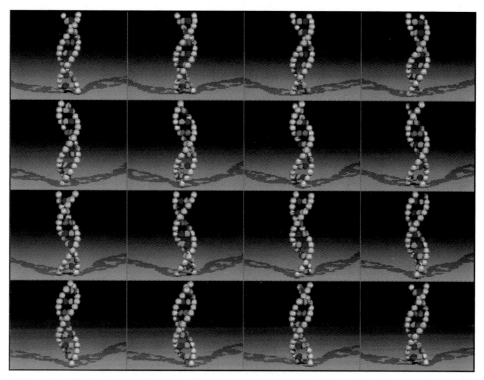

Plate 15. Spinning a Section of a Ray-traced DNA Molecule

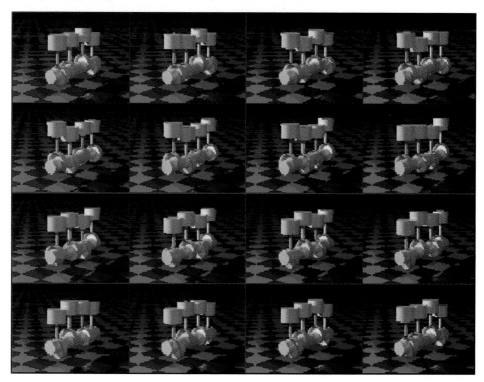

Plate 16. Ray-traced Animation of the Cylinders of an Engine

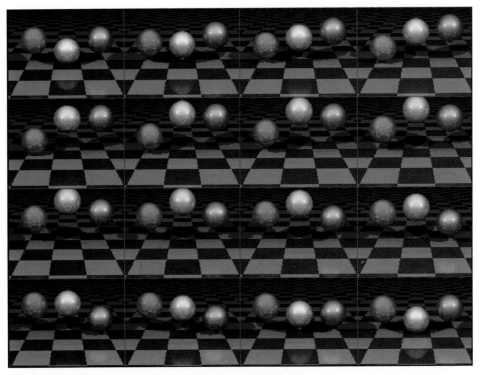

Plate 13. Three Bouncing Ray-traced Opaque Spheres

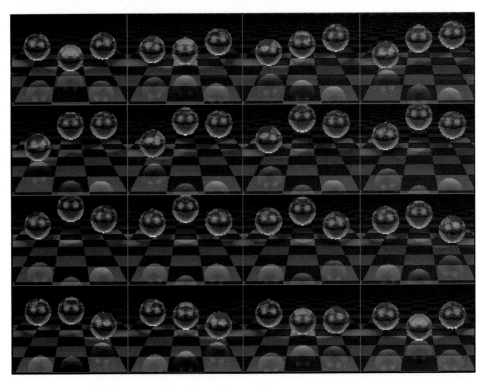

Plate 14. Three Bouncing Ray-traced Glass Spheres

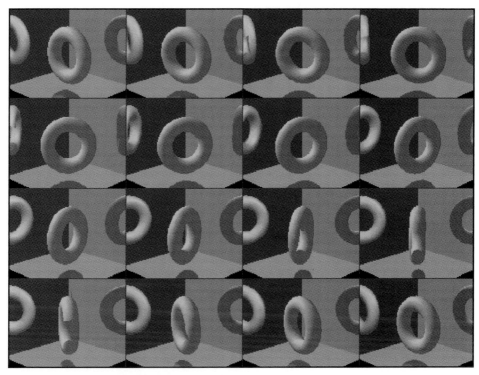

Plate 11. 3-D Modeled Spinning Toroid

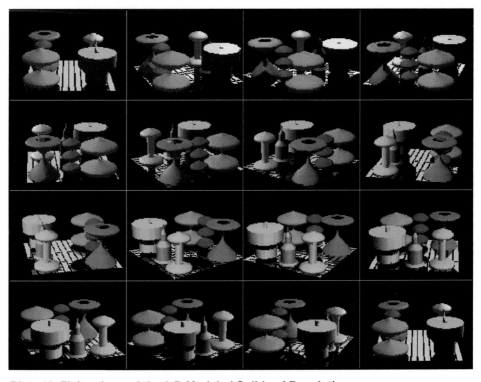

Plate 12. Flying Around the 3-D Modeled Solids of Revolution

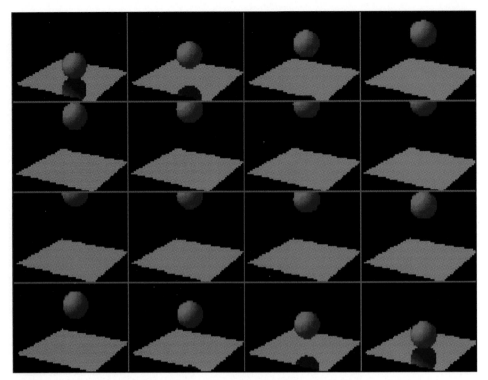

Plate 9. 3-D Modeled Sphere Bouncing on a Reflective Plane

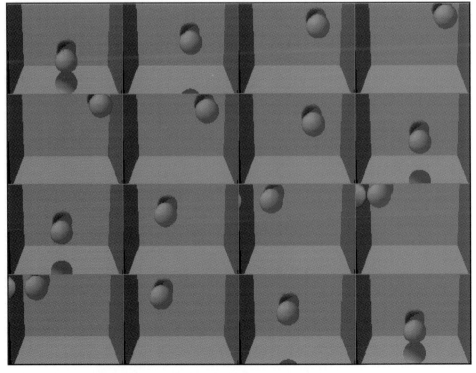

Plate 10. 3-D Modeled Sphere Bouncing off Reflective Walls

Plate 7. A Sierpinski Image Generated Through Cellular Automata

Plate 8. Image of a City Generated Through Cellular Automata

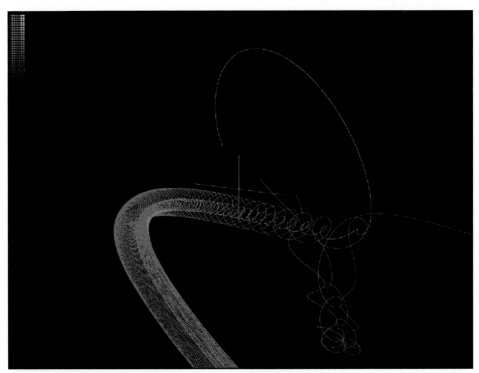

Plate 5. Three-dimensional Three-particle Orbit Trails

Plate 6. Flowering Plant Generated with the Recursive Plant Generator

Plate 25. Ray-traced M&T Logo

Plate 26. Ray-traced Rock-like Structures in Ocean Waves

Plate 27. Ray-traced Office Scene with a Desk

Plate 28. Ray-traced Scene of a Piano and a Mirror

Plate 29. Ray-traced Pool Table with Cue and Pool Balls

Plate 30. Ray-traced Recursive Tetrahedron of Tetradedrons

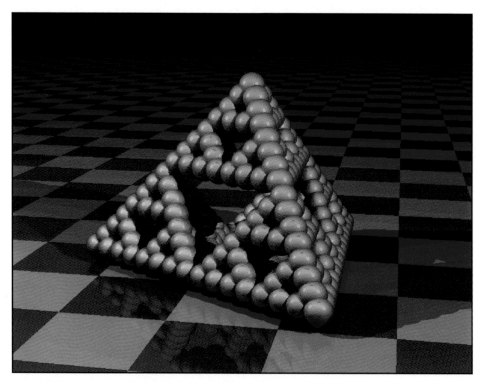

Plate 31. Ray-traced Recursive Tetrahedron of Spheres

Plate 32. Ray-traced Textured and Glass Orbs above the Ocean

```
                {
                        ReflectedObjects=true;
Mirroring=true;
AffineTransformation(ObjList[ObjectNum].Translate,
ObjList[ObjectNum].Scale, ObjList[ObjectNum].Rotate);
PlaceObjectOnScreen();
InvAffineTransformation(ObjList[ObjectNum].Translate,
ObjList[ObjectNum].Scale, ObjList[ObjectNum].Rotate);
                }
                else
                        Mirroring=false;
strcpy(LastObjectName, ObjList[ObjectNum].ObjectName);
        }
}
void DisplayReflections()
{
for(ObjectNum=FirstObject; ObjectNum<=LastObject; ObjectNum++)
        {
if(strcmp(ObjList[ObjectNum].ObjectName, LastObjectName)!=0) {
InitVertexBuffer(); LoadData(ObjList[ObjectNum].ObjectName);
                }
                if(ObjList[ObjectNum].Reflection)
                {
                        Reflect=true;
Mirroring=ObjList[ObjectNum].Mirror;
AffineTransformation(ObjList[ObjectNum].Translate,
ObjList[ObjectNum].Scale, ObjList[ObjectNum].Rotate);
PlaceObjectOnScreen();
InvAffineTransformation(ObjList[ObjectNum].Translate,
ObjList[ObjectNum].Scale, ObjList[ObjectNum].Rotate);
                }
                else
                        Reflect=false;
strcpy(LastObjectName, ObjList[ObjectNum].ObjectName);
        }
}
void DisplayActualImages()
{
for(ObjectNum=FirstObject; ObjectNum<=LastObject; ObjectNum++)
        {
```

```
if(strcmp(ObjList[ObjectNum].ObjectName, LastObjectName)!=0) {
InitVertexBuffer(); LoadData(ObjList[ObjectNum].ObjectName);
        }
        if(!((ObjectNum==1) && ObjList[ObjectNum].Mirror))
        {
            Reflect=false;
Mirroring=ObjList[ObjectNum].Mirror;
AffineTransformation(ObjList[ObjectNum].Translate,
ObjList[ObjectNum].Scale, ObjList[ObjectNum].Rotate);
PlaceObjectOnScreen();
InvAffineTransformation(ObjList[ObjectNum].Translate,
ObjList[ObjectNum].Scale, ObjList[ObjectNum].Rotate);
        }
strcpy(LastObjectName, ObjList[ObjectNum].ObjectName);
    }
}
void DefineReflection(Boolean XRef, Boolean YRef, Boolean ZRef)
{
    XReflectedObject=XRef;
    YReflectedObject=YRef;
    ZReflectedObject=ZRef;
}
void DisplayObjectsInScene()
{
    PrepareSort();
    DefineReflection(false, false, false);
    if(Sorting)
        SortObjectsBackToFront();
    DisplayReflectiveSurfaces();
    if(ReflSurface)
    {
        DefineReflection(false, false, true);
if(Sorting && VerticalSort) SortTopToBottom();
if(ReflectedObjects) DisplayReflections();
        if(NumMirrors>1)
        {
DefineReflection(false, true, false); if(Sorting)
SortObjectsFrontToBackInY();
if(Sorting && VerticalSort) SortBottomToTop();
if(ReflectedObjects) DisplayReflections();
DefineReflection(true, false, false); if(Sorting)
```

```
SortObjectsFrontToBackInX();
if(Sorting && VerticalSort) SortBottomToTop();
if(ReflectedObjects) DisplayReflections();
        }
    }

DefineReflection(false, false, false);
if(Sorting) SortObjectsBackToFront();
if(Sorting && VerticalSort)
SortBottomToTop();
DisplayActualImages();
}
Name SceneFile;
Name Temp_File;
Name Pic_File;
FILE *Out_File;
void Get_Scene_File_Name()
{
    Byte x, y;
textcolor(YELLOW); textbackground(BLUE);
    gotoxy(1, 8);
cprintf("Enter File Name -> "); x=wherex();
    y=wherey();
textcolor(WHITE+BLINK); cprintf("%s", "SPHRPLAN");
textcolor(YELLOW);
    gotoxy(x, y);
    while(!(kbhit()));
    cprintf("              ");
    gotoxy(x, y);
gets(SceneFile); if(!(strcmp(SceneFile, "")))
strcpy(SceneFile, "SPHRPLAN");
    strupr(SceneFile);
strcpy(Pic_File, SceneFile); strcpy(Temp_File, SceneFile);
strcat(SceneFile, ".SCN"); strcat(Temp_File, ".TMP");
strcat(Pic_File, ".ANI");
}
void WriteTmpFile()
{
    Byte x, y;
    Word LineBuf[160];
    Word col, r, g, b;
    for(y=0; y<100; y++)
```

```
     {
          for(x=0; x<160; x++)
          {
r=Red_Plane[xy]&62; g=Green_Plane[xy]&62; b=Blue_Plane[xy]&62;
col=((r>>1)|(g<<4)|(b<<9)); LineBuf[x]=col;
          }
     fwrite(LineBuf, sizeof(LineBuf), 1, Out_File); }
}
Byte Last_Frame_Num, Frame_Num;
Palette_Register PalArray;
void Clear_Screen()
{
     Set_Graphics_Mode(160, 100);
     Init_Palette(PalArray);
     Set_Palette(PalArray);
}
#include "process.h"
```

/*

```
┌──────────────────────────────────────────────────────────────┐
│  ┌────────────────────────────────────────────────────────┐   │
│  │                                                         │   │
│  │                     Main Program                        │   │
│  │                                                         │   │
│  └────────────────────────────────────────────────────────┘   │
└──────────────────────────────────────────────────────────────┘
```

*/

```
void main()
{
     char com[81];
     Allocate_Memory();
     Title();
     printf("Three Dimensional Modeling Program\n\n");
     printf("Program by Christopher D. Watkins\n\n");
     printf("'C' Conversion by Larry Sharp\n\n");Clear_Planes();
     InitObjectBuffer();
     InitReflectionBuffer();
     InitVertexBuffer();
     Get_Scene_File_Name();
     Clear_Screen();
if((In_File=fopen(SceneFile, "rt"))==NULL)
     {
          ungetch(32);
```

```
                  Exit_Graphics();
printf("Can't open Input File -> %s!\nHit any key to
exit....\n", SceneFile); getch();
                  exit(1);
      }
      if((Out_File=fopen(Temp_File, "wb"))==NULL)
      {
                  ungetch(32);
                  Exit_Graphics();
printf("Can't open Output File -> %s!\nHit any key to
exit....\n", Out_File); getch();
                  exit(1);
      }
      fgets(com, 80, In_File);
      fgets(com, 80, In_File);
fscanf(In_File, "%d", &Last_Frame_Num); putc(Last_Frame_Num,
Out_File);
for(Frame_Num=0; Frame_Num<Last_Frame_Num; Frame_Num++)
      {
                  AddObjectsToScene();
                  DisplayObjectsInScene();
                  WriteTmpFile();
                  Clear_Planes();
                  InitReflectionBuffer();
                  InitObjectBuffer();
                  Clear_Screen();
      }
      fclose(Out_File);
      fclose(In_File);
      Process_File();
      remove(Temp_File);
      Exit_Graphics();
      Free_Memory();
```

Listing 8-1. Listing of the *3DModel.C* Program.

At this point, *Process_File* is called to handle the color processing of each image in the *.TMP* file, and store the final displayable screen images in the *.ANI* file. Finally, we call *Exit_Graphics* to return to text mode, then finish up by clearing out our memory. We now have an animation file suitable for use by the animation program.

Usage of the software may seem a bit tricky, for there are many files that must be generated to produce a rendering. Refer to Figure 8-1 as well as Appendix B for further information on working with the files. In the next chapter we'll look at ways to simplify object creation using object database generators. Later, in Chapter 10, we'll put it all together and create some animation sequences with the objects.

Objects for a Scene	*.C Data File Generators ⟶	.DAT files
The Scene	SCRSCR.C Script File Generator ⟶	.SCN file that reference .DAT object files
	3DMODEL.C Modeling Program ⟶	.ANI animation file output .SCN/.DAT input

Figure 8-1. Data flow for *3DModel.C.*

CHAPTER 9

Creating Object Databases

The preceding chapters covered the procedures for adding objects to a scene, sorting them for display, and rendering them to create a finished display. In this chapter, we'll take a look at some programs that simplify the process of creating objects. In addition, a program called *MakeObjc.C* is provided that lets you interactively create your own faceted models by entering facet data directly. Before we examine these object database generators, however, let's look at some of the functions they use. These functions are contained in the *ShpMk.H* header file.

Adding Vertices

As discussed earlier, objects are assembled from planar facets defined by a set of three-dimensional vertices. The various utility programs described in this chapter create a *Facet* array to store the facet description of whatever object they create. The unique facet vertices are stored in a separate *Vertex* array, whereas the *Facet* array stores indices into the *Vertex* array. By storing only the unique vertices of an object, we can significantly reduce both the amount of memory needed to store the object internally and the size of the data file. For example, a model of a cube has only eight unique vertices. By storing just these eight vertices rather than storing each vertex separately for each cube face, we reduce the amount of storage needed by nearly a factor of three.

The object creation programs use the function *AddVertex* to simplify the process of identifying the unique vertices. As the program creates facets, *AddVertex* is called to add the vertex to the *Vertex* array. *AddVertex* starts by checking the *x*, *y*, and *z* components of the vertex to make sure each is between -1.0 and 1.0. If any are out of range, an error flag is set; the program will later notify you of the error and exit. Otherwise, the data is scaled using the variable *ScaleData*, which gives us the integer version of the coordinate ranging from -32,768 to 32,767.

Next, we call *CheckForRepeatingVertices* to compare the vertex against the previously entered vertices for this object to see if it matches one of them. If the vertex is a duplicate, its number is entered in the *Facet* array. Otherwise, the vertex is vectorized, the total vertex count is incremented by 1, and this number is placed in the *Facet* array.

AddVertex also provides a simple line-drawing display of an object while it's being created. As each vertex is processed, *Cartesian_Plot_3D* is called to plot a point in three-dimensional space representing the current vertex. Once all the vertices have been defined, we'll see an outline of the object on the screen.

Initializing the Vertex Database Maker

Before calling *AddVertex* for a new object, we must initialize the vertex processing with a call to *InitVertexMaker*. This function calls other functions to set up our screen and internal buffers:

Init_Graphics sets up our 320-by-200 screen with 256 colors. The image will fall within a 160 by 100 block in the center of the screen.

Init_Plotting and *Init_Perspective* initialize the three-dimensional plotting functions.

Put_Axis_And_Palette tells the program to display the 256-color palette and a three-dimensional axis.

Axis_And_Palette is called to place the axis and palette on the screen.

InitVertexBuffer initializes the *Vertex* buffer.

ReduceRepeatedVertices sets the *RepeatedVertexCheck* flag to true. This forces *AddVertex* to check for repeated vertices.

These are the primary support functions for the object database generators. Now let's look at the object database generators and see how various types of objects are created.

Creating Objects with *MakeObjs.C*

The *MakeObjs.C* program (Listing 9-1) is used to define and create simple objects like planes and cubes; other utility programs are provided later in the chapter for creating more complex objects, such as spheres and cones. The program is also limited to the entry of four-sided facets.

MakeObjs.C lets you type in the coordinates of any number of facets. It's a good idea to map out your facets beforehand so you can simply type them in. As you practice making objects, you'll find this process easier if you map them out first. And because manually entering coordinates for a large number of facets can become quite tedious, you'll also probably want to adapt some of the later programs when creating more complex objects. *MakeObjs.C* is provided to let you experiment right away with some simple models before moving on to more complex shapes.

The program begins by allocating memory to hold the object we're about to create. (This object resides in the *Facet* array described earlier.) Next, we call *Title* to create our opening screen and set the text colors. You're then asked for a file name for the object. If you simply press the return key, the program uses the default name *NewObj.DAT*. Otherwise, you can choose your own file name (always enter the name with a *.DAT* extension). You're then asked for the number of facets in the object, and *InitVertexMaker* is called to set up and initialize the screen and buffers.

Next, we call *SetUpObject* to initialize the object variables.

VertexNum and *VertexNumInFacet* are set to 1.

LastFacet is set equal to *NumOfFacets*, the number of facets in the object.

LastVertexNumInFacet is set to 4 because each facet has four vertices.

LastVertex is set equal to *LastFacet* multiplied by *LastVertexNumInFacet*, or *LastFacet* multiplied by 4.

Now we call *MakeObjectDatabase* to start data entry for our object. At this point, we begin a set of nested loops, the first ranging from 1 to *LastFacet* and the second ranging from 1 to *LastVertexNumInFacet*. On each iteration you must enter the *x*, *y*, and *z* coordinates of each vertex. The program is relatively unforgiving of typing mistakes, so be careful here! If you hit Enter on a line and then discover you've made

199

a mistake, you must start the program over. (You can use the backspace key to make corrections while you're still on the line, however.) As you enter each vertex, a point is plotted on the screen to indicate the position of the vertex. After all the vertices have been entered for the facets, the object file is saved. Finally, *MakeObjs* exits graphics mode, frees up all allocated memory, and exits.

For an example of how to enter an object, see Chapter 5 (where we discussed entering the data to make a plane). This section also describes the data that's written to the completed object file.

While this program will allow you to create an object, entering more complex objects with many facets is fairly difficult. The programs described in the following sections are more suitable for creating complex mathematical objects, which can then be combined using the scene-generation capability and affine transforms.

```
/*
```

```
                          Make Objects

                          Program by
                     Christopher D. Watkins

                         'C' conversion by
                          Larry Sharp
```

```
*/
    #include "stdio.h"
    #include "dos.h"
    #include "conio.h"
    #include "math.h"
    #include "string.h"
    #include "malloc.h"
    #include "defs.h"
    #include "globals.h"
    #include "mathb.h"
    #include "graphb.h"
    #include "modelsup.h"
```

```
#include "shpmk.h"
Name ObjF;
void GetObjF()
{
    int i;
    Byte x, y;
    printf("\nEnter File Name -> ");
    x=wherex();
    y=wherey();
    gets(ObjF);
    if(!(strcmp(ObjF, "")))
    {
            strcpy(ObjF, "NEWOBJ");
            gotoxy(x, y);
            puts(ObjF);
    }
    puts("");
    strcat(ObjF, ".DAT");
    strupr(ObjF);
}
int NumberOfFacets;
void GetNumberOfFacets()
{
    printf("\nNumber of Facets => ");
    scanf("%d", &NumberOfFacets);
}
void SetupObject(int NumOfFacets)
{
    VertexNum=1;
VertexNumInFacet=1; LastFacet=NumOfFacets;
LastVertexNumInFacet=4;
LastVertex=LastFacet*LastVertexNumInFacet;
}
void MakeObjectDataBase()
{
    int T;
    float x, y, z;
    for(FacetNum=1; FacetNum<=LastFacet; FacetNum++)
    {
            for(T=1; T<=LastVertexNumInFacet; T++)
```

```
                {
                    scanf("%f %f %f", &x, &y, &z);
                    AddVertex(x, y, z);
                }
                VertexNumInFacet=1;
        }
    }
/*
```

```
┌─────────────────────────────────────────────────────────┐
│  ┌───────────────────────────────────────────────────┐  │
│  │                                                     │  │
│  │                   Main Program                      │  │
│  │                                                     │  │
│  └───────────────────────────────────────────────────┘  │
└─────────────────────────────────────────────────────────┘
```

```
*/
    void main()
    {
    Facet=farcalloc((((MaxFacet+1)*(MaxVertexNumInFacet+1)),
    sizeof(int));
        Title();
        printf("Make Object Databases\n\n");
        GetObjF();
        GetNumberOfFacets();
        InitVertexMaker();
        SetupObject(NumberOfFacets);
        MakeObjectDataBase();
        SaveData(ObjF);
        Exit_Graphics();
        farfree(Facet);
    }
```

Listing 9-1. Listing of the *MakeObjs.C* Program.

Generating Cone and Pyramid Data Files

ConePyrm.C (Listing 9-2) creates both cone and pyramid objects. We can specify a pyramid exactly because its sides are planar facets. A cone does not have planar sides, due to its circular base, so we can only create an approximation of it. We do this by dividing the circle into several equal triangular wedges. For instance, we can break the circle into a 10-sided figure by creating wedges with an angle of 36 degrees (360/10) each. The more wedges we create, the better the approximation of the circle.

Facets for the sides of the cone are created by connecting every pair of points on the base to the apex of the cone, resulting in sets of triangular facets. We define the base of the cone by connecting sets of four wedge endpoints on the circle. We form facets by using the endpoints of opposite facing wedges. Instead of drawing them as two wedges, we can draw them as one trapezoidal facet by connecting all four points. We then proceed up both sides of the base, connecting sets of wedges, until the entire base is covered. This produces less than half as many facets as if we had used the wedges themselves.

As an example, we can create a triangular pyramid simply by setting our angular increment (wedge size) to 120 degrees, thereby dividing the cone into only three wedges. Further, we'll only have one slice at the base of the cone (the last slice is always connected to the point at the top of the cone). This will create the three sides of the pyramid, and the base will be created by "connecting the dots" of the wedges' endpoints on the bottom slice.

ConePyrm.C starts with the standard initialization call to *InitVertexMaker*. Next, the function *SetUpCone* is called with a value of 4 to create a triangular base pyramid object. The number passed to this function represents the number of facets in the object. *SetUpCone* first sets the initial vertex and facet variables for the object, then creates the variables *DTheta* and *HalfDTheta*. These represent the angular increments around the base of the cone: *DTheta* corresponds to the wedge angle, in this case 120 degrees, while *HalfDTheta* is half of this value, or 60 degrees. The constant *Theta* represents the starting angle.

MakeConeDatabase is then called to create the cone facets. It begins with a loop ranging from 1 to *LastFacet*, calling *AddVertex* on each iteration to add newly computed vertices to the vertex list. For the pyramid, the locations of these vertices are *(cos(Theta-HalfDTheta), sin(Theta-HalfDTheta), -1)*; *(cos(Theta+HalfDTheta), sin(Theta+HalfDTheta), -1)*; and (0, 0, - 1). For a cone with more wedges, the program would add *DTheta* to *Theta* and generate the next set of vertices for the next facet around this new angular position. This process would continue until *Theta* had gone all the way around the circle.

After all the facets have been calculated, we call *EndCap* to produce the facet covering the base of the cone. It uses the procedure just described to produce the set of trapezoidal facets covering the base. Again, we loop around the circle, incrementing *Theta* by *DTheta* for each new facet generated. Once the loop terminates, the pyramid database is saved to disk. We then call *SetUpCone* with a value of 180 to produce a cone, this time using a much finer value of *DTheta* to produce a more realistic circular shape. The process of generating the cone is the same as for the pyramid. Finally, we save the cone object to disk, return to text mode, and free up any allocated memory before exiting.

```
/*
```

```
                    Cone and Pyramid Database Generator


                                Program by
                          Christopher D. Watkins

                             'C' conversion by
                               Larry Sharp
```

```
*/
    #include "stdio.h"
    #include "dos.h"
    #include "conio.h"
    #include "math.h"
    #include "string.h"
    #include "malloc.h"
    #include "defs.h"
    #include "globals.h"
    #include "mathb.h"
    #include "graphb.h"
    #include "modelsup.h"
    #include "shpmk.h"
    int Theta, DTheta, HalfDTheta;
    void SetupCone(int NumOfFacets)
    {
        VertexNum=1;
        VertexNumInFacet=1;
        LastFacet=NumOfFacets;
```

```
        LastVertexNumInFacet=4;
        LastVertex=LastFacet*LastVertexNumInFacet;
        DTheta=360/LastFacet;
        HalfDTheta=DTheta/2;
        Theta=HalfDTheta;
}
int NumFacetsOnEndCap, T;
void EndCap()
{
        int tmp;
        NumFacetsOnEndCap=LastFacet/2-1;
        tmp=NumFacetsOnEndCap&1;
        if(tmp==1)
                Theta=-90+HalfDTheta;
        else
                Theta=-90+DTheta;
        if(LastFacet==4)
                NumFacetsOnEndCap=2;
        for(T=1; T<=NumFacetsOnEndCap; T++)
        {
AddVertex(CosD(Theta+HalfDTheta), SinD(Theta+HalfDTheta), -
1.0); AddVertex(CosD(Theta-HalfDTheta), SinD(Theta-HalfDTheta),
-1.0);
AddVertex(CosD(180-Theta+HalfDTheta), SinD(180-
Theta+HalfDTheta), -1.0); AddVertex(CosD(180-Theta-HalfDTheta),
SinD(180-Theta-HalfDTheta), -1.0); ++FacetNum;
                ++LastFacet;
                VertexNumInFacet=1;
                Theta+=DTheta;
        }
}


void MakeConeDatabase()
{
        for(FacetNum=1; FacetNum<=LastFacet; FacetNum++)
        {
AddVertex(CosD(Theta-HalfDTheta), SinD(Theta-HalfDTheta), -
1.0); AddVertex(CosD(Theta+HalfDTheta), SinD(Theta+HalfDTheta),
-1.0); AddVertex(0.0, 0.0, 1.0);
                AddVertex(0.0, 0.0, 1.0);
```

```
                Theta+=DTheta;
                VertexNumInFacet=1;
        }
        EndCap();
    }
```
/*
```
                                Main Program
```
*/
```
    void main()
    {
    Facet=farcalloc((((MaxFacet+1)*(MaxVertexNumInFacet+1)),
    sizeof(int));
        InitVertexMaker();
        SetupCone(4);
        MakeConeDatabase();
        SaveData("PYRAMID.DAT");
        SetupCone(180);
        MakeConeDatabase();
        SaveData("CONE.DAT");
        Exit_Graphics();
        farfree(Facet);
    }
```

Listing 9-2. Listing of the *ConePyrm.C* Program.

Generating a Cylinder Data File

The program to generate cylinders, *Cylinder.C*, is similar to *ConePyrm.C*, but now we must treat both ends of the cylinder as circles. Instead of generating triangular facets, we'll generate rectangular ones connecting the two ends of the cylinder. We move around the circle as before, incrementing *Theta* by *DTheta* for each new facet. The facet is created by connecting the points at angles *(Theta + HalfDTheta)* and *(Theta - HalfDTheta)* on the lower end ($z = -1$) with those on the upper end ($z = 1$). Note that we do this in such a way that we proceed counterclockwise around the facet; this is to ensure that the surface normal faces out from the center of the cylinder.

Another major difference is that we have a function, *EndCaps*, to generate capping facets at both ends of the cylinder. In all other respects, this program proceeds exactly like *ConePyrm.C*.

```
/*
```

```
                    Cylinder Database Generator

                          Program by
                    Christopher D. Watkins

                       'C' conversion by
                         Larry Sharp
```

```
*/
    #include "stdio.h"
    #include "dos.h"
    #include "conio.h"
    #include "math.h"
    #include "string.h"
    #include "malloc.h"
    #include "defs.h"
    #include "globals.h"
    #include "mathb.h"
    #include "graphb.h"
    #include "modelsup.h"
    #include "shpmk.h"
    int Theta, DTheta, HalfDTheta;
    void SetupCylinder(int NumOfFacets)
    {
        VertexNum=1;
        VertexNumInFacet=1;
        LastFacet=NumOfFacets;
        LastVertexNumInFacet=4;
        LastVertex=LastFacet*LastVertexNumInFacet;
```

```
        DTheta=360/LastFacet;
        HalfDTheta=DTheta/2;
        Theta=HalfDTheta;
    }
int NumFacetsOnEndCap, T;
void EndCaps()
{
        int tmp;
        NumFacetsOnEndCap=LastFacet/2-1;
        tmp=NumFacetsOnEndCap&1;
        if(tmp==1)
                Theta=-90+HalfDTheta;
        else
                Theta=-90+DTheta;
        for(T=1; T<=NumFacetsOnEndCap; T++)
        {
AddVertex(CosD(Theta-HalfDTheta), SinD(Theta-HalfDTheta), 1.0);
AddVertex(CosD(Theta+HalfDTheta), SinD(Theta+HalfDTheta), 1.0);
AddVertex(CosD(180-Theta-HalfDTheta), SinD(180-Theta-
HalfDTheta), 1.0); AddVertex(CosD(180-Theta+HalfDTheta),
SinD(180-Theta+HalfDTheta), 1.0); ++FacetNum;
                ++LastFacet;
                VertexNumInFacet=1;
AddVertex(CosD(Theta+HalfDTheta), SinD(Theta+HalfDTheta), -
1.0); AddVertex(CosD(Theta-HalfDTheta), SinD(Theta-HalfDTheta),
-1.0);
AddVertex(CosD(180-Theta+HalfDTheta), SinD(180-
Theta+HalfDTheta), -1.0); AddVertex(CosD(180-Theta-HalfDTheta),
SinD(180-Theta-HalfDTheta), -1.0); ++FacetNum;
                ++LastFacet;
                VertexNumInFacet=1;
                Theta+=DTheta;
        }
}
void MakeCylinderDatabase()
{
        for(FacetNum=1; FacetNum<=LastFacet; FacetNum++)
        {
AddVertex(CosD(Theta-HalfDTheta), SinD(Theta-HalfDTheta), -
1.0); AddVertex(CosD(Theta+HalfDTheta), SinD(Theta+HalfDTheta),
-1.0); AddVertex(CosD(Theta+HalfDTheta),
```

```
SinD(Theta+HalfDTheta), 1.0); AddVertex(CosD(Theta-HalfDTheta),
SinD(Theta-HalfDTheta), 1.0); Theta+=DTheta;
            VertexNumInFacet=1;
    }
    EndCaps();
}
/*
```

```
┌─────────────────────────────────────────────────────────────┐
│ ┌─────────────────────────────────────────────────────────┐ │
│ │                      Main Program                       │ │
│ └─────────────────────────────────────────────────────────┘ │
└─────────────────────────────────────────────────────────────┘
```

```
*/
    void main()
    {
    Facet=farcalloc(((MaxFacet+1)*(MaxVertexNumInFacet+1)),
    sizeof(int));
        InitVertexMaker();
        SetupCylinder(90);
        MakeCylinderDatabase();
        SaveData("CYLINDER.DAT");
        Exit_Graphics();
        farfree(Facet);
    }
```

Listing 9-3. Listing of the *Cylinder.C* Program.

Generating a Sphere Data File

Generating a unit sphere (having a radius of 1) is slightly more difficult, but *Sphere.C* (Listing 9-4) is still similar to *Cylinder.C*. Just as we divided the circle into wedges, we break up the sphere into angular pieces, both in the *XY* plane, using the angle *Theta*, and in pitch (the angle with respect to the *Z* axis), using the angle *Phi*. We proceed in a doubly nested loop in which the outer loop corresponds to changes in the angle *Phi* and the inner one to changes in the angle *Theta*. For given values of *Theta* and *Phi*, we compute the vertex coordinate using the following equations:

```
x = cos(Phi) * cos(Theta)
y = cos(Phi) * sin(Theta)
z = sin(Phi)
```
Equation 9-1

209

Theta and *Phi* are referred to as the *spherical coordinates* for the point *(x, y, z)*. We generate a facet by using the points at the following angles:

```
(Theta - HalfDTheta, Phi - HalfDPhi)
(Theta + HalfDTheta, Phi - HalfDPhi)
(Theta + HalfDTheta, Phi + HalfDPhi)
(Theta - HalfDTheta, Phi + HalfDPhi)
```

The program fixes the number of facets in *Theta* at 60 (three-degree increments) and in *Phi* at 45 (four-degree increments), for a total of 2,700 facets. The program processes facets in the same manner as *Cylinder.C* except that it uses this doubly nested loop to increment all values of *Theta* and *Phi*.

```
/*



            Sphere Database Generator


                  Program by
            Christopher D. Watkins


              'C' conversion by
                Larry Sharp



*/
    #include "stdio.h"
    #include "dos.h"
    #include "conio.h"
    #include "math.h"
    #include "string.h"
    #include "malloc.h"
    #include "defs.h"
    #include "globals.h"
    #include "mathb.h"
    #include "graphb.h"
    #include "modelsup.h"
    #include "shpmk.h"
```

```
int Theta, DTheta, HalfDTheta;
int Phi, DPhi, HalfDPhi;
int HorzLoop, VertLoop;
int Horz, Vert;
float SinPhi, CosPhi;
void SetupSphere(int Horizontal, int Vertical)
{
    VertexNum=1;
    VertexNumInFacet=1;
    HorzLoop=Horizontal;
    VertLoop=Vertical;
    LastFacet=HorzLoop*VertLoop;
LastVertexNumInFacet=MaxVertexNumInFacet;
LastVertex=LastFacet*LastVertexNumInFacet;
    DTheta=360/HorzLoop;
    HalfDTheta=DTheta/2;
    Theta=HalfDTheta;
    DPhi=180/VertLoop;
    HalfDPhi=DPhi/2;
    Phi=HalfDPhi;
}
void MakeSphereDatabase()
{
    Horz=1;
    Vert=1;
    for(FacetNum=1; FacetNum<=LastFacet; FacetNum++)
    {
            SinPhi=SinD(Phi+HalfDPhi);
            CosPhi=CosD(Phi+HalfDPhi);
AddVertex(SinPhi*CosD(Theta-HalfDTheta), SinPhi*SinD(Theta-
HalfDTheta), CosPhi); AddVertex(SinPhi*CosD(Theta+HalfDTheta),
SinPhi*SinD(Theta+HalfDTheta), CosPhi); SinPhi=SinD(Phi-
HalfDPhi);
            CosPhi=CosD(Phi-HalfDPhi);
AddVertex(SinPhi*CosD(Theta+HalfDTheta),
SinPhi*SinD(Theta+HalfDTheta), CosPhi);
AddVertex(SinPhi*CosD(Theta-HalfDTheta), SinPhi*SinD(Theta-
HalfDTheta), CosPhi); Theta+=DTheta;
            VertexNumInFacet=1;
            ++Horz;
```

```
                    if(Horz>HorzLoop)
                    {
                        Horz=1;
                        ++Vert;
                        Theta=HalfDTheta;
                        Phi+=DPhi;
                    }
                }
            }
        }
/*
```

```
                        Main Program
```

```
*/
    void main()
    {
    Facet=farcalloc(((MaxFacet+1)*(MaxVertexNumInFacet+1)),
    sizeof(int));
        InitVertexMaker();
        SetupSphere(60, 45);
        MakeSphereDatabase();
        SaveData("SPHERE.DAT");
        Exit_Graphics();
        farfree(Facet);
    }
```

List 9-4. Listing of the *Sphere.C* Program.

Generating a Toroid Data File

A torus is a mathematically precise donut-shaped object. A torus is made here from cylinders of radius R that form a circular path. The main axis of the cylinder now lies along a circle of radius *Rho* in the *XY* plane. As with the sphere, we define a torus using the angles *Theta* and *Phi*, with *Theta* representing the angle around the center of the donut. *Phi*, however, is now the angle with respect to the center of the cylinder that intersects a line at angle *Theta* from the center of the donut. We compute the *(x, y, z)* point on the torus for a given *Theta* and *Phi* using the following equations:

212

```
x = (Rho+R*cos(Phi))*cos(Theta)
y = (Rho+R*cos(Phi))*sin(Theta)
z = R*sin(Phi)
```
Equation 9-2

Other than using this new set of equations for a toroid, the program (Listing 9-5) proceeds exactly like *Sphere.C*—in a doubly nested loop that runs through all values of *Theta* and *Phi*, using their corresponding increments. Note that *Phi* runs from 0 to 360 degrees in this case, while for the sphere it runs from -90 to +90 degrees.

```
/*
```

```
                    Toroid Database Generator

                          Program by
                    Christopher D. Watkins

                       'C' conversion by
                         Larry Sharp
```

```
*/
    #include "stdio.h"
    #include "dos.h"
    #include "conio.h"
    #include "math.h"
    #include "string.h"
    #include "malloc.h"
    #include "defs.h"
    #include "globals.h"
    #include "mathb.h"
    #include "graphb.h"
    #include "modelsup.h"
    #include "shpmk.h"
    int Theta, DTheta, HalfDTheta;
    int Phi, DPhi, HalfDPhi;
    int HorzLoop, VertLoop;
    void SetupToroid(int Horizontal, int Vertical) {
        VertexNum=1;
```

```
      VertexNumInFacet=1;
      HorzLoop=Horizontal;
  VertLoop=Vertical; LastFacet=HorzLoop*VertLoop;
  LastVertexNumInFacet=MaxVertexNumInFacet;
  LastVertex=LastFacet*LastVertexNumInFacet; DTheta=360/HorzLoop;
  HalfDTheta=DTheta/2; Theta=HalfDTheta+45+45;
      DPhi=360/VertLoop;
      HalfDPhi=DPhi/2;
      Phi=HalfDPhi;
  }
  void MakeToroidDatabase(float Rho, float R) {
      float CosThetaMinus, SinThetaMinus;
      float CosThetaPlus, SinThetaPlus;
      float RCosPhiMinus, RSinPhiMinus;
      float RCosPhiPlus, RSinPhiPlus;
      float x, y, z;
      FacetNum=0;
      do
      {
  Phi=HalfDPhi;
  CosThetaMinus=CosD(Theta-HalfDTheta); SinThetaMinus=SinD(Theta-
  HalfDTheta); CosThetaPlus=CosD(Theta+HalfDTheta);
  SinThetaPlus=SinD(Theta+HalfDTheta); do
  {   RCosPhiMinus=R*CosD(Phi-HalfDPhi);
  RSinPhiMinus=R*SinD(Phi-HalfDPhi);
  RCosPhiPlus=R*CosD(Phi+HalfDPhi);
  RSinPhiPlus=R*SinD(Phi+HalfDPhi); ++FacetNum;
  x=(Rho+RCosPhiMinus)*CosThetaMinus;
  y=(Rho+RCosPhiMinus)*SinThetaMinus; z=RSinPhiMinus;
  AddVertex(x, y, z); x=(Rho+RCosPhiMinus)*CosThetaPlus;
  y=(Rho+RCosPhiMinus)*SinThetaPlus; z=RSinPhiMinus;
  AddVertex(x, y, z); x=(Rho+RCosPhiPlus)*CosThetaPlus;
  y=(Rho+RCosPhiPlus)*SinThetaPlus; z=RSinPhiPlus;
  AddVertex(x, y, z); x=(Rho+RCosPhiPlus)*CosThetaMinus;
  y=(Rho+RCosPhiPlus)*SinThetaMinus; z=RSinPhiPlus;
  AddVertex(x, y, z); VertexNumInFacet=1;
                  Phi+=DPhi;
              }
  while(Phi<360+HalfDPhi); Theta+=DTheta;
      }
```

```
        while(Theta<360+HalfDTheta+90);
    }
/*
```

```
    ┌─────────────────────────────────────────────────────┐
    │  ┌───────────────────────────────────────────────┐  │
    │  │                                               │  │
    │  │               Main Program                    │  │
    │  │                                               │  │
    │  └───────────────────────────────────────────────┘  │
    └─────────────────────────────────────────────────────┘
```

```
*/
    void main()
    {
    Facet=farcalloc(((MaxFacet+1)*(MaxVertexNumInFacet+1)),
    sizeof(int));
        InitVertexMaker();
        SetupToroid(60, 60);
        MakeToroidDatabase(0.75, 0.25);
        SaveData("TOROID.DAT");
        Exit_Graphics();
        farfree(Facet);
    }
```

Listing 9-5. Listing of the *Toroid.C* Program.

Generating a Solid-of-Revolution Data File

A solid of revolution is a three-dimensional object created by taking a two-dimensional curve and rotating it in a circle about a coordinate axis (in *SolOfRev.C*, it's the Z axis). For example, the cylinder is a solid of revolution generated by rotating a vertical line about the Z axis; a sphere is a solid of revolution formed by rotating the equation of a circle about the Z axis. This program provides a more general way to create a solid object from a silhouette definition. We'll rotate the function of a single variable, in this case considered to be a function of z. Thus the function will represent the radius of our solid for a given value of z.

The program proceeds in much the same way as *Cylinder.C* except that now we're creating 60 cylinders stacked on top of one another (hence, no caps are needed on the ends of the cylinders). We use a *DTheta* of three degrees (60 steps) to move around a circle whose radius depends on the current value of z, running from 0 to 1. We also increment z by *Dz* (again using 60 steps for z).

The function *RadialArray* is called to fill the function values array, *RS*, with data for the selected object. You can select an object by removing the comment marks around it and placing comment marks around the previously selected object. The default object is a chess pawn, but you're encouraged to experiment with your own solids of revolution.

After the *RS* array has been filled in, *DisplayRadialArray* is called to display a silhouette of the selected object on the screen. The program then proceeds as *Sphere.C* does, using a doubly nested loop to increment *Z* in the outer loop and run around the circle using *Theta* in the inner loop. Once all the values of *Z* have been processed, we save the object to disk and exit the program.

Generating a Grid Data File

The final object-generating program, *Grid.C*, (Listing 9-6) represents a two-dimensional grid of regularly spaced rectangular facets for the *xy* plane. This lets you paint a suitable reference grid to see the dimensions of any other objects in your scene.

The function is defined over a region extending in *X* from *Xlft* to *Xrgt* and in *Y* from *Ybot* to *Ytop*. We specify the number of steps we desire using the variables *HorzContours* and *VertContours*. The variable *offset* controls the width of each grid line. The program uses a doubly nested loop in which the outer loop runs from *Xlft* to *Xrgt* and the inner loop runs from *Ybot* to *Ytop*. The *SetUpGrid* routine computes the increment variables *Dx* and *Dy* based on the number of steps specified by *HorzContours* and *VertContours*. *HalfDx* and *HalfDy* are computed as half of *Dx* and *Dy*, respectively, multiplied by the factor:

```
1.0 / (offset + 1.0)
```

The default *offset* value of 0.5 gives a facet width of one-third the step size. You can decrease the facet width with larger values of *offset* and increase it with smaller values (down to 0.0).

We have defined several constants to produce a unit-spaced grid that's the same in both *X* and *Y*. The constant *Span* specifies the maximum absolute value of the range of *X* and *Y* that we wish to use. Therefore, *Xlft* = -*Span*, *Xrgt* = +*Span*, *Ybot* = -*Span*, and *Ytop* = +*Span*. To center the squares over the integer coordinate pairs, we specify a *Contour* value of 13 for both axes. A contour is a constant that gets passed to *VertContours* and that in effect determines the density of the grid by controlling the step values described in the last paragraph. If we wanted to space them at every half unit, we would use a value of 25.

The function *MakeGridDatabase* then proceeds through the loops, making rectangles centered at points *(Dx, Dy)* apart in the *XY* plane (*z* = 0). Each rectangle will have a width of *HalfDX*2.0* and a height of *HalfDy*2.0*.

We have now covered the tools you need to produce your own modeled scenes. To help get you started, this chapter has given you some sample scenes so you can familiarize yourself with how scene scripts are created. In the next chapter, we'll look at the sample scripts and the program you'll use to make your own scene scripts.

```
/*
```

```
                         Grid Database Generator


                              Program by
                         Christopher D. Watkins


                          'C' conversion by
                             Larry Sharp
```

```
*/
    #include "stdio.h"
    #include "dos.h"
    #include "conio.h"
    #include "math.h"
    #include "string.h"
    #include "malloc.h"
    #include "defs.h"
    #include "globals.h"
    #include "mathb.h"
    #include "graphb.h"
    #include "modelsup.h"
```

```
    #include "shpmk.h"
/*

┌─────────────────────────────────────────────────────────┐
│ ┌─────────────────────────────────────────────────────┐ │
│ │                                                     │ │
│ │                     Equations                       │ │
│ │                                                     │ │
│ └─────────────────────────────────────────────────────┘ │
└─────────────────────────────────────────────────────────┘

*/
    #define Span 5.0
    #define Contour 13
    #define Offset 0.5
    float Dx, HalfDx;
    float Dy, HalfDy;
    float x, y;
    float sx, sy;
    float ix, iy;
    float ex, ey;
    void SetupGrid(float Xlft, float Xrgt,
                float Ybot, float Ytop,
    int HorzContours, int VertContours, float offset)
    {
        VertexNum=1;
    VertexNumInFacet=1; LastFacet=HorzContours*VertContours;
    LastVertexNumInFacet=MaxVertexNumInFacet;
    LastVertex=LastFacet*LastVertexNumInFacet; sx=20.0/((Xrgt-
    Xlft)*11.0); sy=20.0/((Ytop-Ybot)*11.0); Dx=(Xrgt-Xlft)/
    (float)(HorzContours-1); Dy=(Ybot-Ytop)/(float)(VertContours-
    1); HalfDx=Dx/((offset+1.0)*2.0); HalfDy=Dy/((offset+1.0)*2.0);
        ix=Xlft;
        iy=Ytop;
        ex=Xrgt;
        ey=Ybot;
    }

    void MakeGridDatabase()
    {
        float XMinus, XPlus;
        float YMinus, YPlus;
        FacetNum=0;
```

```
        x=ix;
        do
        {
XMinus=sx*(x-HalfDx); XPlus=sx*(x+HalfDx);
            y=iy;
            do
            {
++FacetNum; YMinus=sy*(y-HalfDy); YPlus=sy*(y+HalfDy);
AddVertex(XMinus, YPlus, 0.0); AddVertex(XPlus, YPlus, 0);
AddVertex(XPlus, YMinus, 0); AddVertex(XMinus, YMinus, 0);
VertexNumInFacet=1;
                y+=Dy;
            }
            while(y>=ey);
            x+=Dx;
        }
        while(x<=ex);
    }
/*
```

```
┌─────────────────────────────────────────────────────────┐
│ ┌─────────────────────────────────────────────────────┐ │
│ │                                                     │ │
│ │                   Main Program                      │ │
│ │                                                     │ │
│ │                                                     │ │
│ └─────────────────────────────────────────────────────┘ │
└─────────────────────────────────────────────────────────┘
```

```
*/
    void main()
    {
Facet=farcalloc(((MaxFacet+1)*(MaxVertexNumInFacet+1)),
sizeof(int));
        InitVertexMaker();
SetupGrid(-Span, Span, -Span, Span, Contour, Contour, Offset);
MakeGridDatabase();
        SaveData("GRID.DAT");
        Exit_Graphics();
        farfree(Facet);
    }
```

List 9-6. Listing of the *Grid.C* Program.

CHAPTER 10

Editing Scene Files

In the previous chapters, we discussed how scenes are created for the modeling program. This process requires a *.SCN* file to describe the viewer position, environment (such factors as lighting and reflections), and object positions. These variables must be set on a frame-by-frame basis in an animated sequence.

This chapter describes the *SCNSCR.C* program, which allows interactive editing of a *.SCN* file. With this utility, you can quickly alter the scene parameters, create a new *.SCN* file, and view the results. It's often more convenient than simply editing the text file, especially when you're adding or removing frames from an animation sequence. The program is also a good example of how to read and write *.SCN* files from a C program. You may wish to extend it to produce more complex animation sequences involving multiple moving objects, moving viewpoints, moving light sources, or a combination of these.

Generating Animation Scripts

The *SCNSCR.C* program (Listing 10-2) is a menu-driven program for editing script (*.SCN*) files. The menu gives you five options:

> 1 - Create a new script
>
> 2 - Load in an existing script
>
> 3 - Edit a script
>
> 4 - Save a script to disk
>
> 5 - Exit

Option 1 starts a new script from scratch. Option 2 lets you load in an existing script for editing. Option 3, the interactive scene editor, lets you edit any object attributes, add new attributes, examine individual frames of the animation, and add or delete frames from a sequence. Option 4 lets you save your finished sequence in a new or existing .*SCN* file on disk. Finally, Option 5 exits the program. Each of the menu options is discussed in detail in the following subsections.

The program uses two basic structures to hold the frame and object descriptions: a *Frame_Record* and an *Object_Record*. (These structures correspond to those described in Chapter 6 for holding descriptions of frames and objects.) At any given time, we're editing at most one frame and one object within the current frame. The variables *Frame_Num* and *Object_Num* keep track of the current frame and object number being edited. A *Frame_List* array contains descriptions of all the frames (up to *Max_Frames*). Within each *Frame_Record*, an *Object_List* array (up to *Max_Objects*) holds descriptions of the objects in that frame.

While a frame or object is being edited, only the information in these arrays is altered. New data is written to disk only when option 4 is selected from the main menu. *SCNSCR.C* runs entirely in text mode on the screen. Once the .*SCN* file is updated, you can run the modeler to see the effect of your changes.

Let's look at the effect of each option on the .*SCN* file being created or edited.

Creating a Scene File

Choose option 1 from the main menu to start a new scene file. The program will ask for the name of the scene file you wish to create, then create empty versions of two files—a .*SCN* and an .*ORG*—using that name. *SCNSCR.C* creates the .*ORG* as a backup file before the editing process begins. It also does this when you load a file using option 2. This way, you always have a backup version of the .*SCN* file as it existed before you made any changes, much as most text editors create .*BAK* versions of your files before you modify them. If you make a mistake and want to start over, you exit *SCNSCR.C*, delete the .*SCN* file you were working on, and rename (or copy) the .*ORG* file to the .*SCN* file. After selecting option 1 and entering the name of the new file, use option 3 ("Edit a script") to enter new data.

Loading an Existing Scene File

Option 2 lets you load an existing *.SCN* file into memory for editing. It will ask you for the name of the file, then read that file into memory. If the file can be read with no errors, it is saved as both the backup *.ORG* file and the current *.SCN* file. It can then be edited using option 3.

Editing a Scene File

Option 3 is the heart of the program. Once this option is selected, you use the following keys to edit the frame descriptions :

Up/down arrow	Select objects within a frame
Left/right arrow	Select a new frame number to use
Plus key	Add a new object to the frame
Minus key	Delete the current object from the frame
A key	Add a new frame
D key	Delete current frame
Space key	Enable editing of this object
Esc key	Exit to main menu

The screen display shows the object and frame attributes described in Chapter 6. The data items are displayed on separate lines, each of which begins with a number. If you enter one of these line numbers, the cursor is positioned after the item description and the value is highlighted. You can now enter a new value. If there are multiple values (such as in the viewer or object position), separate them with commas. Once the values are entered, press Return. (The data isn't saved to disk until option 4 is entered from the main menu.) If you attempt an illegal operation, such as adding more than the maximum number of frames, the program will issue an extended beep and abort the operation. To exit the editing option altogether, simply press the Escape key.

Saving a Scene File to Disk

Option 4 lets you save the edited *.SCN* file to disk using the name you entered with option 1 or 2. If an error occurs while the data is being written, the program issues a warning beep and aborts the operation. (This typically happens when you run out of disk space.) Once the problem has been corrected, try saving the file again. (In some cases it may be necessary to save the file to a different drive.) When you're through editing, use option 5 to exit the program. The *.SCN* file you created or edited is now ready for the modeler.

The Animation Scripts

To get you started, this chapter includes the *.SCN* files that were used to generate some of the sequences and images in this book. Copy a sample *.SCN* file to one of your own, like *TEST.SCN,* and edit it using *SCNSCR.C.* Try simple changes initially, like altering the viewer position or the sun angle, then add new objects to the scene and adjust the various animation parameters. This utility lets you quickly and easily alter the environment to suit your taste and needs. Experimentation is an excellent way to familiarize yourself with how each of the parameters affects the produced scene.

Let's take a closer look at these sample files.

SPHRPLAN.SCN

SPHRPLAN.SCN produces a very basic scene of a red ball bouncing on a reflective plane. The plane, of course, reflects the ball as it bounces. Plate 9 shows 16 of the 30 frames produced by the animation program. Compare the images in Plate 9 (left to right, top to bottom) with the *.SCN* file in Listing 10-1.

SPHRWALL.SCN

SPHRWALL.SCN extends *SPHRPLAN.SCN* to include a reflective floor, two reflective walls, and one nonreflective wall. Plate 11 shows 16 of the 30 frames of the animation. In this sequence, the ball bounces between one of the reflective walls and the nonreflective wall as well as hitting the reflective floor. This animation is similar to the well-known "Boink" program, which displays a ball bouncing between two walls and a checkered floor.

SPINTOR.SCN

This animation uses two reflective walls, a reflective floor, and a bright yellow toroid. The toroid is in the middle of the floor, spinning about its center. Plate 12 shows 16 of the 30 frames of the animation. The scene's perspective is such that the toroid is reflected on the walls.

SOLOFREV.SCN

Our final sample modeling script uses various solids of revolution. In this scene, the solids are all sitting on a reflective grid. For variety, the entire scene also rotates. This is a good test for the *SCNSCR.C* program because we must now modify the viewing angle as opposed to just the positions of the objects. Examine how the various parameters—notably the rotation angles of the grid—vary from frame to frame. Try changing the rates of rotation, the colors, and the lighting. The results can be astounding.

Obviously, you can create a wide variety of images using the three-dimensional modeling tools. Try experimenting with them to create even more interesting special effects. With the proper tools, three-dimensional modeling and computer graphics can be quite fun. In the next chapter, we'll use the more advanced ray-tracing program to produce very realistic images of some very unreal things.

```
┌─────────────────────────────────────────────────────────────┐
│  ┌───────────────────────────────────────────────────────┐  │
│  │     Red Sphere sitting on a Reflective Gray Plane      │  │
│  └───────────────────────────────────────────────────────┘  │
└─────────────────────────────────────────────────────────────┘
```

```
30

TRUE 3 -18 350 500 240 18
-35 45
FALSE
FALSE
FALSE
0.8800
0.7000

2

Plane.Dat
0.2000 0.2000 0.2000
0.5000 0.5000 0.5000
0.3000 0.3000 0.3000
10
40.0000 40.0000 40.0000
-0.0000 -0.0000 -0.0000
-0.0000 -0.0000 -0.0000
FALSE
FALSE
TRUE

Sphere.Dat
0.3000 0.0000 0.0000
0.5000 0.0000 0.0000
0.2000 0.0000 0.0000
5
12.0000 12.0000 12.0000
-0.0000 -0.0000 -0.0000
-0.0000 -0.0000 12.0000
TRUE
FALSE
FALSE

TRUE 3 -18 350 500 240 18
-35 45
TRUE
FALSE
FALSE
0.8800
0.7000
```

```
2

Plane.Dat
0.2000 0.2000 0.2000
0.5000 0.5000 0.5000
0.3000 0.3000 0.3000
10
40.0000 40.0000 40.0000
-0.0000 -0.0000 -0.0000
-0.0000 -0.0000 -0.0000
FALSE
FALSE
TRUE

Sphere.Dat
0.3000 0.0000 0.0000
0.5000 0.0000 0.0000
0.2000 0.0000 0.0000
5
12.0000 12.0000 12.0000
-0.0000 -0.0000 -0.0000
-0.0000 -0.0000 22.0000
TRUE
FALSE
FALSE

TRUE 3 -18 350 500 240 18
-35 45
40.0000 40.0000 40.0000
-0.0000 -0.0000 -0.0000
-0.0000 -0.0000 -0.0000
TRUE
FALSE
FALSE
0.8800
0.7000

2

Plane.Dat
0.2000 0.2000 0.2000
0.5000 0.5000 0.5000
0.3000 0.3000 0.3000
10
FALSE
FALSE
TRUE
```

```
Sphere.Dat
0.3000 0.0000 0.0000
0.5000 0.0000 0.0000
0.2000 0.0000 0.0000
5
12.0000 12.0000 12.0000
-0.0000 -0.0000 -0.0000
-0.0000 -0.0000 32.0000
TRUE
FALSE
FALSE

TRUE 3 -18 350 500 240 18
-35 45
TRUE
FALSE
FALSE
0.8800
0.7000


2

Plane.Dat
0.2000 0.2000 0.2000
0.5000 0.5000 0.5000
0.3000 0.3000 0.3000
10
40.0000 40.0000 40.0000
-0.0000 -0.0000 -0.0000
-0.0000 -0.0000 -0.0000
FALSE
FALSE
TRUE

Sphere.Dat
0.3000 0.0000 0.0000
0.5000 0.0000 0.0000
0.2000 0.0000 0.0000
5
12.0000 12.0000 12.0000
-0.0000 -0.0000 -0.0000
-0.0000 -0.0000 41.0000
TRUE
FALSE
FALSE

TRUE 3 -18 350 500 240 18
-35 45
TRUE
```

```
FALSE
FALSE
0.8800
0.7000

2

Plane.Dat
0.2000 0.2000 0.2000
0.5000 0.5000 0.5000
0.3000 0.3000 0.3000
10
40.0000 40.0000 40.0000
-0.0000 -0.0000 -0.0000
-0.0000 -0.0000 -0.0000
FALSE
FALSE
TRUE

Sphere.Dat
0.3000 0.0000 0.0000
0.5000 0.0000 0.0000
0.2000 0.0000 0.0000
5
12.0000 12.0000 12.0000
-0.0000 -0.0000 -0.0000
-0.0000 -0.0000 49.0000
TRUE
FALSE
FALSE

TRUE 3 -18 350 500 240 18
-35 45
TRUE
FALSE
FALSE
0.8800
0.7000

2

Plane.Dat
0.2000 0.2000 0.2000
0.5000 0.5000 0.5000
0.3000 0.3000 0.3000
10
40.0000 40.0000 40.0000
-0.0000 -0.0000 -0.0000
```

```
-0.0000 -0.0000 -0.0000
FALSE
FALSE
TRUE

Sphere.Dat
0.3000 0.0000 0.0000
0.5000 0.0000 0.0000
0.2000 0.0000 0.0000
5
12.0000 12.0000 12.0000
-0.0000 -0.0000 -0.0000
-0.0000 -0.0000 55.0000
TRUE
FALSE
FALSE

TRUE 3 -18 350 500 240 18
-35 45
TRUE
FALSE
FALSE
0.8800
0.7000

2

Plane.Dat
0.2000 0.2000 0.2000
0.5000 0.5000 0.5000
0.3000 0.3000 0.3000
10
40.0000 40.0000 40.0000
-0.0000 -0.0000 -0.0000
-0.0000 -0.0000 -0.0000
FALSE
FALSE
TRUE

Sphere.Dat
0.3000 0.0000 0.0000
0.5000 0.0000 0.0000
0.2000 0.0000 0.0000
5
12.0000 12.0000 12.0000
-0.0000 -0.0000 -0.0000
-0.0000 -0.0000 59.0000
TRUE
FALSE
FALSE
```

```
TRUE 3 -18 350 500 240 18
-35 45
TRUE
FALSE
FALSE
0.8800
0.7000

2

Plane.Dat
0.2000 0.2000 0.2000
0.5000 0.5000 0.5000
0.3000 0.3000 0.3000
10
40.0000 40.0000 40.0000
-0.0000 -0.0000 -0.0000
-0.0000 -0.0000 -0.0000
FALSE
FALSE
TRUE

Sphere.Dat
0.3000 0.0000 0.0000
0.5000 0.0000 0.0000
0.2000 0.0000 0.0000
5
12.0000 12.0000 12.0000
-0.0000 -0.0000 -0.0000
-0.0000 -0.0000 61.0000
TRUE
FALSE
FALSE

TRUE 3 -18 350 500 240 18
-35 45
TRUE
FALSE
FALSE
0.8800
0.7000

2

Plane.Dat
0.2000 0.2000 0.2000
0.5000 0.5000 0.5000
0.3000 0.3000 0.3000
10
40.0000 40.0000 40.0000
```

```
-0.0000 -0.0000 -0.0000
-0.0000 -0.0000 -0.0000
FALSE
FALSE
TRUE

Sphere.Dat
0.3000 0.0000 0.0000
0.5000 0.0000 0.0000
0.2000 0.0000 0.0000
5
12.0000 12.0000 12.0000
-0.0000 -0.0000 -0.0000
-0.0000 -0.0000 61.0000
TRUE
FALSE
FALSE

TRUE 3 -18 350 500 240 18
-35 45
TRUE
FALSE
FALSE
0.8800
0.7000

2

Plane.Dat
0.2000 0.2000 0.2000
0.5000 0.5000 0.5000
0.3000 0.3000 0.3000
10
40.0000 40.0000 40.0000
-0.0000 -0.0000 -0.0000
-0.0000 -0.0000 -0.0000
FALSE
FALSE
TRUE

Sphere.Dat
0.3000 0.0000 0.0000
0.5000 0.0000 0.0000
0.2000 0.0000 0.0000
5
12.0000 12.0000 12.0000
-0.0000 -0.0000 -0.0000
-0.0000 -0.0000 59.0000
TRUE
FALSE
```

```
FALSE

TRUE 3 -18 350 500 240 18
-35 45
TRUE
FALSE
FALSE
0.88000
.7000

2

Plane.Dat
0.2000 0.2000 0.2000
0.5000 0.5000 0.5000
0.3000 0.3000 0.3000
10
40.0000 40.0000 40.0000
-0.0000 -0.0000 -0.0000
-0.0000 -0.0000 -0.0000
FALSE
FALSE
TRUE

Sphere.Dat
0.3000 0.0000 0.0000
0.5000 0.0000 0.0000
0.2000 0.0000 0.0000
5
12.0000 12.0000 12.0000
-0.0000 -0.0000 -0.0000
-0.0000 -0.0000 55.0000
TRUE
FALSE
FALSE

TRUE 3 -18 350 500 240 18
-35 45
TRUE
FALSE
FALSE
0.8800
0.7000

2

Plane.Dat
0.2000 0.2000 0.2000
0.5000 0.5000 0.5000
0.3000 0.3000 0.3000
```

```
10
40.0000  40.0000  40.0000
-0.0000  -0.0000  -0.0000
-0.0000  -0.0000  -0.0000
FALSE
FALSE
TRUE

Sphere.Dat
0.3000  0.0000  0.0000
0.5000  0.0000  0.0000
0.2000  0.0000  0.0000
5
12.0000  12.0000  12.0000
-0.0000  -0.0000  -0.0000
-0.0000  -0.0000  49.0000
TRUE
FALSE
FALSE

TRUE  3  -18  350  500  240  18
-35  45
TRUE
FALSE
FALSE
0.8800
0.7000

2

Plane.Dat
0.2000  0.2000  0.2000
0.5000  0.5000  0.5000
0.3000  0.3000  0.3000
10
40.0000  40.0000  40.0000
-0.0000  -0.0000  -0.0000
-0.0000  -0.0000  -0.0000
FALSE
FALSE
TRUE

Sphere.Dat
0.3000  0.0000  0.0000
0.5000  0.0000  0.0000
0.2000  0.0000  0.0000
5
12.0000  12.0000  12.0000
-0.0000  -0.0000  -0.0000
-0.0000  -0.0000  41.0000
```

234

```
TRUE
FALSE
FALSE

TRUE 3 -18 350 500 240 18
-35 45
TRUE
FALSE
FALSE
0.8800
0.7000

2

Plane.Dat
0.2000 0.2000 0.2000
0.5000 0.5000 0.5000
0.3000 0.3000 0.3000
10
40.0000 40.0000 40.0000
-0.0000 -0.0000 -0.0000
-0.0000 -0.0000 -0.0000
FALSE
FALSE
TRUE

Sphere.Dat
0.3000 0.0000 0.0000
0.5000 0.0000 0.0000
0.2000 0.0000 0.0000
5
12.0000 12.0000 12.0000
-0.0000 -0.0000 -0.0000
-0.0000 -0.0000 32.0000
TRUE
FALSE
FALSE

TRUE 3 -18 350 500 240 18
-35 45
TRUE
FALSE
FALSE
0.8800
0.7000

2
```

```
Plane.Dat
0.2000  0.2000  0.2000
0.5000  0.5000  0.5000
0.3000  0.3000  0.3000
10
40.0000  40.0000  40.0000
-0.0000  -0.0000  -0.0000
-0.0000  -0.0000  -0.0000
FALSE
FALSE
TRUE

Sphere.Dat
0.3000  0.0000  0.0000
0.5000  0.0000  0.0000
0.2000  0.0000  0.0000
5
12.0000  12.0000  12.0000
-0.0000  -0.0000  -0.0000
-0.0000  -0.0000  22.0000
TRUE
FALSE
FALSE
```

Listing 10-1. The *SphrPlan.SCN* Scene File.

```
/*
```

```
┌──────────────────────────────────────────────────┐
│ ┌──────────────────────────────────────────────┐ │
│ │              Scene Script Generator           │ │
│ │                                               │ │
│ │      by Christopher D. Watkins and Larry Sharp │ │
│ └──────────────────────────────────────────────┘ │
└──────────────────────────────────────────────────┘
```

```
*/
```

```c
#include "stdio.h"
#include "dos.h"
#include "conio.h"
#include "math.h"
#include "string.h"
#include "malloc.h"
#include "defs.h"

typedef char String[32];
```

```
/*
```

```
┌──────────────────────────────────────────────────┐
│ ┌──────────────────────────────────────────────┐ │
│ │              Math and Screen Routines          │ │
│ └──────────────────────────────────────────────┘ │
└──────────────────────────────────────────────────┘
```

```
*/
```

```c
void Vec(float r, float s, float t, TDA A)
{
  A[0]=r;
  A[1]=s;
  A[2]=t;
}

void VecCopy(TDA A, TDA B)
{
  B[0]=0.0+A[0];
  B[1]=0.0+A[1];
  B[2]=0.0+A[2];
}

void VecScalMult(float r, TDA A, TDA B)
{
  B[0]=r*A[0];
  B[1]=r*A[1];
  B[2]=r*A[2];
}

void VecNull(TDA A)
```

```
{
  A[0]=0.0;
  A[1]=0.0;
  A[2]=0.0;
}

void Set_Text_Screen(int tc, int tb)
{
  textcolor(tc);
  textbackground(tb);
  clrscr();
}

/*
```

```
┌─────────────────────────────────────────────────────────────┐
│                                                               │
│                      Load a .SCN File                         │
│                                                               │
└─────────────────────────────────────────────────────────────┘
```

```
*/
```

```
    .3D and .SCN FORMAT:

A description of the XXXXXXXX.Scn file.  This is the first line.

1                               Number of Frames in sequence

TRUE   0   0  500  500          Do Perspective   Mx  My  Mz  D
  245  25                       Viewing Angle and Tilt
   45  45                       Light Angle and Tilt
FALSE                           Perform Vertical Sort
FALSE                           Place Edge Reflectors
FALSE                           Place Edge Reflectors at Zero

1                               Number of Objects in Frame

Grid.Dat                        Object File Name
     0.3    0.3    0.3          Ambient Color
     0.5    0.5    0.5          Diffuse Color
     0.2    0.2    0.2          Specular Color
     5                          Gloss
    50.0   50.0   50.0          Scale
     0.0    0.0    0.0          Rotate
    50.0   50.0    0.0          Translate
FALSE                           Object is reflected in mirrors
FALSE                           Allow Sort of Object
TRUE                            Object is a mirror
*/

#define  Max_Frame 30L
#define  Max_Objects 20
```

```
typedef struct{
  char Object_Name[14];
  TDA Translate;
  TDA Rotate;
  TDA Scale;
  Boolean Reflection;
  TDA Amb_Color;
  TDA Dif_Color;
  TDA Spc_Color;
  Byte Gloss;
  Boolean Sortable;
  Boolean Mirror;
} Object_Record;

Byte Object_Num, Frame_Num;

typedef struct{
  Boolean Perspective;
  int Mx;
  int My;
  int Mz;
  int D;
  int View_Angle;
  int View_Tilt;
  int Light_Angle;
  int Light_Tilt;
  Boolean Vert_Sort;
  Boolean Add_Edge_Reflectors;
  Boolean Add_Edge_Reflectors_At_Zero;
  float Mix;
  float Darken;
  Byte Last_Object;
  Object_Record Object_List[Max_Objects];
} Frame_Record;

static Frame_Record far *Frame_List;

Byte Object_Num, Frame_Num;
Byte Last_Frame_Num;
char Comment[80];

#define Frame Frame_List[Frame_Num]
#define Frame_Object Frame_List[Frame_Num].Object_List[Object_Num]

void Init_Frame_Buffer()
{
  strcpy(Comment, "");
  for(Frame_Num=0; Frame_Num<Max_Frame; Frame_Num++)
  {
```

```
         Frame.Perspective=false;
         Frame.Mx=0;
         Frame.My=0;
         Frame.Mz=0;
         Frame.D=0;
         Frame.View_Angle=0;
         Frame.View_Tilt=0;
         Frame.Light_Angle=0;
         Frame.Vert_Sort=0;
         Frame.Add_Edge_Reflectors=false;
         Frame.Add_Edge_Reflectors_At_Zero=false;
         Frame.Mix=0;
         Frame.Darken=0;
         Frame.Last_Object=1;
         for(Object_Num=0; Object_Num<Max_Objects; Object_Num++)
         {
           strcpy(Frame_Object.Object_Name, "");
           VecNull(Frame_Object.Translate);
           VecNull(Frame_Object.Rotate);
           VecNull(Frame_Object.Scale);
           Frame_Object.Reflection=false;
           VecNull(Frame_Object.Amb_Color);
           VecNull(Frame_Object.Dif_Color);
           VecNull(Frame_Object.Spc_Color);
           Frame_Object.Gloss=0;
           Frame_Object.Sortable=false;
           Frame_Object.Mirror=false;
         }
       }
       Frame_Num=1;
       Last_Frame_Num=1;
       Object_Num=1;
    }

    void Scale(float x, float y, float z)
    {
      Vec(x, y, z, Frame_Object.Scale);
    }

    void Rotate(float x, float y, float z)
    {
      Vec(x, y, z, Frame_Object.Rotate);
    }

    void Translate(float x, float y, float z)
    {
      Vec(x, y, z, Frame_Object.Translate);
    }

    void Reflect_Object(Boolean state)
```

```
{
  Frame_Object.Reflection=state;
}

void Obj_Amb_Color(float r, float g, float b)
{
  Vec(r, g, b, Frame_Object.Amb_Color);
}

void Obj_Dif_Color(float r, float g, float b)
{
  Vec(r, g, b, Frame_Object.Dif_Color);
}

void Obj_Spc_Color(float r, float g, float b)
{
  Vec(r, g, b, Frame_Object.Spc_Color);
}

void Obj_Gloss(Byte gls)
{
  Frame_Object.Gloss=gls;
}

void Allow_Sort(Boolean state)
{
  Frame_Object.Sortable=state;
}

void Mirrored(Boolean state)
{
  Frame_Object.Mirror=state;
}

/*
```

```
┌──────────────────────────────────────────────────┐
│          Load Scene from .SCN Disk File           │
└──────────────────────────────────────────────────┘
```

```
*/

FILE *In_File;
FILE *Out_File;

Boolean Duplicate;
char b2s[8];

Boolean Bool(char B[8])
{
  if((B[0]=='F') || (B[0]=='f'))
    return(false);
```

```
      else
        return(true);
    }

  void Bool_To_String(Boolean b)
  {
    if(b==false)
      strcpy(b2s, "false");
    else
      strcpy(b2s, "true");
  }

  Byte Get_Num()
  {
    char c[8];
    int Sel1, Sel2;
    Byte Sel;

    do
    {
      while(!isdigit(c[0]))
      {
        while(!kbhit());
        c[0]=getch();
      }
      Sel1=10*((c[0])-48);
      c[0]='a';
      while(!isdigit(c[0]))
      {
        while(!kbhit());
        c[0]=getch();
      }
      Sel2=(c[0])-48;
      Sel=Sel1+Sel2;
    }
    while(Sel>20);
    return(Sel);
  }

  #define Frame0 Frame_List[0]
  #define Frame_Object0 Frame_List[0].Object_List[Object_Num]

  void Duplication()
  {
    for(Frame_Num=1; Frame_Num<Max_Frame; Frame_Num++)
    {
      Frame.Perspective=Frame0.Perspective;
      Frame.Mx=Frame0.Mx;
      Frame.My=Frame0.My;
      Frame.Mz=Frame0.Mz;
```

```
      Frame.D=Frame0.D;
      Frame.View_Angle=Frame0.View_Angle;
      Frame.View_Tilt=Frame0.View_Tilt;
      Frame.Light_Angle=Frame0.Light_Angle;
      Frame.Light_Tilt=Frame0.Light_Tilt;
      Frame.Vert_Sort=Frame0.Vert_Sort;
      Frame.Add_Edge_Reflectors=Frame0.Add_Edge_Reflectors;
      Frame.Add_Edge_Reflectors_At_Zero=Frame0.Add_Edge_Reflectors_At_Zero;
      Frame.Mix=Frame0.Mix;
      Frame.Darken=Frame0.Darken;
      Frame.Last_Object=Frame0.Last_Object;
      for(Object_Num=1; Object_Num<Max_Objects; Object_Num++)
      {
        strcpy(Frame_Object.Object_Name, Frame_Object0.Object_Name);
        VecCopy(Frame_Object0.Translate, Frame_Object.Translate);
        VecCopy(Frame_Object0.Rotate, Frame_Object.Rotate);
        VecCopy(Frame_Object0.Scale, Frame_Object.Scale);
        Frame_Object.Reflection=Frame_Object0.Reflection;
        VecCopy(Frame_Object0.Amb_Color, Frame_Object.Amb_Color);
        VecCopy(Frame_Object0.Dif_Color, Frame_Object.Dif_Color);
        VecCopy(Frame_Object0.Spc_Color, Frame_Object.Spc_Color);
        Frame_Object.Sortable=Frame_Object0.Sortable;
        Frame_Object.Mirror=Frame_Object0.Mirror;
      }
   }
}

void File_IO_Error()
{
  sound(1000);
  delay(500);
  nosound();
  clrscr();
  printf("File I/O Error!\nHit any key to exit....");
  getch();
  exit(1);
}

void Load_Scene_File(String File_Name)
{
  char B[8];
  int i1, i2, i3, i4;
  float f1, f2, f3;
  char Object_File_Name[82];
  char blank[82];

  if((In_File=fopen(File_Name, "rt"))==NULL)
    File_IO_Error();
  fgets(Comment, 80, In_File);
  fgets(blank, 80, In_File);
```

```
fscanf(In_File, "%d", &Last_Frame_Num);
if(Last_Frame_Num==1)
  Duplicate=true;
else
  Duplicate=false;
for(Frame_Num=0; Frame_Num<Last_Frame_Num; Frame_Num++)
{
  fgets(blank, 80, In_File);
  fscanf(In_File, "%s %d %d %d %d", B, &i1, &i2, &i3, &i4);
  Frame.Perspective=Bool(B);
  Frame.Mx=i1;
  Frame.My=i2;
  Frame.Mz=i3;
  Frame.D=i4;
  fscanf(In_File, "%d %d", &i1, &i2);
  Frame.View_Angle=i1;
  Frame.View_Tilt=i2;
  fscanf(In_File, "%d %d", &i1, &i2);
  Frame.Light_Angle=i1;
  Frame.Light_Tilt=i2;
  fscanf(In_File, "%s", B);
  Frame.Vert_Sort=Bool(B);
  fscanf(In_File, "%s", B);
  Frame.Add_Edge_Reflectors=Bool(B);
  fscanf(In_File, "%s", B);
  Frame.Add_Edge_Reflectors_At_Zero=Bool(B);
  fscanf(In_File, "%f", &f1);
  Frame.Mix=f1;
  fscanf(In_File, "%f", &f1);
  Frame.Darken=f1;
  fgets(blank, 80, In_File);
  fscanf(In_File, "%d", &i1);
  Frame.Last_Object=i1;
  for(Object_Num=0; Object_Num<Frame.Last_Object; Object_Num++)
  {
    fgets(blank, 80, In_File);
    fgets(blank, 80, In_File);
    fgets(Object_File_Name, 80, In_File);
    strcpy(Frame_Object.Object_Name, Object_File_Name);
    fscanf(In_File, "%f %f %f", &f1, &f2, &f3);
    Obj_Amb_Color(f1, f2, f3);
    fscanf(In_File, "%f %f %f", &f1, &f2, &f3);
    Obj_Dif_Color(f1, f2, f3);
    fscanf(In_File, "%f %f %f", &f1, &f2, &f3);
    Obj_Spc_Color(f1, f2, f3);
    fscanf(In_File, "%d", &i1);
    Obj_Gloss(i1);
    fscanf(In_File, "%f %f %f", &f1, &f2, &f3);
    Scale(f1, f2, f3);
    fscanf(In_File, "%f %f %f", &f1, &f2, &f3);
```

```
      Rotate(f1, f2, f3);
      fscanf(In_File, "%f %f %f", &f1, &f2, &f3);
      Translate(f1, f2, f3);
      fscanf(In_File, "%s", B);
      Reflect_Object(Bool(B));
      fscanf(In_File, "%s", B);
      Allow_Sort(Bool(B));
      fscanf(In_File, "%s", B);
      Mirrored(Bool(B));
    }
  }
  fclose(In_File);
  if(Duplicate)
    Duplication();
}

void Save_Scene_File(String File_Name)
{
  char B[8];
  int i1, i2, i3, i4;
  float f1, f2, f3;
  String Object_File_Name;
  String blank;

  if((Out_File=fopen(File_Name, "wt"))==NULL)
    File_IO_Error();
  fprintf(Out_File, "%s", Comment);
  fprintf(Out_File, "\n");
  fprintf(Out_File, "%d\n", Last_Frame_Num);
  for(Frame_Num=0; Frame_Num<Last_Frame_Num; Frame_Num++)
  {
    fprintf(Out_File, "\n");
    Bool_To_String(Frame.Perspective);
    fprintf(Out_File, "%s %d %d %d %d\n", b2s,
                                 Frame.Mx,
                                 Frame.My,
                                 Frame.Mz,
                                 Frame.D);
    fprintf(Out_File, "%d %d\n", Frame.View_Angle, Frame.View_Tilt);
    fprintf(Out_File, "%d %d\n", Frame.Light_Angle, Frame.Light_Tilt);
    Bool_To_String(Frame.Vert_Sort);
    fprintf(Out_File, "%s\n", b2s);
    Bool_To_String(Frame.Add_Edge_Reflectors);
    fprintf(Out_File, "%s\n", b2s);
    Bool_To_String(Frame.Add_Edge_Reflectors_At_Zero);
    fprintf(Out_File, "%s\n", b2s);
    fprintf(Out_File, "%4.4f\n", Frame.Mix);
    fprintf(Out_File, "%4.4f\n", Frame.Darken);
    fprintf(Out_File, "\n");
    fprintf(Out_File, "%d\n", Frame.Last_Object);
```

245

```
    for(Object_Num=0; Object_Num<Frame.Last_Object; Object_Num++)
    {
      fprintf(Out_File, "\n");
      fprintf(Out_File, "%s", Frame_Object.Object_Name);
      fprintf(Out_File, "%4.4f %4.4f %4.4f\n", Frame_Object.Amb_Color[0],
                                Frame_Object.Amb_Color[1],
                                Frame_Object.Amb_Color[2]);
      fprintf(Out_File, "%4.4f %4.4f %4.4f\n", Frame_Object.Dif_Color[0],
                                Frame_Object.Dif_Color[1],
                                Frame_Object.Dif_Color[2]);
      fprintf(Out_File, "%4.4f %4.4f %4.4f\n", Frame_Object.Spc_Color[0],
                                Frame_Object.Spc_Color[1],
                                Frame_Object.Spc_Color[2]);
      fprintf(Out_File, "%d\n", Frame_Object.Gloss);
      fprintf(Out_File, "%4.4f %4.4f %4.4f\n", Frame_Object.Scale[0],
                                Frame_Object.Scale[1],
                                Frame_Object.Scale[2]);
      fprintf(Out_File, "%4.4f %4.4f %4.4f\n", -Frame_Object.Rotate[0],
                                -Frame_Object.Rotate[1],
                                -Frame_Object.Rotate[2]);
      fprintf(Out_File, "%4.4f %4.4f %4.4f\n", -Frame_Object.Translate[0],
                                -Frame_Object.Translate[1],
                                -Frame_Object.Translate[2]);
      Bool_To_String(Frame_Object.Reflection);
      fprintf(Out_File, "%s\n", b2s);
      Bool_To_String(Frame_Object.Sortable);
      fprintf(Out_File, "%s\n", b2s);
      Bool_To_String(Frame_Object.Mirror);
      fprintf(Out_File, "%s\n", b2s);
    }
  }
  fclose(Out_File);
}

String Scene_File, Org_File, tmp;

void Get_Scene_File_Name()
{
  Byte x, y;

  textcolor(YELLOW);
  textbackground(BLUE);
  gotoxy(1, 8);
  cprintf("Enter File Name -> ");
  x=wherex();
  y=wherey();
  textcolor(WHITE+BLINK);
  cprintf("%s", "SPHRPLAN");
  textcolor(YELLOW);
  gotoxy(x, y);
```

```
      while(!(kbhit()));
      cprintf("                    ");
      gotoxy(x, y);
      gets(Scene_File);
      if(!(strcmp(Scene_File, "")))
        strcpy(Scene_File, "SPHRPLAN");
      strupr(Scene_File);
      strcpy(Org_File, Scene_File);
    }

  void Create_Script()
  {
    clrscr();
    printf("3D Modeler Script File Generator\n\nCreate Script\n\n");
    Get_Scene_File_Name();
    strcpy(tmp, Scene_File);
    strcat(Scene_File, ".ORG");
    Save_Scene_File(Scene_File);
    strcpy(Scene_File, tmp);
    strcat(Scene_File, ".SCN");
    Save_Scene_File(Scene_File);
  }

  void Load_Script()
  {
    clrscr();
    printf("3D Modeler Script File Generator\n\nLoad Script\n\n");
    Frame_Num=0;
    Get_Scene_File_Name();
    strcat(Scene_File, ".SCN");
    Load_Scene_File(Scene_File);
  }

  void Display()
  {
    clrscr();
    printf("<Lft/Rgt> +/- Frm - <Dn/Up> +/- Obj - <A/D> Add/Del Frm - <+/-
> Add/Del Obj\n");
    printf("——————— <Spc> Edit - <Esc> Menu ———————\n");
    printf("<00> Comment = %s", Comment);
    printf("——> Frame %d <——\n", Frame_Num);
    Bool_To_String(Frame.Perspective);
    printf("<01> Perspective = %s\n", b2s);
    printf("<02> Mx, My, Mz D = %d %d %d %d\n", Frame.Mx, Frame.My,
                                                Frame.Mz,Frame.D);
    printf("<03> View Angle & Tilt = %d %d\n", Frame.View_Angle,Frame.View_Tilt);
    printf("<04> Light  Angle  &  Tilt  =  %d %d\n", Frame.Light_Angle,
Frame.Light_Tilt);
    Bool_To_String(Frame.Vert_Sort);
    printf("<05> Vertical Sort = %s\n", b2s);
```

```
        Bool_To_String(Frame.Add_Edge_Reflectors);
        printf("<06> Edge Reflectors          = %s\n", b2s);
        Bool_To_String(Frame.Add_Edge_Reflectors_At_Zero);
        printf("<07> Edge Reflectors At Zero = %s\n", b2s);
        printf("<08> Mix    = %4.4f\n", Frame.Mix);
        printf("<09> Darken = %4.4f\n", Frame.Darken);
        printf("———> Object %d <———\n", Object_Num);
        printf("<10> Name = %s",Frame_Object.Object_Name);
        printf("<11> Ambient Color  = %4.4f %4.4f %4.4f\n",
Frame_Object.Amb_Color[0],

        Frame_Object.Amb_Color[1],

        Frame_Object.Amb_Color[2]);
        printf("<12>  Diffuse  Color  =  %4.4f  %4.4f  %4.4f\n",
Frame_Object.Dif_Color[0],

        Frame_Object.Dif_Color[1],

        Frame_Object.Dif_Color[2]);
        printf("<13>  Specular  Color  =  %4.4f  %4.4f  %4.4f\n",
Frame_Object.Spc_Color[0],

        Frame_Object.Spc_Color[1],

        Frame_Object.Spc_Color[2]);
        printf("<14> Gloss = %d\n",Frame_Object.Gloss);
        printf("<15> Scale    = %4.4f %4.4f %4.4f\n", Frame_Object.Scale[0],
                                        Frame_Object.Scale[1],
                                        Frame_Object.Scale[2]);
        printf("<16> Rotate    = %4.4f %4.4f %4.4f\n", -Frame_Object.Rotate[0],
                                        -Frame_Object.Rotate[1],
                                        -Frame_Object.Rotate[2]);
        printf("<17> Translate = %4.4f %4.4f %4.4f\n", -Frame_Object.Translate[0],
                                        -Frame_Object.Translate[1],
                                        -Frame_Object.Translate[2]);
        Bool_To_String(Frame_Object.Reflection);
        printf("<18> Object will Reflect   = %s\n", b2s);
        Bool_To_String(Frame_Object.Sortable);
        printf("<19> Object is Sortable   = %s\n", b2s);
        Bool_To_String(Frame_Object.Mirror);
        printf("<20> Object is a Reflector = %s", b2s);
    }

    void Edit_Script()
    {
      String B;
      Boolean Fin2, Edit;
      Word Sel;
      Byte Dir;
```

```
clrscr();
printf("3DModeler Script File Gnerator\n\nEdit Script\n\n\n");
Frame_Num=0;
Object_Num=0;
Display();
Fin2=false;
Edit=false;
while(!Fin2)
{
  while(!kbhit());
  Dir=getch();
  switch(Dir)
  {
    case 'M' : if(Frame_Num==(Last_Frame_Num-1))
                 Frame_Num=0;
               else
                 ++Frame_Num;
               break;
    case 'K' : if(Frame_Num==0)
                 Frame_Num=(Last_Frame_Num-1);
               else
                 -Frame_Num;
               break;
    case 'P' : if(Object_Num==(Frame.Last_Object-1))
                 Object_Num=0;
               else
                 ++Object_Num;
               break;
    case 'H' : if(Object_Num==0)
                 Object_Num=(Frame.Last_Object-1);
               else
                 -Object_Num;
               break;
    case ' ' : Edit=true;
               break;
    case 27  : Fin2=true;
               break;
    case '+' : if(Frame.Last_Object==Max_Objects)
               {
                 sound(1000);
                 delay(200);
                 nosound();
               }
               else
               {
                 ++Frame.Last_Object;
                 Object_Num=(Frame.Last_Object-1);
               }
               break;
```

```
      case '-' : if(Frame.Last_Object==0)
            {
              sound(1000);
              delay(200);
              nosound();
            }
            else
            {
              -Frame.Last_Object;
              Object_Num=(Frame.Last_Object-1);
            }
          break;
      case 'a' : if(Last_Frame_Num==Max_Frame)
            {
              sound(1000);
              delay(200);
              nosound();
            }
            else
            {
              ++Last_Frame_Num;
              Frame_Num=(Last_Frame_Num-1);
            }
          break;
      case 'd' : if(Last_Frame_Num==0)
            {
              sound(1000);
              delay(200);
              nosound();
            }
            else
            {
              -Last_Frame_Num;
              Frame_Num=(Last_Frame_Num-1);
            }
          break;
}
if(!Fin2)
{
  Display();
  if(Edit)
  {
Sel=Get_Num();
switch(Sel)
{
  case 0  : gotoxy(1, 3);
            printf("<00> Comment = ");
            gets(Comment);
            gotoxy(1, 3);
            printf("<00> Comment = %s", Comment);
```

```
          break;
case 1  : gotoxy(1, 5);
          printf("<01> Perspective = ");
          gets(B);
          Frame.Perspective=Bool(B);
          gotoxy(1, 5);
          printf("<01> Perspective = %s", B);
          break;
case 2  : gotoxy(1, 6);
          printf("<02> Mx, My, Mz, D = ");
          scanf("%d %d %d %d", &Frame.Mx, &Frame.My,
                          &Frame.Mz, &Frame.D);
          gotoxy(1, 6);
          printf("<02> Mx, My, Mz, D = %d %d %d %d", Frame.Mx,
                                            Frame.My,
                                            Frame.Mz,
                                            Frame.D);
          break;
case 3  : gotoxy(1, 7);
          printf("<03> ViewAngle, ViewTilt = ");
          scanf("%d %d", &Frame.View_Angle, &Frame.View_Tilt);
          gotoxy(1, 7);
          printf("<03> ViewAngle, ViewTilt = %d %d",
                          Frame.View_Angle, Frame.View_Tilt);
          break;
case 4  : gotoxy(1, 8);
          printf("<04> LightAngle, LightTilt = ");
          scanf("%d %d", &Frame.Light_Angle, &Frame.Light_Tilt);
          gotoxy(1, 8);
          printf("<04> LightAngle, LightTilt = %d %d",
                          Frame.Light_Angle,Frame.Light_Tilt);
          break;
case 5  : gotoxy(1, 9);
          printf("<05> Vertical Sort = ");
          gets(B);
          Frame.Vert_Sort=Bool(B);
          gotoxy(1, 9);
          printf("<05> Vertical Sort = %s", B);
          break;
case 6  : gotoxy(1, 10);
          printf("<06> Edge Reflectors = ");
          gets(B);
          Frame.Add_Edge_Reflectors=Bool(B);
          gotoxy(1, 10);
          printf("<06> Edge Reflectors = %s", B);
          break;
case 7  : gotoxy(1, 11);
          printf("<07> Edge Reflectors At Zero = ");
          gets(B);
          Frame.Add_Edge_Reflectors_At_Zero=Bool(B);
```

```
                gotoxy(1, 11);
                printf("<07> Edge Reflectors = %s", B);
                break;
     case 8  : gotoxy(1, 12);
                printf("<08> Mix = ");
                scanf("%f", &Frame.Mix);
                gotoxy(1, 12);
                printf("<08> Mix = %4.4f", Frame.Mix);
                break;
     case 9  : gotoxy(1, 13);
                printf("<09> Darken = ");
                scanf("%f", &Frame.Darken);
                gotoxy(1, 13);
                printf("<09> Darken = %4.4f", Frame.Darken);
                break;
     case 10 : gotoxy(1, 15);
                printf("<10> Name = ");
                gets(Frame_Object.Object_Name);
                gotoxy(1, 15);
                printf("<10> Name = %s", Frame_Object.Object_Name);
                break;
     case 11 : gotoxy(1, 16);
                printf("<11> Ambient Color = ");
                scanf("%f %f %f", &Frame_Object.Amb_Color[0],
                            &Frame_Object.Amb_Color[1],
                            &Frame_Object.Amb_Color[2]);
                gotoxy(1, 16);
                printf("<11> Ambient Color = %4.4f %4.4f %4.4f",
                            Frame_Object.Amb_Color[0],
                            Frame_Object.Amb_Color[1],
                            Frame_Object.Amb_Color[2]);
                break;
     case 12 : gotoxy(1, 17);
                printf("<12> Diffuse Color = ");
                scanf("%f %f %f", &Frame_Object.Dif_Color[0],
                            &Frame_Object.Dif_Color[1],
                            &Frame_Object.Dif_Color[2]);
                gotoxy(1, 17);
               printf("<12> Diffuse Color = %4.4f %4.4f %4.4f",
                            Frame_Object.Dif_Color[0],
                            Frame_Object.Dif_Color[1],
                            Frame_Object.Dif_Color[2]);
                break;
     case 13 : gotoxy(1, 18);
                printf("<13> Specular Color = ");
                scanf("%f %f %f", &Frame_Object.Spc_Color[0],
                            &Frame_Object.Spc_Color[1],
                            &Frame_Object.Spc_Color[2]);
                gotoxy(1, 18);
               printf("<13> Specular Color = %4.4f %4.4f %4.4f",
```

```
                                Frame_Object.Spc_Color[0],
                                Frame_Object.Spc_Color[1],
                                Frame_Object.Spc_Color[2]);
                break;
case 14 : gotoxy(1, 19);
                printf("<14> Gloss = ");
                scanf("%d", &Frame_Object.Gloss);
                gotoxy(1, 19);
                printf("<14> Gloss = %d", Frame_Object.Gloss);
                break;
case 15 : gotoxy(1, 20);
                printf("<15> Scale    = ");
                scanf("%f %f %f", &Frame_Object.Scale[0],
                                &Frame_Object.Scale[1],
                                &Frame_Object.Scale[2]);
                gotoxy(1, 20);
              printf("<15> Scale    = %4.4f %4.4f %4.4f",
                                Frame_Object.Scale[0],
                                Frame_Object.Scale[1],
                                Frame_Object.Scale[2]);
                break;
case 16 : gotoxy(1, 21);
                printf("<16> Rotate    = ");
                scanf("%f %f %f", &Frame_Object.Rotate[0],
                                &Frame_Object.Rotate[1],
                                &Frame_Object.Rotate[2]);
                gotoxy(1, 21);
              printf("<16> Rotate    = %4.4f %4.4f %4.4f",
                                Frame_Object.Rotate[0],
                                Frame_Object.Rotate[1],
                                Frame_Object.Rotate[2]);
                break;
case 17 : gotoxy(1, 22);
                printf("<17> Translate = ");
                scanf("%f %f %f", &Frame_Object.Translate[0],
                                &Frame_Object.Translate[1],
                                &Frame_Object.Translate[2]);
                gotoxy(1, 22);
              printf("<17> Translate = %4.4f %4.4f %4.4f",
                                Frame_Object.Translate[0],
                                Frame_Object.Translate[1],
                                Frame_Object.Translate[2]);
                break;
case 18 : gotoxy(1, 23);
                printf("<18> Object will Reflect   = ");
                gets(B);
                Frame_Object.Reflection=Bool(B);
                gotoxy(1, 23);
                printf("<18> Object will Reflect   = %s", B);
                break;
```

```
    case 19 : gotoxy(1, 24);
              printf("<19> Object is Sortable    = ");
              gets(B);
              Frame_Object.Sortable=Bool(B);
              gotoxy(1, 24);
              printf("<19> Object is Sortable    = %s", B);
              break;
    case 20 : gotoxy(1, 25);
              printf("<20> Object is a Reflector = ");
              gets(B);
              Frame_Object.Mirror=Bool(B);
              gotoxy(1, 25);
              printf("<20> Object is a Reflector = %s", B);
              break;
    }
      }
    }
    Edit=false;
    Display();
  }
}

void Save_Script()
{
  clrscr();
  printf("3D Modeler Script File Generator\n\nSave Script\n\n");
  Get_Scene_File_Name();
  strcat(Org_File, ".ORG");
  Save_Scene_File(Org_File);
  strcat(Scene_File, ".SCN");
  Save_Scene_File(Scene_File);
}

Boolean Fin;

void Exit_Program()
{
  clrscr();
  printf("Exiting 3DModeler Script File Generator\n\n");
  Fin=true;
}

void Menu()
{
  int Sel;
  char c[5]="\n\n";

  clrscr();
  printf("3DModeler Script File Generator\n\nBy Christopher D.
                    Watkins\n\n");printf(">>>>> Menu <<<<<\n\n");
```

```
   printf("<1> Create Script\n");
   printf("<2> Load Script\n");
   printf("<3> Edit Script\n");
   printf("<4> Save Script\n");
   printf("<5> Exit\n");
   do
   {
     while(!isdigit(c[0]))
     {
       while(!kbhit());
       c[0]=getch();
     }
     Sel=(c[0])-48;
   }
   while((Sel>5) || (Sel<1));
   switch(Sel)
   {
     case 1 : Create_Script(); break;
     case 2 : Load_Script();   break;
     case 3 : Edit_Script();   break;
     case 4 : Save_Script();   break;
     case 5 : Exit_Program();  break;
   }
}

void main()
{
   Frame_List=farcalloc(Max_Frame, sizeof(Frame_Record));
   Set_Text_Screen(YELLOW, BLUE);
   Init_Frame_Buffer();
   Fin=false;
   while(Fin==false)
     Menu();
   farfree(Frame_List);
   Set_Text_Screen(LIGHTGRAY, BLACK);
}
```

Listing 10-2. Scene Script Generator.

```
printf("<1> Create Script\n");
printf("<2> Load Script\n");
printf("<3> Edit Script\n");
printf("<4> Save Script\n");
printf("<5> Exit\n");
do
{
  while(!isdigit(c[0]))
  {
    while(!kbhit());
    c[0]=getch();
  }
  Sel=(c[0])-48;
}
while((Sel>5) || (Sel<1));
switch(Sel)
{
  case 1 : Create_Script(); break;
  case 2 : Load_Script();   break;
  case 3 : Edit_Script();   break;
  case 4 : Save_Script();   break;
  case 5 : Exit_Program();  break;
}
}

void main()
{
  Frame_List=farcalloc(Max_Frame, sizeof(Frame_Record));
  Set_Text_Screen(YELLOW, BLUE);
  Init_Frame_Buffer();
  Fin=false;
  while(Fin==false)
    Menu();
  farfree(Frame_List);
  Set_Text_Screen(LIGHTGRAY, BLACK);
}
```

Listing 10-2. Scene Script Generator.

RAY TRACING

Ray-Tracing Theory

Ray tracing allows you to produce near-photorealistic images and animation. Unlike the modeling program, the ray tracer can accurately model such lighting effects as shadows, reflection and refraction, magnification, mirrors, and textured surfaces.

This chapter presents the basic theories and algorithms involved in producing a ray-traced image. It also discusses various performance issues and ways to improve rendering performance.

The Fundamentals of Ray Tracing

Like the modeling program, ray tracing creates a two-dimensional picture of a three-dimensional world. As you may recall from the previous chapters, the modeling program produces these images by projecting three-dimensional facets onto the two-dimensional screen and filling in, or *scan converting*, the projected areas on the screen. Ray tracing takes a very different approach: the scene is projected in reverse, from the viewer to the world.

Think about how a camera takes a picture. The light from every point in a scene is projected to the camera lens and then to the film, where a permanent record is made. With ray tracing, the process is reversed; a "light" ray is cast from the viewer's eye to the screen for each pixel on the screen and then on to whatever object in the scene it hits first. If the object is reflective, the ray is reflected from the surface. That creates a new ray, which is cast from the object surface to other objects or light sources. We continue tracing the ray's path through the scene until it hits a light source or leaves the scene altogether (in essence, by hitting the global-illumination light source). Each time the ray is reflected, we note the color of the object that was hit; this will determine the color we eventually see for that screen pixel. We may have colored light sources that must be accounted for as well. Once all the screen pixels have been processed, we have a realistic two-dimensional picture of the scene, complete with shadows and reflections.

Ray tracing is a powerful technique because it models how light physically interacts with objects in a scene. Generating such effects as refraction and multiple-object interreflections (reflections between object surfaces) is virtually impossible with the modeler.

To see how this works, imagine a scene composed of various primitive objects and light sources. An observer, stationed at a specified point in the coordinate system, is looking at the scene through a translucent screen. Each tiny point on the screen (corresponding to a pixel on a color monitor display) appears to have some color associated with it; that's actually the color of the ray of light that intersects the screen and is projected into the observer's eye. This is how a camera works, but it's inefficient for the computer to trace the light rays from the light sources to the objects. That's because millions of these rays don't intersect the screen and then continue to the viewers eye, so they're not involved in picture creation. Therefore, we work in the reverse direction, projecting light rays backward from the observer to the screen and then in a straight line to the nearest object. That way, we consider only those rays that are essential for the picture.

The fundamental operation in a ray-tracing program is to determine where a ray intersects an object. The first task is to determine whether or not a given ray intersects an object. If it does, we find out exactly where on the object the intersection occurs. That means we need to break a scene down into relatively primitive objects (spheres, parallelograms, triangles, fractals, and so forth) that can be described by simple mathematical equations. Our problem is then reduced to that of determining the intersection of a line with each primitive. We must also be able to specify how a ray is reflected from each of these surfaces to account for light reflections. These primitives—together with patterns to be projected on surfaces, light sources, and the position of the observer—provide the information we need to define a scene so that the ray tracer can trace every beam of light, and therefore create the complex shadows and reflections that make up a real-life scene.

The color of the ray where it intersects an object isn't easily determined; it often depends not only on the inherent color of the object, but also on what happens to the light ray before it reaches the object. If the light is emitted entirely by the object (the object would then be a light source) and is a specified color, our problem is solved. This is seldom the case, however. More often, the object is illuminated by external light sources or ambient light (or both). If the surface is partially transparent, the color is determined by a combination of colors based on transmitted light and the surface color itself. A surface like glass can both transmit and reflect, so the final ray color will be some combination of light reflected onto the surface and light transmitted through the glass. We must therefore trace all the rays until they intersect a light source or the lighting "background." This is a very complex task, but it's not beyond the capabilities of our PCs.

Figure 11-1 shows the geometry of a simple ray-traced scene. In Figure 11-2, a few objects and light sources, along with shadows and some reflections, have been added. Already things are beginning to get more complex. Considering that a realistic scene may contain thousands of objects, computing all the light-ray interactions for every screen pixel is quite a task. Fortunately, we only have to position the primitive objects that define a scene; the complicated interactions of light and shadows are computed by the program.

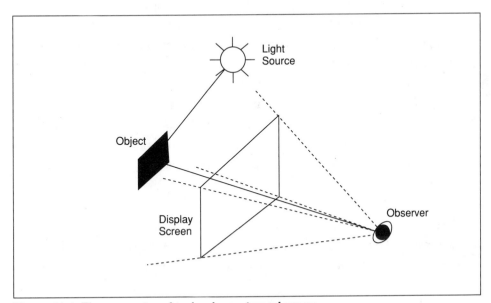

Figure 11-1. The geometry of a simple ray-traced scene.

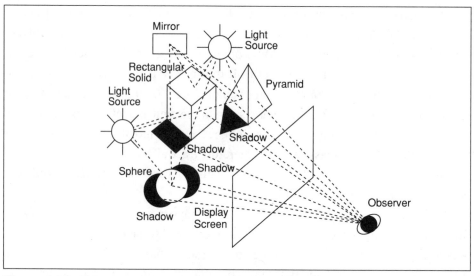

Figure 11-2. The geometry of a complex ray-traced scene with light sources and shadows.

Even though ray tracing is a compute-intensive task, it can be accomplished within the constraints of an IBM PC or compatible in a matter of a few hours. All we need is the proper software, and we're in the picture-generating business. We must, however, define a scene in terms of some primitive geometric objects. We'll exploit the unique properties of these objects in our ray-tracing computations.

As in the modeling program, we may apply affine transformations to scale, position, and rotate these primitives, but we must still perform the basic ray/object intersection calculation for each type of primitive. For any primitive, the method is basically the same no matter what type of affine transform is applied. However, each primitive is processed using the most appropriate method.

Calculating the Ray/Object Intersection

The math for determining the intersection of a ray with a given shape is different for each shape. To simplify the problem, let's represent the equation of the ray in parametric form. The usual equation of a line in three dimensions is of the form:

```
Ax + By + Cz + D = 0
```
                                                    (Equation 11-1)

We make this a parametric equation by introducing a new variable, t, and writing x, y, and z as functions of t:

$$x = x_1 t + x_0 \qquad\qquad \text{(Equation 11-2)}$$

$$y = y_1 t + y_0 \qquad\qquad \text{(Equation 11-3)}$$

$$z = z_1 t + z_0 \qquad\qquad \text{(Equation 11-4)}$$

The coordinates (x_0, y_0, z_0) are those of the starting point of the ray, while the coordinates (x_1, y_1, z_1) represent a unit vector in the direction in which the ray is traveling. One way to interpret the parameter t (and hence the term *parametric representation*) is as *time*. Thus, at zero time, the ray is at its origin. When $t = 1$, the ray is a unit distance away; as time passes, the ray travels further and further along its path.

Sphere Intersections

If the ray intersects an object, there will be a value of t such that the point (x, y, z) of the ray is also a point on the object. Our task is to determine whether or not the ray intersects the object and then find the appropriate value of t. This concept is simplest to understand if we use one of our primitives. The equation of a sphere, centered at $(0, 0, 0)$ and having a radius r, is:

$$x^2 + y^2 + z^2 - r^2 = 0 \qquad\qquad \text{(Equation 11-5)}$$

We now substitute the parametric equations of the ray into this equation (using the same coordinate system, whose origin is the center of the sphere). The result is the following quadratic equation:

$$(x_1{}^2 + y_1{}^2 + z_1{}^2)t^2 + 2(x_0 x_1 + y_0 y_1 + z_0 z_1)t$$
$$+ (x_0{}^2 + y_0{}^2 + z_0{}^2) - 1 = 0 \qquad\qquad \text{(Equation 11-6)}$$

The roots of this equation (in the variable t) are the values of t for which the ray intersects the sphere. Obtaining a straightforward solution of the quadratic equation gives us two roots, the smaller of which represents the nearest intersection.

We'll use this substitution method to determine our object intersections. The equation of the line is substituted in the equation of the object. The resulting equation is then solved in the variable t. If there are no real-valued solutions, the ray doesn't intersect the object; otherwise, we have the value of t that corresponds to an intersection point. We can then use this value in the parametric definition of the line to determine the (x, y, z) coordinates at the point of intersection.

Quadratic Surface Intersections

Consider the intersection of a ray with a quadratic curve. It's similar to the sphere intersection because the sphere is a degenerate case of the general quadratic curve. The most common quadratic shapes are the cone and the cylinder, which can be represented by the following generalized equation:

$$ax^2 + 2bxy + 2cxz + 2dxw + ey^2 + 2fyz$$

$$+ 2gyw + hz^2 + 2izw + jw^2 = 0 \qquad \text{(Equation 11-7)}$$

Although this equation covers every possible kind of quadratic curve, it's too complex for this simple ray-tracing program to handle easily. Fortunately, most of the common quadratic surfaces can be represented by the following simplified equation:

$$Ax^2 + By^2 + Cz^2 + Ey = D \qquad \text{(Equation 11-8)}$$

Using the same technique of substituting the parametric ray equations into the equation of the quadratic and then solving the resulting quadratic equation, we produce one of two equations depending on which parameters are defined. The possible equations are:

$$t^2(Ax_1^2 + By_1^2 + Cz_1^2) + 2t(Ax_0x_1 + By_0y_1 + Cz_0z_1)$$

$$+ (Ax_0^2 + By_0^2 + Cz_0^2 - D) = 0 \qquad \text{(Equation 11-9)}$$

and

$$t^2(Ax_1^2 + Cz_1^2) + 2t(Ax_0x_1 - Ey_1 + Cz_0z_1)$$
$$+ (Ax_0^2 - Ey_0 + Cz_0^2) = 0 \qquad \text{(Equation 11-10)}$$

Again, the solutions to these equations must be real-valued for an intersection to occur. With complex-valued roots (those with a nonzero imaginary component), the ray doesn't intersect the object. We can test for this by looking at the coefficient for which the square root must be calculated. If the coefficient is negative, the root is complex; hence, no object intersection occurs.

Planar Object Intersections

Next, let's consider an intersection of a ray with a ring lying in a plane. The ring has an inner and an outer radius. First, we determine where the ray intersects the plane containing the ring. The equation for a plane is:

$$ax + by + cz + d = 0 \qquad \text{(Equation 11-11)}$$

We substitute the parametric equations of the ray into the equation of the plane, giving:

$$t = \frac{ax_0 + by_0 + cz_0 + d}{ax_1 + by_1 + cz_1 + d} \qquad \text{(Equation 11-12)}$$

This is the general equation, but we may choose a coordinate system centered at the middle of the plane, forcing the parameter d to always be 0. One nice feature of this equation is that the vector (a, b, c) is the surface normal for the plane. Consequently, the equation's denominator is the dot product of the surface normal to the plane and the ray direction; the numerator is the dot product of the surface normal to the plane and the difference between the origin of the plane coordinate system and the origin of the ray.

After substituting the value of *t* from above, we generate a vector from the plane coordinate origin to the point of intersection. As we discussed in Chapter 3, we find the length of this vector by taking the square root of the dot product of the vector with itself. We'll refer to this length as the variable *rad*. If *rad* falls between the values of the inner and outer radii of the ring, the ray intersects the ring.

Parallelogram Intersections

The process of determining the intersection point of the ray with a parallelogram is similar to that for the ring. We first determine whether the ray intersects the plane containing the parallelogram. If so, we determine whether it also intersects the parallelogram (in other words, whether the point of intersection lies within the parallelogram). This is generally more complex than determining the plane intersection point because we must compare the point position with all four sides of the parallelogram.

A result derived from the Jordan curve theorem can simplify this problem somewhat. This method states that if we project a line from the intersection point in an arbitrary direction and the line has an odd number of intersections with the line segments that compose our object (in this case, a parallelogram), the intersection point is inside the object. If the number of intersections is even, the intersection point is outside the object.

To simplify the problem further, we project both the parallelogram and the intersection point onto a plane defined by two axes of the coordinate system. We first decide which of the three coordinate axes should be discarded; it should be the one with the largest value for any of the vertices of the parallelogram. This is the *dominant* axis. We then project the parallelogram and intersection point onto the plane formed by the other two coordinates for each vertex of the parallelogram.

We then compute the location of each vertex in the new system with respect to the parallelogram coordinate system. The first vertex, by definition, is always at (0, 0). Taking into consideration the dominant axis, we compute the coordinates of each vertex in terms of a coordinate system centered at the intersection point. The vertices in the new coordinate system are stored in *(gu[n], gv[n])*, where *n* is the vertex number from 0 to 3. The new coordinate system axes are referred to as *u* and *v* (see Figure 11-3). This means that the refracted ray has angle theta 2 from the surface normal if the ray enters at theta 1. With this knowledge of the angle from the surface normal, the refracted ray vector can be computed. Examine *CalcDirOfRefl* ray and *CalcDirOfTran* ray to see these calculations.

For simplicity, the test ray is here projected along the *u* axis. The function *EvenCrossings* is then used to check the test ray against the line segment between each pair of adjacent vertices. The test ray and the line segment connecting adjacent vertices can intersect only if *gv[i]* and *gv[j]* have opposite signs. (This puts one vertex on one side of the *u* axis and the other on the opposite side, assuring that the *u* axis is crossed.) If both *gu[i]* and *gu[j]* are positive, we know the crossing of the *u* axis is also a crossing of the test ray; therefore, we increment the number of crossings.

If one of the vertex *u* coordinates is positive and the other is negative, we then compute the value of the *u* coordinate for the intersection of the line segment with the *u* axis. If it's positive, we have an intersection with the test ray and therefore increment the number of crossings; if it's negative, no intersection with the test ray has occurred, so the number of crossings is not changed.

After completing the test for all adjacent line-segment pairs, the function returns true if the number of crossings is even (indicating no intersection) and false if not (indicating that the intersection point was inside the object).

We can easily generalize this method to apply to any planar object, such as a triangle, quadrilateral, or polygon.

Once we have determined the intersection point, we must determine where the reflected and/or refracted rays from this surface go (unless the object is a light source, in which case we're finished). Thus, every ray/object intersection generates new rays that go out from the point of intersection and interact with other objects and light sources. The material properties of the surface determine the intensity and color of the reflected rays. For materials such as glass, rays are also generated in the direction in which light would be refracted through the glass. Thus, a single ray may generate two or more new rays (depending on the number of light sources), each of which must be traced through the scene to find the color at the point of intersection. The net pixel color is a weighted sum of the contributions of each ray added to the intrinsic material properties of the object. Reflected rays are computed based on the surface normal of the object at the intersection point. (See Figure 11-4.) Note that the angle of

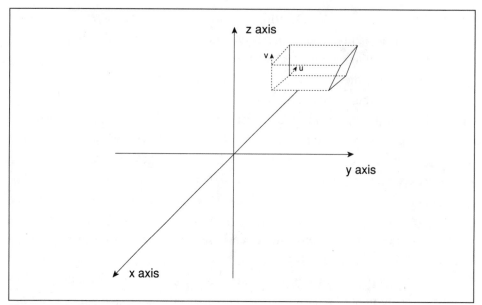

Figure 11-3. Planar Intersection.

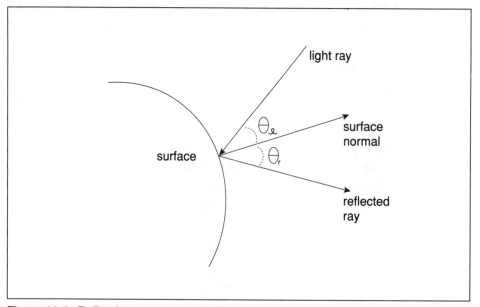

Figure 11-4. Reflection.

reflection (θ_r) is equal to the angle of incidence of the light ray (θ_i). For refracted rays such as rays entering glass, the process is more complex. Light rays refract when they go from a medium of one density like air, to a medium of another density like water. What occurs is that the travelling light changes velocity as it enters the new medium. Snell's Law of Refraction addresses this problem by stating ($n_1 \sin \theta_1 = n_2 \sin \theta_2$). (See Figure 11-5.)

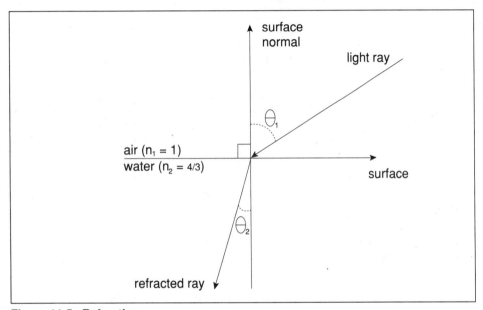

Figure 11-5. Refraction.

The Ray-Tracing Algorithm

We now have methods for determining ray/object intersections for spheres, cylinders, cones, and various planar objects. The basic algorithm is straightforward:

1. For each pixel of the screen, cast a ray into the scene.

2. For each primitive object in the scene, determine whether the ray intersects that object and, if so, where.

3. If the surface is reflective, generate new rays from the object surface based on the surface normal of the object at the point of intersection. If

the surface is refractive, generate new rays according to the physical laws of reflection and refraction.

4. Continue generating rays until no more objects are intersected or you reach a light source.

Generating new rays is similar to the method used to compute the lighting models in Chapter 7. The same laws of reflection apply to the cast rays. Additionally, we're allowing for refraction by materials such as glass to generate new rays that are bent according to the refractive index of the material.

It's important at this point to note several features of the ray-tracing algorithm. First, ray tracing is compute-intensive. Second, the methodology is highly suggestive of object-oriented programming. In other words, the approach is to specify operations on various types of objects and let the programming language handle the mechanics of determining the type of object for each operation. In particular, a separate method is defined for each ray/object intersection calculation as appropriate for a particular type of object. Because our goal was to create code that would work in the most recent versions of C without major modifications, we didn't use the latest object-oriented capabilities of Turbo C++ or Borland C++. If you have one of these compilers, you may want to try modifying the ray-tracing program to work in object-oriented mode. To begin with, however, try running the program in its original state and become familiar with specifying scenes for the ray tracer to translate.

One method used to improve the overall performance of the programs in this book involves *bounding objects*. Each object in the scene may have associated with it a bounding object (like a parallelepiped) containing a more complicated object that may be composed of many primitives. The ray tracer first checks to see if a ray intersects the bounding object. If not, there's no need to test the other objects within the bounding object; otherwise, the ray tracer proceeds as usual and tests the individual objects inside the bounding object. This technique can tremendously accelerate the generation of a complicated scene.

The ray tracer can take other factors into account to reduce the necessary computations. The first is the number of reflections a ray can go through before it is no longer making a significant contribution. As a ray is reflected, it is usually attenuated (reduced in intensity and hence in its contribution to overall color). After several reflections, it is usually too low to contribute significantly to the overall color of the pixel it represents. Thus, you can control how many reflections of a single ray are allowed before the program begins to ignore any additional reflections. The number of levels depends on the nature of the objects in the scene; a scene with many highly reflective objects may need more reflection computations than one with just a few.

Similarly, the ray tracer can reject rays that are too weak to make a significant contribution. For instance, if the ray reflects off a diffuse or poorly lit surface, its intensity will be too low to add significantly to the final color. The ray tracer can therefore stop processing the ray and move on to the next one.

As with the modeler, animations can be created with the ray tracer. By ray-tracing a scene full of objects, storing the image to a file, moving the objects and viewer position, and ray-tracing the new scene (repeating the last three steps for the desired number of frames), you can create animated sequences that look startlingly real.

Having covered the fundamentals of the ray-tracing algorithm, we can move on to Chapter 12 and a detailed description of the ray-tracer code.

Ray Tracing Program

The ray-tracing program, *RAYTRACE.C*, brings together the theory presented in Chapter 11. Formatting constraints of the *.RT* file, used to define the scene in terms of objects and materials; and loading of the *.RT* file and formats for the objects are discussed. When we discuss how the ray tracer produces animation sequences, you'll see the many features of the *.RT* file format and how it can be set up to produce both single-frame images and animation sequences. Finally, we'll discuss how images are written out to disk, both in their preprocessed form (in the *.TMP* file) and in their final *.ANI* or *.RGB* format.

Let's begin by looking at the format of the input script file.

Defining a Scene: The *.RT* File

Before we can begin generating an image, we need to define the scene to be ray-traced. We do this with an *.RT* file. Because it's a text file, you can create one on your text editor as long as it allows ASCII output. The order in which objects and set up parameters are specified, and what constants should appear on each line are constrained.

Once you try out these scenes and get an idea of how they were created, you can create your own scenes made up of the primitive objects defined in the appropriate files. Later in this chapter, you'll see how the ray-tracing program uses this file and what the options are.

Formatting Constraints

The files that appear in Listing 12-2 are text files that are read into the ray-tracing program using C's *fscanf* function in the standard C library. This makes it easy to create and process the files but requires a set arrangement of elements and set positioning of the various elements on a line. The categories that are flush left in the listing are the object definitions that may occur in any order in the file. However, once you have specified one of these objects, like a sphere, certain numerical values or names must occur at the exact positions where they are shown. For instance, for the sphere the first argument is its location. Therefore, location is found on the following line in the .RT file along with three numbers that define its location. The fastest way to see this is to examine a sample file. We'll look at *BOUNCE.RT* here, but the constraints are similar for all files. The parameters are:

STATS. Note that on the following two lines are the parameters *XRES* and *YRES*. When the program reads this file, it takes the eight characters beginning at column 14 of the first line below *STATS* and sets them up as the integer value for *x* resolution. The eight characters beginning at column 14 on the next line will be the integer value of *y* resolution. (The names *XRES* and *YRES* are only there for readability; the ray tracer doesn't interpret them. If you made the second line *XRES*, the output would still be the *YRES* for the output file.) To avoid confusing what parameters and constants go on which lines, use one of the sample files as a template. And be sure to start your inputs at column 14; if you don't, the numbers the program stores won't be the ones you expected.

FRAMES defines the number of animation frames the ray tracer will create. If *NUMBER* equals 1, a single-frame rendering at any SVGA resolution can be created. If *NUMBER* is between 2 and 30 (inclusive), that many frames of 160 x 100 animation will be produced (independent of the *XRES* and *YRES* settings).

ENVIRONMENT uses five weighting factors to determine when a ray is no longer making a significant contribution to the overall light. In addition, a depth factor indicates how many recursions (computations of reflected rays) should take place before the ray is no longer significant. Note that the sample files use the same values for these parameters. Until you've studied the ray-tracing program carefully and understand how these factors interact, it's best to leave them as they are.

LAMPS lets you control the reflectivity of the light sources (a light bulb might reflect an image, for example) and how brightness at a given point is attenuated based on distance from the light source. *REFLAMP* determines whether or not all lamps in the scene can reflect light from other sources. If *REFLAMP* is true, the TDA *LAMPREF* sets the amount of red, green, and blue light that can reflect from the light source. *DISTEFF*, the attenuation factor, allows a light's intensity to decay based on distance from the light source.

OBSERVER's first parameter is the focal length. This value doesn't relate directly to focal length values of real lenses, but the principle is the same. Large focal-length values give telephoto effects with a narrow angular view and much distance compression, while small focal lengths give large angular coverage (the wide-angle effect) and cause considerable distortion. A value of 3.4 is similar to the effect of a lens on a 35mm camera. As the focal length changes, however, so does the coverage, so you may have to move the observer position to compensate. The next parameters are the observer position vector, the observer rotation angle, and the observer tilt angle. All three affect the appearance of the scene.

SKY has two vector parameters, defining the color of the sky at the horizon and at the zenith, and a *CLOUDS* flag. If your scene doesn't include sky, you don't need to worry about this parameter. If you want clouds in the scene, set *CLOUDS* to true.

A *LAMP* parameter is needed for each light source (including the sun or moon if this is an outdoor scene). Its parameters are a vector marking the position of the light source, the radius of the light source, and a color vector indicating the red, green, and blue color components of the light source. A light source is modeled as a colored, spherical bulb placed somewhere in the scene. If *REFLAMP* is true, the bulb itself can reflect rays from other objects in the scene.

A *MATERIAL* parameter is needed for every type of material you plan to define. Its first parameter is any material type name you choose, while the second parameter is one of the following texture names:

SMOOTH
CHECKER
GRIT
MARBLE
WOOD
SHEETROCK
PARTICLE
OCEANWAVES
POOLWAVES
WAVES

The texture name is followed by three vectors defining the colors of the ambient, diffuse, and spectral reflections from the material. Next is the gloss factor (the exponent used in the Phong shading model described for the modeler), followed by special definitions based on the chosen texture. If *CHECKER* is chosen, two color vectors indicating the red, green, and blue color components of the checkerboard tiles are required. A tiling periodicity (individual tile size) is also required. If *OCEANWAVES* is chosen as a texture, the ocean amplitude and phase are required. If we desire *POOLWAVES*, we require not only the pool amplitude and phase but an *(X,Y)* position for the center of the "splash" as well. Finally, if *WAVES* is chosen, the Z position is required in addition to all the parameters for *POOLWAVES*.

The remainder of each file defines the primitive objects that make up the scene. For example, a *SPHERE* object only requires the location of the center of the sphere, its radius, and its material. Most scenes require a ground level for other objects to be placed. *GROUND* requires only a material designation. If you look at the sample files, you'll see the various parameters needed to define the other primitive objects. These parameters are also listed in the following section.

Loading the .*RT* File

To see how an .*RT* file is loaded into the ray tracer, look at the section of the *RAYTRACE* program called "Load an *.*RT* File." It describes the principal function, *GetDataForFrame*. At the beginning of this function are a number of other functions, each of which loads a particular type of data. We'll look at a few of these now and the rest later, when we get into the details of the *GetDataForFrame* function.

The first function is *LoadTDA*, which starts by reading a line from the text file into five string buffers. It creates a vector assigning the last three buffers to the elements of a TDA array after converting them to floating point. This means that the text descriptor beginning at the file line is completely ignored and that the three numbers comprising the vector must be in certain positions in the file.

The next function, *LoadReal*, also reads a line from the text file into a buffer. It then converts the eight characters beginning at position 14 into a real number. The text descriptor is ignored, and the positioning of the numerical data in the file is critical. The next function, *LoadInteger*, also reads a line from the text file into a buffer but then converts the eight characters beginning at position 14 into an integer. Again, the text descriptor is ignored and the positioning of the numerical data in the file is critical. The function *LoadText* also reads a line from the text file into a buffer, then creates a text string from the 30 characters beginning at position 14 of the line. The text descriptor is ignored, and the string data's position in the file is critical.

GetDataForFrame opens the designated data file, then begins a loop that repeats until the end of the file is encountered. On each iteration of the loop, the function reads a line from the file into a buffer. The rest of the loop is a series of *if* statements, one for each type of information that might be encountered in the buffer as a heading for a section of the line.

The first is *STATS*. If this parameter is encountered, the function reads two lines of integers indicating the horizontal and vertical resolution of the desired display. If the buffer contains *FRAMES*, then *NumberOfFrames* holds the number of frames of animation the ray tracer will produce. If the buffer contains *ENVIRONMENT*, the function reads five vectors—*LoclWgt*, *ReflWgt*, *TranWgt*, *MinWgt*, and *MaxWgt*—followed by the integer *MaxDepth*.

If the buffer contains *LAMPS*, the *REFLAMPS* flag is either set (true) or reset (false). If it's set, the lamp reflectivity color vector, *LAMPREF*, is set. The distance-effect variable, *DISTEFF*, is also initialized.

If the buffer contains *OBSERVER*, the function reads the real variable *FocalLength* followed by the vector *ObsPos* and the real-number angles *ObsRotate* and *ObsTilt*. Unlike the modeler, the ray tracer lets us position the observer anywhere in the environment by specifying an *(x, y, z)* position in space, a rotation angle (a compass direction in which the observer is to look), and a tilt angle (look up, down, or level). The function *GetViewDir* uses this information to generate a vector indicating the direction the viewer is looking from wherever it's positioned. From this vector, we can generate the necessary transformations to convert from three dimensions to the two-dimensional screen coordinates.

Returning to the *GetDataForFrame* function, if the buffer contains *SKY*, the color vectors for the horizon and zenith colors are read.

If the buffer contains *MATERIAL*, the function first increments the count of material types. It then loads the appropriate members of the *Matl* array at the new count location; these are the name of the material type and texture, the vectors representing the ambient, diffuse, and specular colors of the material, and the real number representing its gloss power. The function then reads any other variables required when special textures (like the choice of *CHECKER* where tile color vectors and the tile periodicity must also be entered) are selected.

If the buffer contains *GROUND*, *GetDataForFrame* loads the material type for the ground and calls *GetMatlNum*. This function searches the list of materials until it encounters one with the specified name, then assigns its number to the proper member of the ground array. It in turn calls *GetTexNum* to assign a texture number corresponding to the texture specified for the designated material.

If the buffer contains *LAMP*, the function increments the number of lamps and loads the variables needed to define a lamp into the proper members of the lamp array.

For each of the planar object types—*TRIANGLE*, *PARALLELOGRAM*, *CIRCLE*, and *RING*—*GetDataForFrame* increments the number of these objects being loaded and loads the variables needed to define those objects. For any planar object,

276

the surface normal must be generated. We calculate the surface normal here in order to increase the efficiency of the ray tracer. If we didn't calculate the surface normal here a surface normal calculation would have to be made every time that the object is intersected. Thus resulting in as many as a thousand surface normal calculations. This function does that for *TRIANGLE* and *PARALLELOGRAM* by computing the vector cross-product of the two vectors that define the object. For the *CIRCLE* and *RING* objects, it generates two vectors from the object center and computes their cross-product to produce the surface normal. For *PARALLELOGRAM*, *GetDataForFrame* computes and stores the dot product of the surface normal and the location vector (from the origin to the first point). Recall that this value is used in the ray/object intersection calculation for *PARALLELOGRAM*. Finally, *GetDataForFrame* calls *GetMatlNum* and *GetTexNum* to obtain the material and texture numbers.

If the buffer contains *SPHERE*, the function increments the number of spheres and loads the variables needed to define a sphere into the proper members of the sphere array. It then calls *GetMatlNum* and *GetTexNum* to get the material and texture numbers.

The *CONE* and *CYLINDER* objects are actually quadratic surfaces, but entering quadratic coefficients isn't a particularly natural way to specify them. Instead, a cone is specified in terms of the location and radius of its base circle and the location and radius of its apex. A cylinder is almost identical except that an apex circle radius is specified as well. *GetDataForFrame* loads these parameters and automatically computes the coefficients for the quadratic surface equation. It then increments the number of cones (or cylinders), loads the variables needed to define the quadratic into the proper members of the array, and calls *GetMatlNum* and *GetTexNum* to obtain the material and texture numbers.

If the buffer contains *BOX*, the function loads the location vector and the three vectors needed to define the shape and position of the box. It calls *GetMatlNum* and *GetTexNum* to obtain the material and texture numbers, then determines the characteristics of the six parallelograms that define the sides of the box. It performs on each parallelogram the same operations it performs for a single parallelogram.

If the buffer contains *PYRAMID*, the function reads the location vector, the two side vectors, and the height to define the shape and position of the pyramid. It calls *GetMatlNum* and *GetTexNum*, then determines the characteristics of the four triangles that define the sides of the pyramid and the parallelogram that defines the base. It performs the same operations on them as for a single triangle and a single parallelogram.

If the buffer contains *TETRA*, the function reads the location vector, the height, and the radial distance from the center. These are needed to define the shape and position of the tetrahedron. It then calls *GetMatlNum* and *GetTexNum*, determines the characteristics of the four triangles that define the sides of the tetrahedron, and performs the same operations on each that it would ordinarily perform for a single triangle.

If the buffer contains *BOUNDINGSPHERETEST*, then the flag *BoundingSphereTest* is set to true to create a bounding sphere around the object. The ray tracer checks to see if a ray intersects this bounding sphere and, if not, removes the object from further processing for that ray.

If the buffer contains *BOUNDINGPRISMTEST*, *BoundingPrismTest* is set to true. This places a bounding prism around the object. For objects that have one dimension that's much longer or shorter than the other two, the prism test is more efficient. For those that are approximately uniform in shape, the bounding-sphere test is simpler and therefore more efficient.

If the buffer contains *TETRAEXTENTS*, the *TetraExtent1*, *TetraExtent2*, *TetraExtent3*, and *TetraExtent4* TDA typed variables are loaded with the three-dimensional points that bound the object, and *BoundingTetraTest* is set to true. The tetrahedron bounding object is even more efficient than the prism bounding object, but it does require that you calculate the location of the four tetrahedron corners and ensure that the object is entirely contained within this prism. The ray tracing program for tetrahedron-shaped objects generates the bounding prism automatically by looking at the maximum object extent in all three dimensions.

If the buffer contains *ENDFRAME*, the software renders the frame as defined by all the earlier objects and conditions read into the database.

You'll find a list of objects and their structures in Listing 12-1.

```
GROUND
     MATL    =     PLASTICTILE

LAMP
     LOC     =     550.000  -550.000     550.000
     RADIUS  =     100.000
     INTENS  =     0.970    0.970        0.930

TRIANGLE
     LOC     =     -108.000    -108.000     0.000
     V1      =     27.000      0.000       0.000
     V2      =     0.000       27.000      0.000
     MATL    =     MOUNTAINGRAY

PARALLELOGRAM
     LOC     =     -150.000    280.000  130.000
     V1      =     300.000     0.000    0.000
     V2      =     0.000       0.000    150.000
     MATL    =     MIRROR

CIRCLE
     LOC     =     0.000    -130.000    75.000
     V1      =     1.000    0.000       0.000
     V2      =     0.000    0.000       1.000
     RADIUS  =     20.000
     MATL    =     STEEL

RING
     LOC     =     -70.000 0.000    105.000
     V1      =     0.000   1.000    0.000
     V2      =     -0.325  0.000    0.946
     RAD1    =     15.000
     RAD2    =     20.000
     MATL    =     CANNONBLACK

SPHERE
     LOC     =     0.000    -98.000 110.000
     RADIUS  =     5.000
     MATL    =     STEEL
```

```
CONE
        BASELOC     =    0.000    -130.000    75.000
        BASERAD     =    20.000
        APEXLOC     =    0.000     130.000    75.000
        APEXRAD     =    1.000
        MATL        =    STEEL

CYLINDER
        BASELOC     =    0.000    -130.000    75.000
        RADIUS      =    20.000
        APEXLOC     =    0.000     130.000    75.000
        MATL        =    STEEL

    BOX
        LOC         =    -125.000   -75.000  0.000
        V1          =    250.000     0.000   0.000
        V2          =    0.000     150.000   0.000
        V3          =    0.000       0.000  80.000
        MATL        =    ITALIANMARBLE

    PYRAMID
        LOC         =    0.000     0.000    0.000
        V1          =    400.000   0.000    0.000
        V2          =    0.000     400.000  0.000
        HEIGHT      =    200.000
        MATL        =    SANDBLOCK

    TETRA
        LOC         =    0.000     0.000    0.000
        HEIGHT      =    200.000
        RADIAL      =    130.000
        MATL        =    SANDBLOCK
```

Listing 12-1. Objects available to the ray tracer.

The Ray-Tracing Program

The ray-tracing program, *RAYTRACE.EXE*, is produced from the source file *RAYTRACE.C* (Listing 12-2). It reads in one of the scene description (*.RT*) files and uses it to produce an *.RGB* or *.TMP* file containing color information for the pixels comprising the picture.

While the image is being rendered, a monochrome version of the image is simultaneously generated on the screen display. This gives you an idea of how the full-color display will look; that way, if there are problems with your scene description, you can make the necessary modifications without running *DISP.EXE* (produced from the source file *DISP.C* and used for single-frame renderings) or *PROCESS.EXE* (produced from *PROCESS.C* and used for animation) to see what the finished image will look like.

Single-frame renderings output to *.RGB* files may be displayed using the *DISPRGB.C* program described in Chapter 16. This program lets you see the image detail and resolution the ray tracer can produce.

The *PROCESS.C* program, also described in Chapter 16, transforms the detailed color information in the *.TMP* file to produce a full-color animation-sequence file. You can then use the animation program to display the sequences on your screen. These sequences offer some of the best examples of how the ray tracer models the complex interaction of light, shadow, and interobject reflections and refraction. The animation program is discussed in detail in Chapters 14 and 15.

Constants and Variables

The most direct way to see how the ray-tracing program works is to start near the end of the program listing, where the main program begins. First, however, let's take a quick look at some of the constants and variables defined at the beginning of the program.

The first of these is *LampReflects*. This Boolean variable indicates whether or not the lamps in the program will reflect light. If the light source is supposed to be the sun, it's obviously far too bright to reflect any other light sources; in this case, you would set *LampReflects* to false. Less intense light sources, like some street lamps, could possibly reflect part of the light cast on them, so you would set the variable to true. If *LampReflects* is true, the TDA *LampRefl* contains the red, green, and blue percentages of light this light source can reflect.

The next variable is *DistEffect*, the fractional effect of distance on lamp intensity. The further away the light source is from the object surface, the less intense the light will be. This variable lets you control how quickly the light intensity is reduced as a function of distance from the source. Increasing the value makes the light source appear brighter, while decreasing the value dims the light source.

DistEffect is followed by two real numbers, *XAspDivFocLen* and *YAspDivFocLen*. These parameters determine the coverage of the scene area and are essentially the inverse of the focal length: the larger the focal-length values, the more restricted the area covered by the "camera lens"; the larger the values for these parameters, the larger the area covered and thus the smaller the focal length. Unlike the focal length of a lens, however, these parameters can be set separately for the *x* and *y* directions (from within the code), thereby permitting selective distortions of the scene that would be difficult with real lenses.

The next parameters determine the weighting of the color components for a particular scene. These are *LoclWgt*, the weighting of the object color component; *ReflWgt*, the weighting of the reflected color component; *TranWgt*, the weighting of the transmitted (refracted) color component; *MinWgt*, the minimum weighting of colors in the scene; and *MaxWgt*, the maximum weighting of colors in the scene. Each is a vector having values for the red, green, and blue components. We also have the integer variable *MaxDepth*, which is the maximum depth of the scene. The color at the output pixel is determined by a weighted sum of the contributions from each ray and from the surface itself. These coefficients determine the relative contributions of each type of ray.

Next, the focal length and viewer position are defined. The geometry for ray tracing is the same as for solid modeling: the variable *ObsPos* is the observer position (a three-dimensional vector), while *ObsRotate* (the observer rotate angle) and *ObsTilt* (the observer tilt angle) are *ViewTheta* and *ViewPhi,* respectively. From these we can compute the variable *ViewDir* (the viewer direction from the origin) as well as *ViewU* and *ViewV* (the transformations from the scene coordinate system to a viewer-centered system).

The sky colorings are defined next. These are *HorCol* (the color of the sky at the horizon) and *ZenCol* (the color of the sky at the zenith). Clouds can be turned on by setting the *CLOUDS* flag to *True*. The program then sets up variables for tiling with a checkerboard pattern. These are *TILE1* and *TILE2* (the two checkerboard colors) and *TILE*, the size of the side of the checkerboard square. Other variables for wave texturing are also found here, as are the wave amplitudes and phases and the two- and three-dimensional positions from which the waves start.

Next, the program sets up a maximum value of 20 for the number of types of material that may be defined and then defines the variables that make up a material type, the name of its texture type, the ambient, diffuse, and reflected color values, and the gloss factor. Attenuation of the light through the object and the materials index of refraction are also found here. The program then creates an array of these material records.

Next, the maximum number of textures is set to 10. These textures are *SMOOTH*, *CHECKER*, *GRIT*, *MARBLE*, *WOOD*, *SHEETROCK*, *PARTICLE*, *OCEANWAVES*, *POOLWAVES*, and *WAVES*. The program establishes the number of primitive shapes as eight plus the ground; these shapes are *LAMP*, *TRIANGLE*, *PARALLELO-GRAM*, *CIRCLES*, *RING*, *SPHERE*, *CONE*, *CYLINDER*, and *GROUND*.

The maximum value for each shape is then specified. Only one ground is possible, but there can be 10 lamps, 512 triangles, 50 parallelograms, 50 circles, 50 rings, 256 spheres, 50 cones, and 50 cylinders.

Next, the parameters associated with each primitive object are defined. These include its position, vectors defining its extent and orientation, radii (if appropriate), intensity (for lamps), surface normal, material, texture, dot product of the surface normal and location vector (precalculated here to accelerate ray/object intersection computations), and any other parameters needed to define the object and compute its intersections with light rays. The program then sets up an array containing all the primitive objects that may be defined. Finally, the program defines the *.RT* disk file containing the scene definition data.

The Main Program

Now we're ready to deal with the relatively simple main program, which begins by calling *InitNoise*. This function sets up the noise function that will be used to create wood and marble textures and texture our sky with clouds. It then calls *ClearMemory* to initialize the program parameters. This function simply zeros out the variables and arrays described earlier. The data for the arrays is allocated using the *Allocate_Memory* function.

It then calls *InitLineBuffer*, which initializes a buffer to store the red, green, and blue components for all the pixels in a given scan line. As each scan line is rendered, it's written to the disk as one line of an *.RGB* single-frame rendering file.

Next, *GetSceneFile* is called to display "Enter File Name =>" and read the *.RT* file name the user types in. If the user simply pressed Return, the program uses the file *BOUNCE.RT* by default. (Note that the file name should be entered without the *.RT* extension.) The resulting file name is stored and used throughout the program.

ClearScreen is called next. It calls *Set_Graphics_Mode* to prepare for graphics display at whatever resolution has been selected for this run of the program, then calls *Init_Palette* and *Set_Palette* to set up the SVGA color registers for the gray-scale display.

Next, the program calls *GetDataForFrame*, passing the designated file name as a parameter. This function loads all the data from the selected scene data file into the program. Based on the value of *NumberOfFrames*, either a single-frame rendering (in which an *.RGB* file is created) or a *.TMP* file (creating animation screens) will result. In either case, *InitBoundingObjects* is called to sort through the objects in the scene and create a larger bounding object to contain all the objects. *PreCalculation* is called to initialize variables related to projection, such as the aspect ratio.

If only one frame is to be scanned, the ray tracer renders the image once to produce an *.RGB* file; otherwise, it processes *NumberOfFrames* frames to produce an animation *.TMP* file. The *.RGB* file can be displayed with *DISPRGB.C*, while the *.TMP* file must be processed by *PROCESS.C* to produce an *.ANI* file of screens with the appropriate colors for animation. The *.ANI* file may then be displayed using the *ANIMATE.C* program found in Chapter 15.

Finally, the ray tracer calls the function *Exit_Graphics* to exit from graphics mode, and the program terminates.

Initializing the Noise Function

The texture functions use a technique known as *color modulation* to create their effects. Basically, they modify the color at a point on the surface by *perturbing*, or slightly altering, its value using some well-defined function. To speed up the computation, we'll define our function using lookup tables that are indexed according to the position on the surface.

The textures the ray tracer uses correspond to a simple class of functions known as *noise* functions. Essentially, these are random over the surface but are repeatable and have some desirable characteristics. The technique used here follows that described by Alan Watt in his book *Fundamentals of Three-Dimensional Computer Graphics* (Addison-Wesley, 1989).

We'll begin with a 28 x 28 x 28 matrix. The function uses three nested *for* loops to fill every member of this array with a random number between 0 and 12,000. This is all taken care of in the first statement of the innermost loop. The remainder of the function is designed so that whenever one of the three indices of the matrix reaches its maximum value, the matrix element is filled with the number contained in the corresponding matrix element where the index value is zero. This assures that the beginning and end of the array are the same (the function is now repeatable or cyclical), thus enabling us to cycle without any undue effects.

The array is now initialized. You'll see how to use it in the section "Creating a Textured Surface" later in this chapter.

Scanning the Scene

The function *Scan*, which scans the pixel display, begins by calling *PreCalculation*. This function sets up variables that relate to the projection of the image onto the screen and define the *ViewVec* viewing vector. *ViewVec* is used to send out the initial eye-ray from the viewer position, through the given pixel on the screen, and into the scene. It points the observer's eye to the center of the screen, which is computed in this routine to yield *CentreX* and *CentreY*.

PreCalculation also handles aspect correction; this is necessary because the horizontal and vertical pixel dimensions are the same in the high-resolution mode but not in the low-resolution mode. Thus, if we have specified the correct picture proportions for the high-resolution mode, one of the dimensions must be scaled for the picture to have the same proportions in a lower resolution. The program then computes the scaling factors *XAspDivFocLen* and *YAspDivFocLen*, which provide the appropriate correction factors.

Scan's next task is to open and prepare to write the designated output file. The function starts two nested *for* loops that iterate once for each pixel location on the display screen. On each iteration the function calls *GetInitialDir*, which performs the necessary mathematical operations to compute a normalized vector, *InitialDir*. This vector points from the observer to the screen pixel being processed.

The *Scan* function now calls *TraceRay* to project this vector into the scene until it intersects an object. *TraceRay* returns the resulting color for the pixel. The returned color is either 0 or 1 and is scaled to the range 0 to 63, making it suitable for storage in the output file. To produce the monochrome screen display, the function averages the red, green, and blue color values and plots this average intensity on the screen.

When the loops are completed and every pixel has been processed, we have a complete gray-scale image of the scene on the screen and a complete file of color data on disk. If we're producing an animation sequence, the rendering process is repeated for each frame to produce a *.TMP* file containing color data for every frame of the animation.

Tracing the Ray

TraceRay performs the actual chore of tracing from the observer to the objects in the scene. It begins by calling the function *ShootRay*, which uses two nested *for* loops to examine every type of shape and every object of every type in the database. For each object, it calls *Intersect* to determine the distance at which the current ray from the observer intersects the object. We must find the nearest object the ray strikes, so for each object we compute the distance from the eye to the intersection point. If this distance is less than the last object the ray intersected (or is the first object to be intersected), this object is saved for processing. If the distance is greater, we continue processing objects until the nearest object is found.

Note that bounding objects can be placed around the objects in the scene to increase rendering speed. Three objects can be used as bounding objects: the *BoundingSphere*, the *BoundingPrism*, and the *BoundingTetra*. Bounding objects are processed like ordinary objects. If the ray intersects the bounding object, we check the objects inside the bounding object for intersection. If our *BoundingSphere*, for instance, bounds 1,000 triangles, imagine the increase in rendering speed!

Where the *BoundingSphere* is simply a single sphere around all the objects, the *BoundingPrism* is a rectangular prism similar to a box. Intersection tests are performed on all six sides of the box, but this is still faster than doing 1,000 intersection tests for 1,000 triangles for every pixel of the screen instead of just the pixels that would intersect the *BoundingPrism*.

The *BoundingTetra* is a tetrahedron used to bound the recursive tetrahedron objects generated by *TETRA.C* and *TETSPHR2.C* (described in Chapter 13). Note that the corners of the tetrahedron must be defined. *TETRA.C* is a good example of how a bounding tetrahedron is generated for an object. Again, although the four triangles that make up the tetrahedron must be tested, it's still much faster than testing 1,000 triangles for every screen pixel.

As mentioned earlier, *Intersect* incorporates a bounding-object scheme to improve performance. Let's see what really happens to each of the objects in *Intersect*. Essentially, a switch statement tests the ray against each type of object *Intersect* supports. As you recall, we run through all objects in the scene to see if the ray intersects the object. *Intersect* takes the definition of the ray and tests to see where the intersection occurs, if at all.

At some point in our computations, we need to determine exactly where the ray intersects an object's surface. (Refer to Chapter 11 for details on the mathematics of ray/object intersections.) *Intersect* returns the distance at which the ray intercepts the designated object, then *ShootRay* completes the loops by identifying the object intersected and the distance to it from the ray origin. This information is returned to *TraceRay*.

If no intersection with an object occurred, *Sky* is called. This function interpolates the horizon and zenith sky colors as appropriate for the position in the sky toward which the ray is pointing, then returns the proper color. Clouds are created using the noise function used to create wood and marble textures. If the ray did intersect an object, the function *GetIntrPt* is called to establish the coordinates of the point of intersection using the method described in Chapter 11.

Once the intersection point is determined, we need to get (or compute) the surface normal at the point of intersection. This vector will be used in color calculations and to generate the reflected and transmitted rays from the object

surface. The function *GetSrfNrm* is called to determine the surface normal vector. The mathematics for obtaining the surface normal differ for each object; to see what's involved, study the function in the listing. (See Figure 12-2.) For instance, a sphere's surface normal at the intersection point is the normalized vector from the sphere center to that intersection point.

Determining the Color

The next thing *TraceRay* does is call the function *GetLoclCol*, which returns the local color of the object at the point of intersection. At this point, the function calls are rather convoluted; you'll need to trace carefully through the listing to understand all the necessary interactions.

GetLoclCol begins by seeing if the object intersected by the ray is a lamp. If so, we don't need to go any further. The color is set to that of the lamp, with its intensity decreased by the square root of the distance from the lamp to the viewer and by the cosine of the angle between the lamp to the viewer direction and the surface normal to the lamp surface. This calculation decreases the intensity of the lamp based on your distance from the lamp.

If the object intersected by the light ray isn't a lamp, the function enters a *case* statement by calling *MaterialNumbs* to determine the material code for the intersected surface. The contribution of ambient light to the total light vector is determined from the appropriate material properties. The *GetLoclCol* function then enters a *for* loop that iterates once for each lamp (light source) in the scene, thereby determining the contributions of all the light sources to the lighting on the object where the light ray intersects it. On each iteration of the loop, a new light ray is created from the point of intersection on the object surface toward the lamp being processed.

For each lamp, *GetLoclCol* calls *ShootRay* to determine the closest object hit by the ray from the intersection point to the lamp. If it intersects an object other than the lamp itself, the initial intersection is shadowed from this light source; therefore, it doesn't contribute to the color vector. If the new light ray doesn't intersect with anything or if it intersects with the lamp itself, there is a color contribution from this light source. In this case, the function determines that we have an *unshadowed surface*.

We now add the lamp's contribution using the ambient, diffuse, and specular components, just as we did in the modeler. The total color vector now has the diffuse and specular contributions. If the texture of the object first intersected is smooth, we have determined the total color vector and return to *TraceRay*. If the surface is textured, we call *Texture* to perturb the color that we obtained from the ambient diffuse and specular calculations thus far determined. This determines how the object itself and the lamp contribute to the color at the surface.

Creating a Textured Surface

The function *Texture* modifies the color for each point on a surface to give the appearance of one of the defined textures. The function consists of a *case* statement that permits the proper operations to be performed for the defined texture. The first case is *CHECKER*, which produces a checkerboard pattern. For this case, *Texture* processes the intersection point to determine which colored square of the checkerboard it falls within and returns the proper color. That color will be used to modify the local color information and obtain the final pixel color.

The next case is *Grit*, which produces a slightly varied color over the surface (similar to that of a grassy surface or dirt). All that happens here is that a random number between 0.8 and 1.0 is selected and used to multiply each component of the total color vector.

To obtain a marble texture, we call *MarbleTex*. This function first separates the point-of-intersection vector into its three components (x, y, and z). It then calls the noise function using the values $0.2x$, $0.1y$, and $0.1z$. The noise function takes the real-valued arguments and uses them to interpolate values from the previously generated noise matrix. The integer portion of the passed arguments index into the noise table. The function then uses the fractional components to determine how to weight the values from adjacent corners of the matrix. By building a noise matrix, the function will automatically wrap around the noise matrix elements % modular operator if the arguments are larger than the matrix size. The returned noise value is modified and used to create a vector (having the same value for each of its three components) that multiplies the results of the local color value containing the ambient, diffuse, and specular calculations.

The next case is *Wood*. To obtain this texture, we call the function *WoodTex*; it's the same as the function for marble except that the contribution of the noise is only one-third of that for marble.

The next case is *Sheetrock*, which is the same as *Grit* except that the random scalar is set to between 0.9 and 1.0 instead of 0.8 and 1.0.

The next case, *Particle*, is also the same as *Grit* except that the random scalar is set to between 0.85 and 1.0 and the red, green, and blue components of the color vector are independently colored.

OceanWaves, *PoolWaves*, and *Waves* all fall into another classification of texturing called *bump mapping* or *bump texturing*. Here, we perturb (or "bump") the surface normal for the object at the intersection point instead of simply changing the color. If the surface normal perturbation is based on some mathematical equation that relates to the three-dimensional position where the equation starts, we can create realistic water waves and other phenomena. *OceanWaves* produces realistic ocean waves given just an amplitude and a phase. By changing the phase from frame to frame, we create a windswept ocean. *PoolWaves* produces a water-droplet effect using amplitude, phase, and a two-dimensional location where the imaginary ball bearing was dropped into the water. Finally, *Waves* produces a three-dimensional wave texture (seen in Chapter 13's *WAVYORB.C*) specified with amplitude, phase, and a three-dimensional starting point for the wave. This type of texturing requires the surface normal, so it's processed in the *TraceRay* procedure.

Completing the Ray Trace

We're now back in the *TraceRay* function with a color for the pixel. If we've reached the maximum depth of recursion (explained in a moment) or the weighting of the color on this pass is insignificant, we accept the current pixel color and terminate the function.

Otherwise, if the object material has a specular reflection capability, the function calls *CalcDirOfReflRay* to determine the direction of a ray from the intersection point of the original ray and the object. If the object material has a transmission capability, like glass, the function calls *CalcDirOfTranRay*, which determines the direction of a ray from the intersection point of the original ray into the object. The

direction of this ray is based on the index of refraction of the surface as well as the surface normal at the intersection point.

The weight of the reflected ray's contribution to color is then computed, and *TraceRay* is called recursively (with the depth increased by 1) to determine that color contribution. Similarly, we determine the color contribution of the transmitted ray by tracing it through the scene. This is why a ray-tracing program is fundamentally recursive: each newly generated ray is traced just like the ones originating from the viewer position until the number of reflections exceeds the maximum depth factor or the rays intersect a light source. The reason for having a depth parameter is that we don't want the recursive process to go on forever; thus, when the depth reaches the maximum depth (usually 5), the recursion ceases.

Next, *Comb* is called to combine all the color contributions into a single, final color vector. *TraceRay* is now completed, and we return either one level higher in the recursion or, if we're at the top of the recursive stack, to *Scan*.

```
/*
    ┌─────────────────────────────────────────────────────────────────┐
    │  ┌───────────────────────────────────────────────────────────┐  │
    │  │              Recursive Ray Tracing Program                │  │
    │  │          Renders Reflective And Transmissive Objects      │  │
    │  │   Uses Spheres, Prisms and Tetrahedrons for Bounding Objects │  │
    │  │                                                           │  │
    │  │          Creates 160x100 16-bit Animation Sequences       │  │
    │  │            (c) 1990, 1991, 1992 Christopher D. Watkins     │  │
    │  │                 'C' conversion by Larry Sharp              │  │
    │  └───────────────────────────────────────────────────────────┘  │
    └─────────────────────────────────────────────────────────────────┘
*/

#include "stdio.h"
#include "stdlib.h"
#include "dos.h"
#include "conio.h"
#include "malloc.h"
#include "mem.h"
#include "math.h"
#include "string.h"
#include "defs.h"
#include "globals.h"
#include "mathb.h"
#include "graphb.h"


/*
    ┌─────────────────────────────────────────────────────────────────┐
    │  ┌───────────────────────────────────────────────────────────┐  │
    │  │              Declare Constants and Variables              │  │
    │  └───────────────────────────────────────────────────────────┘  │
    └─────────────────────────────────────────────────────────────────┘
*/

typedef char Name[32];

Word ScanXRes;                    /* Stats */
Word ScanYRes;
float XAspDivFocLen;
float YAspDivFocLen;
Word Xo, Yo;
Word CenterX, CenterY;
TDA ViewVec;

Byte NumberOfFrames;
```

```
TDA LoclWgt;                    /* Environment */
TDA ReflWgt;
TDA TranWgt;
TDA MinWgt;
TDA MaxWgt;
Byte MaxDepth;

Boolean LampReflects;           /* Lamps */
TDA LampRefl;
float DistEffect;

float FocalLength;              /* Observer */
TDA ObsPos;
float ObsRotate;
float ObsTilt;
TDA ViewDir;
TDA ViewU, ViewV;

TDA HorCol;     /* Sky Horizon to Zenith Coloration */
TDA ZenCol;
Boolean Clouds;
Boolean SkyExists;

TDA Tile1;      /* Checkerboard tiling coloration */
TDA Tile2;
float Tile;

float OceanWaveAmpl;
float OceanWavePhase;

float PoolWaveAmpl;
float PoolWavePhase;
float PoolWaveXPos;
float PoolWaveYPos;

float WaveAmpl;
float WavePhase;
float WaveXPos;
float WaveYPos;
float WaveZPos;

Boolean GroundExists;
```

```
TDA TetraExtent1;
TDA TetraExtent2;
TDA TetraExtent3;
TDA TetraExtent4;

Boolean BoundingSphereTest;
Boolean BoundingPrismTest;
Boolean BoundingTetraTest;

#define MaxMaterial 20            /* Maximum Types of Materials */

typedef struct {
   Name MType;
   Name Textur;
   TDA   AmbRfl;
   TDA   DifRfl;
   TDA   SpcRfl;
   float Gloss;
   TDA Trans;
   float Index;
} MaterialList;

static MaterialList far *Matl;

#define MaxTexture 10     /* Maximum Number of Textures */

#define Smooth     1     /* Texture Number */
#define Checker    2
#define Grit       3
#define Marble     4
#define Wood       5
#define Sheetrock  6
#define Particle   7
#define OceanWaves 8
#define PoolWaves  9
#define Waves      10

#define MaxShapeType 8    /* Maximum Number of Shape Types */

#define Ground 0          /* Ground is Shape Type 0 - a high speed calc */

#define Lamp       1  /* Shape Type Number */
#define Triangle   2
```

```
#define Parallelogram 3
#define Circles    4
#define Ring       5
#define Sphere     6
#define Cone       7
#define Cylinder   8


#define MaxLamp       10
#define MaxTriangle   512 /* Max Count of Objects for any one Shape Type */
#define MaxParallelogram  50
#define MaxCircles        50
#define MaxRing           50
#define MaxSphere         256
#define MaxCone           50
#define MaxCylinder       50

typedef struct {
   Byte MtlNum;
   Byte TexNum;
} GroundList;

typedef struct {
   TDA Loc;
   float Rad;
   float RadSqr;
   TDA Intens;
} LampList;

typedef struct {
   TDA Loc;
   TDA v1;
   TDA v2;
   TDA Norm;
   float NdotLoc;
   Byte MtlNum;
   Byte TexNum;
} TriangleList;

typedef struct {
   TDA Loc;
   TDA v1;
   TDA v2;
   TDA Norm;
```

```
        float NdotLoc;
        Byte MtlNum;
        Byte TexNum;
    }  ParallelogramList;

    typedef struct {
        TDA Loc;
        TDA v1;
        TDA v2;
        TDA Norm;
        float NdotLoc;
        float Radius;
        Byte MtlNum;
        Byte TexNum;
    }   CircleList;

    typedef struct {
        TDA Loc;
        TDA v1;
        TDA v2;
        TDA Norm;
        float NdotLoc;
        float Rad1;
        float Rad2;
        Byte MtlNum;
        Byte TexNum;
    }   RingList;

    typedef struct {
            TDA Loc;                        /* special case quadratic */
        float Rad;
        float RadSqr;
        Byte MtlNum;
        Byte TexNum;
    } SphereList;

    typedef struct {
        TDA BaseLoc;
        float BaseRad;
        float BaseD;
        TDA ApexLoc;
        float ApexRad;
            TDA U, V, W;                    /* vector along cone axis */
```

```
   float Height;
   float Slope;
   float MinD;
   float MaxD;
    Boolean InSNrm;                   /* inward facing surface normal */
   Byte MtlNum;
   Byte TexNum;
} QuadraticList;
typedef QuadraticList ConeList;
typedef QuadraticList CylinderList;
int ObjCnt[MaxShapeType+1];
GroundList Gnd;
static LampList far *Lmp;
static TriangleList far *Tri;
static ParallelogramList far *Para;
static CircleList far *Cir;
static RingList far *Rng;
static SphereList far *Sphr;
static ConeList far *Con;
static CylinderList far *Cyl;

FILE *DiskFile;
FILE *TextDiskFile;

/*
```

```
┌──────────────────────────────────────────────────────────────┐
│                                                                │
│        Pixel Buffer for a 160 x 100 Frame of Animation         │
│                                                                │
└──────────────────────────────────────────────────────────────┘
```

```
 */
   static Byte far *Red_Plane;              /* Red Components of Pixels */
   static Byte far *Green_Plane;            /* Green Components of Pixels
*/      static Byte far *Blue_Plane;          /* Blue Components of Pixels
*/

#define xy (yc*160)+xc

void PutGrayScalePixel(Word xc, Word yc, TDIA Intens)
{
   Byte Col;

Red_Plane[xy]=(Intens[0]&255)>>2;
Green_Plane[xy]=(Intens[1]&255)>>2;
Blue_Plane[xy]=(Intens[2]&255)>>2;
Col=((Intens[0]+Intens[1]+Intens[2])/3)>>2;
```

```
    Plot(xc, yc, Col);
    }

    void GrayScalePixel(Word xc, Word yc, TDIA Intens) {
      Byte Col;

    Col=((Intens[0]+Intens[1]+Intens[2])/3)>>2;

    Plot(xc, yc, Col);

    }

    void Clear_Planes()
    {
      _fmemset(Red_Plane, 0, 16000);
      _fmemset(Green_Plane, 0, 16000);
      _fmemset(Blue_Plane, 0, 16000);
    }

    /*
```

```
    ┌──────────────────────────────────────────────────┐
    │                                                    │
    │               Clear all Variables                  │
    │                                                    │
    │        ClearMemory - clear all variables           │
    │                                                    │
    └──────────────────────────────────────────────────┘
```

```
    */

    void ClearQuadratic(QuadraticList *List)
    {
      VecNull(List->BaseLoc);
      List->BaseRad=0.0;
      List->BaseD=0.0;
      VecNull(List->ApexLoc);
      List->ApexRad=0.0;
      VecNull(List->U);
      VecNull(List->V);
      VecNull(List->W);
      List->Height=0.0;
      List->Slope=0.0;
      List->MinD=0.0;
      List->MaxD=0.0;
      List->InSNrm=false;
      List->MtlNum=0;
```

```
      List->TexNum=0;
   }

   void ClearMemory()
   {
      int i;

      VecNull(LoclWgt);
      VecNull(ReflWgt);
      VecNull(TranWgt);
      VecNull(MinWgt);
      VecNull(MaxWgt);
      MaxDepth=0;
      LampReflects=false;        /* will the surface of a lamp reflect light? */
VecNull(LampRefl);             /* percentage of light a lamp reflects */
      DistEffect=0.0;           /* percentage of distance effect on lamp */
FocalLength=0.0;
      VecNull(ObsPos);
      ObsRotate=0.0;
      ObsTilt=0.0;
      VecNull(ViewDir);
      VecNull(ViewU);
      VecNull(ViewV);
      VecNull(HorCol);
      VecNull(ZenCol);
      Clouds=false;
      SkyExists=false;
      VecNull(Tile1);
      VecNull(Tile2);
      Tile=0.0;
      OceanWaveAmpl=0.0;
      OceanWavePhase=0.0;
      PoolWaveAmpl=0.0;
      PoolWavePhase=0.0;
      PoolWaveXPos=0.0;
      PoolWaveYPos=0.0;
      WaveAmpl=0.0;
      WavePhase=0.0;
      WaveXPos=0.0;
      WaveYPos=0.0;
      WaveZPos=0.0;
      GroundExists=false;
      VecNull(TetraExtent1);
      VecNull(TetraExtent2);
```

```
VecNull(TetraExtent3);
VecNull(TetraExtent4);
BoundingSphereTest=false;
BoundingPrismTest=false;
BoundingTetraTest=false;
for(i=0; i<=MaxMaterial; i++)
{
   strcpy(Matl[i].MType, "");
   strcpy(Matl[i].Textur, "");
   VecNull(Matl[i].AmbRfl);
   VecNull(Matl[i].DifRfl);
   VecNull(Matl[i].SpcRfl);
   Matl[i].Gloss=0.0;
   VecNull(Matl[i].Trans);
   Matl[i].Index=0.0;
}
for(i=0; i<=MaxShapeType; i++)
   ObjCnt[i]=0;
Gnd.MtlNum=0;
Gnd.TexNum=0;
for(i=0; i<=MaxLamp; i++)
{
   VecNull(Lmp[i].Loc);
   Lmp[i].Rad=0.0;
   Lmp[i].RadSqr=0.0;
   VecNull(Lmp[i].Intens);
}
for(i=0; i<=MaxTriangle; i++)
{
   VecNull(Tri[i].Loc);
   VecNull(Tri[i].v1);
   VecNull(Tri[i].v2);
   VecNull(Tri[i].Norm);
   Tri[i].NdotLoc=0.0;
   Tri[i].MtlNum=0;
   Tri[i].TexNum=0;
}
                  for(i=0; i<=MaxParallelogram; i++)
   {
VecNull(Para[i].Loc);
VecNull(Para[i].v1);
VecNull(Para[i].v2);
VecNull(Para[i].Norm);
Para[i].NdotLoc=0.0;
```

```
Para[i].MtlNum=0;
Para[i].TexNum=0;
   }
   for(i=0; i<=MaxCircles; i++)
   {
VecNull(Cir[i].Loc);
VecNull(Cir[i].v1);
VecNull(Cir[i].v2);
VecNull(Cir[i].Norm);
Cir[i].NdotLoc=0.0;
Cir[i].Radius=0.0;
Cir[i].MtlNum=0;
           Cir[i].TexNum=0;
   }
   for(i=0; i<=MaxRing; i++)
   {
VecNull(Rng[i].Loc);
VecNull(Rng[i].v1);
VecNull(Rng[i].v2);
VecNull(Rng[i].Norm);
Rng[i].NdotLoc=0.0;
Rng[i].Rad1=0.0;
           Rng[i].Rad2=0.0;
           Rng[i].MtlNum=0;
           Rng[i].TexNum=0;
   }
   for(i=0; i<=MaxSphere; i++)
   {
VecNull(Sphr[i].Loc);
Sphr[i].Rad=0.0;
Sphr[i].RadSqr=0.0;
Sphr[i].MtlNum=0;
Sphr[i].TexNum=0;
   }
for(i=0; i<=MaxCone; i++)
   ClearQuadratic(&Con[i]);
for(i=0; i<=MaxCylinder; i++)
   ClearQuadratic(&Cyl[i]);
}

/*
```

```
┌─────────────────────────────────────────────────────┐
│                  Load an *.RT File                    │
└─────────────────────────────────────────────────────┘
```

```
*/
```

```
char Buf1[256], Buf2[256], Buf3[256], Buf4[256], Buf5[256];
int dummy;
Name MtlName;
FILE *InFile;

void Clear_Buffers()
{
  strset(Buf1, 0);
  strset(Buf2, 0);
  strset(Buf3, 0);
  strset(Buf4, 0);
  strset(Buf5, 0);
}

void LoadTDA(TDA A)
{
  Clear_Buffers();
    fscanf(InFile, "%s %s %s %s %s", Buf1, Buf2, Buf3, Buf4, Buf5);
  A[0]=atof(Buf3);
  A[1]=atof(Buf4);
  A[2]=atof(Buf5);
}

void LoadReal(float *a)
{
  Clear_Buffers();
  fscanf(InFile, "%s %s %s", Buf1, Buf2, Buf3);
  *a=atof(Buf3);
}

void LoadInteger(int *a)
{
  Clear_Buffers();
  fscanf(InFile, "%s %s %s", Buf1, Buf2, Buf3);
  *a=atoi(Buf3);
}

void LoadWord(Word *a)
{
  Clear_Buffers();
  fscanf(InFile, "%s %s %s", Buf1, Buf2, Buf3);
  *a=atoi(Buf3);
}
```

```
void LoadByte(Byte *a)
{
   Clear_Buffers();
   fscanf(InFile, "%s %s %s", Buf1, Buf2, Buf3);
   *a=atoi(Buf3);
}

void LoadText(Name a)
{
   Clear_Buffers();
   fscanf(InFile, "%s %s %s", Buf1, Buf2, Buf3);
   strcpy(a, Buf3);
}

Boolean LoadBoolean()
{
   Name a;

   LoadText(a);
   if((a[0]=='T') || (a[0]=='t'))
        return(true);
   else
        return(false);
}

void LoadRTHeader()

{
   Byte t, cnt;

   XRes=0;
   YRes=0;
   ScanXRes=0;
   ScanYRes=0;
   NumberOfFrames=0;
   cnt=0;
   do
   {
        Clear_Buffers();
   fscanf(InFile, "%s", Buf1);
   if(!strcmp(Buf1, "STATS"))
        {
             LoadWord(&ScanXRes);
```

```
            LoadWord(&ScanYRes);
            ++cnt;
         }
         if(!strcmp(Buf1, "FRAMES"))
         {
            LoadByte(&NumberOfFrames);
            ++cnt;
         }
      }
   while(cnt<2);
}
#define Small 1E-01    /* Constants for removal of precision error effects */

TDA PrecCor={1.0, 1.0, 1.0};

Byte MtlCount;            /* Number of Materials Loaded */

void GetViewDir(float Angl, float Tilt, TDA View, TDA U, TDA V)
{
   float Phi, Theta;
   float x, y, z;

   Phi=Radians(Angl);
   Theta=Radians(Tilt);
   x=cos(Theta)*sin(Phi);
   y=cos(Theta)*cos(Phi);
   z=-sin(Theta);
   Vec(x, y, z, View);
   x=cos(Phi);
   y=-sin(Phi);
   z=0.0;
   Vec(x, y, z, U);
   x=sin(Theta)*sin(Phi);
   y=sin(Theta)*cos(Phi);
   z=cos(Theta);
   Vec(x, y, z, V);
}


void GetMatlNum(char Mat[], Byte *MatNum) {
   Byte i;

   /* Associate Materials to Objects */
```

```
    for(i=1; i<=MtlCount; i++)
    {
        if(!strcmp(Matl[i].MType, Mat))
            *MatNum=i;
    }
}

void GetTexNum(char Tex[], Byte *TexNum)
{
if(!strcmp(Tex, "SMOOTH"))
  *TexNum=Smooth;
else if(!strcmp(Tex, "CHECKER"))
  *TexNum=Checker;
else if(!strcmp(Tex, "GRIT"))
  *TexNum=Grit;
else if(!strcmp(Tex, "MARBLE"))
  *TexNum=Marble;
else if(!strcmp(Tex, "WOOD"))
  *TexNum=Wood;
else if(!strcmp(Tex, "SHEETROCK"))
  *TexNum=Sheetrock;
else if(!strcmp(Tex, "PARTICLE"))
   *TexNum=Particle;
else if(!strcmp(Tex, "OCEANWAVES"))
  *TexNum=OceanWaves;
else if(!strcmp(Tex, "POOLWAVES"))
  *TexNum=PoolWaves;
else if(!strcmp(Tex, "WAVES"))
  *TexNum=Waves;
}

void OrientQuadratic(QuadraticList *List)
{
   TDA Temp;
   float RTmp;

/* Inward facing normal */
if((List->BaseRad<0.0) || (List->ApexRad<0.0))
{
   List->BaseRad=fabs(List->BaseRad);
   List->ApexRad=fabs(List->ApexRad);
   List->InSNrm=true;
}
```

305

```
        else
            List->InSNrm=false;
VecSub(List->ApexLoc, List->BaseLoc, List->W);
List->Height=VecLen(List->W);
VecNormalize(List->W);
List->Slope=(List->ApexRad-List->BaseRad)/List->Height;
List->BaseD=-VecDot(List->BaseLoc, List->W);
Vec(0.0, 0.0, 1.0, Temp);
RTmp=fabs(fabs(VecDot(Temp, List->W))-1.0);
if(RTmp<Small)
    Vec(0.0, 1.0, 0.0, Temp);

/* Find two axes which are at right angles to W */

VecCross(List->W, Temp, List->U);
VecCross(List->U, List->W, List->V);
VecNormalize(List->U);
VecNormalize(List->V);
List->MinD=VecDot(List->W, List->BaseLoc);
List->MaxD=VecDot(List->W, List->ApexLoc);
if(List->MaxD<List->MinD)
{
    RTmp=List->MaxD;
    List->MaxD=List->MinD;
    List->MinD=RTmp;
    }
}

void GetDataForFrame()
{
    float Radial, Hgt;
    TDA ShapeLoc, TempLoc;
    TDA vec1, vec2, vec3;
    TDA pt1, pt2, pt3, pt4;
    Byte MtlNumber, TexNumber;

MtlCount=0;
do
{
    Clear_Buffers();
    fscanf(InFile, "%s", Buf1);
    if(!strcmp(Buf1, "ENVIRONMENT"))
    {
```

```
        LoadTDA(LoclWgt);
        LoadTDA(ReflWgt);
        LoadTDA(TranWgt);
        LoadTDA(MinWgt);
        LoadTDA(MaxWgt);
        LoadByte(&MaxDepth);
}
if(!strcmp(Buf1, "LAMPS"))
{
        LampReflects=LoadBoolean();
        LoadTDA(LampRefl);
        LoadReal(&DistEffect);
}
if(!strcmp(Buf1, "OBSERVER"))
{
        LoadReal(&FocalLength);
        LoadTDA(ObsPos);
        LoadReal(&ObsRotate);
        LoadReal(&ObsTilt);
        GetViewDir(ObsRotate, ObsTilt, ViewDir, ViewU, ViewV);
}
if(!strcmp(Buf1, "SKY"))
{
        LoadTDA(HorCol);
        LoadTDA(ZenCol);
        Clouds=LoadBoolean();
        SkyExists=true;
}
if(!(strcmp(Buf1, "MATERIAL")))
{
        MtlCount+=1;
        LoadText(Matl[MtlCount].MType);
        LoadText(Matl[MtlCount].Textur);
        LoadTDA(Matl[MtlCount].AmbRfl);
        LoadTDA(Matl[MtlCount].DifRfl);
        LoadTDA(Matl[MtlCount].SpcRfl);
        LoadReal(&Matl[MtlCount].Gloss);
        LoadTDA(Matl[MtlCount].Trans);
        LoadReal(&Matl[MtlCount].Index);
        if(!strcmp(Matl[MtlCount].Textur, "CHECKER"))
        {
            LoadTDA(Tile1);
            LoadTDA(Tile2);
            LoadReal(&Tile);
```

```
    }
    if(!strcmp(Matl[MtlCount].Textur, "OCEANWAVES"))
    {
        LoadReal(&OceanWaveAmpl);
        LoadReal(&OceanWavePhase);
    }
    if(!strcmp(Matl[MtlCount].Textur, "POOLWAVES"))
    {
        LoadReal(&PoolWaveAmpl);
        LoadReal(&PoolWavePhase);
        LoadReal(&PoolWaveXPos);
        LoadReal(&PoolWaveYPos);
    }
    if(!strcmp(Matl[MtlCount].Textur, "WAVES"))
    {
        LoadReal(&WaveAmpl);
        LoadReal(&WavePhase);
        LoadReal(&WaveXPos);
        LoadReal(&WaveYPos);
        LoadReal(&WaveZPos);
    }
}
if(!strcmp(Buf1, "GROUND"))
{
    GroundExists=true;
    ++ObjCnt[Ground];
    LoadText(MtlName);
    GetMatlNum(MtlName, &Gnd.MtlNum);
    GetTexNum(Matl[Gnd.MtlNum].Textur, &Gnd.TexNum);
}
if(!strcmp(Buf1, "LAMP"))
{
    ++ObjCnt[Lamp];
    LoadTDA(Lmp[ObjCnt[Lamp]].Loc);
    LoadReal(&Lmp[ObjCnt[Lamp]].Rad);
    Lmp[ObjCnt[Lamp]].RadSqr=SqrFP(Lmp[ObjCnt[Lamp]].Rad);
    LoadTDA(Lmp[ObjCnt[Lamp]].Intens);
}
if(!strcmp(Buf1, "TRIANGLE"))
{
    ++ObjCnt[Triangle];
    LoadTDA(Tri[ObjCnt[Triangle]].Loc);
    LoadTDA(Tri[ObjCnt[Triangle]].v1);
    LoadTDA(Tri[ObjCnt[Triangle]].v2);
```

```
VecCross(Tri[ObjCnt[Triangle]].v1, Tri[ObjCnt[Triangle]].v2,
                                    Tri[ObjCnt[Triangle]].Norm);
VecNormalize(Tri[ObjCnt[Triangle]].Norm);
Tri[ObjCnt[Triangle]].NdotLoc=VecDot(Tri[ObjCnt[Triangle]].Norm,
Tri[ObjCnt[Triangle]].Loc); LoadText(MtlName);
GetMatlNum(MtlName, &Tri[ObjCnt[Triangle]].MtlNum);
GetTexNum(Matl[Tri[ObjCnt[Triangle]].MtlNum].Textur,
                                &Tri[ObjCnt[Triangle]].TexNum);
}
if(!strcmp(Buf1, "PARALLELOGRAM"))
{
   ++ObjCnt[Parallelogram];
   LoadTDA(Para[ObjCnt[Parallelogram]].Loc);
   LoadTDA(Para[ObjCnt[Parallelogram]].v1);
   LoadTDA(Para[ObjCnt[Parallelogram]].v2);
VecCross(Para[ObjCnt[Parallelogram]].v1,\Para[ObjCnt[Parallelogram]].v2,
                             Para[ObjCnt[Parallelogram]].Norm);
VecNormalize(Para[ObjCnt[Parallelogram]].Norm);
Para[ObjCnt[Parallelogram]].NdotLoc=VecDot(
Para[ObjCnt[Parallelogram]].Norm,
Para[ObjCnt[Parallelogram]].Loc); LoadText(MtlName);
GetMatlNum(MtlName, &Para[ObjCnt[Parallelogram]].MtlNum);
GetTexNum(Matl[Para[ObjCnt[Parallelogram]].MtlNum].Textur,
                             &Para[ObjCnt[Parallelogram]].TexNum);
}
if(!strcmp(Buf1, "CIRCLE"))
{
   ++ObjCnt[Circles];
   LoadTDA(Cir[ObjCnt[Circles]].Loc);
   LoadTDA(Cir[ObjCnt[Circles]].v1);
   VecNormalize(Cir[ObjCnt[Circles]].v1);
   LoadTDA(Cir[ObjCnt[Circles]].v2);
   VecNormalize(Cir[ObjCnt[Circles]].v2);
   VecCross(Cir[ObjCnt[Circles]].v1, Cir[ObjCnt[Circles]].v2,
                             Cir[ObjCnt[Circles]].Norm);
   VecNormalize(Cir[ObjCnt[Circles]].Norm);
   Cir[ObjCnt[Circles]].NdotLoc=VecDot(Cir[ObjCnt[Circles]].Norm,
                             Cir[ObjCnt[Circles]].Loc);
   LoadReal(&Cir[ObjCnt[Circles]].Radius);
   LoadText(MtlName);
   GetMatlNum(MtlName, &Cir[ObjCnt[Circles]].MtlNum);
   GetTexNum(Matl[Cir[ObjCnt[Circles]].MtlNum].Textur,
                             &Cir[ObjCnt[Circles]].TexNum);
}
```

```
if(!strcmp(Buf1, "RING"))
{
   ++ObjCnt[Ring];
   LoadTDA(Rng[ObjCnt[Ring]].Loc);
   LoadTDA(Rng[ObjCnt[Ring]].v1);
   VecNormalize(Rng[ObjCnt[Ring]].v1);
   LoadTDA(Rng[ObjCnt[Ring]].v2);
   VecNormalize(Rng[ObjCnt[Ring]].v2);
   VecCross(Rng[ObjCnt[Ring]].v1, Rng[ObjCnt[Ring]].v2,
                                   Rng[ObjCnt[Ring]].Norm);
   VecNormalize(Rng[ObjCnt[Ring]].Norm);
   Rng[ObjCnt[Ring]].NdotLoc=VecDot(Rng[ObjCnt[Ring]].Norm,
                                   Rng[ObjCnt[Ring]].Loc);
   LoadReal(&Rng[ObjCnt[Ring]].Rad1);
   LoadReal(&Rng[ObjCnt[Ring]].Rad2);
   LoadText(MtlName);
   GetMatlNum(MtlName, &Rng[ObjCnt[Ring]].MtlNum);
   GetTexNum(Matl[Rng[ObjCnt[Ring]].MtlNum].Textur,
                                   &Rng[ObjCnt[Ring]].TexNum);
}
if(!strcmp(Buf1, "SPHERE"))
{
   ++ObjCnt[Sphere];
   LoadTDA(Sphr[ObjCnt[Sphere]].Loc);
   LoadReal(&Sphr[ObjCnt[Sphere]].Rad);
   Sphr[ObjCnt[Sphere]].RadSqr=SqrFP(Sphr[ObjCnt[Sphere]].Rad);
   LoadText(MtlName);
   GetMatlNum(MtlName, &Sphr[ObjCnt[Sphere]].MtlNum);
   GetTexNum(Matl[Sphr[ObjCnt[Sphere]].MtlNum].Textur,
                                   &Sphr[ObjCnt[Sphere]].TexNum);
}
if(!strcmp(Buf1, "CONE"))
{
   ++ObjCnt[Cone];                     /* hyxy - 2ryyy + hyzy = 0 */
   LoadTDA(Con[ObjCnt[Cone]].BaseLoc);
   LoadReal(&Con[ObjCnt[Cone]].BaseRad);
   LoadTDA(Con[ObjCnt[Cone]].ApexLoc);
   LoadReal(&Con[ObjCnt[Cone]].ApexRad);
   OrientQuadratic(&Con[ObjCnt[Cone]]);
   LoadText(MtlName);
   GetMatlNum(MtlName, &Con[ObjCnt[Cone]].MtlNum);
   GetTexNum(Matl[Con[ObjCnt[Cone]].MtlNum].Textur,
                                   &Con[ObjCnt[Cone]].TexNum);
}
```

```
    if(!strcmp(Buf1, "CYLINDER"))
    {
      ++ObjCnt[Cylinder];                    /* hxxy - 2ryyy + hyzy = 0 */
      LoadTDA(Cyl[ObjCnt[Cylinder]].BaseLoc);
      LoadReal(&Cyl[ObjCnt[Cylinder]].BaseRad);
      LoadTDA(Cyl[ObjCnt[Cylinder]].ApexLoc);
      Cyl[ObjCnt[Cylinder]].ApexRad=Cyl[ObjCnt[Cylinder]].BaseRad;
      OrientQuadratic(&Cyl[ObjCnt[Cylinder]]);
      LoadText(MtlName);
      GetMatlNum(MtlName, &Cyl[ObjCnt[Cylinder]].MtlNum);
      GetTexNum(Matl[Cyl[ObjCnt[Cylinder]].MtlNum].Textur,
                                  &Cyl[ObjCnt[Cylinder]].TexNum);
    }
    if(!strcmp(Buf1, "BOX"))
    {
      LoadTDA(ShapeLoc);            /* Constructed of 6 parallelograms */
      LoadTDA(vec1);
      LoadTDA(vec2);
      LoadTDA(vec3);
      LoadText(MtlName);
      GetMatlNum(MtlName, &MtlNumber);
      GetTexNum(Matl[MtlNumber].Textur, &TexNumber);
      ++ObjCnt[Parallelogram];
      VecCopy(ShapeLoc, Para[ObjCnt[Parallelogram]].Loc);
      VecCopy(vec1, Para[ObjCnt[Parallelogram]].v1);
      VecCopy(vec3, Para[ObjCnt[Parallelogram]].v2)
      VecCross(Para[ObjCnt[Parallelogram]].v1, Para[ObjCnt[Parallelogram]].v2,
Para[ObjCnt[Parallelogram]].Norm);
      VecNormalize(Para[ObjCnt[Parallelogram]].Norm);
Para[ObjCnt[Parallelogram]].NdotLoc=VecDot(Para[ObjCnt[Parallelogram]].Norm,
      Para[ObjCnt[Parallelogram]].Loc);
      Para[ObjCnt[Parallelogram]].MtlNum=MtlNumber;
      Para[ObjCnt[Parallelogram]].TexNum=TexNumber;
      ++ObjCnt[Parallelogram];
      VecCopy(ShapeLoc, Para[ObjCnt[Parallelogram]].Loc);
      VecCopy(vec3, Para[ObjCnt[Parallelogram]].v1);
      VecCopy(vec1, Para[ObjCnt[Parallelogram]].v2);
      VecCross(Para[ObjCnt[Parallelogram]].v1, Para[ObjCnt[Parallelogram]].v2,
Para[ObjCnt[Parallelogram]].Norm);
      VecNormalize(Para[ObjCnt[Parallelogram]].Norm);
      Vec(0.0, vec2[1], 0.0, TempLoc);
      VecAdd(TempLoc, Para[ObjCnt[Parallelogram]].Loc
      Para[ObjCnt[Parallelogram]].Loc);
Para[ObjCnt[Parallelogram]].NdotLoc=VecDot(Para[ObjCnt[Parallelogram]].Norm,
```

```
Para[ObjCnt[Parallelogram]].Loc);
    Para[ObjCnt[Parallelogram]].MtlNum=MtlNumber;
    Para[ObjCnt[Parallelogram]].TexNum=TexNumber;
    ++ObjCnt[Parallelogram];
    VecCopy(ShapeLoc, Para[ObjCnt[Parallelogram]].Loc);
    VecCopy(vec3, Para[ObjCnt[Parallelogram]].v1);
    VecCopy(vec2, Para[ObjCnt[Parallelogram]].v2);
    VecCross(Para[ObjCnt[Parallelogram]].v1, Para[ObjCnt[Parallelogram]].v2,
Para[ObjCnt[Parallelogram]].Norm);
    VecNormalize(Para[ObjCnt[Parallelogram]].Norm);
    Para[ObjCnt[Parallelogram]].NdotLoc=VecDot(Para[ObjCnt
                                        [Parallelogram]].Norm,
Para[ObjCnt[Parallelogram]].Loc);
    Para[ObjCnt[Parallelogram]].MtlNum=MtlNumber;
    Para[ObjCnt[Parallelogram]].TexNum=TexNumber;
    ++ObjCnt[Parallelogram];
    VecCopy(ShapeLoc, Para[ObjCnt[Parallelogram]].Loc);
    VecCopy(vec2, Para[ObjCnt[Parallelogram]].v1);
    VecCopy(vec3, Para[ObjCnt[Parallelogram]].v2);
    VecCross(Para[ObjCnt[Parallelogram]].v1,
    Para[ObjCnt[Parallelogram]].v2,
Para[ObjCnt[Parallelogram]].Norm);
    VecNormalize(Para[ObjCnt[Parallelogram]].Norm);
    Vec(vec1[0], 0.0, 0.0,TempLoc);
    VecAdd(TempLoc,Para[ObjCnt[Parallelogram]].Loc,
                                Para[ObjCnt[Parallelogram]].Loc);
    Para[ObjCnt[Parallelogram]].NdotLoc=VecDot
                            (Para[ObjCnt[Parallelogram]].Norm,
Para[ObjCnt[Parallelogram]].Loc);
    Para[ObjCnt[Parallelogram]].MtlNum=MtlNumber;
    Para[ObjCnt[Parallelogram]].TexNum=TexNumber;
    ++ObjCnt[Parallelogram];
    VecCopy(ShapeLoc, Para[ObjCnt[Parallelogram]].Loc);
    VecCopy(vec2, Para[ObjCnt[Parallelogram]].v1);
    VecCopy(vec1,
    Para[ObjCnt[Parallelogram]].v2VecCross(Para[ObjCnt[Parallelogram]].v1,
    Para[ObjCnt[Parallelogram]].v2, Para[ObjCnt[Parallelogram]].Norm);
    VecNormalize(Para[ObjCnt[Parallelogram]].Norm);
    Para[ObjCnt[Parallelogram]].NdotLoc=VecDot
                            (Para[ObjCnt[Parallelogram]].Norm,
Para[ObjCnt[Parallelogram]].Loc);
        Para[ObjCnt[Parallelogram]].MtlNum=MtlNumber;
        Para[ObjCnt[Parallelogram]].TexNum=TexNumber;
        ++ObjCnt[Parallelogram];
```

```
    VecCopy(ShapeLoc, Para[ObjCnt[Parallelogram]].Loc);
    VecCopy(vec1, Para[ObjCnt[Parallelogram]].v1);
    VecCopy(vec2, Para[ObjCnt[Parallelogram]].v2);
    VecCross(Para[ObjCnt[Parallelogram]].v1,Para[ObjCnt[Parallelogram]].v2,
Para[ObjCnt[Parallelogram]].Norm);
    VecNormalize(Para[ObjCnt[Parallelogram]].Norm);
    Vec(0.0, 0.0, vec3[2], TempLoc);
    VecAdd(TempLoc,Para[ObjCnt[Parallelogram]].Loc,
                            Para[ObjCnt[Parallelogram]].Loc);
Para[ObjCnt[Parallelogram]].NdotLoc=VecDot
                            (Para[ObjCnt[Parallelogram]].Norm,
Para[ObjCnt[Parallelogram]].Loc);
    Para[ObjCnt[Parallelogram]].MtlNum=MtlNumber;
    Para[ObjCnt[Parallelogram]].TexNum=TexNumber;
   }
  if(!strcmp(Buf1, "PYRAMID"))
  {
    LoadTDA(ShapeLoc);          /* Constructed of 1 parallelogram *
    LoadTDA(vec1);              /* and 4 triangles */
    LoadTDA(vec2);
    LoadReal(&Hgt);
    LoadText(MtlName);
    GetMatlNum(MtlName, &MtlNumber);
    GetTexNum(Matl[MtlNumber].Textur, &TexNumber);
    ++ObjCnt[Parallelogram];
    VecCopy(ShapeLoc, Para[ObjCnt[Parallelogram]].Loc);
    VecCopy(vec2, Para[ObjCnt[Parallelogram]].v1);
    VecCopy(vec1, Para[ObjCnt[Parallelogram]].v2);
    VecCross(Para[ObjCnt[Parallelogram]].v1,Para[ObjCnt[Parallelogram]].v2,
Para[ObjCnt[Parallelogram]].Norm);
  VecNormalize(Para[ObjCnt[Parallelogram]].Norm);
  Para[ObjCnt[Parallelogram]].NdotLoc=VecDot
                            (Para[ObjCnt[Parallelogram]].Norm,
Para[ObjCnt[Parallelogram]].Loc);
  Para[ObjCnt[Parallelogram]].MtlNum=MtlNumber;
  Para[ObjCnt[Parallelogram]].TexNum=TexNumber;
  ++ObjCnt[Triangle];
  VecCopy(ShapeLoc, Tri[ObjCnt[Triangle]].Loc);
  VecCopy(vec1, Tri[ObjCnt[Triangle]].v1);
  Vec(0.5*vec1[0], 0.5*vec2[1], Hgt, Tri[ObjCnt[Triangle]].v2);
  VecCross(Tri[ObjCnt[Triangle]].v1, Tri[ObjCnt[Triangle]].v2,
                            Tri[ObjCnt[Triangle]].Norm);
  VecNormalize(Tri[ObjCnt[Triangle]].Norm);
  Tri[ObjCnt[Triangle]].NdotLoc=VecDot(Tri[ObjCnt[Triangle]].Norm,
```

```
Tri[ObjCnt[Triangle]].Loc);
      Tri[ObjCnt[Triangle]].MtlNum=MtlNumber;
      Tri[ObjCnt[Triangle]].TexNum=TexNumber;
      ++ObjCnt[Triangle];
      Tri[ObjCnt[Triangle]].Loc[0]=ShapeLoc[0]+vec1[0];
      Tri[ObjCnt[Triangle]].Loc[1]=ShapeLoc[1]+vec2[1];
      Tri[ObjCnt[Triangle]].Loc[2]=ShapeLoc[2];
      VecScalMult(-1.0, vec1, Tri[ObjCnt[Triangle]].v1);
      Vec(-0.5*vec1[0], -0.5*vec2[1], Hgt, Tri[ObjCnt[Triangle]].v2);
      VecCross(Tri[ObjCnt[Triangle]].v1, Tri[ObjCnt[Triangle]].v2,
                                        Tri[ObjCnt[Triangle]].Norm);
      VecNormalize(Tri[ObjCnt[Triangle]].Norm);
      Tri[ObjCnt[Triangle]].NdotLoc=VecDot(Tri[ObjCnt[Triangle]].Norm,
Tri[ObjCnt[Triangle]].Loc);
      Tri[ObjCnt[Triangle]].MtlNum=MtlNumber;
      Tri[ObjCnt[Triangle]].TexNum=TexNumber;
      ++ObjCnt[Triangle];
      Tri[ObjCnt[Triangle]].Loc[0]=ShapeLoc[0]+vec1[0];
      Tri[ObjCnt[Triangle]].Loc[1]=ShapeLoc[1]+vec2[1];
      Tri[ObjCnt[Triangle]].Loc[2]=ShapeLoc[2];
      Vec(-0.5*vec1[0], -0.5*vec2[1], Hgt, Tri[ObjCnt[Triangle]].v1);
      VecScalMult(-1.0, vec2, Tri[ObjCnt[Triangle]].v2);
      VecCross(Tri[ObjCnt[Triangle]].v1, Tri[ObjCnt[Triangle]].v2,
                                        Tri[ObjCnt[Triangle]].Norm);
      VecNormalize(Tri[ObjCnt[Triangle]].Norm)
      Tri[ObjCnt[Triangle]].NdotLoc=VecDot(Tri[ObjCnt[Triangle]].Nor
Tri[ObjCnt[Triangle]].Loc);
      Tri[ObjCnt[Triangle]].MtlNum=MtlNumber;
      Tri[ObjCnt[Triangle]].TexNum=TexNumber;
      ++ObjCnt[Triangle];
      VecCopy(ShapeLoc, Tri[ObjCnt[Triangle]].Loc);
      Vec(0.5*vec1[0], 0.5*vec2[1], Hgt, Tri[ObjCnt[Triangle]].v1);
      VecCopy(vec2, Tri[ObjCnt[Triangle]].v2);
      VecCross(Tri[ObjCnt[Triangle]].v1, Tri[ObjCnt[Triangle]].v2,
                                        Tri[ObjCnt[Triangle]].Norm);
      VecNormalize(Tri[ObjCnt[Triangle]].Norm);
      Tri[ObjCnt[Triangle]].NdotLoc=VecDot(Tri[ObjCnt[Triangle]].Norm
Tri[ObjCnt[Triangle]].Loc);
      Tri[ObjCnt[Triangle]].MtlNum=MtlNumber;
      Tri[ObjCnt[Triangle]].TexNum=TexNumber;
   }
   if(!strcmp(Buf1, "TETRA"))
   {
      LoadTDA(ShapeLoc);                   /* Contructed of 4 triangles */
```

```
        LoadReal(&Hgt);
        LoadReal(&Radial);
        LoadText(MtlName);
        GetMatlNum(MtlName, &MtlNumber);
        GetTexNum(Matl[MtlNumber].Textur, &TexNumber);
        Vec(ShapeLoc[0], ShapeLoc[1], ShapeLoc[2]+Hgt, pt1);
        Vec(ShapeLoc[0], ShapeLoc[1]+Radial, ShapeLoc[2], pt2);
        Vec(ShapeLoc[0]-Radial*0.707, ShapeLoc[1]-Radial*0.707, ShapeLoc[2], pt3);
        Vec(ShapeLoc[0]+Radial*0.707, ShapeLoc[1]-Radial*0.707, ShapeLoc[2], pt4);
        ++ObjCnt[Triangle];
        VecCopy(pt3, Tri[ObjCnt[Triangle]].Loc);
        VecSub(pt1, pt3, Tri[ObjCnt[Triangle]].v1);
        VecSub(pt2, pt3, Tri[ObjCnt[Triangle]].v2);
        VecCross(Tri[ObjCnt[Triangle]].v1, Tri[ObjCnt[Triangle]].v2,
                                            Tri[ObjCnt[Triangle]].Norm);
        VecNormalize(Tri[ObjCnt[Triangle]].Norm);
        Tri[ObjCnt[Triangle]].NdotLoc=VecDot(Tri[ObjCnt[Triangle]].Norm,
Tri[ObjCnt[Triangle]].Loc);
        Tri[ObjCnt[Triangle]].MtlNum=MtlNumber;
        Tri[ObjCnt[Triangle]].TexNum=TexNumber;
        ++ObjCnt[Triangle];
        VecCopy(pt2, Tri[ObjCnt[Triangle]].Loc);
        VecSub(pt1, pt2, Tri[ObjCnt[Triangle]].v1);
        VecSub(pt4, pt2, Tri[ObjCnt[Triangle]].v2);
        VecCross(Tri[ObjCnt[Triangle]].v1, Tri[ObjCnt[Triangle]].v2,
                                            Tri[ObjCnt[Triangle]].Norm);
        VecNormalize(Tri[ObjCnt[Triangle]].Norm);
        Tri[ObjCnt[Triangle]].NdotLoc=VecDot(Tri[ObjCnt[Triangle]].Norm,
Tri[ObjCnt[Triangle]].Loc);
        Tri[ObjCnt[Triangle]].MtlNum=MtlNumber;
        Tri[ObjCnt[Triangle]].TexNum=TexNumber;
        ++ObjCnt[Triangle];
        VecCopy(pt4, Tri[ObjCnt[Triangle]].Loc);
        VecSub(pt1, pt4, Tri[ObjCnt[Triangle]].v1);
        VecSub(pt3,pt4,Tri[ObjCnt[Triangle]].v2);
        VecCross(Tri[ObjCnt[Triangle]].v1, Tri[ObjCnt[Triangle]].v2,
                                            Tri[ObjCnt[Triangle]].Norm);
        VecNormalize(Tri[ObjCnt[Triangle]].Norm);
        Tri[ObjCnt[Triangle]].NdotLoc=VecDot(Tri[ObjCnt[Triangle]].Norm,
Tri[ObjCnt[Triangle]].Loc);
        Tri[ObjCnt[Triangle]].MtlNum=MtlNumber;
        Tri[ObjCnt[Triangle]].TexNum=TexNumber;
        ++ObjCnt[Triangle];
        VecCopy(pt3, Tri[ObjCnt[Triangle]].Loc);
```

```
    VecSub(pt2, pt3, Tri[ObjCnt[Triangle]].v1);
    VecSub(pt4, pt3, Tri[ObjCnt[Triangle]].v2);
    VecCross(Tri[ObjCnt[Triangle]].v1, Tri[ObjCnt[Triangle]].v2,
                                  Tri[ObjCnt[Triangle]].Norm);
    VecNormalize(Tri[ObjCnt[Triangle]].Norm);
    Tri[ObjCnt[Triangle]].NdotLoc=VecDot(Tri[ObjCnt[Triangle]].Norm,
Tri[ObjCnt[Triangle]].Loc);
    Tri[ObjCnt[Triangle]].MtlNum=MtlNumber;
    Tri[ObjCnt[Triangle]].TexNum=TexNumber;
  }
  if(!strcmp(Buf1, "TETRAEXTENTS"))
  {
    LoadTDA(TetraExtent1);    /* Extents for bounding tetrahedron */
    LoadTDA(TetraExtent2);
    LoadTDA(TetraExtent3);
    LoadTDA(TetraExtent4);
    BoundingTetraTest=true;
  }
  if(!strcmp(Buf1, "BOUNDINGSPHERETEST"))
    BoundingSphereTest=true;
  if(!strcmp(Buf1, "BOUNDINGPRISMTEST"))
    BoundingPrismTest=true;
  }
  while(strcmp(Buf1, "ENDFRAME"));
  }


  /*
  ┌─────────────────────────────────────────────────────────────┐
  │ ┌─────────────────────────────────────────────────────────┐ │
  │ │            Calculate Directions of Reflected Rays        │ │
  │ └─────────────────────────────────────────────────────────┘ │
  └─────────────────────────────────────────────────────────────┘

    CalcDirOfReflRay - calculate the direction of a reflected ray
    CalcDirOfTranRay - calculate the direction of a transmitted ray
  */

  void CalcDirOfReflRay(TDA Dir, TDA SrfNrm, TDA ReflRay)
  {
    float Tmp;

    Tmp=-2.0*VecDot(Dir, SrfNrm);
    VecAddScalMult(Tmp, SrfNrm, Dir, ReflRay);
  }


  void CalcDirOfTranRay(TDA Dir, TDA SrfNrm, Byte Mtl, TDA TranRay)
```

```
{
    float ni=1.000; /* air */
    float NdotV, nmult;   /* N=SrfNrm      V=Dir */
    TDA cosV, sinT, temp;
    float lsinT, NdotT;
    float nt;

  /* Based on Snell's Law of Refraction   n1 x sin(θ1) = n2 x sin(θ2) */

    VecScalMult(-1.0, Dir, Dir);  /* Flip for calculations */
    NdotV=VecDot(SrfNrm, Dir);
    nt=Matl[Mtl].Index;
    if(NdotV>0.0)
        nmult=ni/nt;
    else
        nmult=nt;            /* nt/ni  where ni=1 */
    VecScalMult(NdotV, SrfNrm, cosV);
    VecSub(cosV, Dir, temp);
    VecScalMult(nmult, temp, sinT);
    lsinT=VecDot(sinT, sinT);
    if(lsinT>=1.0)
        VecNull(TranRay);           /* internal reflections */
    else
    {
        NdotT=sqrt(1.0-lsinT);
        if(NdotV<0.0)
            NdotT=-NdotT;
        VecScalMult(NdotT, SrfNrm, temp);
        VecSub(sinT, temp, TranRay);
    }
}

void QuadraticSrfNrm(TDA IntrPt, TDA SrfNrm, QuadraticList *List)
{
    float t;
    TDA ProjPt;;

t=-(VecDot(IntrPt, List->W)+List->BaseD);  /* Project IntrPt onto the*/
VecAddScalMult(t, List->W, IntrPt, ProjPt);    /* plane of the Base */
VecSub(ProjPt, List->BaseLoc, SrfNrm); /* The surface normal is a vector */
VecNormalize(SrfNrm);                   /* from BaseLoc through the point */
                                        /* projected, plus slope times W */
VecAddScalMult(-List->Slope, List->W, SrfNrm, SrfNrm); VecNormalize(SrfNrm);
```

```
        if(List->InSNrm)               /* Inward facing normal */
        VecNegate(SrfNrm);
    }


    void GetSrfNrm(int Shp, int Obj, TDA IntrPt, TDA SrfNrm)
    {
        switch(Shp)
        {
            case Ground          : Vec(0.0, 0.0, 1.0, SrfNrm);
                                   break;


                        /* lamp = | IntrPt - Loc | */

            case Lamp            : VecSub(IntrPt, Lmp[Obj].Loc, SrfNrm);
        VecNormalize(SrfNrm);
                                   break;

                        /* triangle = | v1 X v2 | */

            case Triangle        : VecCopy(Tri[Obj].Norm, SrfNrm);
                                   break;

                        /* parallelogram = |v1 X v2 | */

            case Parallelogram : VecCopy(Para[Obj].Norm, SrfNrm);
                                   break;

                        /* circles = | v1 X v2 | */

            case Circles         : VecCopy(Cir[Obj].Norm, SrfNrm);
                                   break;

                        /* ring = | v1 X v2 | */

            case Ring            : VecCopy(Rng[Obj].Norm, SrfNrm);
                                   break;

                        /* sphere = | IntrPt - Loc | */

            case Sphere          : VecSub(IntrPt, Sphr[Obj].Loc, SrfNrm);
           VecNormalize(SrfNrm);             break;
        case Cone                : QuadraticSrfNrm(IntrPt, SrfNrm, &Con[Obj]);
                                   break;
```

```
      case Cylinder      : QuadraticSrfNrm(IntrPt, SrfNrm, &Cyl[Obj]);
                                break;
   }
}


/*
   ┌──────────────────────────────────────────────────────────────┐
   │                                                                │
   │              Intersection of Ray with Objects                  │
   │                                                                │
   └──────────────────────────────────────────────────────────────┘

GetIntrPt - find the intersection point given a point, direction and dist
GetSrfNrm - find the surface normal given the point of intersection
Intersect - determine if an object has been hit by a ray
*/

void GetIntrPt(TDA Pt, TDA Dir, float Dist, TDA IntrPt)
{
   VecAddScalMult(Dist, Dir, Pt, IntrPt);
}


FDA gu, gv;

Boolean EvenCrossings(Byte Sides)
{
   Byte i, j;
   Word crossings;

   crossings=0;
   for(i=0; i<Sides; i++)
   {
        j=(i+1) % Sides;
        if(((gv[i]<0) && (gv[j]>=0)) || ((gv[j]<0) && (gv[i]>=0)))
        {
                if((gu[i]>=0) && (gu[j]>=0))
                        ++crossings;
                else
                {
                        if((gu[i]>=0) || (gu[j]>=0))
                        {
                                if((gu[i]-gv[i]*(gu[j]-gu[i])/(gv[j]-
                                        gv[i]))>0)++crossings;
                        }
                }
        }
   }
```

```
        }
    if((crossings%2)==0)
        return(true);
    else
        return(false);
}


TDA delta;

void SetUpTriangle(Byte p1, Byte p2, int Obj)
{
    gu[0]=-delta[p1];
    gv[0]=-delta[p2];
    gu[1]=Tri[Obj].v1[p1]-delta[p1];
    gv[1]=Tri[Obj].v1[p2]-delta[p2];
    gu[2]=Tri[Obj].v2[p1]-delta[p1];
    gv[2]=Tri[Obj].v2[p2]-delta[p2];
}


void SetUpParallelogram(Byte p1, Byte p2, int Obj) {
    gu[0]=-delta[p1];
    gv[0]=-delta[p2];
    gu[1]=Para[Obj].v1[p1]-delta[p1];
    gv[1]=Para[Obj].v1[p2]-delta[p2];
    gu[2]=Para[Obj].v2[p1]+Para[Obj].v1[p1]-delta[p1];
    gv[2]=Para[Obj].v2[p2]+Para[Obj].v1[p2]-delta[p2];
    gu[3]=Para[Obj].v2[p1]-delta[p1];
    gv[3]=Para[Obj].v2[p2]-delta[p2];
}


float t1, t2;

float QuadraticIntersectionCheck()
{
    float intersection;

    if(((!(t1>Small)) && (!(t2>Small)))
        intersection=-1.0;
    else
    {
        if(t1>t2)
        {
            if(t2<Small)
```

```
                    t2=t1;
        }
        else
        {
            if(t1>Small)
                    t2=t1;
        }
        intersection=t2;
    }
    return(intersection);
}


TDA IntrPoint, temp;
float a, b, c, d;
float disc, sroot;
float t;


float QuadraticIntersection(QuadraticList *List, TDA Pt, TDA Dir)
{
    TDA NewPnt, NewDir;
    float SqrSlope;

    /* Parts of this conical-section intersection routine are based on */
    /* ideas from Mark Terrence VandeWettering's MTV raytracer          */

    VecSub(Pt, List->BaseLoc, temp);  /* Get the coordinates of the ray */
    NewPnt[0]=VecDot(temp, List->U);  /* origin in the objects space. */
    NewPnt[1]=VecDot(temp, List->V);
    NewPnt[2]=VecDot(temp, List->W);
    NewDir[0]=VecDot(Dir, List->U);
    NewDir[1]=VecDot(Dir, List->V);
    NewDir[2]=VecDot(Dir, List->W);
    SqrSlope=SqrFP(List->Slope);
    a=SqrFP(NewDir[0])+SqrFP(NewDir[1])-SqrFP(NewDir[2])*SqrSlope;
    b=2.0*(NewPnt[0]*NewDir[0]+
        NewPnt[1]*NewDir[1]-
        NewDir[2]*(NewPnt[2]*SqrSlope-List->BaseRad*List->Slope));
    c=SqrFP(NewPnt[0])+SqrFP(NewPnt[1])-SqrFP(NewPnt[2]*List->Slope+List-
                                                >BaseRad);
if(a==0)
{
    if(b==0)
        return(-1.0);
```

```
       t2=-c/b;
       if(t2<Small)
             return(-1.0);
       else
             t1=-1.0;
   }
   else
   {
       disc=SqrFP(b)-4.0*a*c;
       if(disc<0.0)
             return(-1.0);
       else
       {
             sroot=sqrt(disc);
             t=1.0/(a+a);
             t1=(-b-sroot)*t;
             t2=(-b+sroot)*t;
             if((t1<0.0) && (t2<0.0))
                 return(-1.0);
             else
             {
                 if(t1>t2)
                 {
                         /* make t1 the nearest root */
                         t=t1;
                         t1=t2;
                         t2=t;
                 }
             }
       }
   }
   if(t1>Small)
   {
      /* Hit object */
      GetIntrPt(Pt, Dir, t1, IntrPoint);
      d=VecDot(List->W, IntrPoint);
      if((!(d<List->MinD)) && (!(d>List->MaxD)))
             return(t1);
   }
   if(t2>Small)
   {
      /* Hit object */
      GetIntrPt(Pt, Dir, t2, IntrPoint);
      d=VecDot(List->W, IntrPoint);
```

```
   if(((!(d<List->MinD)) && (!(d>List->MaxD)))
        return(t2);
   }
   return(-1.0);
}


float Intersect(TDA Pt, TDA Dir, int Shp, int Obj) {
   float intersection;
   float rad, dot;
   float pos1, pos2;

   switch(Shp)
   {
       case Ground :     if(Dir[2]==0.0)
                         intersection=-1.0;
                   else
                   {
                         t=-Pt[2]/Dir[2];
                         if(t>Small)
                         intersection=t;
                   else
                         intersection=-1.0;
                   }
                         break;
       case Lamp : VecSub(Lmp[Obj].Loc, Pt, temp);
                   b=VecDot(Dir, temp)*-2.0;
                   c=VecDot(temp, temp)-Lmp[Obj].RadSqr;
                   disc=SqrFP(b)-4.0*c;
                   if(disc<=0.0)
                         intersection=-1.0;
                   else
                   {
                         sroot=sqrt(disc);
                         t1=(-b-sroot)*0.5;
t2=(-b+sroot)*0.5; intersection=QuadraticIntersectionCheck();
                   }
                   break;
       case Triangle :   dot=VecDot(Tri[Obj].Norm, Dir);
                         if(fabs(dot)<Small)
                         intersection=-1.0;
                   else
                   {
                         pos1=Tri[Obj].NdotLoc;
                         pos2=VecDot(Tri[Obj].Norm, Pt);
```

```
                        t=(pos1-pos2)/dot;
                        GetIntrPt(Pt, Dir, t, IntrPoint);
                        VecSub(IntrPoint, Tri[Obj].Loc, delta);
                          if((fabs(Tri[Obj].Norm[0])>fabs(Tri[Obj].
                                                    Norm[1])) &&
                            (fabs(Tri[Obj].Norm[0])>fabs(Tri[Obj].
                                                    Norm[2])))
                         SetUpTriangle(1, 2, Obj);
                  else
                  {
                        if(fabs(Tri[Obj].Norm[1])>=fabs(Tri[Obj].
                                                    Norm[2]))
                                SetUpTriangle(0, 2, Obj);
                        else
                                SetUpTriangle(0, 1, Obj);
                        }
                  }
                  if(EvenCrossings(3))
                        intersection=-1.0;
                  else
                        intersection=t;
                  break;
        case Parallelogram : dot=VecDot(Para[Obj].Norm, Dir);
                        if(fabs(dot)<Small)
                         intersection=-1.0;
                  else
                  {
                        pos1=Para[Obj].NdotLoc;
                        pos2=VecDot(Para[Obj].Norm, Pt);
                        t=(pos1-pos2)/dot;
                        GetIntrPt(Pt, Dir, t, IntrPoint);
                        VecSub(IntrPoint, Para[Obj].Loc, delta);
                        if((fabs(Para[Obj].Norm[0])>fabs(Para[Obj].
                                                    Norm[1])) &&
                        (fabs(Para[Obj].Norm[0])>fabs(Para[Obj].
                                                    Norm[2])))
                            SetUpParallelogram(1, 2, Obj);
                  else
                  {
                        if(fabs(Para[Obj].Norm[1])>=fabs(Para[Obj].
                                                    Norm[2]))
                            SetUpParallelogram(0, 2, Obj);
                  else
                            SetUpParallelogram(0, 1, Obj);
```

```
                    }
            }
            if(EvenCrossings(4))
                    intersection=-1.0;
            else
                    intersection=t;
            break;
case Circles :       dot=VecDot(Cir[Obj].Norm, Dir);
            if(fabs(dot)<Small)
                    intersection=-1.0;
            else
            {
                    pos1=Cir[Obj].NdotLoc;
                    pos2=VecDot(Cir[Obj].Norm, Pt);
                    t=(pos1-pos2)/dot;
                    GetIntrPt(Pt, Dir, t, IntrPoint);
                    VecSub(IntrPoint, Cir[Obj].Loc, delta);
                                                rad=VecLen(delta);
                    if(rad>Cir[Obj].Radius)
                            intersection=-1.0;
            else
                            intersection=t;
            }
            break;
case Ring :dot=VecDot(Rng[Obj].Norm, Dir);
            if(fabs(dot)<Small)
                    intersection=-1.0;
            else
            {
                    pos1=Rng[Obj].NdotLoc;
                    pos2=VecDot(Rng[Obj].Norm, Pt);
                    t=(pos1-pos2)/dot;
                    GetIntrPt(Pt, Dir, t, IntrPoint);
                    VecSub(IntrPoint, Rng[Obj].Loc, delta);
                    rad=VecLen(delta);
                    if((rad<Rng[Obj].Rad1) || (rad>Rng[Obj].Rad2))
                            intersection=-1.0;
            else
                            intersection=t;
            }
            break;
case Sphere :VecSub(Sphr[Obj].Loc, Pt, temp);
            b=VecDot(Dir, temp)*-2.0;
            c=VecDot(temp, temp)-Sphr[Obj].RadSqr;
```

325

```
            disc=SqrFP(b)-4.0*c;
            if(disc<=0.0)
                    intersection=-1.0;
            else
            {
                    sroot=sqrt(disc);
                    t1=(-b-sroot)*0.5;
                    t2=(-b+sroot)*0.5;
                    intersection=QuadraticIntersectionCheck();
            }
            break;
    case Cone :intersection=QuadraticIntersection(&Con[Obj], Pt, Dir);
            break;
    case Cylinder:intersection=QuadraticIntersection(&Cyl[Obj], Pt, Dir);
            break;
    }
    return(intersection);
}


/*

        ┌──────────────────────────────────────────────────────────┐
        │                                                          │
        │          Initial Eye-to-Pixel Ray Calculation           │
        │                                                          │
        │       GetInitialDir - calculation of initial eye-to-pixel ray │
        │                                                          │
        └──────────────────────────────────────────────────────────┘
*/

void GetInitialDir(float i, float j, TDA Dir)
{
    float x, y;
    TDA EyeToPixVec;

x=(i-(float)CenterX)*XAspDivFocLen; y=((float)CenterY-j)*YAspDivFocLen;
    VecLinComb(x, ViewU, y, ViewV, EyeToPixVec);
    VecAdd(ViewVec, EyeToPixVec, Dir);
    VecNormalize(Dir);
}


/*

    ┌──────────────────────────────────────────────────────────────┐
    │ Bounding Objects Scheme to Reduce the Number of Intersection Tests │
    └──────────────────────────────────────────────────────────────┘
        BoundingBoxes                    - find bounding box for an object
```

```
          GetMinimumAndMaximumPoints - find min and max points for all objects
*/
 void QuadraticBound(QuadraticList *List, TDA Minimum, TDA Maximum)
 {
    TDA Qmin, Qmax;
    float MaxRad;

    VecMin(List->BaseLoc, List->ApexLoc, Qmin);
    VecMax(List->BaseLoc, List->ApexLoc, Qmax);
    MaxRad=MAX(List->BaseRad, List->ApexRad);
    Minimum[0]=Qmin[0]-MaxRad;
    Minimum[1]=Qmin[1]-MaxRad;
    Minimum[2]=Qmin[2]-MaxRad;
    Maximum[0]=Qmax[0]+MaxRad;
    Maximum[1]=Qmax[1]+MaxRad;
    Maximum[2]=Qmax[2]+MaxRad;
 }

 void BoundingBoxes(int Shp, int Obj, TDA Minimum, TDA Maximum)
 {
    TDA p2, p3, p4;

    switch(Shp)
    {
    case Triangle      :VecAdd(Tri[Obj].Loc, Tri[Obj].v1, p2);
                        VecAdd(Tri[Obj].Loc, Tri[Obj].v2, p3);
                        Minimum[0]=MIN3(Tri[Obj].Loc[0], p2[0], p3[0]);
                        Minimum[1]=MIN3(Tri[Obj].Loc[1], p2[1], p3[1]);
                        Minimum[2]=MIN3(Tri[Obj].Loc[2], p2[2], p3[2]);
                        Maximum[0]=MAX3(Tri[Obj].Loc[0], p2[0], p3[0]);
                        Maximum[1]=MAX3(Tri[Obj].Loc[1], p2[1], p3[1]);
                        Maximum[2]=MAX3(Tri[Obj].Loc[2], p2[2], p3[2]);
                        break;
    case Parallelogram : VecAdd(Para[Obj].Loc, Para[Obj].v1, p2);
                        VecAdd(Para[Obj].Loc, Para[Obj].v2, p3);
                        VecAdd3(Para[Obj].Loc, Para[Obj].v1, Para[Obj].v2, p4);
                        Minimum[0]=MIN4(Para[Obj].Loc[0], p2[0], p3[0], p4[0]);
                        Minimum[1]=MIN4(Para[Obj].Loc[1], p2[1], p3[1], p4[1]);
                        Minimum[2]=MIN4(Para[Obj].Loc[2], p2[2], p3[2], p4[2]);
                        Maximum[0]=MAX4(Para[Obj].Loc[0], p2[0], p3[0], p4[0]);
                        Maximum[1]=MAX4(Para[Obj].Loc[1], p2[1], p3[1], p4[1]);
                        Maximum[2]=MAX4(Para[Obj].Loc[2], p2[2], p3[2], p4[2]);
                        break;
    case Circles:      Vec(-Cir[Obj].Radius, -Cir[Obj].Radius, -
```

```
                                           Cir[Obj].Radius, Minimum);
                        Vec(Cir[Obj].Radius, Cir[Obj].Radius, Cir[Obj].Radius,
                                           Maximum);
                        VecAdd(Minimum, Cir[Obj].Loc, Minimum);
                        VecAdd(Maximum, Cir[Obj].Loc, Maximum);
                        break;
      case Ring      : Vec(-Rng[Obj].Rad2, -Rng[Obj].Rad2, -Rng[Obj].Rad2,
                                           Minimum);
                        Vec(Rng[Obj].Rad2, Rng[Obj].Rad2, Rng[Obj].Rad2, Maximum);
                        VecAdd(Minimum, Rng[Obj].Loc, Minimum);
                        VecAdd(Maximum, Rng[Obj].Loc, Maximum);
                        break;
      case Sphere    : Vec(-Sphr[Obj].Rad, -Sphr[Obj].Rad, -Sphr[Obj].Rad,
                                           Minimum);
                        Vec(Sphr[Obj].Rad, Sphr[Obj].Rad, Sphr[Obj].Rad,Maxmum);
                        VecAdd(Minimum, Sphr[Obj].Loc, Minimum);
                        VecAdd(Maximum, Sphr[Obj].Loc, Maximum); break;
      case Cone      : QuadraticBound(&Con[Obj], Minimum, Maximum); break;
      case Cylinder  : QuadraticBound(&Cyl[Obj], Minimum, Maximum); break;
      }
}


void GetMinAndMaxPoints(TDA Minimum, TDA Maximum)
{
    int ShapeNum, ObjectNum;
    TDA MinPt, MaxPt;

    VecNull(MinPt);
    VecNull(MaxPt);
    VecNull(Minimum);
    VecNull(Maximum);

    /* find min and max coords, don't include ground or lamps */

    for(ShapeNum=2; ShapeNum<=MaxShapeType; ShapeNum++)
    {
        for(ObjectNum=1; ObjectNum<=ObjCnt[ShapeNum]; ObjectNum++)
        {
        BoundingBoxes(ShapeNum, ObjectNum, MinPt, MaxPt);
        if((ShapeNum==2) && (ObjectNum==1))
        {
            VecCopy(MinPt, Minimum);
            VecCopy(MaxPt, Maximum);
        }
```

```
        else
        {
            VecMin(MinPt, Minimum, Minimum);
            VecMax(MaxPt, Maximum, Maximum);
        }
    }
  }
/* decrease minimum and increase maximum to */
/*  compensate for precision error */
VecSub(Minimum, PrecCor, Minimum);
VecAdd(Maximum, PrecCor, Maximum);
}
```

```
/*
```

```
┌──────────────────────────────────────────────────────┐
│ ┌──────────────────────────────────────────────────┐ │
│ │                                                    │ │
│ │                 Bounding Sphere                    │ │
│ │                                                    │ │
│ │      CreateBoundingSphere - setup bounding sphere  │ │
│ │                                                    │ │
│ └──────────────────────────────────────────────────┘ │
└──────────────────────────────────────────────────────┘
```

```
*/
```

```
typedef struct{
    TDA Center;
    float RadSqr;
} SphereType;

void CreateBoundingSphere(SphereType *sphere)
{
    TDA Minimum, Maximum;
    TDA temp;

    GetMinAndMaxPoints(Minimum, Maximum);
    VecSub(Maximum, Minimum, temp);  /* find center of bounding sphere */
    VecScalMult(0.5, temp, temp);
    VecAdd(Minimum, temp, sphere->Center);
    sphere->RadSqr=VecDot(temp, temp);/* find square of the radius of the */
                                /* bounding sphere - note Sqr(Sqrt()) */

}
```

```
/*
```

```
                     Bounding Prism

        CreateBoundingPrism - setup bounding prism
```

```
*/
```

```c
typedef struct{
   TDA Loc;
   TDA v1;
   TDA v2;
   TDA Norm;
   float NdotLoc;
} PrismFace;

typedef PrismFace PrismType[7];

void CreateBoundingPrism(PrismType Prism)
{
   Byte i, j;
   float dot[7];
   TDA Minimum, Maximum;
   TDA vec1, vec2, vec3;
   TDA span;
   TDA PrismLoc, temploc;
   TDA InitDir;
   PrismFace tempface;
   float tempdot;


GetMinAndMaxPoints(Minimum, Maximum);
/* find the 3 vectors that represent the edges of the bounding Prism and
                                   the Prism's location */
VecNull(vec1);
VecNull(vec2);
VecNull(vec3);
VecSub(Maximum, Minimum, span);
Vec(span[0], 0.0, 0.0, vec1);
Vec(0.0, span[1], 0.0, vec2);
Vec(0.0, 0.0, span[2], vec3);
VecCopy(Minimum, PrismLoc);
/* find 6 parallelograms that make up the faces of the bounding Prism*/
for(i=1; i<7; i++)
{
```

```
  VecNull(Prism[i].Loc);
  VecNull(Prism[i].v1);
  VecNull(Prism[i].v2);
  VecNull(Prism[i].Norm);
  Prism[i].NdotLoc=0.0;
}
VecCopy(PrismLoc, Prism[1].Loc);
VecCopy(vec1, Prism[1].v1);
VecCopy(vec3, Prism[1].v2);
VecCross(Prism[1].v1, Prism[1].v2, Prism[1].Norm);
VecNormalize(Prism[1].Norm);
Prism[1].NdotLoc=VecDot(Prism[1].Norm, Prism[1].Loc);
VecCopy(PrismLoc, Prism[2].Loc);
VecCopy(vec3, Prism[2].v1);
VecCopy(vec1, Prism[2].v2);
VecCross(Prism[2].v1, Prism[2].v2, Prism[2].Norm);
VecNormalize(Prism[2].Norm);
Vec(0.0, vec2[1], 0.0, temploc);
VecAdd(temploc, Prism[2].Loc, Prism[2].Loc);
Prism[2].NdotLoc=VecDot(Prism[2].Norm, Prism[2].Loc);
VecCopy(PrismLoc, Prism[3].Loc);
VecCopy(vec3, Prism[3].v1);
VecCopy(vec2, Prism[3].v2);
VecCross(Prism[3].v1, Prism[3].v2, Prism[3].Norm);
VecNormalize(Prism[3].Norm);
Prism[3].NdotLoc=VecDot(Prism[3].Norm, Prism[3].Loc);
VecCopy(PrismLoc, Prism[4].Loc);
VecCopy(vec2, Prism[4].v1);
VecCopy(vec3, Prism[4].v2);
VecCross(Prism[4].v1, Prism[4].v2, Prism[4].Norm);
VecNormalize(Prism[4].Norm);
Vec(vec1[0], 0.0, 0.0, temploc);
VecAdd(temploc, Prism[4].Loc, Prism[4].Loc);
Prism[4].NdotLoc=VecDot(Prism[4].Norm, Prism[4].Loc);
VecCopy(PrismLoc, Prism[5].Loc);
VecCopy(vec2, Prism[5].v1);
VecCopy(vec1, Prism[5].v2);
VecCross(Prism[5].v1, Prism[5].v2, Prism[5].Norm);
VecNormalize(Prism[5].Norm);
Prism[5].NdotLoc=VecDot(Prism[5].Norm, Prism[5].Loc);
VecCopy(PrismLoc, Prism[6].Loc);
VecCopy(vec1, Prism[6].v1);
VecCopy(vec2, Prism[6].v2);
VecCross(Prism[6].v1, Prism[6].v2, Prism[6].Norm);
```

```
VecNormalize(Prism[6].Norm);
Vec(0.0, 0.0, vec3[2], temploc);
VecAdd(temploc,Prism[6].Loc,
Prism[6].Loc);Prism[6].NdotLoc=VecDot(Prism[6].Norm, Prism[6].Loc);

/* Order Prisms for the intersection testing based on the direction of the
   initial eye ray -> this is the creation of the priority queue */

GetInitialDir((float)ScanXRes/2, (float)ScanYRes/2, InitDir);
for(i=1; i<7; i++)

   dot[i]=VecDot(InitDir, Prism[i].Norm);

/* Bubble sort based on closest opposite direction since rays approach
          closest opposite direction is when dot approaches -1.0 */

   for(j=1; j<7; j++)
   {
       for(i=1; i<6; i++)
       {
           if(dot[i]>dot[i+1])
           {
                   memcpy(&tempface, &Prism[i], sizeof(PrismFace));
                                                      /* swap */
                   memcpy(&Prism[i], &Prism[i+1], sizeof(PrismFace));
                   memcpy(&Prism[i+1], &tempface, sizeof(PrismFace));
                   tempdot=dot[i];
                   dot[i]=dot[i+1];
                   dot[i+1]=tempdot;
           }
       }
   }
}


/*
┌─────────────────────────────────────────────────────────────────┐
│                                                                   │
│                      Bounding Tetrahedron                         │
│      CreateBoundingTetra - setup bounding tetrahedron from loaded │
│                         TetraExtents                              │
│                                                                   │
└─────────────────────────────────────────────────────────────────┘
*/

typedef struct{
   TDA Loc;
```

```
   TDA v1;
   TDA v2;
   TDA Norm;
   float NdotLoc;
 } TetraFace;


typedef TetraFace TetraType[5];


void CreateBoundingTetra(TetraType Tetra)
{
   Byte i, j;
   float dot[5];
   TDA TetraLoc;
   TDA InitDir;
   TDA temp;
   TetraFace tempface;
   float tempdot;


/* Loaded are 4 extents for a bounding tetrahedron - TetraExtent<n> */
/* increase size of extents to compensate for precision error *

VecScalMult(1.1, TetraExtent1, TetraExtent1);
VecScalMult(1.1, TetraExtent2, TetraExtent2);
VecScalMult(1.1, TetraExtent3, TetraExtent3);
VecScalMult(1.1, TetraExtent4, TetraExtent4);


/* find 4 triangles that make up the faces of the bounding Tetrahedron*/

for(i=1; i<5; i++)
{
       VecNull(Tetra[i].Loc);
       VecNull(Tetra[i].v1);
       VecNull(Tetra[i].v2);
       VecNull(Tetra[i].Norm);
       Tetra[i].NdotLoc=0.0;
}
VecAdd3(TetraExtent1, TetraExtent2, TetraExtent3, temp);
VecScalMult(1.0/3.0, temp, TetraLoc);
VecAdd(TetraLoc, TetraExtent1, Tetra[1].Loc);
VecSub(TetraExtent2, TetraExtent1, Tetra[1].v1);
VecSub(TetraExtent4, TetraExtent1, Tetra[1].v2);
VecCross(Tetra[1].v1, Tetra[1].v2, Tetra[1].Norm);
VecNormalize(Tetra[1].Norm);
```

```
Tetra[1].NdotLoc=VecDot(Tetra[1].Norm, Tetra[1].Loc);
VecAdd(TetraLoc, TetraExtent2, Tetra[2].Loc);
VecSub(TetraExtent3, TetraExtent2, Tetra[2].v1);
VecSub(TetraExtent4, TetraExtent2, Tetra[2].v2);
VecCross(Tetra[2].v1, Tetra[2].v2, Tetra[2].Norm);
VecNormalize(Tetra[2].Norm);
Tetra[2].NdotLoc=VecDot(Tetra[2].Norm, Tetra[2].Loc);
VecAdd(TetraLoc, TetraExtent3, Tetra[3].Loc);
VecSub(TetraExtent1, TetraExtent3, Tetra[3].v1);
VecSub(TetraExtent4, TetraExtent3, Tetra[3].v2);
VecCross(Tetra[3].v1, Tetra[3].v2, Tetra[3].Norm);
VecNormalize(Tetra[3].Norm);
Tetra[3].NdotLoc=VecDot(Tetra[3].Norm, Tetra[3].Loc);
VecAdd(TetraLoc, TetraExtent1, Tetra[4].Loc);
VecSub(TetraExtent3, TetraExtent1, Tetra[4].v1);
VecSub(TetraExtent2, TetraExtent1, Tetra[4].v2);
VecCross(Tetra[4].v1, Tetra[4].v2, Tetra[4].Norm);
VecNormalize(Tetra[4].Norm);
Tetra[4].NdotLoc=VecDot(Tetra[4].Norm, Tetra[4].Loc);

/* Order Tetrahedrons for the intersection testing based on the direction
of the initial eye ray -> this is the creation of the priority queue */

GetInitialDir((float)ScanXRes/2, (float)ScanYRes/2, InitDir);
for(i=1; i<5; i++)
   dot[i]=VecDot(InitDir, Tetra[i].Norm);

 /* Bubble sort based on closest opposite direction since rays approach
          closest opposite direction is when dot approaches -1.0 */

for(j=1; j<5; j++)
{
   for(i=1; i<4; i++)
   {
      if(dot[i]>dot[i+1])
   {
      memcpy(&tempface, &Tetra[i], sizeof(TetraFace));       /* swap */
      memcpy(&Tetra[i], &Tetra[i+1], sizeof(TetraFace));
      memcpy(&Tetra[i+1], &tempface, sizeof(TetraFace));
      tempdot=dot[i];
      dot[i]=dot[i+1];
      dot[i+1]=tempdot;
   }
}
```

```
  }
}
  /*
```

```
    ShootRay - check ray Intersect against all objects and return nearest

       Bounding Sphere and Bounding Prism or
       Bounding Sphere and Bounding Tetrahedron or
       Bounding Sphere or Bounding Prism or Bounding Tetrahedron
  */

  SphereType BoundingSphere;
  PrismType BoundingPrism;
  TetraType BoundingTetra;

  void InitBoundingObjects()
  {
     if(BoundingSphereTest)
         CreateBoundingSphere(&BoundingSphere);
     if(BoundingPrismTest)
         CreateBoundingPrism(BoundingPrism);
     if(BoundingTetraTest)
         CreateBoundingTetra(BoundingTetra);
  }

  Boolean InitialRay;

  void SetUpTri(Byte i, Byte p1, Byte p2)
  {
     gu[0]=-delta[p1];
     gv[0]=-delta[p2];
     gu[1]=BoundingTetra[i].v1[p1]-delta[p1];
     gv[1]=BoundingTetra[i].v1[p2]-delta[p2];
     gu[2]=BoundingTetra[i].v2[p1]-delta[p1];
     gv[2]=BoundingTetra[i].v2[p2]-delta[p2];
  }

  void SetUpPara(Byte i, Byte p1, Byte p2)
  {
     gu[0]=-delta[p1];
     gv[0]=-delta[p2];
     gu[1]=BoundingPrism[i].v1[p1]-delta[p1];
```

```
          gv[1]=BoundingPrism[i].v1[p2]-delta[p2];
          gu[2]=BoundingPrism[i].v2[p1]+BoundingPrism[i].v1[p1]-delta[p1];
          gv[2]=BoundingPrism[i].v2[p2]+BoundingPrism[i].v1[p2]-delta[p2];
          gu[3]=BoundingPrism[i].v2[p1]-delta[p1];
          gv[3]=BoundingPrism[i].v2[p2]-delta[p2];
     }


Boolean HitBoundingSphere;

void DoBoundingSphereTest(TDA Start, TDA Dir)
{
VecSub(BoundingSphere.Center, Start, temp);    /* check hit with */
b=VecDot(Dir, temp)*-2.0;                       /* bounding sphere */
c=VecDot(temp, temp)-BoundingSphere.RadSqr;
disc=SqrFP(b)-4.0*c;
if(disc<=0.0)
   HitBoundingSphere=false;
else
{
   sroot=sqrt(disc);
   t1=(-b-sroot)*0.5;
   t2=(-b+sroot)*0.5;
   if((!(t1>Small)) && (!(t2>Small)))
        HitBoundingSphere=false;
   else
        HitBoundingSphere=true;
}
}
floatdot;
float pos1, pos2;
Boolean HitBoundingPrism;

void DoBoundingPrismTest(TDA Start, TDA Dir)
{
   Byte i, last;

   if(InitialRay)
   {
        InitialRay=false;
        last=4;
   }
   else
        last=7;
   i=1;
```

```
    do
    {
         dot=VecDot(BoundingPrism[i].Norm, Dir);
         if(fabs(dot)<Small)
             HitBoundingPrism=false;
         else
         {
             pos1=BoundingPrism[i].NdotLoc;
             pos2=VecDot(BoundingPrism[i].Norm, Start);
             t=(pos1-pos2)/dot;
             GetIntrPt(Start, Dir, t, IntrPoint);
             VecSub(IntrPoint, BoundingPrism[i].Loc, delta);
             if((fabs(BoundingPrism[i].Norm[0])>fabs(BoundingPrism[i].
                                                       Norm[1])) &&
             (fabs(BoundingPrism[i].Norm[0])>fabs(BoundingPrism[i].
                                                       Norm[2])))
               SetUpPara(i, 1, 2);
             else
             {
               if(!(fabs(BoundingPrism[i].Norm[1])<fabs(BoundingPrism[i].
                                                       Norm[2])))
                     SetUpPara(i, 0, 2);
                else
                     SetUpPara(i, 0, 1);
             }
             if(EvenCrossings(4))
                     HitBoundingPrism=false;
             else
                     HitBoundingPrism=true;
         }
         ++i;
    }
  while((i!=last) && (HitBoundingPrism==false));
}

Boolean HitBoundingTetra;

void DoBoundingTetraTest(TDA Start, TDA Dir)
{
  Byte i, last;

  if(InitialRay)
  {
       InitialRay=false;
```

```
            last=4;
    }
    else
            last=5;
    i=1;
    do
    {
            dot=VecDot(BoundingTetra[i].Norm, Dir);
            if(fabs(dot)<Small)
                HitBoundingTetra=false;
            else
            {
pos1=BoundingTetra[i].NdotLoc;
pos2=VecDot(BoundingTetra[i].Norm, Start);
t=(pos1-pos2)/dot;
GetIntrPt(Start, Dir, t, IntrPoint);
VecSub(IntrPoint, BoundingTetra[i].Loc, delta);
if((fabs(BoundingTetra[i].Norm[0])>fabs(BoundingTetra[i].Norm[1]))&&
 (fabs(BoundingTetra[i].Norm[0])>fabs(BoundingTetra[i].Norm[2])))
    SetUpTri(i, 1, 2);
else
{
    if(!(fabs(BoundingTetra[i].Norm[1])<fabs(BoundingTetra[i].Norm[2])))
      SetUpTri(i, 0, 2);
    else
      SetUpTri(i, 0, 1);
    }
    if(EvenCrossings(3))
            HitBoundingTetra=false;
    else
            HitBoundingTetra=true;
    }
    ++i;
    }
    while((i!=last) && (HitBoundingTetra==false));
}


void IntersectTest(TDA Start, TDA Dir, int *Shp, int *Obj, float *Dist,
                                        Boolean *ObjHit)
{
    int ShapeNum;
    int ObjectNum;
    float NewDist;
```

```
    *ObjHit=false;
    for(ShapeNum=0; ShapeNum<=MaxShapeType; ShapeNum++)
    {
         for(ObjectNum=1; ObjectNum<=ObjCnt[ShapeNum]; ObjectNum++)
         {
              NewDist=Intersect(Start, Dir, ShapeNum, ObjectNum);
              if(NewDist>Small)
              {
                   if(*Dist==-1.0)
                   {
                        *ObjHit=true;
                        *Dist=NewDist;
                        *Shp=ShapeNum;
                        *Obj=ObjectNum;
                   }
                   else
                   {
                        /* find closest object */
                        if(NewDist<*Dist)
                        {
                             *Dist=NewDist;
                             *Shp=ShapeNum;
                             *Obj=ObjectNum;
                        }
                   }
              }
         }
    }
}

void IntersectGroundTest(TDA Start, TDA Dir, int *Shp, int *Obj, float
                                   *Dist, Boolean *ObjHit)
{
    float NewDist;

    *ObjHit=false;
    NewDist=Intersect(Start, Dir, Ground, 1);
    if(NewDist>Small)
    {
         *ObjHit=true;
         *Dist=NewDist;
         *Shp=Ground;
         *Obj=1;
    }
```

```
      }

void ShootRay(TDA Start, TDA Dir, int *Shp, int *Obj, float *Dist,
                                             Boolean *ObjHit)
{
   Byte i;

   *Shp=-1;
   *Obj=-1;
   *Dist=-1.0;
   *ObjHit=false;
   if((!BoundingSphereTest) && (!BoundingPrismTest) && (!BoundingTetraTest))
        IntersectTest(Start, Dir, Shp, Obj, Dist, ObjHit);
   else if(BoundingSphereTest)
   {
        DoBoundingSphereTest(Start, Dir);
        if((HitBoundingSphere) && (BoundingPrismTest))
        {
           DoBoundingPrismTest(Start, Dir);
           if(HitBoundingPrism)
             IntersectTest(Start, Dir, Shp, Obj, Dist, ObjHit);
           else if(GroundExists)
             IntersectGroundTest(Start, Dir, Shp, Obj, Dist, ObjHit);
           }
           else if((HitBoundingSphere) && (BoundingTetraTest))
           {
                   DoBoundingTetraTest(Start, Dir);
                   if(HitBoundingTetra)
                     IntersectTest(Start, Dir, Shp, Obj, Dist, ObjHit);
                   else if(GroundExists)
        IntersectGroundTest(Start, Dir, Shp, Obj, Dist, ObjHit);
                   }
           else if(HitBoundingSphere)
                   IntersectTest(Start, Dir, Shp, Obj, Dist, ObjHit);
           else if(GroundExists)
                   IntersectGroundTest(Start, Dir, Shp, Obj, Dist, ObjHit);
   }
   else if(BoundingPrismTest)
   {
           DoBoundingPrismTest(Start, Dir);
           if(HitBoundingPrism)
                   IntersectTest(Start, Dir, Shp, Obj, Dist, ObjHit);
           else if(GroundExists)
                   IntersectGroundTest(Start, Dir, Shp, Obj, Dist, ObjHit);
```

```
        }
    else if(BoundingTetraTest)
    {
            DoBoundingTetraTest(Start, Dir);
            if(HitBoundingTetra)
                    IntersectTest(Start, Dir, Shp, Obj, Dist, ObjHit);
            else if(GroundExists)
                    IntersectGroundTest(Start, Dir, Shp, Obj, Dist, ObjHit);

    }
}


/*
```

```
    ┌──────────────────────────────────────────────────────────────┐
    │   Calculate Contribution of Local Color Model at Intersection Point │
    └──────────────────────────────────────────────────────────────┘

        GetLoclCol - calculate ambient, diffuse, reflection and specular
                                    reflection
*/
#define  MaxNoise 28
Word NoiseMatrix[MaxNoise][MaxNoise][MaxNoise];
void InitNoise()
{
    Byte x, y, z;
    Byte i, j, k;

    randomize();
    for(x=0; x<=MaxNoise-1; x++)
    {
            for(y=0; y<=MaxNoise-1; y++)
            {
                    for(z=0; z<=MaxNoise-1; z++)
                    {
                    NoiseMatrix[x][y][z] = random(12000);
                    if(x==MaxNoise-1)
                            i=0;
                    else
                            i=x;
                    if(y==MaxNoise-1)
                            j=0;
                    else
                            j=y;
                    if(z==MaxNoise-1)
                            k=0;
                    else
```

```
                              k=z;
                    NoiseMatrix[x][y][z]=NoiseMatrix[i][j][k];
                    }
              }
        }
}


int Noise(float x, float y, float z)
{
```

/* harmonic and random functions combined to create a noise function based
   on Perlin's (1985) noise function - ideas found in Alan Watt's
         Fundamentals of Three-Dimensional Computer Graphics */

```
   int ix, iy, iz;
   float ox, oy, oz;
   int p000, p001;
   int p010, p011;
   int p100, p101;
   int p110, p111;
   int p00, p01;
   int p10, p11;
   int p0, p1;
   int d00, d01;
   int d10, d11;
   int d0, d1;
   int d;

   x=fabs(x);
   y=fabs(y);
   z=fabs(z);
   ix=Trunc(x)%MaxNoise; iy=Trunc(y)%MaxNoise; iz=Trunc(z)%MaxNoise;
   ox=x-(int)x;
   oy=y-(int)y;
   oz=z-(int)z;
   p000=NoiseMatrix[ix][iy][iz];
   p001=NoiseMatrix[ix][iy][iz+1];
   p010=NoiseMatrix[ix][iy+1][iz];
   p011=NoiseMatrix[ix][iy+1][iz+1];
   p100=NoiseMatrix[ix+1][iy][iz];
   p101=NoiseMatrix[ix+1][iy][iz+1];
   p110=NoiseMatrix[ix+1][iy+1][iz];
   p111=NoiseMatrix[ix+1][iy+1][iz+1];
```

```
      d00=p100-p000;
      d01=p101-p001;
      d10=p110-p010;
      d11=p111-p011;
      p00=Trunc((float)d00*ox)+p000;
      p01=Trunc((float)d01*ox)+p001;
      p10=Trunc((float)d10*ox)+p010;
      p11=Trunc((float)d11*ox)+p011;
      d0=p10-p00;
      d1=p11-p01;
      p0=Trunc((float)d0*oy)+p00;
      p1=Trunc((float)d1*oy)+p01;
      d=p1-p0;
      return((Trunc((float)d*oz)+p0));
}

void MarbleTex(TDA Pt, TDA RGB)
{
   float i, d;
   float x, y, z;

   UnVec(Pt, &x, &y, &z);
   x*=0.2;
   d=x+0.0006*(float)Noise(x, y*0.1, z*0.1);
   d*=(float)(Trunc(d)%25);
   i=0.5+0.05*fabs(d-10.0-20.0*(float)Trunc(d*0.05));
   if (i > 1.0)
       i = 1.0;
   Vec(i, i, i, RGB);
}

void WoodTex(TDA Pt, TDA RGB)
{
   float i, d;
   float x, y, z;

   UnVec(Pt, &x, &y, &z);
   x*=0.2;
   d=x+0.0002*(float)Noise(x, y*0.1, z*0.1);
   d*=(float)(Trunc(d)%25);
   i=0.7+0.05*fabs(d-10.0-20.0*(float)Trunc(d*0.05));
   if (i > 1.0)
       i = 1.0;
   Vec(i, i, i, RGB);
```

```
      }

Byte TextureNumbs(int Shp, int Obj)
{
   Byte tex;

   switch(Shp)
   {
        case Ground : tex=Gnd.TexNum;
                        break;
        case Triangle     : tex=Tri[Obj].TexNum;
                        break;
        case Parallelogram : tex=Para[Obj].TexNum;
                        break;
        case Circles      : tex=Cir[Obj].TexNum;
                        break;
        case Ring   : tex=Rng[Obj].TexNum;
                        break;
        case Sphere : tex=Sphr[Obj].TexNum;
                        break;
        case Cone   : tex=Con[Obj].TexNum;
                        break;
        case Cylinder     : tex=Cyl[Obj].TexNum;
                        break;
   }
   return(tex);
}

Byte MaterialNumbs(int Shp, int Obj)
{
   Byte mtl;

   switch(Shp)
   {
        case Ground : mtl=Gnd.MtlNum;
                        break;
        case Triangle     : mtl=Tri[Obj].MtlNum;
                        break;
        case Parallelogram : mtl=Para[Obj].MtlNum;
                        break;
        case Circles      : mtl=Cir[Obj].MtlNum;
                        break;
        case Ring   : mtl=Rng[Obj].MtlNum;
```

```
                            break;
            case Sphere : mtl=Sphr[Obj].MtlNum;

                            break;
            case Cone   : mtl=Con[Obj].MtlNum;
                            break;
            case Cylinder   : mtl=Cyl[Obj].MtlNum;
                            break;
    }
    return(mtl);
}

void Texture(TDA IntrPt, int Tex, TDA Texturing)
{
    int x, y, z, rt;
    float lev, lev1, lev2, lev3, r;

    switch(Tex)
    {
    case Checker    : x=Round(fabs(IntrPt[0])*Tile)%10000;
                    y=Round(fabs(IntrPt[1])*Tile)%10000;
                    z=Round(fabs(IntrPt[2])*Tile)%10000;
                    if(((x+y+z)%2)==1)
                            VecCopy(Tile1, Texturing);
                    else
                            VecCopy(Tile2, Texturing); break;
    case Grit       : rt=random(32767);
                    r=(float) rt/32768.0; lev=r*0.2+0.8;
                    Vec(lev, lev, lev, Texturing);
                    break;
    case Marble     : MarbleTex(IntrPt, Texturing); break;
    case Wood       : WoodTex(IntrPt, Texturing);
                    break;
    case Sheetrock  : rt=random(32767);
                    r=(float) rt/32768.0; lev=r*0.1+0.9;
                    Vec(lev, lev, lev, Texturing);
                    break;
    case Particle   : rt=random(32767);
                    r=(float) rt/32768.0;
                    lev1=r*0.15+0.85;
                    lev2=r*0.15+0.85;
                    lev3=r*0.15+0.85;
                    Vec(lev1, lev2, lev3, Texturing);
                    break;
```

```
      }
   }

   Boolean ObjHitTransmissive(Byte Mtl)
   {
   if((Matl[Mtl].Trans[0]==0.0) &&
      (Matl[Mtl].Trans[1]==0.0) &&
      (Matl[Mtl].Trans[2]==0.0))
      return(false);
   else
      return(true);
   }

   void GetLoclCol(int Shp, int Obj,
                   TDA Dir, TDA IntrPt, TDA SrfNrm,
                   float Dist, TDA LoclCol)
   {
      int Mtl, Tex, Src;
      Boolean ObjHit, HitItself;
      float IntensFactor;
      TDA LmpDir;
      TDA Addition;
      TDA Total;
      float Lamb;
      TDA Spec, Diff;
      TDA Temp;
      float cone, Glint;
      int ShadShp;
      int ShadObj;
      float ShadDist;
      TDA ShadIntrPt;
      TDA ShadSrfNrm;
      float Alpha;
      TDA ColorTexture;


      if(Shp==Lamp)
      {
         if(DistEffect==0.0)
            IntensFactor=1.0;
         else
            IntensFactor=(1.0-DistEffect)+DistEffect*(-VecDot(SrfNrm, Dir)/
                                                     sqrt(Dist));
         VecScalMult(IntensFactor, Lmp[Obj].Intens, LoclCol);
```

```
}
else
{

    Mtl=MaterialNumbs(Shp, Obj);
        /* Ambient Component */
    VecCopy(Matl[Mtl].AmbRfl, Total);
    for(Src=1; Src<=ObjCnt[Lamp]; Src++)
    {
        VecSub(Lmp[Src].Loc, IntrPt, LmpDir);
        VecNormalize(LmpDir);
        ShootRay(IntrPt, LmpDir, &ShadShp, &ShadObj, &ShadDist, &ObjHit);

    /* There is no need to check beyond lamp since the closest
    object is returned. If the shadow feeler hits the lamp that
    is in the direction of the lamp (itself), then the hit is ignored.

    If the shadow feeler hits a transmissive object, then the
    lamp's contribution is attenutated by α and by the transmis
    sion factor - no refraction in the object is taken into ac
    count. Note that α represents a percentage of transmission
    based on the angle between LmpDir and the obstructing object's
    surface normal and that α also has a constant component.
    */

    if((ObjHit) && ((ShadShp==Lamp) && (ShadObj==Src)))
        HitItself=true;
    else
        HitItself=false;
    if((!(ObjHit)) || HitItself)
    {
        /* Unshadowed surface */
        Lamb=VecDot(SrfNrm, LmpDir);            /* N - L */ if(Lamb<=0.0)
        {
                    VecNull(Spec);
                VecNull(Diff);
    }
    else
    {
        /* Diffuse Component */
        VecElemMult(Lamb, Matl[Mtl].DifRfl, Lmp[Src].Intens, Diff);

        /* Specular Component */
        VecSub(LmpDir, Dir, Temp);
        VecScalMult(0.5, Temp, Temp);           /* H = (L + V) / 2 */
```

347

```
                VecNormalize(Temp);
                cone=VecDot(SrfNrm, Temp);
                if(cone>0.5)
                {
                        Glint=exp(Matl[Mtl].Gloss*Log(cone));
                        VecElemMult(Glint, Matl[Mtl].SpcRfl, Lmp[Src].Intens,
                                                                Spec);
                }
                else
                        VecNull(Spec);
        }
        VecAdd(Diff, Spec, Addition);
        VecAdd(Total, Addition, Total);
    }
    else if(ShadShp!=Lamp)
    {
        Mtl=MaterialNumbs(ShadShp, ShadObj);
        if(ObjHitTransmissive(Mtl))
        {
        /* Light through transmissive object */
        GetIntrPt(IntrPt, LmpDir, ShadDist, ShadIntrPt);
        GetSrfNrm(ShadShp, ShadObj, ShadIntrPt, ShadSrfNrm);
         Alpha=0.7*fabs(VecDot(LmpDir, ShadSrfNrm))+0.2;
        VecElemMult(Alpha, Lmp[Src].Intens, Matl[Mtl].Trans, Addition);
        VecAdd(Total, Addition, Total);
    }
  Mtl=MaterialNumbs(Shp, Obj);
 }
}
Tex=TextureNumbs(Shp, Obj);
if((Tex==Smooth) || (Tex==OceanWaves) || (Tex==PoolWaves) || (Tex==Waves))
   VecCopy(Total, LoclCol);              /* don't modify color */
else
{
   Texture(IntrPt, Tex, ColorTexture);
   VecElemMult(1.0, Total, ColorTexture, LoclCol);
}
}
}
/*
```

```
┌─────────────────────────────────────────────────────────────┐
│                                                               │
│                         Calculate Sky                         │
│                                                               │
└─────────────────────────────────────────────────────────────┘
```

Sky   - blend a sky color from the horizon to the zenith

```
    CloudySky - noise function clouds with blended sky color
*/

void Sky(TDA Dir, TDA Col)
{
    float small2=1E-03;
    float sin2, cos2;
    float x2, y2, z2;

    x2=SqrFP(Dir[0]);
    y2=SqrFP(Dir[1]);
    z2=SqrFP(Dir[2]);
    if(z2==0)
            z2=small2;
    sin2=z2/(x2+y2+z2);
    cos2=1.0-sin2;
    VecLinComb(cos2, HorCol, sin2, ZenCol, Col);
}

void CloudySky(TDA Dir, TDA SkyCol)
{
    float small2=1E-03;
    float sin2, cos2;
    float x2, y2, z2;
    TDA Col;
    TDA Col1, Col2;
    float x, y, z;
    float d, f;

    UnVec(Dir, &x, &y, &z);
    x2=SqrFP(Dir[0]);
    y2=SqrFP(Dir[1]);
    z2=SqrFP(Dir[2]);
    if(z2==0)
            z2=small2;
    sin2=z2/(x2+y2+z2);
    cos2=1.0-sin2;
    VecLinComb(cos2, HorCol, sin2, ZenCol, Col);
    x*=10.0;
    y*=10.0;
    z*=400.0;
    d=z+0.0006*Noise(x, y, z);
    d*=(float)(Trunc(d)%25);
```

```
       f=0.06*fabs(d-10.0-20.0*(float)Trunc(d*0.05)); if(f>1.0)
       f=1.0;
       Vec(Col[2], Col[2], Col[2], Col1); /* Grey scale white for clouds */
                                          /*  based on blue level */
       VecCopy(Col, Col2);               /* color = sky blue */
       VecLinComb(f, Col1, 1.0-f, Col2, SkyCol);
}


/*
```

```
┌────────────────────────────────────────────────────────────┐
│ ┌──────────────────────────────────────────────────────────┐ │
│ │                    Recursive Ray Tracer                  │ │
│ └──────────────────────────────────────────────────────────┘ │
└────────────────────────────────────────────────────────────┘
```

```
       TraceRay - perform recursive ray tracing

*/

void Comb(TDA A, TDA B, TDA C, TDA D, TDA E, TDA F, TDA Col)
{
   TDA T1, T2, T3;

   VecElemMult(1.0, A, B, T1);
   VecElemMult(1.0, C, D, T2);
   VecElemMult(1.0, E, F, T3);
   VecAdd3(T1, T2, T3, Col);
}

Boolean WgtMin(TDA TotWgt)
{
   if((TotWgt[0]<=MinWgt[0])&&
         (TotWgt[1]<=MinWgt[1])&&
         (TotWgt[2]<=MinWgt[2]))
      return(true);
   else
      return(false);
}

Boolean MaterialSpecular(int Shp, Byte Mtl)
{
   if(!(Shp==Lamp))
   {
       if((Matl[Mtl].SpcRfl[0]==0.0)&&
          (Matl[Mtl].SpcRfl[1]==0.0)&&
          (Matl[Mtl].SpcRfl[2]==0.0))
```

```
      return(false);
    else
      return(true);
    }
    else
      return(true);
}


Boolean MaterialTransmissive(int Shp, Byte Mtl)
{
    if(!(Shp==Lamp))
    {
        if((Matl[Mtl].Trans[0]==0.0)&&
           (Matl[Mtl].Trans[1]==0.0)&&
           (Matl[Mtl].Trans[2]==0.0))
          return(false);
        else
          return(true);
    }
    else
      return(false);
}


void TraceRay(TDA Start, TDA Dir, TDA TotWgt, Byte Depth, TDA Col)
{
    TDA LoclCol, ReflCol, TranCol;
    TDA ReflDir, TranDir, Wgt;
    TDA IntrPt, SrfNrm;
    int Shp, Obj;
    float Dist;
    Byte Mtl, Tex;
    float f1, f2, f3, f4;
    float Ampl, Dampen, Dampen2;
    TDA OnesVec={1.0, 1.0, 1.0};
    TDA Temp;
    Boolean ObjHit;
    Boolean Dummy;

    ShootRay(Start, Dir, &Shp, &Obj, &Dist, &ObjHit);
    if(ObjHit)
    {

        GetIntrPt(Start, Dir, Dist, IntrPt);
        GetSrfNrm(Shp, Obj, IntrPt, SrfNrm);
```

```
Tex=TextureNumbs(Shp, Obj); if(Tex==OceanWaves)
{
    /* Bump Surface Normal for Texture */
    f1=sin(Radians(IntrPt[0]+IntrPt[1]+OceanWavePhase));
    f2=sin(Radians(2.5*IntrPt[0]+IntrPt[1]+OceanWavePhase));
    f3=sin(Radians(IntrPt[0]+1.7*IntrPt[1]+OceanWavePhase));
    f4=sin(Radians(1.5*IntrPt[0]+4.1*IntrPt[1]+OceanWavePhase));
    Ampl=OceanWaveAmpl*(f1+f2+f3+f4)*0.25;
    SrfNrm[0]+=Ampl;
    SrfNrm[1]+=Ampl;
    VecNormalize(SrfNrm);
}
if(Tex==PoolWaves)
{
/* Bump Surface Normal for Texture */
Dampen=sqrt(SqrFP(IntrPt[0]-PoolWaveXPos)+SqrFP(IntrPt[1]-
                                        PoolWaveYPos));
Dampen2=Dampen*1E-02;
if(Dampen2<1.0)
  Dampen2=1.0;
Ampl=PoolWaveAmpl*sin(Radians(2.5*Dampen+PoolWavePhase))/Dampen2;
SrfNrm[0]+=Ampl;
SrfNrm[1]+=Ampl;
VecNormalize(SrfNrm);
}
if(Tex==Waves)
{
    /* Bump Surface Normal for Texture */
    Dampen=sqrt(SqrFP(IntrPt[0]-WaveXPos)+
    SqrFP(IntrPt[1]-WaveYPos)+
    SqrFP(IntrPt[2]-WaveZPos));
    Dampen2=Dampen*1E-02;
    if(Dampen2<1.0)
    Dampen2=1.0;
    Ampl=WaveAmpl*cos(Radians(60.0*Dampen+WavePhase))/Dampen2;
                                        SrfNrm[0]+=Ampl;
    SrfNrm[1]+=Ampl;
    SrfNrm[2]+=Ampl;
    VecNormalize(SrfNrm);
}
if((Shp==Lamp) && (!(LampReflects)))
    GetLoclCol(Shp, Obj, Dir, IntrPt, SrfNrm, Dist, Col);
else
{
```

```
GetLoclCol(Shp, Obj, Dir, IntrPt, SrfNrm, Dist, LoclCol);
if((Depth==MaxDepth) || (WgtMin(TotWgt)))
     VecElemMult(1.0, LoclCol, LoclWgt, Col);
else
{
if((Shp!=Lamp) || ((Shp==Lamp) && LampReflects))
{
     Mtl=MaterialNumbs(Shp, Obj);
     if(MaterialSpecular(Shp, Mtl))
     {
         CalcDirOfReflRay(Dir, SrfNrm, ReflDir);
         VecElemMult(1.0, TotWgt, ReflWgt, Wgt);
         TraceRay(IntrPt, ReflDir, Wgt, Depth+1, ReflCol);
         if(Shp!=Lamp)
         {
              VecSub(OnesVec, Mtl[Mtl].Trans, Temp);
              VecElemMult(1.0, ReflCol, Temp, ReflCol);
         }
     }
     else
         VecNull(ReflCol);
     if(MaterialTransmissive(Shp, Mtl))
     {
         /* take ray through object and exit the other side */
         CalcDirOfTranRay(Dir, SrfNrm, Mtl, TranDir);
         ShootRay(IntrPt, TranDir, &Shp, &Obj, &Dist, &Dummy);
         GetIntrPt(IntrPt, TranDir, Dist, IntrPt);
         GetSrfNrm(Shp, Obj, IntrPt, SrfNrm);
         CalcDirOfTranRay(TranDir, SrfNrm, Mtl, TranDir);
         VecElemMult(1.0, TotWgt, TranWgt, Wgt);
         TraceRay(IntrPt, TranDir, Wgt, Depth+1, TranCol);
         VecElemMult(1.0, TranCol, Mtl[Mtl].Trans, TranCol);
     }
     else
         VecNull(TranCol);
     }
     else
     {
         VecNull(ReflCol);
         VecNull(TranCol);
     }
     if((Shp==Lamp) && LampReflects)
     {
         VecSub(OnesVec, LampRefl, Temp);
```

```
                    VecElemMult(1.0, Temp, LoclCol, LoclCol);
                    VecElemMult(1.0, LampRefl, ReflCol, ReflCol);
                    VecAdd(LoclCol, ReflCol, Col);
                }
            else
                Comb(LoclCol, LoclWgt,
                        ReflCol, ReflWgt,
                        TranCol, TranWgt, Col);
                }
            }
        }
    else
    {
        if(SkyExists)
        {
            if(Clouds)
                    CloudySky(Dir, Col);
            else
                    Sky(Dir, Col);
        }
        else
            VecNull(Col);
    }
}


/*

    ┌─────────────────────────────────────────────────────────┐
    │                                                         │
    │      General Screen and Viewing Vector Calculations     │
    │                                                         │
    └─────────────────────────────────────────────────────────┘
*/

void PreCalculation()
{
    float Scale;

    XAspDivFocLen=Asp/FocalLength;
    YAspDivFocLen=1.0/FocalLength;
    CenterX=ScanXRes>>1;
    CenterY=ScanYRes>>1;
    Scale=(float)CenterX;
    VecScalMult(Scale, ViewDir, ViewVec);
}
```

```
Palette_Register PalArray;

void ClearScreen()
{
   Set_Graphics_Mode(ScanXRes, ScanYRes);
   Init_Palette(PalArray);
   Set_Palette(PalArray);
}
```

```
/*
┌─────────────────────────────────────────────────────┐
│ ┌─────────────────────────────────────────────────┐ │
│ │                  RGB File Buffer                │ │
│ └─────────────────────────────────────────────────┘ │
└─────────────────────────────────────────────────────┘
*/
```

```
#define MaxBufLen 3*ScanXRes

Word BufLen;
Byte Buffer[3072];
Word BufIndex;

void InitLineBuffer()
{
   for(BufIndex=0; BufIndex<MaxBufLen; BufIndex++)
           Buffer[BufIndex]=0;
   BufIndex=0;
   BufLen=3*ScanXRes;
}


FILE *RGBFile;

void PutRGBHeader()
{
   putw(ScanXRes, RGBFile);
   putw(ScanYRes, RGBFile);
   BufIndex=0;
}

void AddToLineBuffer(TDIA Colr)
{
   Buffer[BufIndex++]=(Colr[0]&255)>>2;    /* Red */
   Buffer[BufIndex++]=(Colr[1]&255)>>2;    /* Green */
```

```
    Buffer[BufIndex++]=(Colr[2]&255)>>2;   /* Blue */
}


void WriteLineBufferToRGBFile()
{
    fwrite(Buffer, 3*XRes, 1, RGBFile);
    BufIndex=0;
}


/*
```

```
┌─────────────────────────────────────────────────────────────┐
│ ┌───────────────────────────────────────────────────────────┐ │
│ │              Allocated Memory Management                  │ │
│ └───────────────────────────────────────────────────────────┘ │
└─────────────────────────────────────────────────────────────┘
```

```
*/

void Allocate_Memory()
{
Matl=farcalloc(MaxMaterial, sizeof(MaterialList));
Lmp=farcalloc(MaxLamp, sizeof(LampList));
Tri=farcalloc(MaxTriangle, sizeof(TriangleList));
Para=farcalloc(MaxParallelogram, sizeof(ParallelogramList));
Cir=farcalloc(MaxCircles, sizeof(CircleList));
Rng=farcalloc(MaxRing, sizeof(RingList));
Sphr=farcalloc(MaxSphere, sizeof(SphereList));
Con=farcalloc(MaxCone, sizeof(ConeList));
Cyl=farcalloc(MaxCylinder, sizeof(CylinderList));
if((Matl==NULL) || (Lmp==NULL) || (Tri==NULL) || (Para==NULL) ||
   (Cir==NULL) || (Rng==NULL) || (Sphr==NULL) || (Con==NULL) || (Cyl==NULL))
{
    Exit_Graphics();
    printf("Cannot allocate enough memory!\n\n Hit any key to exit.");
    getch();
    exit(1);
}
Red_Plane=farmalloc(16000);
Green_Plane=farmalloc(16000);
Blue_Plane=farmalloc(16000);
if((Red_Plane==NULL) || (Green_Plane==NULL) || (Blue_Plane==NULL))
{
    Exit_Graphics();
    printf("Cannot allocate enough memory for planes!\n\n Hit any key to
                                               exit.");
    getch();
```

```
    exit(1);
    }
}

void Free_Memory()
{
    farfree(Matl);
    farfree(Lmp);
    farfree(Tri);
    farfree(Para);
    farfree(Cir);
    farfree(Rng);
    farfree(Sphr);
    farfree(Con);
    farfree(Cyl);
    farfree(Red_Plane);
    farfree(Green_Plane);
    farfree(Blue_Plane);
}


/*
```

```
                        Scan Pixel Display
```

```
*/

Boolean SingleFrame;

void Scan()
{
    TDA InitialDir;
    TDA Col;
    TDIA Colr;
    Word Xp, Yp;
    Word X, Y;
    Boolean Inside;

    PreCalculation();
    randomize();
    for(Yp=0; Yp<ScanYRes; Yp++)
    {
        for(Xp=0; Xp<ScanXRes; Xp++)
        {
```

```
                if(kbhit())
                {
                        fcloseall();
                        ungetch(32);
                        Free_Memory();
                        Exit_Graphics();
                        exit(1);
                }
                GetInitialDir((float)Xp, (float)Yp, InitialDir);
                InitialRay = true;
                TraceRay(ObsPos, InitialDir, MaxWgt, 1, Col);
                if(Col[0]>1.0)
                        Col[0]=1.0;
                if(Col[1]>1.0)
                        Col[1]=1.0;
                if(Col[2]>1.0)
                        Col[2]=1.0;
                VecScalMultInt(255.0, Col, Colr);
                if(SingleFrame)
                {
                        AddToLineBuffer(Colr);
                        GrayScalePixel(Xp, Yp, Colr);
                }
                else
                        PutGrayScalePixel(Xp, Yp, Colr);
        }
        if(SingleFrame)
            WriteLineBufferToRGBFile();
    }
}

Name InFileName;            /* .RT scene descriptions for frames file */
Name TempFileName;          /* .TMP file written here and read in Process.C*/
Name RGBFileName;           /* .RGB file for large non-animated images
                                                        Disp.C */

void GetSceneFile()
{
    Byte x, y;

    textcolor(YELLOW);
    textbackground(BLUE);
    gotoxy(1, 8);
```

```
    cprintf("Enter File Name -> ");
    x=wherex();
    y=wherey();
    textcolor(WHITE+BLINK);
    cprintf("%s", "BOUNCE");
    textcolor(YELLOW);
    gotoxy(x, y);
    while(!(kbhit()));
    cprintf("               ");
    gotoxy(x, y);
gets(InFileName); if(!(strcmp(InFileName, "")))
    strcpy(InFileName, "BOUNCE");
strupr(InFileName); strcpy(TempFileName, InFileName);
strcpy(RGBFileName, InFileName);
strcat(InFileName, ".RT"); strcat(TempFileName, ".TMP");
strcat(RGBFileName, ".RGB");
}


FILE *TempFile;

#define XY (y*160)+x
void WriteTMPFile()
{
    Word LineBuf[160];
    Word i;
    Word xc, yc;
    Word x, y;
    Word ColorNum;
    Word rc, gc, bc;

    for(y=0; y<100; y++)
    {
        for(i=0; i<160; i++)
            LineBuf[i]=0;
        for(x=0; x<160; x++)
        {
            ColorNum=0;
            rc=Red_Plane[XY]&62;          /* 32 levels of each color */
            gc=Green_Plane[XY]&62;        /* yields 32768 colors */
            bc=Blue_Plane[XY]&62;
            ColorNum=((rc>>1)|(gc<<4)|(bc<<9));
            LineBuf[x]=ColorNum;
        }
        fwrite(LineBuf, sizeof(Word), 160, TempFile);
```

```
    }
  }

  /*
  ┌──────────────────────────────────────────────────────────────┐
  │                                                              │
  │                        Main Program                          │
  │                                                              │
  └──────────────────────────────────────────────────────────────┘
  */

Palette_Register PalArray;
Byte FrameNum, LastFrameNum;

void main()
{
   Title();
   printf("Recursive Ray Tracing Program\n\n");
   printf("Program by Christopher D. Watkins\n\n");
   printf("'C' Conversion by Larry Sharp\n\n");
   Allocate_Memory();
   Clear_Planes();
   InitNoise();          /* Noise function for Wood and Marble Textures */
   ClearMemory();
   InitLineBuffer();
   GetSceneFile();
   InFile=fopen(InFileName, "rt");        /* Scene .RT file */
   if(InFile==NULL)
   {
        ungetch(32);
        Exit_Graphics();
        printf("Can't open .RT file %s.\n", InFileName);
        exit(1);
   }
   LoadRTHeader();
   ClearScreen();
   if((NumberOfFrames==1) || (!(ScanXRes<=160)) || (!(ScanYRes<=100)))
        SingleFrame=true;
   else
        SingleFrame=false;
   if(SingleFrame)
   {
RGBFile=fopen(RGBFileName, "wb");  /* .RGB image file */ if(RGBFile==NULL)
        {
             ungetch(32);
```

```
            Exit_Graphics();
            printf("Can't open .RGB file.\n");
            exit(1);
        }
        InitLineBuffer();                    /* Buffers for RGB File */
        PutRGBHeader();
        GetDataForFrame();
        PreCalculation();
        InitBoundingObjects();
        Scan();
        fclose(RGBFile);
        fclose(InFile);
        Free_Memory();
    }
    else
    {
        TempFile=fopen(TempFileName, "wb"); /* .TMP temporary file */
        if(TempFile==NULL)
    {
        ungetch(32);
        Exit_Graphics();
        printf("Can't open .RGB file.\n");
        exit(1);
    }
    LastFrameNum=NumberOfFrames;
    putc(LastFrameNum, TempFile);
    for(FrameNum=0; FrameNum<LastFrameNum; FrameNum++)
    {
        ClearMemory();
        GetDataForFrame();
        PreCalculation();
        InitBoundingObjects();
        Scan();
        WriteTMPFile();              /* Write 32768 Color Frames to File */
    }
    fclose(TempFile);
    fclose(InFile);
    Free_Memory();
    }
    Exit_Graphics();
}
```

Listing 12-2. *RAYTRACE.C.*

CHAPTER 13

Image and Animation Creation with the Ray Tracer

At last, we're ready to put our work to the test by using the ray-tracing program to produce animation sequences and single-frame renderings. But first, let's review some useful trigonometry for the unit circle.

A unit circle is a circle with a radius of 1. We can move a point around the perimeter of the unit circle using *sine* and *cosine*. These functions are used extensively to translate circular or angular motion back to Cartesian coordinates (X, Y, Z) and vice versa. By changing the angle argument for *sine* and *cosine*, we can set an object to any position on the unit circle. If we increment the argument from 0 to 360 degrees, we span a complete circle—in other words, we end up where we started. This is how we produce *periodic motion* (motion that repeats itself over time). We'll see many examples of this in the sample scripts that follow.

The following equation represents the coordinate transformation from a *(radius (r), angle θ* coordinate on a circle (often referred to as *polar coordinates*) to *(x, y)* Cartesian coordinates:

```
x = r cos θ
y = r sin θ                                    (Equation 13-1)
```

Figure 13-1 illustrates the process.

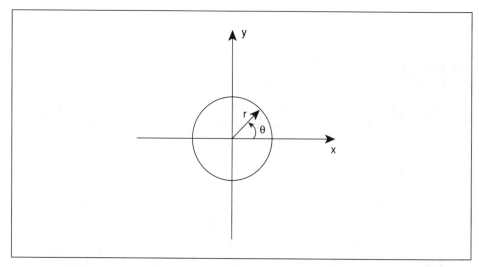

Figure 13-1. Using Sin and Cos to draw a circle.

This conversion and its inverse are powerful tools where rotation is concerned. Many of the animation sequences in this chapter were generated quickly and elegantly with these functions, which are used to create spinning objects, particular physical models of motion, orbits, and animation of mechanical parts. They allow us to specify the positions of parts of objects by a convenient angle and convert this angle to the Cartesian coordinates needed by the ray-tracing program. We'll see how angles are used when we examine the actual programs that generate the ray-tracer animation scripts.

Let's look at how animation files are created for the ray tracer.

Ray-Tracer Animation File Creators

Animation sequences are defined for the ray tracer using an .*RT* file that specifies the number of frames for the animation along with the image resolution and a scene designation for each frame. The scene designation describes the placement and orientation of every object in the scene, the lighting, and the viewing conditions. One or more objects can change position and color from frame to frame, and the observer can change position and viewing direction from frame to frame. The resolution of choice for our computer's memory scheme (640K) is 160 horizontal pixels by 100 vertical pixels, with 30 frames of animation. This resolution allows a reasonable number of frames to be stored within the finite memory available to the animator program. Larger frame resolutions mean fewer frames in a single animation; for example, a 320-by-200-pixel frame requires four times the amount of memory, allowing us to produce only one-quarter the number of animation frames.

The *.RT* animation sequence definition files allow the ray tracer to produce the temporary file of screens. This *.TMP* file contains high-color resolution (that is, the number of colors a pixel might be, for instance, 8 bit = 256 levels of gray) data for each screen (five bits each for red, green, and blue, stored as a 16-bit word for each pixel). The data is later reduced to 256 colors for storage in an animation sequence file of screens by *PROCESS.C*, described in Chapter 16. This *.ANI* file may then be read in and displayed by the animation program.

The programs that generate animation sequences all have the same basic structure. First, a general header describing the desired output resolution (normally 160 by 100 pixels) and the number of frames is written out with the *WriteHeader* function. The program indexes through the frame numbers and generates the new data describing the given frame. Within the loop, the *WriteStudio* function sets the *ENVIRONMENT*, *LAMPS*, *OBSERVER*, *SKY*, *MATERIAL*, *GROUND*, and *LAMP* variables to appropriate values for the sequence being generated. At the end of each frame's data, an *ENDFRAME* is written to the output file as a signal to the ray tracer. The file is closed, and the ray tracer can use it to generate the *.TMP* output image file.

The rest of this chapter explains how the sample animation sequences and their corresponding *.RT* files are created. We begin with the bouncing-balls sequence produced by *BOUNCE.C*.

BOUNCE.C

The *BOUNCE.C* program generates the file *BOUNCE.RT*, which contains the information the ray tracer needs to produce a 30-frame, 160-by-100-pixel animation of three bouncing, opaque orbs (see Listing13-1). After writing out the header information, a loop of *Theta* from 0 to 180 degrees begins. We use this kind of loop (a loop of degree changes) rather than a loop of frame numbers to allow for the periodic motion of the bouncing balls; since the relative degree changes from one ball to the next makes the balls bounce out of phase. We want the balls to bounce up, reach a maximum altitude, and then fall down to their starting position. The animator can repeat the animation sequence indefinitely to produce the illusion that the balls are continuously bouncing.

For this example, we'll change the z position of each ball from frame to frame to produce the periodic motion. All other scene parameters are held constant. To produce the periodic change in the z coordinate, we'll use the *sinD* function applied to an angle, *Theta*. We'll vary *Theta* from 0 to 180 and produce an animation frame whenever that angle is a multiple of six. We do this by producing a frame only when the equation:

```
(Theta % (180 / NumberOfFrames))                (Equation 13-2)
```

is equal to 0, where *Theta* is incremented 0 to 180 degrees and *NumberOfFrames* is 30 (*180/NumberOfFrames* therefore equals 6). Note that % is the C modulo operator; it returns the remainder when the second argument is divided into the first. This technique lets us change *NumberOfFrames* and still get the same motion in z, though with a finer step size (for a larger number of frames) or a larger step (fewer frames). The step size controls how much the balls move from one frame to another and thus determines the smoothness of the animation.

Every six iterations of the loop for *Theta*, we generate a frame with new z positions computed as a function of *Theta* using the following equation:

```
z = SinD(Theta + <phase term>)                  (Equation 13-3)
```

As *Theta* changes, the orb positions change in a periodic fashion because of the *SinD*. The phase term, which represents a time delay between the orbs' contact with the ground, keeps the balls from bouncing in perfect synchronicity to make the animation sequence more pleasing. Each ball has a different phase term. Examples of these relative phase terms might be that one ball is at the 0^0 phase, the next at 60^0 phase, and the next at -60^0 phase. This would make the balls strike the ground at different times.

Because we're using spherical balls, bounding-sphere tests speed up the ray tracer by reducing the time spent testing intersections with objects. Here in order to create the bounding sphere, we find all of the extents of the objects that make up the scene; in this case, the three spheres. By finding the minimum and maximum possible extents of these spheres by building a box around each sphere; we can find the minimum and maximum points that all objects fit within. By finding the center of these points, we then know the center of a sphere and its radius (half the distance between the points) that bound all of the objects in the scene. Rendering packages use these tests extensively to improve performance and eliminate unnecessary computations.

```
/*
```

```
                              Bounce
                     by Christopher D. Watkins
```

```
*/

    #include "stdio.h"
    #include "dos.h"
    #include "math.h"
    #include "defs.h"

    #define piover180 0.01745

    float SinD(Word a)
    {
        return sin(a * piover180);
    }

    typedef char name[32];

    FILE *textdiskfile;
    name filename;

    Word xresolution  = 160;
    Word yresolution  = 100;
    Byte numberofframes = 30;

    void writeheader()
    {
```

```
fprintf(textdiskfile,;"  ┌─────────────────────────────────────┐        \n");
fprintf(textdiskfile,   │                                     │        \n");
fprintf(textdiskfile," │               Bounce               │         \n");
fprintf(textdiskfile," │                                     │         \n");
fprintf(textdiskfile," │       by Christopher D. Watkins     │         \n");
fprintf(textdiskfile," │                                     │         \n");
fprintf(textdiskfile," └─────────────────────────────────────┘         \n");
fprintf(textdiskfile,"\n");
fprintf(textdiskfile,"\n");
fprintf(textdiskfile,"STATS\n");
fprintf(textdiskfile,"        XRES    = %d\n",xresolution);
fprintf(textdiskfile,"        YRES    = %d\n",yresolution);
                      fprintf(textdiskfile,"\n");
fprintf(textdiskfile,"\n");
fprintf(textdiskfile,"FRAMES\n");
fprintf(textdiskfile,"        NUMBER  = %d\n",numberofframes);
}


void writestudio()
{
fprintf(textdiskfile,"\n");
fprintf(textdiskfile,"\n");
fprintf(textdiskfile,"ENVIRONMENT\n");
fprintf(textdiskfile,"        LOCLWGT =    0.750  0.750   0.750\n");
fprintf(textdiskfile,"        REFLWGT =    0.250  0.250   0.250\n");
fprintf(textdiskfile,"        TRANWGT =    0.000  0.000   0.000\n");
fprintf(textdiskfile,"        MINWGT  =    0.030  0.030   0.030\n");
fprintf(textdiskfile,"        MAXWGT  =    1.000  1.000   1.000\n");
fprintf(textdiskfile,"        RDEPTH  =    3\n");
fprintf(textdiskfile,"\n");
fprintf(textdiskfile,"\n");
fprintf(textdiskfile,"LAMPS\n");
fprintf(textdiskfile,"        REFLAMP = FALSE\n");
fprintf(textdiskfile,"        LAMPREF =    0.000  0.000   0.000\n");
fprintf(textdiskfile,"        DISTEFF =    0.050\n");
fprintf(textdiskfile,"\n");
fprintf(textdiskfile,"\n");
fprintf(textdiskfile,"OBSERVER\n");
fprintf(textdiskfile,"        FLENGTH =    3.200\n");
fprintf(textdiskfile,"        OBSPOS  =    0.000 -660.000 220.000\n");
fprintf(textdiskfile,"        ROTATE  =    0.000\n");
fprintf(textdiskfile,"        TILT    =   16.000\n");
fprintf(textdiskfile,"\n");
fprintf(textdiskfile,"\n");
fprintf(textdiskfile,"SKY\n");
fprintf(textdiskfile,"        HORCOL  =    0.100  0.100   0.100\n");
fprintf(textdiskfile,"        ZENCOL  =    0.700  0.800   1.000\n");
fprintf(textdiskfile,"        CLOUDS  = TRUE\n");
fprintf(textdiskfile,"\n");
fprintf(textdiskfile,"\n");
```

```
fprintf(textdiskfile,"MATERIAL\n");
fprintf(textdiskfile,"        TYPE    = PLASTICTILE\n");
fprintf(textdiskfile,"        TEXTURE = CHECKER\n");
fprintf(textdiskfile,"        AMBRFL  =    0.100  0.100   0.100\n");
fprintf(textdiskfile,"        DIFRFL  =    0.700  0.700   0.700\n");
fprintf(textdiskfile,"        SPCRFL  =    0.200  0.200   0.200\n");
fprintf(textdiskfile,"        GLOSS   =    8.000\n");
fprintf(textdiskfile,"        TRANS   =    0.000  0.000   0.000\n");
fprintf(textdiskfile,"        INDEX   =    1.000\n");
fprintf(textdiskfile,"        TILE1   =    1.000  0.200   0.200\n");
fprintf(textdiskfile,"        TILE2   =    0.250  0.250   0.250\n");
fprintf(textdiskfile,"        TILE    =    0.012\n");
fprintf(textdiskfile,"\n");
fprintf(textdiskfile,"\n");
fprintf(textdiskfile,"MATERIAL\n");
fprintf(textdiskfile,"        TYPE    = CHROME\n");
fprintf(textdiskfile,"        TEXTURE = SMOOTH\n");
fprintf(textdiskfile,"        AMBRFL  =    0.200  0.200   0.200\n");
fprintf(textdiskfile,"        DIFRFL  =    0.500  0.500   0.500\n");
fprintf(textdiskfile,"        SPCRFL  =    0.300  0.300   0.300\n");
fprintf(textdiskfile,"        GLOSS   =   30.000\n");
fprintf(textdiskfile,"        TRANS   =    0.000  0.000   0.000\n");
fprintf(textdiskfile,"        INDEX   =    1.000\n");
fprintf(textdiskfile,"\n");
fprintf(textdiskfile,"\n");
fprintf(textdiskfile,"MATERIAL\n");
fprintf(textdiskfile,"        TYPE    = BRASS\n");
fprintf(textdiskfile,"        TEXTURE = SMOOTH\n");
fprintf(textdiskfile,"        AMBRFL  =    0.100  0.100   0.100\n");
fprintf(textdiskfile,"        DIFRFL  =    0.300  0.300   0.300\n");
fprintf(textdiskfile,"        SPCRFL  =    0.600  0.500   0.250\n");
fprintf(textdiskfile,"        GLOSS   =   25.000\n");
fprintf(textdiskfile,"        TRANS   =    0.000  0.000   0.000\n");
fprintf(textdiskfile,"        INDEX   =    1.000\n");
fprintf(textdiskfile,"\n");
fprintf(textdiskfile,"\n");
fprintf(textdiskfile,"MATERIAL\n");
fprintf(textdiskfile,"        TYPE    = REDMIRROR\n");
fprintf(textdiskfile,"        TEXTURE = SMOOTH\n");
fprintf(textdiskfile,"        AMBRFL  =    0.200  0.050   0.050\n");
fprintf(textdiskfile,"        DIFRFL  =    0.500  0.100   0.100\n");
fprintf(textdiskfile,"        SPCRFL  =    0.300  0.100   0.100\n");
fprintf(textdiskfile,"        GLOSS   =   25.000\n");
fprintf(textdiskfile,"        TRANS   =    0.000  0.000   0.000\n");
fprintf(textdiskfile,"        INDEX   =    1.000\n");
fprintf(textdiskfile,"\n");
fprintf(textdiskfile,"\n");
fprintf(textdiskfile,"GROUND\n");
fprintf(textdiskfile,"        MATL    = PLASTICTILE\n");
fprintf(textdiskfile,"\n");
fprintf(textdiskfile,"\n");
```

```
fprintf(textdiskfile,"LAMP\n");
fprintf(textdiskfile,"        LOC     =   350.000-350.000 350.000\n");
fprintf(textdiskfile,"        RADIUS  =   100.000\n"); \
fprintf(textdiskfile,"        INTENS  =   0.950   0.950    0.910\n");
fprintf(textdiskfile,"\n");
fprintf(textdiskfile,"\n");
fprintf(textdiskfile,"LAMP\n");
fprintf(textdiskfile,"        LOC     =-350.000-350.000  350.000\n");
fprintf(textdiskfile,"        RADIUS  =100.000\n")\;
fprintf(textdiskfile,"        INTENS  =   0.950   0.950    0.910\n");
}


void make()


{
Word theta;
float x, y, z1;
float z2, z3;
float zoffset;
float rad;


theta = 0;
rad = 40.0;
zoffset = rad;
x = 0.0;
y = 0.0;
z1 = 0.0;
z2 = 0.0;
z3 = 0.0;
for (theta = 0; theta <= 180; theta++)
{
if (((theta % (180 / numberofframes)) == 0))
    {
        writestudio();
        z1 = zoffset + 90 * SinD(theta);
        z2 = zoffset + 70 * fabs(SinD(theta + 30));
        z3 = zoffset + 50 * fabs(SinD(theta - 45));
        fprintf(textdiskfile,"\n");
        fprintf(textdiskfile,"\n");
        fprintf(textdiskfile,"SPHERE\n");
        fprintf(textdiskfile," LOC    = %3.3f %3.3f %3.3f\n",x,y,z1);
        fprintf(textdiskfile," RADIUS = %3.3f\n",rad);
        fprintf(textdiskfile," MATL   = CHROME\n");
        fprintf(textdiskfile,"\n");
        fprintf(textdiskfile,"SPHERE\n");
        fprintf(textdiskfile," LOC    = %3.3f %3.3f %3.3f\n",(x + 2.5 *
                                                    rad),y,z2);
        fprintf(textdiskfile," RADIUS = %3.3f\n",rad);
        fprintf(textdiskfile," MATL   = BRASS\n");

        fprintf(textdiskfile,"\n");
```

370

```
        fprintf(textdiskfile,"SPHERE\n");
        fprintf(textdiskfile," LOC    = %3.3f %3.3f %3.3f\n",(x - 2.5 *
                                                     rad),y,z3);
        fprintf(textdiskfile," RADIUS = %3.3f\n",rad);
        fprintf(textdiskfile," MATL   = REDMIRROR\n");
        fprintf(textdiskfile,"\n");
        fprintf(textdiskfile,"\n");
        fprintf(textdiskfile,"BOUNDINGSPHERETEST\n");
        fprintf(textdiskfile,"\n");
        fprintf(textdiskfile,"\n");
        fprintf(textdiskfile,"ENDFRAME\n");
      }
    }
}


void main()
{
    strcpy(filename,"BOUNCE.RT");
    clrscr();
    printf("Generating %s File\n",filename); printf("\n");
    printf("By Christopher D. Watkins\n"); printf("\n");
    printf("\n");
    printf("Writing %d frames\n",(int)numberofframes);
    textdiskfile=fopen(filename, "wt"); writeheader();
    make();
    fclose(textdiskfile);
}
```

Listing 13-1. *BOUNCE.C*

BOUNCE2.C

BOUNCE2.C is identical to *BOUNCE.C* except the three orbs now have the material type *GLASS* and are therefore translucent. The ray tracer simulates the refraction of light through glass, resulting in interesting lighting effects as the glass orbs bounce up and down and focus light on the checkered floor. Because the glass is curved, it acts as a lens to focus light passing through it. In this case, light from the checkerboard passes through the glass orbs and is reflected back to the viewer, producing a magnifying-glass effect. Look at any surface through a glass marble (or a larger piece of glass) to see this effect for yourself.

371

DNA.C

DNA.C produces an animation file (*DNA.RT*) of a spinning deoxyribonucleic acid (DNA) molecule. This molecule is chemically constructed of the nitrogenous bases (pyrimidine and purine derivatives) *GUANINE*, represented by a green orb; *CYTOSINE*, a blue orb; *THYMINE*, a red orb; and *ADENINE*, a magenta orb. The *PHOSPHATE* bonding elements are represented by smooth, white orbs. The program starts building a DNA model by assigning random molecule types, where a *CYTOSINE* is always paired with a *GUANINE* and an *ADENINE* is always paired with a *THYMINE*. For every other pair of *PHOSPHATE* molecules, a randomly selected *BASE* molecule is generated; the result is DNA's familiar ladder shape.

In our animation, we'll rotate the entire molecule about the Z axis instead of moving it linearly as in *BOUNCE.C*. We use the variable *Phase* to keep track of how far we've rotated about the Z axis as each frame is computed. To produce a continuous, repeatable animation, we want to rotate a full 360 degrees over the 30-frame length of the animation. *Phase* is therefore incremented by:

```
360.0 / NumberOfFrames
```

where *NumberOfFrames* equals 30. The program loops using the frame number and multiplies by the phase incrementation factor to compute the new *Phase*. Once the new phase term is computed, we use the *SinD* and *CosD* functions to compute the new *X,Y* location of each molecule.

An interesting property of the DNA molecule is its double-helix shape. Essentially, each side of the ladder twists about the other in such a way that the sides are still the same distance apart. This requires that each molecule be rotated about the main molecule axis based on where it is along that axis. The way our model is constructed, the molecule is aligned vertically; the additional twist is about the Z axis. As with the rotation, we can add this twist by computing an additional phase term that's a function of the *z* value of each molecule. This molecule-by-molecule phase term is added to the *Phase* variable to keep the molecules in the same position relative to one another. We can vary the degree of twisting by changing the multipliers of *z* used in the *SinD* and *CosD* functions; a larger multiplier will force the molecule to become more twisted, a smaller value less twisted.

As with *BOUNCE.C*, bounding-sphere and prism tests improve performance by reducing the amount of time the ray tracer spends testing intersections with objects.

ENGINE.C

ENGINE.C is a simple animation of a four-cylinder engine. The cam mechanism rotates, pushing the rods, which in turn push the pistons up and down. The cams on the shaft are composed of offset cylinders and circles. *ENGINE.C* is an excellent example of how the *sine* and *cosine* functions cause the synchronous rotation of the various engine parts. *Phase* is used, as in *DNA.C*, to make the cams rotate at the proper times. Note that we use this variable to create the illusion that the engine components are physically connected to one another, when in fact they all move independently. Each moving part has its own phase term that is a constant offset from the global value of *Phase*. Thus, each part moves synchronously with all of the other parts, even though we specify each part's rotation separately.

NEWTCRAD.C

The *NEWTCRAD.C* program is an animation of the popular Newton's cradle. The outer orbs move back and forth in a pendular motion, illustrating the energy transfer from the outer orbs to the inner orbs. As in previous animations, *Phase* provides the proper rotation offsets of the outer orbs. In this case, however, the orb itself is rotating not about its own center but about the point where each pendulum component is attached. The program computes the new position based on the simple pendular motion, $x = x_0 + A\sin(w+)$ taking into account that when one side is struck, the pendulum on the other end moves.

ORBIT.C

The *ORBIT.C* program animates the motions of the three inner planets of our solar system—Mercury, Venus, and Earth—as well as the Earth's moon. Since the Earth takes 365.25 days to orbit the sun, compared to Venus's 224.7 days and Mercury's 88 days, it has the longest period of rotation. We're generating a relatively short animation sequence, so we set the rotational period of Venus to half of the Earth's time and Mercury to one-quarter the time.

Phase is used to compute the new planets' positions for each frame. Here, a separate *Phase* value is stored for each planet. The relative orbiting speed of a particular planet is generated by multiplying the planet's *Phase* value by the ratio of the Earth's orbit time to the other planet's orbit time. The moon's orbit about the Earth is also computed this way. For the animation, we must actually compute the location of the moon relative to the sun. Therefore, we compute first the Earth's new position, then the moon's position relative to the new location of the Earth.

To fit the entire simulation on the screen, the planets' distances from the sun are scaled (divided) by 500,000, their diameters by 1,000, the sun's diameter by 35,000, and the moon's distance from the Earth by 15,000. For this simulation, the planets' orbits are assumed to be in the same plane (which is actually a fairly good approximation).

ROBOT.C

ROBOT.C creates an animation of a walking robot. The robot's arms and legs move, and its head turns back and forth. When you run the program, notice how the floor moves under the robot. This effect is achieved by moving the viewer's position as well as the robot's, keeping the robot from "running away" from the viewer; the viewer moves back at the same relative speed as the robot moves forward. This animation uses the *sine* and *cosine* functions extensively to animate the robot's various body parts. Just as when we computed the moon's orbit in *ORBIT.C*, we must compute rotations in several places to keep those parts connected during the animation. Each individual part's rotation angle is derived from the global Phase value by using a constant offset. Thus, the connected parts will remain connected. For the more complicated motion of the arms, we compute the new positions of the shoulder, and use this as the center about which to rotate the rest of the arm.

SPIN2.C

The *SPIN2.C* program creates a simple animation of a spinning, mechanical, cross-shaped part. The animation is similar to *DNA.C* in that the part rotates 360 degrees about the *z* axis.

WAVES.C

WAVES.C animates a windswept ocean. Instead of using Phase to change an object's rotation, however, it uses the variable to control the location of the ocean texture relative to the origin. If we change this offset smoothly from frame to frame, the texture appears to change. There are two additions to the *MATERIAL* record when *OCEANWAVES* is used as a texture: *AMPL* is the amplitude, and *PHASE* is the phase of the water. The Phase varies from 0 to 360 degrees over the entire animation, producing continuous motion of the water when the animator replays this sequence.

Ray-Traced, Single-Frame Renderings

The preceding animations were all generated in low-resolution mode. The following *.RT* files produce high-resolution, single-frame renderings. The process is identical to that used to produce animation-sequence *.RT* files except that only one frame is generated. Also, the resolution may be any value up to the 1,024 horizontal by 768 vertical pixels. These programs generate *.RGB* files that are read in and displayed by the *DISP.C* program, discussed in Chapter 16. Typically, images rendered in high resolution take four times longer to render. Image generation time is roughly proportional to the number of pixels in the output image.

DIE&CARD.C

The *DIE&CARD.C* program creates a scene of some dice and poker chips, a tumbler, and an ace of spades (see Listing13-2). The spade is generated from two circles and two triangles that are slightly separated from the card. This separation allows the ray tracer to distinguish which object is on the other object (here, the spade is on the card). The stack of poker chips is constructed from circles and cylinders. The tumbler is nothing more than a cylinder with a ring top.

A die is more intricate to produce. First, the eight points that describe the corners are calculated. Next, spheres are placed at the corners and cylinders are used to connect the spheres, creating the rounded corners and edges found on real dice. The sides of this boxlike structure are filled with parallelograms to complete the die. These planes must be offset in certain dimensions by the sphere radius to form a solid die. According to the side being calculated, one or more dots are placed on the die.

Like the spades, the dots are offset by slightly more than the sphere radius to ensure that they're drawn on top of the die face. (The ray tracer cannot distinguish between two planar objects lying in the same plane.) This image illustrates the complexity of objects that can be created using the relatively simple primitives of rectangles, spheres, and cylinders.

```
/*

             Die and Card

        by Christopher D. Watkins

*/

#include "stdio.h"
#include "dos.h"
#include "math.h"
#include "defs.h"
#include "globals.h"
#include "mathb.h"

typedef char name[32];

FILE *textdiskfile;
name filename;

Word xresolution  = 1024;
Word yresolution  = 768;
Byte numberofframes = 1;

void writeheader()
{   fprintf(textdiskfile,"                                    \n");
    fprintf(textdiskfile,"                                    \n");
    fprintf(textdiskfile,"             Die and Card           \n");
    fprintf(textdiskfile,"                                    \n");
    fprintf(textdiskfile,"       by Christopher D. Watkins    \n");
    fprintf(textdiskfile,"                                    \n");
    fprintf(textdiskfile,"                                    \n");
    fprintf(textdiskfile,"\n");
    fprintf(textdiskfile,"\n");
    fprintf(textdiskfile,"STATS\n");
    fprintf(textdiskfile,"XRES    = %d\n",xresolution);
    fprintf(textdiskfile,"YRES    = %d\n",yresolution);
    fprintf(textdiskfile,"\n");
```

```
        fprintf(textdiskfile,"\n");
        fprintf(textdiskfile,"FRAMES\n");
        fprintf(textdiskfile,"NUMBER  = %d\n",numberofframes);
}


void writestudio()
{
        fprintf(textdiskfile,"\n");
        fprintf(textdiskfile,"\n");
        fprintf(textdiskfile,"ENVIRONMENT\n");
        fprintf(textdiskfile,"    LOCLWGT  =  0.800     0.800     0.800\n");
        fprintf(textdiskfile,"    REFLWGT  =  0.200     0.200     0.200\n");
        fprintf(textdiskfile,"    TRANWGT  =  0.000     0.000     0.000\n");
        fprintf(textdiskfile,"    MINWGT   =  0.030     0.030     0.030\n");
        fprintf(textdiskfile,"    MAXWGT   =  1.000     1.000     1.000\n");
        fprintf(textdiskfile,"    RDEPTH   =  2\n");
        fprintf(textdiskfile,"\n");
        fprintf(textdiskfile,"\n");
        fprintf(textdiskfile,"LAMPS\n");
        fprintf(textdiskfile,"    REFLAMP  =  FALSE\n");
        fprintf(textdiskfile,"    LAMPREF  =  0.000     0.000     0.000\n");
        fprintf(textdiskfile,"    DISTEFF  =  0.050\n");
        fprintf(textdiskfile,"\n");
        fprintf(textdiskfile,"\n");
        fprintf(textdiskfile,"OBSERVER\n");
        fprintf(textdiskfile,"    FLENGTH  =  3.300\n");
        fprintf(textdiskfile,"    OBSPOS   =100.000  -800.000  150.000\n");
        fprintf(textdiskfile,"    ROTATE   =-13.000\n");
        fprintf(textdiskfile,"    TILT     =13.000\n");
        fprintf(textdiskfile,"\n");
        fprintf(textdiskfile,"\n");
        fprintf(textdiskfile,"MATERIAL\n");
        fprintf(textdiskfile,"    TYPE= CARPET\n");
        fprintf(textdiskfile,"    TEXTURE  = SHEETROCK\n");
        fprintf(textdiskfile,"    AMBRFL   =  0.100     0.100     0.100\n");
        fprintf(textdiskfile,"    DIFRFL   =  0.450     0.800     0.490\n");
        fprintf(textdiskfile,"    SPCRFL   =  0.000     0.000     0.000\n");
        fprintf(textdiskfile,"    GLOSS    =  0.000\n");
        fprintf(textdiskfile,"    TRANS    =  0.000     0.000     0.000\n");
        fprintf(textdiskfile,"    INDEX    =  1.000\n");
        fprintf(textdiskfile,"\n");
        fprintf(textdiskfile,"\n");
        fprintf(textdiskfile,"MATERIAL\n");
        fprintf(textdiskfile,"    TYPE= WHITE\n");
        fprintf(textdiskfile,"    TEXTURE  = SMOOTH\n");
        fprintf(textdiskfile,"    AMBRFL   =  0.300     0.300     0.300\n");
        fprintf(textdiskfile,"    DIFRFL   =  0.600     0.600     0.600\n");
        fprintf(textdiskfile,"    SPCRFL   =  0.030     0.030     0.030\n");
        fprintf(textdiskfile,"    GLOSSb   =  2.000\n");
        fprintf(textdiskfile,"    TRANS    =  0.000     0.000     0.000\n");
        fprintf(textdiskfile,"    INDEX    =  1.000\n");
```

```
fprintf(textdiskfile,"\n");
fprintf(textdiskfile,"\n");
fprintf(textdiskfile,"MATERIAL\n");
fprintf(textdiskfile,"        TYPE= BLACK\n");
fprintf(textdiskfile,"        TEXTURE = SMOOTH\n");
fprintf(textdiskfile,"        AMBRFL  =   0.200   0.200    0.200\n");
fprintf(textdiskfile,"        DIFRFL  =   0.200   0.200    0.200\n");
fprintf(textdiskfile,"        SPCRFL  =   0.050   0.050    0.050\n");
fprintf(textdiskfile,"        GLOSS   =   2.000\n");
fprintf(textdiskfile,"        TRANS   =   0.000   0.000    0.000\n");
fprintf(textdiskfile,"        INDEX   =   1.000\n");
fprintf(textdiskfile,"\n");
fprintf(textdiskfile,"\n");
fprintf(textdiskfile,"MATERIAL\n");
fprintf(textdiskfile,"        TYPE= RED\n");
fprintf(textdiskfile,"        TEXTURE = SMOOTH\n");
fprintf(textdiskfile,"        AMBRFL  =   0.300   0.100    0.100\n");
fprintf(textdiskfile,"        DIFRFL  =   0.600   0.000    0.000\n");
fprintf(textdiskfile,"        SPCRFL  =   0.150   0.000    0.000\n");
fprintf(textdiskfile,"        GLOSS   =   5.000\n");
fprintf(textdiskfile,"        TRANS   =   0.000   0.000    0.000\n");
fprintf(textdiskfile,"        INDEX   =   1.000\n");
fprintf(textdiskfile,"\n");
fprintf(textdiskfile,"\n");
fprintf(textdiskfile,"MATERIAL\n");
fprintf(textdiskfile,"        TYPE    = CHROME\n");
fprintf(textdiskfile,"        TEXTURE = SMOOTH\n");
fprintf(textdiskfile,"        AMBRFL  =   0.100   0.100    0.100\n");
fprintf(textdiskfile,"        DIFRFL  =   0.700   0.700    0.700\n");
fprintf(textdiskfile,"        SPCRFL  =   0.200   0.200    0.200\n");
fprintf(textdiskfile,"        GLOSS   =  18.000\n");
fprintf(textdiskfile,"        TRANS   =   0.000   0.000    0.000\n");
fprintf(textdiskfile,"        INDEX   =   1.000\n");
fprintf(textdiskfile,"\n");
fprintf(textdiskfile,"\n");
fprintf(textdiskfile,"MATERIAL\n");
fprintf(textdiskfile,"        TYPE= BRASS\n");
fprintf(textdiskfile,"        TEXTURE = SMOOTH\n");
fprintf(textdiskfile,"        AMBRFL  =   0.100   0.100    0.100\n");
fprintf(textdiskfile,"        DIFRFL  =   0.300   0.300    0.300\n");
fprintf(textdiskfile,"        SPCRFL  =   0.600   0.500    0.250\n");
fprintf(textdiskfile,"        GLOSS   =  10.000\n");
fprintf(textdiskfile,"        TRANS   =   0.000   0.000    0.000\n");
fprintf(textdiskfile,"        INDEX   =   1.000\n");
fprintf(textdiskfile,"\n");
fprintf(textdiskfile,"\n");
fprintf(textdiskfile,"GROUND\n");
fprintf(textdiskfile,"        MATL    = CARPET\n");
fprintf(textdiskfile,"\n");
fprintf(textdiskfile,"\n");
fprintf(textdiskfile,"LAMP\n");
```

```
fprintf(textdiskfile,"        LOC     =  0.000 350.000  350.000\n");
fprintf(textdiskfile,"        RADIUS  =120.000\n");
fprintf(textdiskfile,"        INTENS  =  0.650   0.650    0.650\n");
fprintf(textdiskfile,"\n");
fprintf(textdiskfile,"\n");
fprintf(textdiskfile,"LAMP\n");
fprintf(textdiskfile,"        LOC     =  0.000 -500.000 350.000\n");
fprintf(textdiskfile,"        RADIUS  =120.000\n");
fprintf(textdiskfile,"        INTENS  =  0.650   0.650    0.650\n");
}


void sph(TDA pt, float rad)
{
fprintf(textdiskfile,"\n");
fprintf(textdiskfile,"\n");
fprintf(textdiskfile,"SPHERE\n");
fprintf(textdiskfile,"        LOC     = %3.3f%3.3f\ %3.3f\n",pt[0],
                                            pt[1], pt[2]);
fprintf(textdiskfile,"        RADIUS  = %3.3f\n",rad);
fprintf(textdiskfile,"        MATL    = WHITE\n");
}


void cyl(TDA pt1, TDA pt2, float rad)
{
fprintf(textdiskfile,"\n");
fprintf(textdiskfile,"\n");
fprintf(textdiskfile,"CYLINDER\n");
fprintf(textdiskfile,"        BASELOC  = %3.3f %3.3f %3.3f\n", pt1[0],
                                            pt1[1], pt1[2]);
fprintf(textdiskfile,"        BASERAD = %3.3f\n",rad);
fprintf(textdiskfile,"        APEXLOC  = %3.3f %3.3f %3.3f \n", pt2[0],
                                            pt2[1], pt2[2]);
fprintf(textdiskfile,"        MATL     = WHITE\n");
}


void cir(TDA p, float rad, TDA v1, TDA v2)
{
fprintf(textdiskfile,"\n");
fprintf(textdiskfile,"\n");
fprintf(textdiskfile,"CIRCLE\n");
fprintf(textdiskfile,"        LOC      = %3.3f %3.3f %3.3f \n", p[0], p[1],
                                            p[2]);
fprintf(textdiskfile,"        V1       = %3.3f   %3.3f   %3.3f \n", v1[0],
                                            v1[1], v1[2]);
fprintf(textdiskfile,"        V2       = %3.3f   %3.3f   %3.3f \n", v2[0],
                                            v2[1], v2[2]);
fprintf(textdiskfile,"        RADIUS  = %3.3f\n",rad);
fprintf(textdiskfile,"        MATL= RED\n");
}
```

```
void pln(Byte side, float rad, TDA p1, TDA p2, TDA p3, float x, float y,
                                                                float z)
{
  TDA v1, v2, p;
  float dotrad;
  TDA t1, t2, cp;
  TDA cp1, cp2;
  TDA cp3, cp4;
  TDA adj;

  VecSub(p2,p1,v1);
  VecSub(p3,p1,v2);
  Vec(x,y,z,adj);
  VecAdd(p1,adj,p);
  fprintf(textdiskfile,"\n");
  fprintf(textdiskfile,"\n");
  fprintf(textdiskfile,"PARALLELOGRAM\n");
  fprintf(textdiskfile,"  LOC   = %3.3f %3.3f %3.3f\n",p[0],p[1],p[2]);
  fprintf(textdiskfile,"  V1    = %3.3f %3.3f %3.3f\n",v1[0],v1[1],v1[2]);
  fprintf(textdiskfile,"  V2    = %3.3f %3.3f %3.3f\n",v2[0],v2[1],v2[2]);
  fprintf(textdiskfile,"   MATL    = WHITE\n");
  dotrad = rad * 0.65;
  switch (side)
  {
    case 1:VecAdd(p2,p3,t1);
            VecScalMult(0.5,t1,t2);
            VecAdd(t2,adj,cp); p[2] = cp[2] + 0.5;
            cir(cp,dotrad,v1,v2);
            break;
    case 2:VecAdd(p2,p3,t1);
            VecScalMult(0.5,t1,t1);
            VecAdd(p2,t1,t2);
            VecScalMult(0.5,t2,t2);
            VecAdd(t2,adj,cp);
            cp[1] = cp[1] - 0.5;
            cir(cp,dotrad,v1,v2);
            VecAdd(p3,t1,t2);
            VecScalMult(0.5,t2,t2);
            VecAdd(t2,adj,cp);
            cp[1] = cp[1] - 0.5;
            cir(cp,dotrad,v1,v2);
            break;
    case 3:VecAdd(p2,p3,t1);
            VecScalMult(0.5,t1,t1);
            VecAdd(t1,adj,cp);
            cp[0] = cp[0] + 0.5;
            cir(cp,dotrad,v1,v2);
            VecAdd(p2,t1,t2);
            VecScalMult(0.5,t2,t2);
            VecAdd(t2,adj,cp);
```

380

```
                cp[0] = cp[0] + 0.5;
                cir(cp,dotrad,v1,v2);
                VecAdd(p3,t1,t2);
                VecScalMult(0.5,t2,t2);
                VecAdd(t2,adj,cp);
                cp[0] = cp[0] + 0.5;
                cir(cp,dotrad,v1,v2);
                break;
    case 4:VecAdd(p2,p3,t1);
                VecScalMult(0.5,t1,t1);
                VecAdd(p2,t1,t2);
                VecScalMult(0.5,t2,t2);
                VecAdd(t2,adj,cp1);
                cp1[0] = cp1[0] - 0.5;
                cir(cp1,dotrad,v1,v2);
                VecAdd(p3,t1,t2);
                VecScalMult(0.5,t2,t2);
                VecAdd(t2,adj,cp2);
                cp2[0] = cp2[0] - 0.5;
                cir(cp2,dotrad,v1,v2);
                Vec(cp1[0],cp2[1],cp1[2],cp);
                cir(cp,dotrad,v1,v2);
                Vec(cp1[0],cp1[1],cp2[2],cp);
                cir(cp,dotrad,v1,v2);
                break;
    case 5:VecAdd(p2,p3,t1);
                VecScalMult(0.5,t1,t1);
                VecAdd(t1,adj,cp);
                cp[1] = cp[1] + 0.5;
                cir(cp,dotrad,v1,v2);
                VecAdd(p2,t1,t2);
                VecScalMult(0.5,t2,t2);
                VecAdd(t2,adj,cp1);
                cp1[1] = cp1[1] + 0.5;
                cir(cp1,dotrad,v1,v2);
                VecAdd(p3,t1,t2);
                VecScalMult(0.5,t2,t2);
                VecAdd(t2,adj,cp2);
                cp2[1] = cp2[1] + 0.5;
                cir(cp2,dotrad,v1,v2);
                Vec(cp2[0],cp1[1],cp1[2],cp);
                cir(cp,dotrad,v1,v2);
                Vec(cp1[0],cp1[1],cp2[2],cp);
                cir(cp,dotrad,v1,v2);
                break;
    case 6:VecAdd(p2,p3,t1);
                VecScalMult(0.5,t1,t1);
                VecAdd(p2,t1,t2);
                VecScalMult(0.5,t2,t2);
                VecAdd(t2,adj,cp1);
                cp1[2] = cp1[2] - 0.5;
```

```
                cir(cp1,dotrad,v1,v2);
                VecAdd(p3,t1,t2);
                VecScalMult(0.5,t2,t2);
                VecAdd(t2,adj,cp2);
                cp2[2] = cp2[2] - 0.5;
                cir(cp2,dotrad,v1,v2);
                Vec(cp1[0],cp2[1],cp1[2],cp3);
                cir(cp3,dotrad,v1,v2);
                Vec(cp1[0],cp1[1],cp2[2],cp4);
                cir(cp4,dotrad,v1,v2);
                VecAdd(cp1,cp3,t1);
                VecScalMult(0.5,t1,cp);
                cir(cp,dotrad,v1,v2);
                VecAdd(cp2,cp4,t1);
                VecScalMult(0.5,t1,cp);
                cir(cp,dotrad,v1,v2);
                break;
        }
    }


void die(float x, float y, float z, float rad)
{
    TDA p1, p2, p3, p4, p5, p6, p7, p8;

    Vec(x,y,z + rad,p1);
    Vec(x + 4.0 * rad,y,z + rad,p2);
    Vec(x + 4.0 * rad,y + 4.0 * rad,z + rad,p3);
    Vec(x,y + 4.0 * rad,z + rad,p4);
    Vec(x,y,z + rad + 4.0 * rad,p5);
    Vec(x + 4.0 * rad,y,z + rad + 4.0 * rad,p6);
    Vec(x + 4.0 * rad,y + 4.0 * rad,z + rad + 4.0 * rad,p7);
    Vec(x,y + 4.0 * rad,z + rad + 4.0 * rad,p8);
    sph(p1,rad);
    sph(p2,rad);
    sph(p3,rad);
    sph(p4,rad);
    sph(p5,rad);
    sph(p6,rad);
    sph(p7,rad);
    sph(p8,rad);
    cyl(p1,p2,rad);
    cyl(p2,p3,rad);
    cyl(p3,p4,rad);
    cyl(p4,p1,rad);
    cyl(p5,p6,rad);
    cyl(p6,p7,rad);
    cyl(p7,p8,rad);
    cyl(p8,p5,rad);
    cyl(p1,p5,rad);
    cyl(p2,p6,rad);
```

```
    cyl(p3,p7,rad);
    cyl(p4,p8,rad);

    /*    Pln(6, rad, p1, p4, p2,  0.0,  0.0, -rad);  */
    /*  6 - no bottom generation  */
    pln(2,rad,p1,p2,p5,0.0,-rad,0.0);   /*  2  */
    pln(3,rad,p3,p7,p2,rad,0.0,0.0);    /*  3  */
    pln(5,rad,p3,p4,p7,0.0,rad,0.0);    /*  5  */
    pln(4,rad,p1,p5,p4,-rad,0.0,0.0);   /*  4  */
    pln(1,rad,p5,p6,p8,0.0,0.0,rad);    /*  1  */
}
void pokerchip(float x, float y, float z, float rad, char * color)
{
    fprintf(textdiskfile,"\n");
    fprintf(textdiskfile,"\n");
    fprintf(textdiskfile,"CIRCLE\n");
    fprintf(textdiskfile," LOC    = %3.3f %3.3f %3.3f\n",x,y,z);
    fprintf(textdiskfile," V1     =   1.000  0.000  0.000\n");
    fprintf(textdiskfile," V2     =   0.000  1.000  0.000\n");
    fprintf(textdiskfile," RADIUS = %3.3f\n",rad);
    fprintf(textdiskfile," MATL   = %s\n",color);
    fprintf(textdiskfile,"\n");
    fprintf(textdiskfile,"\n");
    fprintf(textdiskfile,"CYLINDER\n");
    fprintf(textdiskfile," BASELOC = %3.3f %3.3f %3.3f\n",x,y,z);
    fprintf(textdiskfile," BASERAD = %3.3f\n",rad);
    fprintf(textdiskfile," APEXLOC = %3.3f %3.3f %3.3f\n",x,y,z - 5.0);
    fprintf(textdiskfile," MATL    = %s\n",color);
}


void spade(float x, float y, float z, float rad, char * color)
{
    fprintf(textdiskfile,"\n");
    fprintf(textdiskfile,"\n");
    fprintf(textdiskfile,"CIRCLE\n");
    fprintf(textdiskfile," LOC    = %3.3f %3.3f %3.3f\n",x,y,z);
    fprintf(textdiskfile," V1     =   1.000  0.000  0.000\n");
    fprintf(textdiskfile," V2     =   0.000  0.000  1.000\n");
    fprintf(textdiskfile," RADIUS = %3.3f\n",rad);
    fprintf(textdiskfile," MATL   = %s\n",color);
    fprintf(textdiskfile,"\n");
    fprintf(textdiskfile,"\n");
    fprintf(textdiskfile,"CIRCLE\n");
    fprintf(textdiskfile," LOC    = %3.3f %3.3f %3.3f\n",(x + 1.7 *
                           rad),y,z);
    fprintf(textdiskfile," V1     =   1.000  0.000  0.000\n");
    fprintf(textdiskfile," V2     =   0.000  0.000  1.000\n");
    fprintf(textdiskfile," RADIUS = %3.3f\n",rad);
    fprintf(textdiskfile," MATL   = %s\n",color);
    fprintf(textdiskfile,"\n");
```

```
    fprintf(textdiskfile,"\n");
    fprintf(textdiskfile,"TRIANGLE\n");
    fprintf(textdiskfile,"  LOC    = %3.3f %3.3f %3.3f\n",(x - rad *
                                0.95),y,(z + 0.33 * rad));
    fprintf(textdiskfile,"  V1     = %3.3f   0.000  0.000\n",(3.6 *
                                rad));
    fprintf(textdiskfile,"  V2     = %3.3f   0.000 %3.3f\n",(1.85 *
                                rad),(3.0 * rad));
    fprintf(textdiskfile,"  MATL   = %s\n",color);
    fprintf(textdiskfile,"\n");
    fprintf(textdiskfile,"\n");
    fprintf(textdiskfile,"TRIANGLE\n");
    fprintf(textdiskfile,"  LOC    = %3.3f %3.3f %3.3f\n",(x + 0.85 *
                                rad),y,(z - 0.34 * rad));
    fprintf(textdiskfile,"  V1     = %3.3f   0.000 %3.3f\n",(-0.75 *
                                rad),(-1.1 * rad));
    fprintf(textdiskfile,"  V2     = %3.3f   0.000 %3.3f\n",(0.75 *
                                rad),(-1.1 * rad));
    fprintf(textdiskfile,"  MATL   = %s\n",color);
}

void make()
{
    Byte t;

    writestudio();

                        /*  Ace of Spades  */

    fprintf(textdiskfile,"\n");
    fprintf(textdiskfile,"\n");
    fprintf(textdiskfile,"PARALLELOGRAM\n");
    fprintf(textdiskfile,"  LOC    = -40.000 -19.000   0.000\n");
    fprintf(textdiskfile,"  V1     =  80.000   0.000   0.000\n");
    fprintf(textdiskfile,"  V2     =   0.000   0.000 128.000\n");
    fprintf(textdiskfile,"  MATL   = WHITE\n");
    spade(-12.0,-20.0,50.0,14.0,"BLACK");

        /*  Stack of Poker Chips  */

    for (t = 1; t <= 12; t++)
        pokerchip(-60.0,-85.0,t * 6.0,25.0,"RED");

        /*  Dice  */

    die(-80.0,-320.0,0.0,7.5);
    die(50.0,-335.0,0.0,7.5);

        /*  Tumbler  */
```

384

```
    fprintf(textdiskfile,"\n");
    fprintf(textdiskfile,"\n"); fprintf(textdiskfile,"CYLINDER\n");
    fprintf(textdiskfile,"   BASELOC = -170.000 -30.000 0.000\n");
    fprintf(textdiskfile,"   BASERAD = 60.000\n");
    fprintf(textdiskfile,"   APEXLOC = -170.000 -30.000 90.000\n");
    fprintf(textdiskfile,"   MATL    = CHROME\n");
    fprintf(textdiskfile,"\n");
    fprintf(textdiskfile,"\n");
    fprintf(textdiskfile,"RING\n");
    fprintf(textdiskfile,"   LOC    = -170.000 -30.000 90.000\n");
    fprintf(textdiskfile,"   V1     =    1.000   0.000   0.000\n");
    fprintf(textdiskfile,"   V2     =    0.000   1.000   0.000\n");
    fprintf(textdiskfile,"   RAD1   = 45.000\n");
    fprintf(textdiskfile,"   RAD2   = 60.000\n");
    fprintf(textdiskfile,"   MATL   = BRASS\n");
    fprintf(textdiskfile,"\n");
    fprintf(textdiskfile,"\n");
    fprintf(textdiskfile,"BOUNDINGSPHERETEST\n");
    fprintf(textdiskfile,"\n");
    fprintf(textdiskfile,"\n"); fprintf(textdiskfile,"ENDFRAME\n");
}

void main()
{
    strcpy(filename,"DIE&CARD.RT");
    clrscr();
    printf("Generating %s File\n",filename);
    printf("\n");
    printf("By Christopher D. Watkins\n");
    printf("\n");
    printf("\n");
    printf("Writing %d frames\n",numberofframes);
    textdiskfile=fopen(filename, "wt");
    writeheader();
    make();
    fclose(textdiskfile);
}
```

Listing 13-2. Listing of *DIE&CARD.C*.

CANNON.C

The *CANNON.C* program creates a scene consisting of a cannon firing a cannonball, a stack of cannonballs, and a flag. The most interesting thing about this program is how the stack of cannonballs is created. The three corner cannonballs on the base are placed at the corners of an equilateral triangle. A simple way to generate these corners is to use three equally spaced points on a circle. These points are computed with the *sine* and *cosine* functions for the angles 0, 120, and 240 degrees. Once the base is established, we generate the next position by averaging the three corner positions. Further positions up the stack are generated by averaging positions from the layer below. This process continues until we reach the top of the stack, with only one ball in the center.

DESERT.C

The *DESERT.C* program creates a moonlit desert scene of pyramids and dunes. The pyramids are different from most of the other objects we've encountered in that they're constructed from other primitive objects, *TRIANGLE* and *PARALLELO-GRAM*. The ray tracer knows how to convert the object *PYRAMID* from an appropriate set of *TRIANGLE*s and *PARALLELOGRAM* primitive objects. Each *PYRAMID* is made up of four *TRIANGLE*s (for the sides) and a *PARALLELOGRAM* (for the base). Thus, *PYRAMID* is an example of an instanced model—one that is made up of smaller primitive objects but can be manipulated as if it were a single primitive object. This technique is commonly available in most advanced graphics software.

The dunes are created using cut spheres (spheres with slices taken out). In this case, we cut a sphere by placing it under the ground, allowing only part of it to extend above the surface. Because the ray tracer intersects only the closest object, the ground hides the remainder of these spheres, leaving just the tops exposed.

The moonlight emanates from a dim *LAMP* placed a great distance above the scene. The moon is a much dimmer source of light than the sun, lending a nighttime feel to the scene.

M&T.C

The *M&T.C* program creates the M&T logo hovering above ocean waves with a backdrop of a cloudy sky. This program illustrates how letters can be created from fundamental shapes. The letters *M* and *T* are created from spheres and cylinders; the ampersand (&) is created only from spheres, which overlap to produce a ribbed texture.

MOUNT.C

The *MOUNT.C* program creates a fractal mountain or rocklike structure emerging from the ocean waves. You can obtain any fractal mountain by selecting the random seed in the *InitRand* function. This program produces a height buffer with a size of *MaxRes* by *MaxRes* elements. Each value in the buffer represents a height above the ground for a particular *x,y* location on the ground. Adjacent sets of four points specify a parallelogram, which is in turn broken into two triangles. An internal perturbation buffer is used to alter the *x* and *y* locations slightly to remove some of the repetition in the image.

A *MinMountainCoverage* variable is used to specify the minimum ratio of land area to sea area. *Roughness* controls the heights of the elements in the *HeightBuffer*, and *NumberLevels* sets the number of binary divisions per side to create the two-dimensional height buffer. *NumberLevels* is now set to 3, yielding a *MaxRes* of 2^3, or 8. This means the height buffer will generate 8 x 8, or 64, parallelograms, so 2 x 64 triangles are required to create the image. The *SC* variable specifies the overall height scaling, and *Perturb* controls the perturbation of the *x* and *y* values (how much they will deviate from evenly spaced values) written to the MOUNT.RT file. *MntRotate* and *MntTilt* specify the location from which we wish to view the scene as well as the rotation and tilt of the preview display generated when we run this program. *MOUNT.C* generates new height values until the minimum land coverage specified by *MinMountainCoverage* is met.

The basic fractal algorithm generates new height points from some initial values at the endpoints of a line. The process consists of three steps. First, two endpoints are generated in the *x* direction (along the *y*=0 axis), averaged, and offset by a small, random amount. This becomes the value at the midpoint of the two original points. Next, the process is repeated in the *y* direction (*x*=0 axis). Finally, the two new values are used to compute a midpoint value along the diagonal between the two midpoints. The entire process is also repeated for the other side of the height buffer, along the *y=MaxRes-1* and *x=MaxRes-1* axes. The subdivision process is recursively repeated up to *NumberLevels* (three) times along both sides of the height buffer. This process thus generates the height values in the height buffer and is referred to as the *midpoint replacement algorithm*.

DESK.C

The *DESK.C* program creates a room scene comprising sheetrock walls, wooden floors, and a marble desk with geometric objects on it. A glass orb demonstrates the ray tracer's ability to generate transmission rays through translucent objects. *WriteHeader* and *WriteStudio* perform the same functions as in the preceding file-creation programs except that the *LAMP*s are no longer part of the *WriteStudio* procedure; here, they're placed in the main *Make* procedure and are described as ceiling lights. Their placement on the ceiling near a large, flat surface helps diffuse the light, providing ambiance. You can create some interesting effects by changing the colors and intensities of the *LAMP*s.

PIANO.C

The *PIANO.C* program creates another room scene, this time with sheetrock walls, marble floors, and a wooden piano with ivory and ebony keys. As in *DESK.C*, the *LAMP*s are not part of the *WriteStudio* procedure.

The interesting part of this program is the way the keyboard is produced. A loop is set up to span the width of the keyboard, periodically placing ivory keys (white *PARALLELOGRAM* objects) in the scene. A second loop again spans the width of the keyboard, starting with a slight offset, to place the smaller ebony keys (black *PARALLELOGRAM* objects) in the scene. A counter omits every third and seventh ebony key position to put the sharps in the proper places.

POOLTABL.C

The *POOLTABL.C* program creates the top surface of a pool table with a rack of pool balls, a cue ball, and a pool cue ready to break. As in the cannonball stack, the positions of the balls are calculated by averaging the base positions, and the *sine* and *cosine* functions are used to compute the position of each ball.

TETRA.C

TETRA.C creates a stack of tetrahedrons using a recursive procedure. The program starts with a single tetrahedron and recursively subdivides it (much like a fractal process) into smaller and smaller sets of tetrahedrons. Each tetrahedron in the stack is assigned a random material and is made of triangles with outward-pointing surface normals. We do this by creating a ray from the center of the tetrahedron to the centerpoint of the triangle, then looking at the surface normal of the triangle face. If the dot product of the two vectors is less than zero, we negate the direction of the surface normal to force it to point outward.

Note that the tetrahedron extents are set by *TETRA.C* and that the tetrahedron test is automatically performed by the ray tracer when *TETRAEXTENTS* is found in the file.

TETSPHR2.C

TETSPHR2.C creates a recursive, tetrahedral stack of spheres. The centers of the spheres are computed by averaging the four corner points of the recursive tetrahedrons produced by *TETRA.C*. At each recursion level, the program checks to make sure the newly generated spheres aren't in the same location as spheres from previous recursion levels. This helps reduce the number of computations the ray tracer needs to perform. Without this check, this particular scene could take days to ray trace. Memory would also be a problem in that we would easily generate more than the maximum allowable number of spheres in any given scene.

WAVYORB.C

The *WAVYORB.C* program creates a sphere textured with the *WAVES* texture. The *MATERIAL* record now contains the new parameters necessary to specify the kind of texture we want: *AMPL* is the amplitude of the wave, *PHASE* is the phase of the wave, and *XPOS*, *YPOS*, and *ZPOS* are the position variables for the wave. The object is viewed through a glass orb floating above the ocean.

Now that we can generate the animation sequences, we'll look next at the animator program. It allows us to view the animations interactively in several different ways.

PART IV

ANIMATION

CHAPTER 14

Animation Techniques

Computers have both broadened and improved the types of animation we can produce. Many processes that are either time-consuming or difficult can be automated with the computer. For instance, we saw in the last chapter how easily we could rotate an animated object. Doing this with hand drawings would be very tedious, especially if the object must have exactly the same shape from frame to frame.

While computer animation opens up new possibilities, it also presents new challenges: It requires that we build a detailed, three-dimensional model of all the elements of our scene. For complex models, this can be a difficult process. This chapter explores several techniques for making animation sequences easier to produce. Many of these techniques have been adapted from those used in cartoon animation. We'll discuss the pros and cons of each method and look at some techniques for improving the image quality of an animation sequence.

Let's begin with a review of how cartoon animation is created.

Computer Animation vs. Manual Animation

For each cell of an animated cartoon, the artist draws characters onto a piece of clear plastic. This material is used so that multiple characters can be overlaid on one another. This saves time because the artist can draw a single fixed background (or a small number of backgrounds if the characters will "run" through it) and then animate the characters on top of it without having to redraw the background for every frame. The characters and other moving objects are drawn onto separate sheets and placed on top of the background. Once the artist has finished the scene, the plastic-film frame is photographed. This process is repeated for every frame in the cartoon. The average cartoon has 24 to 30 frames per second, so a one-minute cartoon requires anywhere from 1,440 to 1,800 individual frames. This is one reason many cartoons take up to a year to create.

The fact that feature-length animated movies can easily require hundreds of thousands of frames is a great motivation to remove some of the more tedious aspects of animation and let the animators concentrate on the more artistic aspects. For example, the latest animated movie from Disney, *Beauty and the Beast*, used computer graphics extensively to render many of the backgrounds. The computer has the advantage of providing consistency and scene realism along with automated production. Many of the backgrounds would have taken much longer using traditional hand animation. In addition, computer-generated imagery is far more flexible when the scene must be edited. Digital pixels are easy to draw and erase, whereas animation cells usually require redrawing. Computer-generated scenes also give the artist great flexibility in changing colors, material attributes, lighting conditions, and so on; in traditional animation, such changes would require complete redrawing by hand.

Probably the biggest advantage of computer animation over manual animation is the ability to construct the scene mathematically and then define the motions of the objects within the scene. These are the most time-consuming tasks in manual animation, requiring that the animator manually position the objects from frame to frame. In computer animation, objects usually move according to a well-defined set of equations (such as when rotating about a center point, periodically moving up and down, or simply moving in a particular direction). Once the motion is defined, the computer can automatically generate the entire animation sequence without human intervention. Thus, the animator can spend more time on the overall look of the animation and devise new and more complex motions.

The animation sequences in this book are generated using scene editors and various mathematically defined motions. You'll see several scenes in which most of the objects are mathematically defined, as in *DIE&CARD.C*, or their placement is defined by a mathematical procedure, as in *CANNON.C*. A more complex example is found in *ROBOT.C*, in which many components must move synchronously to produce the illusion of an animated character. The principal advantage of using a computer is the ability to define the object motions precisely and then produce the entire animated sequence automatically, ensuring accuracy and consistency from frame to frame.

Now let's look at some of the computer animation techniques used by the programs in this book.

Methods of Animation

An animation sequence is a series of images that, when played back quickly enough, gives the illusion of continuous motion. Movies and television depend on this ability to fool the human eye into believing that the images represent continuous motion. From frame to frame in an animation, the scene elements that move do so only slightly. The animation must be replayed fast enough—24 frames per second for motion pictures, 30 for American television—to prevent the eye from perceiving the individual frames, a phenomenon known as flicker. Therefore, a computer-animated sequence must be played back at about 30 frames-per-second to produce the illusion of smooth, continuous motion.

The computer provides two distinct methods for animating images. The first is a technique known as *color cycling*, which uses a single image but changes the color palette from frame to frame. Recall that for our VGA images we use color values, from 0 to 255, as indices into the color palette tables. If we change the table element for 0, all the pixels with that value in our image will be displayed in the new color. The *CLOUDS.C* program uses this technique to make the clouds appear to move.

The colors can be changed in a variety of ways; the simplest is simply to shift all the colors by one table entry. Value 0 would then be displayed with value 1's color, value 1 with value 2's color, and so on up to value 255, which would be displayed with the old value 0 color. We could also shift the table in the opposite direction, or just load an entirely new table for each frame.

Color cycling is a fairly limited technique for a variety of reasons. The first is that it requires a display with a color palette, which some of the older display types (such as CGA) don't provide. The second is that even VGA gives you only 256 colors to manipulate; this can be a serious constraint if you have more than one or two moving objects. Finally, the viewer position normally cannot change because that would cause too much of the scene to change. For these reasons, color cycling is used only for fairly simple animations of short duration, such as the cloud and plasma demonstration programs. Instead, the more traditional technique of generating new frames and playing them back rapidly, as in movies and television, is used.

As mentioned earlier, we must playback a sequence rapidly enough to produce the illusion of smooth motion. This is done on the computer display using a technique known as *page-flipping*. Each animation frame is stored in computer memory (off-screen). The animation program plays back a sequence by copying each frame in turn from memory to the display. Each frame is referred to as a new *page* of memory; the rate at which new frames are copied to the screen is referred to as the *update rate*. This rate is completely under computer control. Lower rates than 30 frames per second will slow down the motion and make it appear less smooth. You can see this effect for yourself by experimenting with the animation program described in the next chapter.

Because we must store the animation frames in computer memory to get the desired playback speed, the number of frames we can have is limited by the amount of memory available. On a standard PC, that's 640K (slightly less due to the presence of DOS and the animation program itself). Our animation frames are 160 by 100 pixels in size, so 30 cells' worth can be stored in memory.

As the program copies the frames from memory to the screen, it can perform other operations on them, such as reversing them from left to right or flipping them upside down. You can experiment with this to vary the animation sequences. This feature illustrates how computer animation provides flexibility not only in how the images are generated but in how the actual animation is processed.

Anti-Aliasing Techniques

Anti-aliasing is a generic term for reducing the various objectionable artifacts that occur in computer-animated imagery and animation. For instance, jagged lines result when a vector is drawn across the screen and the connecting pixels "step" from line to line. One anti-aliasing technique for removing this artifact is known as *image smoothing*: The image is made more fuzzy or blurry, which tends to smooth out the edges of the objects. Thus, the jagged line would look both less jagged and less sharp.

One of the simplest ways to smooth an image is to process it with a *box filter*. We replace the value of every pixel of the image with the average value of its neighbors (which may or may not be the adjacent pixels). The more pixels we average together, the blurrier the image will become. Eventually, the image will look out of focus. If done properly for certain types of animation, this technique can dramatically improve the image quality. You'll need to experiment with different sizes and shapes to find the proper extent of the box filter.

Though many other anti-aliasing techniques are used in computer graphics, they aren't incorporated into the software in this book; they usually require extensive amounts of memory that could not be provided in the animation program without sacrificing displayable animation cells. However, you may use the tools provided in this book along with the description of the *.ANI* file format provided in Chapter 16 to write your own box-filter program and see how it affects an animation sequence.

Now that we've explored the basic computer animation techniques, let's take a closer look at the *ANIMATE.C* animation program itself. This is where we'll actually view the animation sequences we produced with the modeling tool and ray tracer.

CHAPTER 15

The Animation Program

The animation program *ANIMATE.C* loads the *.ANI* files created by *3DMODEL.C* and *RAYTRACE.C* and brings them to life on your screen. It has several useful features, such as forward and reverse animation, the ability to flip the cells upside-down, and a variety of animation speed controls. You'll also learn how to create interesting displays for your own programs.

Unlike most of the other software discussed in this book, *ANIMATE.C* (Listing 15-1) doesn't use the *MATH.C* and *GRAPH.C* modules. The necessary routines were taken from the modules and put directly into the program rather than being linked in. This saves as much memory as possible for the animation frames themselves. A typical animation sequence that we will use stores 30 frames at 160 x 100 (16,000 bytes) resolution. This requires 480K bytes of memory, which is quite a lot considering the 640K limit imposed by DOS 3.3. We therefore wish to make *ANIMATE.C* as small a program as possible. Since the animation program uses very few of the functions in the modules, a large portion of the computer's memory is available for storing the animation cells.

Also, the only header file the program needs is *DEFS.H*, which contains datatype definitions (*TypeDefs*). The easiest way to compile the program is with *MAKE.EXE*, available in the Borland editor. Simply load the source code into the editor and type **Alt C-M**. This will compile and link the necessary files and generate the executable animation program, *ANIMATE.EXE*.

ANIMATE.C Variables

ANIMATE.C's *Cell_Off* and *Cell_Seg* arrays hold 32-bit pointers (memory addresses) to each line of our animation cell. *Cell_Off* contains the first 16 bits (the *offset*) of the pointer, while *Cell_Seg* contains the second 16 bits (the *segment*). We'll use the macro *MK_FP* to unite the two into one 32-bit pointer. The PC uses a segmented memory architecture, meaning that it divides up memory into 64K segments. Since we must address a lot of different segments when copying frames to the screen, pre-calculating these addresses saves time. The 32-bit address created by *MK_FP* allows us to use the 32-bit addressing mode, effectively a huge pointer, without having to use the huge memory model (which is considerably slower) for everything else.

The *Screen_Offsets* buffer is identical to the *GRAPH.C* module's *Pre_Calc_Y** buffers except that it is only used to hold the offsets for the 320 x 200, 256-color VGA mode. Precalculating these offsets will speed up plotting dramatically.

The *Window* array performs the same function as the *Screen* array except that the offsets are the precalculated addresses for the 160x100 animation cell viewing window. Just as the precalculated *Screen* array speeds up plotting, the precalculated *Window* array speeds up the copying of animation cells from memory to the screen.

The *Direction* flag indicates whether the animation sequence is played back in forward or reverse direction. The *Flip* flag determines whether the sequence is presented right-side-up, or upside-down.

D_Rate is the delay rate for the animator; it controls the speed at which new frames are written to the screen. In effect, it controls the playback speed. Once an animation cell is copied to the screen, two loops ranging from 0 to *D_Rate*200* are executed. These loops force the computer to wait a fixed amount of time before displaying the next frame.

Num_Cells holds the number of cells in the animation sequence. If it's greater than 30, the animation sequence is truncated to 30 cells and *Num_Cells* reset to 30. (The 30-cell limit is due to the memory limitations of most PCs.)

Screen is a pointer to the start of the SVGA screen memory. *Cell_Buf* is a pointer to the beginning of the internal animation cell buffer, where the animation frames are stored for subsequent playback.

ANIMATE.C Functions

The following are the various functions the animation program uses. In the next section, we'll actually run the program and see how these functions work together to produce an animation sequence.

Set_Mode

The *Set_Mode* function, taken from the *GRAPH.C* module, simply sets the graphics mode to VGA mode 19 (320x200, 256-color).

Init_Screen

Init_Screen is the equivalent of the *GRAPH.C* module's *Pre_Calc* function; the only difference is that it precalculates the row addresses only for the 320 x 200, 256-color mode (the only mode the animator uses).

Plot

Plot is the same as the 320 x 200-mode *Plot* routine found in the *GRAPH.C* module. Support for the other modes has been removed to reduce the amount of code needed for the animator, thereby increasing the memory available for the animation cells. This function relies on the *Pre_Calc* buffers (from *Init_Screen*) to generate *(x,y)* screen positions correctly.

Set_Palette

Like the *Set_Palette* function in *GRAPH.C*, this function sets the palette to the color values stored at the beginning of the animation file. This palette is used for all the animation frames; setting the palette for each frame would slow down the animation and make it appear choppy.

Init_Graphics

This condensed version of *GRAPH.C*'s *Init_Graphics* function simply calls *Init_Screen* to precalculate the rows. It sets the graphics mode to 19 and calls the *Set_Palette* function to set up the color palette.

Exit_Graphics

Like the function of the same name in the *GRAPH.C* module, *Exit_Graphics* sounds a beep to let you know it has finished, then waits for a keypress.

Set_Text_Screen

This function sets the screen from the graphics mode the animator uses back to text mode. It takes two integers, *tc* and *tb*, as arguments. The text color is set to *tc*, and the text background color is set to *tb*. The screen is then cleared.

Allocate_Memory

Allocate_Memory is called to set aside enough memory for 30 cells of animation. Each element of the *Cell_Buf* array is a pointer to an individual animation cell. *Cell_Buf[0]* points to the first cell, *Cell_Buf[1]* points to the second, and so on. The animator uses this array to locate a particular frame in memory. If enough memory cannot be allocated, an error message is printed and the program terminates after a key is pressed. Otherwise, the function returns with *Cell_Buf* initialized.

Free_Memory

This function frees up the memory *Allocate_Memory* has set aside for our animation cells.

Max

This function simply returns the greater of two values passed to it. The values are of type *word*.

Get_Key

Get_Key is called if a key is pressed while the animation program is running. It returns the key's value in the variable *key*.

Get_ANI_File_Name

When *Get_ANI_File_Name* is called, it displays a blinking file name and asks you to enter the name of the animation file. To accept the displayed file name, simply press Enter. Otherwise, enter the name of the *.ANI* file you wish to view and press Enter.

Init_Cells

The *Init_Cells* function precalculates the 32-bit pointers for each row of each cell. The *Cell_Buf* array contains pointers to the beginning of each cell, while *Cell_Off* and *Cell_Seg* contain pointers to each row of each cell. Each 32-bit pointer comprises a segment selector and an offset; the segment selector refers to the 64K memory segment we're using, and the offset is the address inside that memory segment. We need these pointers to move the cell from memory to the screen quickly. Because the screen's dimensions are different from those of the animation cells, the cells must be moved a row at a time. Having the arrays precalculated makes this operation much faster than if we had to continually compute the addresses.

We could have used the huge memory model rather than two 16-bit pointer arrays. That approach has several drawbacks, however. The first is that the program would run considerably slower because the huge model requires every 32-bit pointer in the program to be normalized. (See the Borland C++ programmer's guide for a description of the huge memory model and normalization.) Normalizing a 32-bit pointer requires some extra computations that would slow down the animation. The second drawback is that some functions in the compiler are incompatible with the huge memory model. For our purposes, calculating our own pointers is faster and easier.

Init_Window

Init_Window precalculates the address of the start of each row inside the 160 x 100 viewing window. This greatly speeds up the process of moving animation cells from memory to the viewing window in the center of the display screen.

Do_Title

This function sets up a simple but unique screen as the opening display of the program.

Find_Brightest_Color

This function finds the brightest color in the *.ANI* file's palette. The animator displays a delay rate meter that should be visible regardless of the palette used by the animation sequence. The color *Find_Brightest_Color* returns is used to draw the meter, ensuring that the meter will be visible on the screen.

H_Line

This function draws a horizontal line from *(x1, y1)* to *(x2, y1)* in the argument color *c* and is used to draw parts of the delay rate meter. The color *c* is determined by the *Find_Brightest_Color* function.

V_Line

V_Line draws a vertical line from *(x1, y1)* to *(x1, y2)* in the color *c*. Like the *H_Line* function, *V_Line* is used to draw part of the delay rate meter.

Draw_D_Meter

This function uses *H_Line* and *V_Line* to build the delay rate meter displayed near the bottom of the screen during animation.

Update_D_Meter

This function updates the delay rate meter by moving the meter pointer left or right, showing how much delay is occurring in each frame. *Update_D_Meter* also uses the *V_Line* function.

Init_D_Meter

Init_D_Meter initializes the delay rate and makes the necessary function calls to initialize the delay rate meter and place it on the screen.

Animate

This function is the heart of the *ANIMATE.C* program and is where the images are actually animated. The routine begins by initializing several variables that enable forward, reverse, and upside-down animation. The variable *NC* contains the number of cells in the animation minus 1, and *CP* is used as a pointer to the next cell to be copied to the screen.

The next two variables are used to flip the animation upside-down. *Nl* contains the maximum number of rows in a cell, and *LP* is a pointer to the current row number of the cell to be sent to the screen. When the animator begins, *CP* is set to 0 (for forward animation) and *LP* to 0 (so that it is right-side-up).

Two loops are now initialized, the first ranges from 0 to *Num_Cells* and the second from 0 to 100 (or the number of rows per cell). During each iteration of the inner loop, one row of data from the current cell is moved to the screen using the *_fmemcpy* function. This function's destination parameter is calculated using the pointer *Screen* (A000H) and the array *Window_Offsets* for the row being copied. The offset value from *Window_Offsets* is added to the value of *Screen*, telling *_fmemcpy* the address at which to start copying the data from the cell.

To find the address of the current row of the animation cell, we use the variables *CP* and *LP*, the arrays *Cell_Off* and *Cell_Seg*, and the macro *MK_FP*. We begin by computing the appropriate index into *Cell_Off* and *Cell_Seg*. Since *CP* is the current cell pointer and each animation frame has 100 rows, we multiply *CP* by 100 and add *LP*, the current row number. This value is the index for row number *LP* from the current frame, *CP*. The two 16-bit values from *Cell_Off* and *Cell_Seg* are then retrieved and passed to the *MK_FP* macro to generate the appropriate 32-bit pointer to the data in memory.

The final parameter (*size*) for *_fmemcpy* is set to 160, the length of one row of a cell. *_fmemcpy* then copies the 160 bytes pointed to by *source* (the row of the current cell in memory) to the destination address on the screen. This operation is repeated for each of the 100 rows in the current cell.

After drawing the cell, the animator waits a fixed amount of time (depending on the value of *D_Rate*) before drawing the next frame. The next frame drawn depends on the *Direction* flag. If *Direction* is true, *CP* is incremented by 1 and the animation proceeds in the forward direction. Otherwise, *CP* is decremented and the animation is reversed. Note that if *CP* is greater than 30, it is reset to 0. If the animation is being displayed backwards, the animator skips from frame 0 to frame 30.

During the inner loop, the animator examines the *Flip* flag to see if the image should be written upside-down. If *Flip* is True, *LP* is decremented; the rows are read in reverse order, displaying the cells upside-down. Otherwise, *LP* is incremented so the cells are displayed in their normal orientation.

During the delay between frames, the animator checks to see if a key has been pressed. If so, the *Get_Key* function is called to find out which key it was. If the animator recognizes the key as a command, it takes the appropriate action. Once the key has been processed, the variable *key* is reset to 0 and the first loop is iterated to draw the next animation frame.

Load_Cells

The *Load_Cells* function opens an *.ANI* file and reads the animation cells into the memory allocated by *Allocate_Memory*. First, *Load_Cells* attempts to open the *.ANI* file. If it cannot open the file, the program prints an error message and exits after a key is pressed. If *Load_Cells* successfully opens the *.ANI* file, it checks the number of cells in the animation sequence to see if it's greater than 30. If so, the program tells you it is truncating the sequence to 30 cells, and the variable *Num_Cells* is set to 30. Otherwise, *Num_Cells* is set to the number of frames in the sequence. *Load_Cells* then loads the color palette from the file and places it in the *Palette_Register Pal_Array*. This palette is used for every frame of the animation.

Now, using the pointers stored in the *Cell_Off* and *Cell_Seg* arrays, we read in each row of each cell from the file and store it in the appropriate memory location. *Direction* is set to its default value of *true* (1) to indicate forward animation; *Flip* is set to its default value of *false* (0) to force the images to be displayed right-side-up. Finally, the *.ANI* file is closed, and we're ready to animate.

Let's look at some of the controls that may be exercised during the animation sequence.

ANIMATE.C Controls

The following are the legal keypresses and their meanings. These controls are active while animation is taking place.

+	decrease the delay rate by 1
-	increase the delay rate by 1
*	decrease the delay rate by 10
/	increase the delay rate by 10
up arrow	return to normal (right-side-up) animation
down arrow	upside-down animation
right arrow	forward animation
left arrow	reverse animation
Escape	stop animation and exit program

Running *ANIMATE.C*

Now that we've explored the individual functions in the animator program, let's run through the program itself. First, *Allocate_Memory* is called to set aside a buffer for the cells in our animation sequence. Next, the text screen colors are set and *Do_Title* is called to display the opening screen. We then retrieve the name of the animation file via a call to *Get_ANI_File_Name*, then call *Init_Cells* and *Init_Window* to set up the offset and pointer arrays.

The cells are loaded into memory from the *.ANI* file using the 32-bit pointer arrays (*Cell_Off* and *Cell_Seg*). Notice that the *MK_FP* macro is used once again to turn two 16-bit pointers into a single 32-bit pointer, dramatically improving performance. The graphics screen is then initialized and the delay meter drawn onto the screen. Next, the *Animate* function is called to begin the actual animation of the sequence. The control keys are now active, so we can perform various special functions (rate control, image flip, and reverse animation) on the animation sequence. After the Escape key is pressed, *Exit_Graphics* is called to return to text mode. Finally, the allocated memory is freed and the program exits.

Having generated animations using both the three-dimensional modeling tool and the ray tracer, we need to examine in greater detail how the 16-bit computed images in the *.TMP* files are color-reduced for display on the eight-bit, 256-color SVGA display. The next chapter explains how this process works as well as its features and limitations.

405

PROGRAMMING IN 3 DIMENSIONS

```
/*
```

```
          Graphics Animation Program
             (c) 1991 Larry Sharp

          Compile using large memory model

          Maximum of 30 cells per animation sequence
                at 160x100 resolution
```

```
*/
```

```
#include "stdio.h"
#include "dos.h"
#include "string.h"
#include "malloc.h"
#include "mem.h"
#include "conio.h"
#include "defs.h"

union  REGS reg;     /* global variables */
struct SREGS inreg;

char File_Name[81];
Byte n, y, key, B_Col;
Byte Num_Cels;
int  Direction, Flip, CP;
int  D_Rate, Old_D_Rate;
Word Cel_Off[3000];
Word Cel_Seg[3000];
Word Window_Offsets[100];
Word Screen_Offsets[200];
Palette_Register Pal_Array;
static Byte far *Screen;
static Byte far *Cel_Buf;
```

```
/*
┌─────────────────────────────────────────────────────────┐
│                                                         │
│                    Graphics Routines                    │
│                                                         │
└─────────────────────────────────────────────────────────┘
*/
void Set_Mode(Byte Mode)
{
    reg.h.ah=0;
    reg.h.al=Mode;
    int86(0x10,&reg,&reg);
}


void Init_Screen()
{
    Byte y;

    for(y=0; y<200; y++)
        Screen_Offsets[y]=320*y;
}

void Plot(int x, int y, Byte color)
{
    Word Offset, Page;
    char far *address;

    if(!((x<0) || (y<0) || (x>(319)) || (y>(200))))
    {
        Offset = Screen_Offsets[y] + x;
        address = (char far *)  (0xA0000000L + Offset);
        *address = color;
    }
}

void Set_Palette(Palette_Register Hue)
{
    reg.x.ax=0x1012;
    segread(&inreg);
    inreg.es=inreg.ds;
    reg.x.bx=0;
```

```
    reg.x.cx=256;
    reg.x.dx=(int)&Hue[0];
    int86x(0x10,&reg,&reg,&inreg);
}

void Init_Graphics()
{
    Init_Screen();
    Set_Mode(19);
    Set_Palette(Pal_Array);
}

void Exit_Graphics()
{
    sound(1000);
    delay(500);
    nosound();
    Set_Mode(3);
}

void Set_Text_Screen(int tc, int tb)
{
    textcolor(tc);
    textbackground(tb);
    clrscr();
}

/*

        Memory Routines

*/

void Allocate_Memory()
{
    if((Cel_Buf=farcalloc(32, 16000))==NULL)
    {
        printf("Not enough memory!\n\nHit any key to
exit....");
        getch();
```

```
            exit(1);
        }
    }

void Free_Memory()
{
    farfree(Cel_Buf);
}

Word Max(Word n1, Word n2)
{
    return((n1>n2) ? n1 : n2);
}

Byte Get_Key()
{
    Byte k;

    key=getch();
    return(key);
}

void Get_ANI_File_Name()
{
    Byte x, y;

    textcolor(YELLOW);
    textbackground(BLUE);
    gotoxy(1, 8);
    cprintf("Enter File Name -> ");
    x=wherex();
    y=wherey();
    textcolor(WHITE+BLINK);
    cprintf("%s", "SPHRPLAN");
    textcolor(YELLOW);
    gotoxy(x, y);
    while(!(kbhit()));
    cprintf("                    ");
    gotoxy(x, y);
    gets(File_Name);
```

```
        if(!(strcmp(File_Name, "")))
            strcpy(File_Name, "SPHRPLAN");
        strupr(File_Name);
        strcat(File_Name, ".ANI");
        gotoxy(1, 8);
        printf("                              ");
        textcolor(WHITE+BLINK);
        gotoxy(1, 8);
        cprintf("Loading ");
        textcolor(YELLOW);
        cprintf("%s", File_Name);
    }


void Init_Cels()
    {
        DWord tmp, NCel_Buf;
        Word n, y, Seg;

        tmp=NCel_Buf=(DWord) Cel_Buf;
        Seg=(Word)((tmp>>16)&65535);
        for(n=0; n<30; n++)
        {
            for(y=0; y<100; y++)
            {
                tmp=(DWord) NCel_Buf;
                tmp+=(DWord)((n*16000)+(y*160));
                Cel_Off[(n*100)+y]=(Word)(tmp&65535);
                if((Cel_Off[(n*100)+y]+160)<Cel_Off[(n*100)+y])
                {
                    tmp+=160;
                    NCel_Buf+=160;
                    Cel_Off[(n*100)+y]=(Word)(tmp&65535);
                    Seg+=0x1000;
                }
                Cel_Seg[(n*100)+y]=Seg;
            }
        }
    }

void Init_Window()
```

```
{
    long tmp;

    Screen=0xA0000000L;
    for(y=50; y<150; y++)
    {
        tmp=(y*320)+80;
        Window_Offsets[y-50]=tmp;
    }
}

void Do_Title()
{
    Byte i, j;
    int B_Colors[3]={RED, WHITE, BLUE};
    int F_Colors[3]={LIGHTGRAY, MAGENTA, YELLOW};

    for(i=0; i<3; i++)
    {
        for(j=0; j<80; j++)
        {
            textcolor(F_Colors[i]);
            textbackground(B_Colors[i]);
            cprintf(" ");
        }
    }
    textcolor(F_Colors[0]);
    textbackground(B_Colors[0]);
    for(i=1; i<32; i++)
    {
        gotoxy(i, 1);
        cprintf(" Animation Software");
        delay(15);
    }
    textcolor(F_Colors[1]);
    textbackground(B_Colors[1]);
    for(i=77; i>38; i--)
    {
        gotoxy(i, 2);
        cprintf("by ");
```

```
        delay(15);
}
textcolor(F_Colors[2]);
textbackground(B_Colors[2]);
for(i=23; i>2; i—)
{
    gotoxy(34, i);
    cprintf("Larry Sharp");
    gotoxy(34, i+1);
    cprintf("                    ");
    delay(15);
}
textcolor(LIGHTGRAY);
gotoxy(35, 20);
cprintf("DIRECTION");
gotoxy(37, 23);
cprintf("SPEED");
textbackground(BLACK);
textcolor(LIGHTRED);
gotoxy(16, 21);
cprintf("Fwd Rvs Flip Up Flip Down");
gotoxy(16, 24);
cprintf("Speed Up Slow Down <10>10 Quit");
textcolor(WHITE);
gotoxy(17, 21);
cprintf("Rgt");
gotoxy(27, 21);
cprintf("Lft");
gotoxy(38, 21);
cprintf("Up");
gotoxy(51, 21);
cprintf("Dwn");
gotoxy(17, 24);
cprintf("+");
gotoxy(29, 24);
cprintf("-");
gotoxy(42, 24);
cprintf("*");
gotoxy(49, 24);
cprintf("/");
```

```
    gotoxy(56, 24);
    cprintf("Esc");
}

void Find_Brightest_Color()
{
    Word h1, h2, h3, i;
    Byte c;

    c=0;
    h3=h1=(Pal_Array[0].Red+Pal_Array[0].Grn+Pal_Array[0].Blu);
for(i=1; i<256; i++)
    {

h2=(Pal_Array[i].Red+Pal_Array[i].Grn+Pal_Array[i].Blu);
h3=Max(h1, h2);
        if(h3==h2)
        {
            c=i;
            h1=h2;
        }
    }
    B_Col=c;
}

void H_Line(Word x1, Word x2, Byte y1, Byte c)
{
    Word i;

    for(i=x1; i<=x2; i++)
    {
        Plot(i, y1, c);
    }
}

void V_Line(Word x1, Byte y1, Byte y2, Byte c)
{
    Word i;

    for(i=y1; i<=y2; i++)
```

```c
        {
            Plot(x1, i, c);
        }
    }

void Draw_Window_Frame()
    {
        H_Line(79, 240, 49, B_Col);
        H_Line(79, 240, 150, B_Col);
        V_Line(79, 49, 150, B_Col);
        V_Line(240, 49, 150, B_Col);
    }

void Draw_D_Meter()
    {
        H_Line(32, 289, 189, B_Col);   /* draw rectangular meter */
        H_Line(32, 289, 199, B_Col);
        V_Line(32, 189, 199, B_Col);
        V_Line(289, 189, 199, B_Col);
        V_Line(32, 183, 187, B_Col);     /* draw '+' */
        H_Line(30, 34, 185, B_Col);
        H_Line(287, 291, 185, B_Col);    /* draw '-' */
    }

void Update_D_Meter(int D_Rate)
    {
        Word i;

        if(Old_D_Rate>D_Rate)
        {
            for(i=Old_D_Rate; i>D_Rate; i—)
                V_Line((i+33), 190, 198, 0);
        }
        else
        {
            for(i=Old_D_Rate; i<=D_Rate; i++)
                V_Line((i+33), 190, 198, 24);
        }
    }
```

```
void Init_D_Meter()
{
    D_Rate=50;                          /* initial delay rate */
    Old_D_Rate=0;
    Find_Brightest_Color();
    Draw_Window_Frame();
    Draw_D_Meter();
    Update_D_Meter(D_Rate);
    Old_D_Rate=D_Rate;
}

void Animate()
{
    Byte n, y, k, tmp, NC, N1;
    int LP;
    Word Del;

    NC=Num_Cels-1;
    CP=0;
    N1=99;
    LP=0;
    while(key!=27)              /* animate until Escape key hit */
    {
        for(n=0; n<Num_Cels; n++)
        {
            for(y=0; y<100; y++)
            {
                _fmemcpy((Screen+(Window_Offsets[y])),
                    MK_FP(Cel_Seg[(CP*100)+LP],
                    Cel_Off[(CP*100)+LP]), 160);
    if(Flip)
    {
        -LP;
        if(LP<0)
            LP=N1;
    }
    else
    {
        ++LP;
        if(LP>N1)
```

```
            LP=0;
    }
}
if(Direction)
{
    ++CP;
    if(CP>NC)
        CP=0;
    }
    else
    {
    —CP;
    if(CP<0)
        CP=NC;
        }
        for(Del=0; Del<(D_Rate*200); Del++);
        for(Del=0; Del<(D_Rate*200); Del++);
        if(kbhit())                /* check for keystroke */
        {
            k=Get_Key();           /* get keystroke */
switch(toupper(k))
            {
                case '+' : Old_D_Rate=D_Rate;   /* faster by 1 */
                    —D_Rate;
                    if(D_Rate<0)
                        D_Rate=0;
                    Update_D_Meter(D_Rate);
                    break;

                case '-' : Old_D_Rate=D_Rate;   /* slower by 1 */
                    ++D_Rate;
                    if(D_Rate>255)
                        D_Rate=255;
                    Update_D_Meter(D_Rate);
                    break;

                case '*' : Old_D_Rate=D_Rate;   /* faster by 10 */
                    D_Rate-=10;
                    if(D_Rate<0)
                        D_Rate=0;
```

```
        Update_D_Meter(D_Rate);
        break;

    case '/' : Old_D_Rate=D_Rate;      /* slower by 10 */
        D_Rate+=10;
        if(D_Rate>255)
            D_Rate=255;
        Update_D_Meter(D_Rate);
        break;

    case 'M' : if(!Direction)          /* forward */
        {
            Direction=1;
            n=NC-n;
        }
        break;

    case 'K' : if(Direction)           /* reverse */
        {
            Direction=0;
            n=NC-n;
        }
        break;

    case 'H' : if(Flip)                /* forward */
        {
            Flip=0;
            LP=0;
        }
        break;

    case 'P' : if(!Flip)               /* reverse */
        {
            Flip=1;
            LP=N1;
        }
        break;
}
k=0;                                   /* set key back to 0 */
}
```

```c
        }
      }
   }

   void Load_Cels()
   {
       FILE *In_File;

       if((In_File=fopen(File_Name,"rb"))==NULL)    /* open anima-
   tion file */
       {
           Exit_Graphics();
           printf("Can't open Animation File %s!\n\nHit any key to
   exit....", File_Name);
           getch();
           Free_Memory();
           exit(1);
       }
       Num_Cels=getc(In_File);       /* get # of cells in sequence
   */
       printf("\n\nThere are %u Cels in this Animation
   sequence.\n", Num_Cels);
       if(Num_Cels>30)                   /* maximum of 30 cells */
       {
           printf("\nTruncating to 30 Cels....\n");
           Num_Cels=30;
       }
       fread(Pal_Array, 1, 768, In_File);  /* load palette for
   animation */
       for(n=0; n<Num_Cels; n++)   /* load cells */
       {
           for(y=0; y<100; y++)
               fread(MK_FP(Cel_Seg[(n*100)+y],
   Cel_Off[(n*100)+y]),
                   160, 1, In_File);
       }
       Direction=1;                          /* go forward to start
   animation */
       Flip=0;
       fclose(In_File);
```

```
}

void main()
{
    Allocate_Memory();              /* get memory for cells */
    Set_Text_Screen(YELLOW, BLUE);  /* set text screen colors
*/
    Do_Title();                         /* opening display and
title */
    Get_ANI_File_Name();            /* get the name of the .ANI
file */
    Init_Cels();                        /* initialize cell
offsets */
    Init_Window();                      /* initialize window
offsets */
    Load_Cels();                        /* load cells from .ANI
file */
    Init_Graphics();                    /* initialize graphics
screen */
    Init_D_Meter();                 /* initialize delay meter
*/
    Animate();                          /* animate! */
    Free_Memory();                      /* free up far memory
*/
}
```

Listing 15-1. *Animate.C.*

PART V

COLOR PROCESSING

CHAPTER 16

Reducing Colors with the Color Histogram Processor

The three-dimensional modeling tool and ray tracer generate images using up to 262,144 unique colors. Since an SVGA graphics card can only display 256 colors, we must take the computed images and find 256 colors that best represent those in the original image. This chapter describes a method for this color reduction and shows how it's implemented in the program *PROCESS.C* and the header file *PROCESS.H*.

Our discussion starts with a look at how the color histogram processor works. We'll examine the *PROCESS.C* and *PROCESS.H* files, then discuss the *.ANI* file format and the *DISPRGB.C* program used to view single-frame, ray-traced renderings.

The Color Histogram Processor

The color reduction method used in this chapter is an implementation of a simple concept: We wish to use the 256 most frequently occurring colors in the image (or images of an animation sequence). For each of the possible colors, we count the number of pixels in the image that have that color. This process produces a frequency count, or *histogram*, that is then sorted from the color having the most pixels to the one having the least. The 256 colors with the greatest number of pixels are the ones we'll use in our palette.

Once the palette is chosen, we process the images to generate new ones for the *.ANI* output file. That file's pixel values are eight-bit quantities that index into our new palette. We examine the pixel color to see which of the 256 colors it is most similar to (in other words, has the nearest red, green, and blue values). The output pixel is assigned the index to that color in the palette. Every pixel of each animation frame is processed this way to convert the *.TMP* file into an *.ANI* file for the animator to display.

The ray tracer and three-dimensional modeler write out images using three bytes for each pixel, one each for red, green, and blue. The values of these bytes range from 0 to 63, for a total of 262,144 (64x64x64) possible unique colors. (The reason this reduction process works is that few images use anywhere near this many colors.) Our job is to find the most commonly occurring colors in this particular set of images.

The first step is to initialize the *ColorHistogram*, *Frequency*, and *Hues* arrays. After we enter the name of the *.TMP* file, *CollectColorData* opens and processes it. This function reads in the red, green, and blue components for each pixel of each image. To reduce the histogram size to fit in the available memory, it truncates the least significant bit. Thus, each color component now has a possible range of 0 to 31, for a total of 32,768 (32x32x32) colors. We can represent this as a single 16-bit value, which is used as an index into the *ColorHistogram* array. The array value at this index is incremented by 1 to indicate that a pixel has this particular color. This continues until all the color components have been read in, and the file is closed.

Now, using a *for* loop, we look at every value stored in the *ColorHistogram* array. An entry of 0 indicates that none of the images had pixels with this color value, so it is ignored. Nonzero entries have the color number stored in the *Hues* array and the count (the number of pixels with this color) stored in the corresponding *Frequency* array. Next, *SortColorData* is called to sort the colors so that the most frequently occurring color is first and the least frequently occurring color is last. The 256 most frequently occurring colors make up the palette for our image. *MakePalette* is called to form our new palette using the *Hues* array and set the display palette.

We must go through the file again to create the *.ANI* file input, converting each pixel into its appropriate index into the new palette. To do this, we use *GetColorHistogramFromFrequency* to replace the frequency-of-occurrence values in the *ColorHistogram* array with the color-register assignments stored in the

Frequency array. In effect, we have created a lookup table that maps the original red, green, and blue components to palette indices.

We're now ready to use the red, green, and blue data in the *.TMP* file to find the correct colors and display the image. We read in the red, green, and blue components of each pixel in the image, drop the least significant bit, and form a 16-bit color value. We'll use this value as an index into the *ColorHistogram* array to find the correct output color for the new palette. The color index value is then written to the output *.ANI* file for subsequent playback.

Let's take a closer look at the *PROCESS.C* program and the *PROCESS.H* include file for the ray tracer and modeler, respectively.

The *PROCESS.C* Program and *PROCESS.H* Include File

PROCESS.C is the program used to color-process the *.TMP* files produced by the ray tracer for animation, while the *PROCESS.H* file is linked directly into the modeling program. The only difference is that the routines in *PROCESS.H* are called by the modeler to process each frame as it is rendered, whereas *PROCESS.C* is a separate program run after the ray tracer has completed. In the case of the modeler, we call the *ProcessTMPFileToANIFile* function to begin the color-reduction process; for the ray tracer, we execute *PROCESS.C* after completing the ray tracing of an animation sequence. Otherwise, the procedure is the same for both.

As with the other software we've examined, the first step is to initialize the necessary arrays. For the color-reduction programs, these arrays are *Hues*, *Frequency*, and *ColorHistogram*. Memory is allocated for each array, each element of which is set to zero. Next, we try to open the *.TMP* file and, if we're successful, retrieve the number of frames in the animation sequence from the file. A loop ranging from 1 to the number of frames in the sequence then begins.

For each iteration of the frame loop, we call *CollectColorData* to read in the red, green, and blue color components for every pixel of the current animation frame and increment the appropriate color index. Once the data from all the frames in the sequence has been collected, we begin another loop to create the *Hues* and *Frequency* arrays. Once again, we examine every color stored in the *ColorHistogram* array. If a color is zero, it is ignored; otherwise, its number is stored in the *Hues* array and the frequency of occurrence (from the *ColorHistogram* array) is stored in the *Frequency* array.

Next, *SortColorData* is called to sort the colors from the most frequently occurring to the least. *MakePalette* is then called to take the first 256 colors (or the 256 most frequently occurring colors) and make a new palette out of them. The new color indices are stored in the corresponding locations in the *Frequency* array. *Set_Palette* is now called to set up our newly formed VGA palette.

Once the palette is set, we must run back through the *.TMP* file and generate the corresponding *.ANI* file using the new palette and the reduced number of colors. The function *GetColorHistogramFromFrequency* does this by copying the *Frequency* array into the *ColorHistogram* array. *Frequency* has the indices for each color input into the new palette. As pixels are again read in from the *.TMP* file, they're used as indices into the *ColorHistogram* array (just as when the histogram was originally computed). *ColorHistogram* now provides the pointer to the correct color number stored in the computed palette. This is the color that's plotted to the screen.

For each frame, we read in 160x100 (16,000) pixels, find the correct color number, and plot the pixel to the screen. This allows us to view the results as the frame is processed. After processing a frame, we write it out to the new *.ANI* file. After all frames have been processed and written to the *.ANI* file, that file is closed and our new animation sequence is ready to be loaded into the animation program.

The *.ANI* File Format

.ANI files have a very simple binary format (in other words, they are not text files that one can type to the screen but have a simple structure which can be read from a program). The first thing in an *.ANI* file is the number of frames in the sequence, stored in one byte. Next is a color palette consisting of 256 red, green, and blue color components, also stored as one byte each. Thus, the palette array is 768 bytes long. Finally, we have the frames that comprise our animation sequence. Each frame is stored as 16,000 bytes: 160 horizontal pixels by 100 vertical pixels, one byte per pixel.

The frames are stored in row order, meaning the first byte corresponds to the first pixel in the top row of the image, the second byte is the next pixel in the row, and so on. Byte 161 corresponds to the first pixel in the second row, and so forth. The frames are stored contiguously in the file. Therefore, if our animation sequence is 30 frames, we read in 16,000 bytes 30 times.

The *DISPRGB.C* Program

DISPRGB.C (Listing 16-1) performs the same basic operations as *PROCESS.C* and *PROCESS.H*; the only difference is that a single-frame rendering from the ray tracer is stored as an *.RGB* file rather than an *.ANI* file. *DISPRGB* lets you view these files directly on the screen, performing the same color histogram processing to reduce the displayable colors to 256.

The first four bytes of the file specify the dimensions of the image (no longer fixed at 160 x 100), using two bytes for each dimension. We don't need a palette because we're storing the red, green, and blue values for each pixel directly. Immediately following the dimensions are the three-byte red, green, and blue color data triplets for each pixel of each animation frame. These values are then processed exactly as described above for the *.TMP* files.

After the image is displayed, we wait for a key to be pressed and then exit the program. This program allows us to view images in any resolution, even high resolution. (Any user-defined resolution up to 1024 x 768 is acceptable.) With *DISPRGB.C*, you can sit back and admire the interesting images the ray tracer can produce at higher resolutions.

About the Graphics Cards

The programs in this chapter use the STB ERGO PowerGraph and Ilon VGA graphics cards. Table 16-1 shows the cards' graphics modes and other data.

Mode	Type	Resolution Characters	Resolution Pixels	Colors	Horizontal Frequency
0,1	Text	40 x 25	320 x 200	16	31.5 KHz
2,3	Text	80 x 25	640 x 200	16	31.5 KHz
4,5	Graphics	40 x 25	320 x 200	4	31.5 KHz
6	Graphics	80 x 25	640 x 200	2	31.5 KHz
7	Text	80 x 25	720 x 350	4	31.5 KHz
8	Text	132 x 25	1056 x 350	16	31.5 KHz
10	Text	132 x 44	1056 x 616	16	31.5 KHz
13	Graphics	40 x 25	320 x 200	16	31.5 KHz
14	Graphics	80 x 25	640 x 200	16	31.5 KHz
15	Graphics	80 x 25	640 x 350	2	31.5 KHz
16	Graphics	80 x 25	640 x 350	16	31.5 KHz
17	Graphics	80 x 30	640 x 480	2	31.5/38.0 KHz
18	Graphics	80 x 30	640 x 480	16	31.5/38.0 KHz
19	Graphics	40 x 25	320 x 200	256	31.5 KHz
34	Text	132 x 44	1056 x 616	16	31.5 KHz
35	Text	132 x 25	1056 x 350	16	31.5 KHz
36	Text	132 x 28	1056 x 400	16	31.5 KHz
41	Graphics	100 x 43	800 x 600	16	35.5/45.0 KHz
45	Graphics	80 x 25	640 x 350	256	31.5 KHz
46	Graphics	80 x 30	640 x 480	256	31.5/38.0 KHz
48	Graphics	100 x 43	800 x 600	256	35.5/45.0 KHz

Table 16-1. Display Modes for PowerGraph ERGO Extended VGA (continued)

Mode	Type	Resolution Characters	Resolution Pixels	Colors	Horizontal Frequency
55	Graphics	128x54	1024x768	16	35.5/48/57 KHz
56	Graphics	128 x 54	1024 x 768	256	35.5/48/57 KHz
106	Graphics	100 x 43	800 x 600	16	35.5/45.0 KHz
120	Graphics	80 x 25	640 x 400	256	31.5 KHz

Table 16-1. Display Modes for PowerGraph ERGO Extended VGA (continued)

As graphics cards become more powerful and less expensive, the ability to display more than 256 colors will become more common. You should be able to adapt the programs in this book to use more advanced displays to better advantage. For the currently available SVGA cards, however, color reduction is a necessary step.

```
/*

        Histogram VGA Color Processor
      Program by Christopher D. Watkins
        'C' Conversion by Larry Sharp

*/

#include "stdio.h"
#include "dos.h"
#include "conio.h"
#include "alloc.h"
#include "mem.h"
#include "math.h"
#include "string.h"
#include "defs.h"
#include "globals.h"
#include "mathb.h"
#include "graphb.h"

Byte Frequency[8192];
```

```
Word Hues[8192];

void Sort(Word First, Word Last)
{
    Word i, j, k;
    Word Pivot, Temp2;
    Byte Temp;

    if(First<Last-1)
    {
        i=First;
        j=Last;
        k=(First+Last)>>1;
        Pivot=(Frequency[i]+Frequency[j]+Frequency[k])/3;
        while(i<j)
        {
            while(Frequency[i]>Pivot)
            ++i;
            while(Frequency[j]<Pivot)
            —j;
            if(i<j)
            {
                Temp=Frequency[i];
                Frequency[i]=Frequency[j];
                Frequency[j]=Temp;
                Temp2=Hues[i];
                Hues[i]=Hues[j];
                Hues[j]=Temp2;
                ++i;
                —j;
            }
        }
        if(j<Last)
        {
            Sort(First,j);
            Sort(j+1,Last);
        }
    }
    if(Frequency[Last]>Frequency[First])
    {
```

```
                Temp=Frequency[First];
                Frequency[First]=Frequency[Last];
                Frequency[Last]=Temp;
                Temp2=Hues[First];
                Hues[First]=Hues[Last];
                Hues[Last]=Temp2;
        }
}

typedef char Name[80];

Name FileName;

void GetFileName()
{
        Byte x, y;

        printf("\nEnter File Name => ");
        x=wherex();
        y=wherey();
        gets(FileName);
        if(strlen(FileName)==0)
        {
                strcpy(FileName,"TEST");
                gotoxy(x, y);
                puts(FileName);
        }
        strcat(FileName, ".RGB");
        puts("");
        puts("");
}

PaletteRegister PalArray;
Word i, j, x, y;
int LastColor;
Word ColorNum;
static Byte
far *ColorHistogram;
Word rc, gc, bc;
FILE *TextDiskFile;
```

```
void CollectColorData()
{
    TextDiskFile=fopen(FileName, "r+b");
    XRes=getw(TextDiskFile);
    YRes=getw(TextDiskFile);
    printf("Image Resolution is %d by %d pixels.\n\n\n", XRes,
                                                          YRes);
    printf("Collecting color data....\n\n");
    for(y=0; y<YRes; y++)
    {
        for(x=0; x<XRes; x++)
        {
            rc=(getc(TextDiskFile))&62;
            gc=(getc(TextDiskFile))&62;
            bc=(getc(TextDiskFile))&62;
            ColorNum=(rc>>1)|(gc<<4)|(bc<<9);
            if(ColorHistogram[ColorNum]<255)

ColorHistogram[ColorNum]=ColorHistogram[ColorNum]+1;
        }
    }
    fclose(TextDiskFile);
    LastColor=-1;
    for(j=0; j<=32767; j++)
    {
        if(ColorHistogram[j]>0)
        {
            ++LastColor;
            Hues[LastColor]=j;
            Frequency[LastColor]=ColorHistogram[j];
        }
    }
}

void SortColorData()
{
    Word d1, Tempd, d2;
    Byte r1, g1, b1;
    Byte r2, g2, b2;
```

```
    printf("There are %d colors.\n\n",LastColor);
    puts("Starting sort.");
    Sort(0, LastColor);
    puts("Sort completed.");
    printf("\nModifying extra colors....\n");
    for(i=0; i<=255; i++)
        Frequency[i]=i;
    for(i=256; i<=LastColor; i++)
    {
        d1=32768;
        for(j=0; j<=255; j++)
        {
            r1=(Hues[i]<<1)&62;
            g1=(Hues[i]>>4)&62;
            b1=(Hues[i]>>9)&62;
            r2=(Hues[j]<<1)&62;
            g2=(Hues[j]>>4)&62;
            b2=(Hues[j]>>9)&62;
            Tempd=Sqr(r1-r2)+Sqr(g1-g2)+Sqr(b1-b2);
            if(Tempd<d1)
            {
                d1=Tempd;
                d2=j;
            }
        }
        Frequency[i]=d2;
    }
}


void MakePalette(PaletteRegister PalArray)
{
    for(j=0; j<=255; j++)
    {
        PalArray[j].Red=(Hues[j]<<1)&62;
        PalArray[j].Grn=(Hues[j]>>4)&62;
        PalArray[j].Blu=(Hues[j]>>9)&62;
    }
}


void GetColorHistogramFromFrequency()
```

```
{
    for(j=0; j<=LastColor; j++)
        ColorHistogram[Hues[j]]=Frequency[j];
}

void Display()
{
    TextDiskFile=fopen(FileName,"r+b");
    XRes=getw(TextDiskFile);
    YRes=getw(TextDiskFile);
    for(y=0; y<YRes; y++)
    {
        for(x=0; x<XRes; x++)
        {
            rc=(getc(TextDiskFile))&62;
            gc=(getc(TextDiskFile))&62;
            bc=(getc(TextDiskFile))&62;
            ColorNum=(rc>>1)|(gc<<4)|(bc<<9);
            Plot(x, y, ColorHistogram[ColorNum]);
        }
    }
    fclose(TextDiskFile);
}

void main(int argc, char **argv)
{
    ColorHistogram=_fmalloc(32768);
    if(ColorHistogram==NULL)
    {
        printf("Not enough memory!\n\n");
        exit(1);
    }
    clrscr();
    printf("\t   Histogram Color Image Processor using Least
                                                Squares Fit\n");
    printf("\t   for VGA 256 Color Modes by Christopher D.
                                                Watkins\n\n");
    if(argc>=2)
    {
        strcpy(FileName, argv[1]);
```

```
                strcat(FileName, ".CPR");
        }
        else
                GetFileName();
        CollectColorData();
        SortColorData();
        Set_Graphics_Mode(XRes, YRes);
        MakePalette(PalArray);
        Set_Palette(PalArray);
        GetColorHistogramFromFrequency();
        Display();
        Exit_Graphics();
        farfree(ColorHistogram);
}
```

Listing 16-1. The *DISPRGB.C* program.

PART VI

APPENDICES

APPENDIX A
Mathematics and Graphics Module Functions

Mathematics Module

```
int Round(double x);
```
round number to nearest integer

```
float Frac(double x);
```
return fractional part of number

```
int Trunc(double x);
```
return integer part of a number

```
float SqrFP(float x);
```
floating-point square root

```
int Sqr(int x);
```
integer square root

```
float Radians(float Angle);
```
convert degrees to radians

```
float Degrees(float Angle);
```
convert radians to degrees

```
float CosD(float Angle);
```
cosine in degrees

```
float SinD(float Angle);
```
   sine in degrees

```
float Power(float Base, int Exponent);
```
   power a^n

```
float Log(float x);
```
   log base 10

```
float Exp10(float x);
```
   exp base 10

```
float Sign(float x);
```
   negative=-1   positive=1   null=0

```
int IntSign(int x);
```
   negative=-1   positive=1   null=0

```
int IntSqrt(int x);
```
   integer square root

```
int IntPower(int Base, int Exponent);
```
   integer power a^n

```
float MIN(float a, float b);
```
   return minimum of two numbers

```
float MAX(float a, float b);
```
   return maximum of two numbers

```
float MIN3(float a, float b, float c);
```
   return minimum of three numbers

```
float MAX3(float a, float b, float c);
```
return maximum of three numbers

```
float MIN4(float a, float b, float c, float d);
```
return minimum of four numbers

```
float MAX4(float a, float b, float c, float d);
```
return maximum of four numbers

```
void Vec(float r, float s, float t, TDA A);
```
make vector

```
void VecInt(int r, int s, int t, TDIA A);
```
make integer vector

```
void UnVec(TDA A, float *r, float *s, float *t)
```
get components of vector

```
void UnVecInt(TDIA A, int *r, int *s, int *t);
```
get components of integer vector

```
float VecDot(TDA A, TDA B);
```
vector dot product

```
void VecCross(TDA A, TDA B, TDA C);
```
vector cross product

```
float VecLen(TDA A);
```
vector length

```
void VecNormalize(TDA A);
```
vector normalize

```
void VecMatxMult(FDA A, Matx4x4 Matrix, FDA B);
```
vector matrix multiply

```
void VecSub(TDA A, TDA B, TDA C);
```
vector subtraction

```
void VecSubInt(TDIA A, TDIA B, TDA C);
```
vector subtraction integer

```
void VecAdd(TDA A, TDA B, TDA C);
```
vector addition of two vectors

```
void VecAdd3(TDA A, TDA B, TDA C, TDA D);
```
vector addition of three vectors

```
void VecCopy(TDA A, TDA B);
```
vector copy

```
void VecCopyInt(TDIA A, TDIA B);
```
vector copy integer vectors

```
void VecLinComb(float r, TDA A, float s, TDA B, TDA C);
```
vector linear combination

```
void VecScalMult(float r, TDA A, TDA B);
```
vector scalar multiple

```
void VecScalMultI(float r, TDIA A, TDA B);
```
vector scalar multiple

```
void VecScalMultInt(float r, TDA A, TDIA B);
```
vector scalar multiple and rounding

```
void VecAddScalMult(float r, TDA A, TDA B, TDA C);
```
vector add scalar multiple

```
void VecNull(TDA A);
```
vector null

```
void VecNullInt(TDIA A);
```
vector null integer

```
void VecElemMult(float r, TDA A, TDA B, TDA C);
```
vector element multiply

```
void VecNegate(TDA A);
```
vector negation

```
void VecMin(TDA a, TDA b, TDA c);
```
create vector of minimum components of two vectors

```
void VecMax(TDA a, TDA b, TDA c);
```
create vector of maximum components of two vectors

```
void ZeroMatrix(Matx4x4 A);
```
zero the elements of a 4x4 matrix

```
void Translate3D(float tx, float ty, float tz, Matx4x4 A);
```
make translation matrix

```
void Scale3D(float sx, float sy, float sz, Matx4x4 A);
```
make scaling matrix

```
void Rotate3D(int m, float Theta, Matx4x4 A);
```
make rotation matrix

```
void Multiply3DMatrices(Matx4x4 A, Matx4x4 B, Matx4x4 C);
```
multiply two 4x4 matrices

```
void MatCopy(Matx4x4 a, Matx4x4 b);
```
copy a matrix to another matrix

```
void PrepareMatrix(float Tx, float Ty, float Tz,
        float Sx, float Sy, float Sz,
        float Rx, float Ry, float Rz,
        Matx4x4 XForm);
```
prepare the transformation matrix (Tm=S*R*T)

```
void PrepareInvMatrix(float Tx, float Ty, float Tz,
        float Sx, float Sy, float Sz,
        float Rx, float Ry, float Rz,
        Matx4x4 XForm);
```
prepare the inverse transformation matrix

```
void Transform(TDA A, Matx4x4 M, TDA B);
```
multipy a vertex by the transformation matrix

```
void InitRand(float Seed);
```
seed random number generator

```
int RandInt(Word Range);
```
get random integer number

```
float Rand();
```
get random floating-point number

Graphics Module

```
void Set_Mode(int Mode);
```
   set graphics mode

```
void Pre_Calc();
```
   initialize scan-line calculations

```
void Plot(Word x, Word y, Byte color);
```
   place pixel to screen

```
void Set_Palette(Palette_Register Hue);
```
   set palette register

```
void Init_Palette(Palette_Register Color);
```
   64 levels of gray, red, green, and blue

```
void Init_Palette_2(Palette_Register Color);
```
   7 colors with 35 intensities each—use with Pixel

```
void Cycle_Palette(Palette_Register Hue);
```
   cycle through palette

```
void Swap(int *first, int *second);
```
   swap two numbers

```
void Circle(Word x, Word y, Word radius, Byte color);
```
   circle-draw routine

```
void Draw(int xx1, int yy1, int xx2, int yy2, Byte color);
```
   line-draw routine

```
void Init_Graphics();
```
   initialize graphics

```
void Set_Graphics_Mode(Word xRes, Word yRes);
```
    used to set the graphics mode based on resolution

```
void Wait_For_Key();
```
    wait for keypress

```
void Exit_Graphics();
```
    sound and wait for keypress before exiting graphics

```
void Title();
```
    set up text screen colors

```
void Init_Plotting(int Ang, int Tlt);
```
    rotation and tilt angles

```
void Init_Perspective(Boolean Perspective, float x, float y,
        float z, float m);
```
    observer location and distances

```
void Map_Coordinates(float X, float Y, float Z, int *Xp, int
        *Yp);
```
    map 3D space onto the 2D screen

```
void Cartesian_Plot_3D(float X, float Y, float Z, Byte Color);
```
    plot a Cartesian system point

```
void Cylindrical_Plot_3D(float Rho, float Theta, float Z, Byte
        Color);
```
    plot a cylindrical system point

```
void Spherical_Plot_3D(float R, float Theta, float Phi, Byte
        Color);
```
    plot a spherical system point

```
void Draw_Line_3D(TDA Pnt1, TDA Pnt2, Byte Color);
```
plot a line from 3D coordinates

```
void Put_Pixel(int x, int y, Byte Color, Byte Intens
```
plot pixel

```
Byte Get_Pixel(Word x, Word y);
```
get pixel

```
Byte Get_Pixel_2(Word x, Word y);
```
another version of Get_Pixel

```
void Put_Axis_And_Palette(Boolean PlaceOnScreen);
```
toggle for axis and palette

```
void Display_Axis();
```
display axis

```
void Display_Palette();
```
display palette on left of screen

```
void Axis_And_Palette();
```
place axis and color palette on screen

Contents of the Code Disk

Directory of C:\BLSC

```
BOOKMISC<DIR>        Chapters 1-4
SCNSCRPT<DIR>        Chapters 9-10
3DMODEL <DIR>        Chapters 5-9
RTSCRPT <DIR>        Chapter  13
RAYTRACE<DIR>        Chapters 11-12
ANIMATE <DIR>        Chapters 14-15
```

Directory of C:\BLSC\BOOKMISC   Chapters 1-4

```
DEFS       H      590     Modules
GLOBALS    H      176
GRAPHB     C      14445
GRAPHB     H      1705
MATHB      C      10772
MATHB      H      2810

3DAVR      C      6568    3D IFS—translation.
3DAVR      DSK    12661
3DAVR      PRJ    5107

3DIFS      C      2506    3D IFS—translation, scaling, and
3DIFS      DSK    12263   rotation.
3DIFS      PRJ    5111

CELL1D     C      3384    Cellular automaton—run WORLD1D to
CELL1D     DSK    17402   create the world, then run either
CELL1D     PRJ    5150    RULE1D or SIER1D to create the
                          rule.
```

RULE1D	C	1896	Run CELL1D to display.
RULE1D	DSK	16412	
RULE1D	PRJ	4986	
SIER1D	C	2231	
SIER1D	DSK	17087	
SIER1D	PRJ	4842	
WORLD1D	C	1651	
WORLD1D	DSK	17272	
WORLD1D	PRJ	4781	
CELL2D	C	4507	Cellular automaton—run WORLD2D to
CELL2D	DSK	17532	create the world, then run either
CELL2D	PRJ	5148	RULE2D or SIER2D to create the
			rule.
RULE2D	C	2497	Run CELL2D to display.
RULE2D	DSK	17437	
RULE2D	PRJ	4778	
SIER2D	C	1684	
SIER2D	DSK	17439	
SIER2D	PRJ	4778	
WORLD2D	C	1859	
WORLD2D	DSK	17634	
WORLD2D	PRJ	4781	
CLOUDS	C	3702	Recursive plasma generator.
CLOUDS	DSK	17681	
CLOUDS	PRJ	5136	
LIFECA	C	5955	Cellular automaton—run LIFRWRLD to
LIFECA	DSK	17695	create the world, then run LIFERULE
LIFECA	PRJ	5148	to create the rule. Run LIFECA to
LIFERULE	C	2549	display.
LIFERULE	DSK	17548	
LIFERULE	PRJ	4780	
LIFEWRLD	C	2788	
LIFEWRLD	DSK	17842	
LIFEWRLD	PRJ	0	
ORB3D-3P	C	5456	Three-dimensional, three-particle
ORB3D-3P	DSK	12147	orbit simulation.
ORB3D-3P	PRJ	5099	

```
PLANT        C      2207    Recursive plant generator.
PLANT        DSK    17762
PLANT        PRJ    5149
```

Directory of C:\BLSC\SCNSCRPT   Chapters 9-10

```
DEFS         H      590     Modules

SCNSCR       C      24960   Scene .SCN script file generator
                            for 3DMODEL.
```

Directory of C:\BLSC\3DMODEL   Chapters 5-9

```
SOLOFREV     SCN    40068   .SCN files for 3DMODEL generated
SPHRPLAN     SCN    13104   by ScnScr.C.
SPHRWALL     SCN    29033
SPINTOR      SCN    23777


DEFS         H      590         Modules
GLOBALS      H      176
GRAPHB       C      14445
GRAPHB       H      1705
MATHB        C      10772
MATHB        H      2810


MODELSUP     H      3351    3DMODEL modeling program. Requires
PROCESS      H      5107    a .SCN file to render and .DAT
3DMODEL      C      31966   object database files to be present
3DMODEL      PRJ    5200    for objects referenced in the .SCN
3DMODEL      DSK    2876    file. Outputs an .ANI file for
3DMODEL      EXE    51244   ANIMATE. .DAT object database
PLANE        DAT    38      files.



CUBE         DAT    102
```

SHPMK	H	2899	Programs to create specific .DAT
CONEPYRM	C	3073	object database files.
CONEPYRM	DSK	17881	
CONEPYRM	PRJ	5195	
CYLINDER	C	2836	
CYLINDER	DSK	17881	
CYLINDER	PRJ	5193	
GRID	C	2638	
GRID	DSK	15962	
GRID	PRJ	5191	
MAKEOBJS	C	2107	
MAKEOBJS	DSK	17745	
MAKEOBJS	PRJ	5195	
SOLOFREV	C	4483	
SOLOFREV	DSK	15958	
SOLOFREV	PRJ	5195	
SPHERE	C	2405	
SPHERE	DSK	14606	
SPHERE	PRJ	5193	
TOROID	C	2935	
TOROID	DSK	17582	
TOROID	PRJ	5193	

Directory of C:\BLSC\RTSCRPT   Chapter 13

DEFS	H	590	Modules
GLOBALS	H	176	
GRAPHB	C	14445	
GRAPHB	H	1705	
MATHB	C	10772	
MATHB	H	2810	
BOUNCE	C	8608	Programs to generate .RT ray tracer
BOUNCE2	C	6986	animation script scene files.
DNA	C	10289	
ENGINE	C	16446	
FLYOVER	C	5166	
NEWTCRAD	C	14435	

ORBIT	C	11006	
ROBOT	C	8917	
SPIN2	C	8815	
WAVES	C	5060	
CANNON	C	15711	Programs to generate .RT ray tracer
DESERT	C	7612	single-frame rendering scene files.
DESK	C	15108	
DIE&CARD	C	17568	
DIE&CARD	DSK	18431	
DIE&CARD	PRJ	5075	
M&T	C	8752	
MOUNT	C	14068	
MOUNT	DSK	18393	
MOUNT	PRJ	5149	
PIANO	C	19198	
POOLTABL	C	19238	
TETRA	C	14711	
TETRA	DSK	18465	
TETRA	PRJ	5147	
TETSPHR2	C	9914	
TETSPHR2	DSK	18443	
TETSPHR2	PRJ	5136	
WAVYORB	C	7052	

Directory of C:\BLSC\RAYTRACE   Chapters 11-12

BOUNCE	RT	72463	.RT files for the ray tracer
BOUNCE2	RT	55723	generated by the animation script
DNA	RT	193463	scene file generators.
ENGINE	RT	155000	
FLYOVER	RT	37418	
NEWTCRAD	RT	127816	
ORBIT	RT	70929	
ROBOT	RT	108062	
SPIN2	RT	71254	
WAVES	RT	35488	

CANNON	RT	6080	.RT files for the ray tracer
DESERT	RT	2751	generated by the single-frame
DESK	RT	6054	rendering scene file generators.
DIE&CARD	RT	18014	
M&T	RT	12698	
MOUNT	RT	20517	
PIANO	RT	15207	
POOLTABL	RT	8158	
TETRA	RT	39857	
TETSPHR2	RT	24894	
WAVYORB	RT	2485	
DEFS	H	590	Modules
GLOBALS	H	176	
GRAPHB	C	14445	
GRAPHB	H	1705	
MATHB	C	10772	
MATHB	H	2810	
RAYTRACE	C	82924	The ray-tracing program. Requires
RAYTRACE	DSK	13372	.RT file for rendering single
			frames
RAYTRACE	PRJ	5237	or animation. Outputs an .RGB file
RAYTRACE	EXE	124138	if a single frame or a .TMP file
			for PROCESS if an animation.
PROCESS	C	6150	Program to perform color reduction
PROCESS	DSK	17817	on the .RT animation scene files.
PROCESS	PRJ	5137	Outputs an .ANI file for ANIMATE.
PROCESS	EXE	34114	
DISP	C	5095	Program to display the .RT single-
DISP	DSK	17767	frame rendering scene files.
DISP	PRJ	5192	
DISP	EXE	33794	

Directory of C:\BLSC\ANIMATE   Chapters 14-15

```
DEFS        H       590     Modules

ANIMATE     C       11333   The animation program. Requires an
ANIMATE     EXE     42499   .ANI file to animate.

SPHRPLAN    ANI     480769  Sample .ANI animation files.
BOUNCE      ANI     480769
DNA         ANI     480769
WAVES       ANI     480769


4677681 bytes total found in 198 files
```

Bibliography

Akeley, Kurt, and Jermoluk, Tom, "High Performance Polygon Rendering,"Computer Graphics (SIGGRAPH '88), Vol. 22, No.4, (August 1988), pp, 239-246.

Blanton, Keith, "Image Extrapolation for Flight Simulator Visual Systems," AIAA Conference, 1988.

Blanton, Keith, "The Design of Videodisc-based Interactive Simulation Visual Systems," SCS Eastern Simulation Conferences, 1988.

Bouville, C., "Bounding Ellipsoids for Ray-Fractal Intersection." (SIGGRAPH '85), Vol. 19, No. 3, (1985), pp. 45-52.

Carpender, L. "Computer Rendering of Fractal Curves and Surfaces." Computer Graphics, (1980), pp. 109 ff.

Demko, S., Hodges, L., and Naylor, B., "Construction of Fractal Objects with Iterated Function Systems." (SIGGRAPH '85), Vol. 19, No. 3, (1985), pp 271-278.

Dewdney, A.K., "Computer Recreations: Exploring the Mandelbrot Set." Computer Graphics, Vol. 20, No. 4, (1985), pp 16 ff.

Escher, M.C., *The World of M.C. ESCHER*, New York: H.N. Abrams, 1971.

Feigenbaum, M.J., "Quantitative Universality for a Class of Non-Linear Transformations." *Journal of Statistical Physics*, Vol. 19, No. 1, (January, 1978), pp. 25-52.

Finlay, Mark, "Fractal Terrain Image Synthesis for Simulation Using Defense Mapping Agency Data," SPIE Technical Symposium on Optics, Electro-Optics, & Sensors, Orlando, FL, 1987.

Finlay, Mark, "Computer Generated 3-D Infrared Background Imagery Model," Report to U.S Army Missile Command, 1983.

Foley, James, van Dam, Andries, Feiner, Steven, and Hughes, John. *Computer Graphics Principles and Practice*, Addison-Wesley, 2nd ed., 1990.

Fournier, Alain, Reeves, William, "A Simple Model of Ocean Waves." Computer Graphics, Vol. 20, No. 4, pp 75-84, 1986.

Glassner, Andrew S., *An Introduction to Ray Tracing*, Academic Press, Ltd., 1989.

Gouraud, H., "Continuous Shading of Curves Surfaces," IEEE Transaction on Computers, Vol. 20, No. 6, (June 1971), pp. 623-628.

Mastin, G.A., Watterberg, P.A., and Mareda, J.F., "Fourier Synthesis of Ocean Scenes." IEEE Computer Graphics and Applications, (March, 1987), pp. 16-24.

Musgrave, F. Kenton, "Uses of Fractional Brownian Motion in Modeling Nature." (SIGGRAPH '91), Course 14 Notes, pp 5-34.

Peitgen, H.O., and Richter, P.H., *The Beauty of Fractals*, Berlin: Springer-Verlag, 1986.

Peitgen, H.O., and Saupe, D., *The Science of Fractal Images*, Berlin: Springer-Verlag, 1988.

Peachy, Darwin, "Modeling Waves and Surf," Computer Graphics, Vol. 20, No. 4, pp. 65-74, 1986.

454

Phong, Bui Tuong, "Illumination for Computer Generated Pictures" Communications of the ACM, Vol. 18, No. 6, (June, 1975), pp. 311-317.

Prusinkiewicz, Przemyslaw, and Hammel, Mark, "Automata, Languages, and Iterated Function Systems." (SIGGRAPH '91), Course 14 Notes, pp 115-143.

Rushmeier, Holly E., "Extending the Radiosity Method to Transmitting and Specularly Reflecting Surfaces." Masters Thesis, Cornell University, 1986.

Saupe, Dietmar, "Simulation und Animation von Wolken mit Fraktalen," GI-19. JAHRESTAGUNG I, Springer-Verlag, 1989.

Watkins, Christopher D., Stevens, Roger T., *Advanced Graphics Programming in Turbo Pascal*, San Mateo: M & T Publishing, 1991.

Watkins, Christopher D., Stevens, Roger T., *Advanced Graphics Programming in C and C++*, San Mateo: M & T Publishing, 1991.

Watt, Alan, *Fundamentals of Three-Dimensional Computer Graphics*, Addison-Wesley, 1989.

Whitted, Turner, "Managing Geometric Complexity with Enhanced Procedural Models." (SIGGRAPH '86), Vol. 20, No. 4, (1986) pp. 189-195.

Index

A Library of Technical References from M&T Books

Fractal Programming in C
by Roger T. Stevens

If you are a programmer wanting to learn more about fractals, this book is for you. Learn how to create pictures that have both beauty and an underlying mathematical meaning. Included are over 50 black and white pictures and 32 full-color fractals. All source code to reproduce these pictures is provided on disk in MS-DOS format requiring an IBM PC or clone with an EGA or VGA card, a color monitor, and a Turbo C, Quick C, or Microsoft C compiler. 580 pp.

Book/Disk (MS-DOS)	**Item #038-9**	**$39.95**
Book only	**Item #037-0**	**$29.95**

Fractal Programming in Turbo Pascal
by Roger T. Stevens

This book equips Turbo Pascal programmers with the tools needed to program dynamic fractal curves. It is a reference that gives full attention to developing the reader's understanding of various fractal curves. More than 100 black and white and 32 full-color fractals are illustrated throughout the book. All source code to reproduce the fractals is available on disk in MS/PC-DOS format. Requires a PC or clone with EGA or VGA, color monitor, and Turbo Pascal 4.0 or later. 462 pp.

Book/Disk (MS-DOS)	**Item #107-5**	**$39.95**
Book	**Item #106-7**	**$29.95**

Graphics Programming in C
by Roger T. Stevens

All the information you need to program graphics in C, including source code, is presented. You'll find complete discussions of ROM BIOS, VGA, EGA, and CGA inherent capabilities; methods of displaying points on a screen; improved, faster algorithms for drawing and filling lines, rectangles, rounded polygons, ovals, circles, and arcs; graphic cursors; and much more! Both Turbo C and Microsoft C are supported. 639 pp.

Book/Disk (MS-DOS)	**Item #019-2**	**$36.95**
Book only	**Item #018-4**	**$26.95**

A Library of Technical References from M&T Books

Advanced Fractal Programming in C
by Roger T. Stevens

Programmers who enjoyed our best-selling *Fractal Programming in C* can move on to the next level of fractal programming with this book. Included are how-to instructions for creating many different types of fractal curves, including source code. Contains 16 pages of full-color fractals. All the source code to generate the fractals is available on an optional disk in MS/PC-DOS format. 305 pp.

Book/Disk (MS-DOS)	Item #097-4	$39.95
Book only	Item #096-6	$29.95

Advanced Graphics Programming in Turbo Pascal
by Roger T. Stevens and Christopher D. Watkins

This new book is must reading for Turbo Pascal programmers who want to create impressive graphic designs on IBM PCs and compatibles. There are 32 pages of full-color graphic displays along with the source code to create these dramatic pictures. Complete explanations are provided on how to tailor the graphics to suit the programmer's needs. Covered are algorithms for creating complex 2-D shapes, including lines, circles and squares; how to create advanced 3-D shapes, wire-frame graphics, and solid images; numerous tips and techniques for varying pixel intensities to give the appearance of roundness to an object; and more. 540 pp.

Book/Disk (MS-DOS)	Item #132-6	$39.95
Book only	Item #131-8	$29.95

1-800-533-4372 (in CA 1-800-356-2002)

ORDER FORM

To Order:

Return this form with your payment to M&T Books, 411 Borel Avenue, Suite 100, San Mateo, CA 94402 or **call toll-free 1-800-533-4372 (in California, call 1-800-356-2002).**

ITEM #	DESCRIPTION	DISK	PRICE

Subtotal	
CA residents add sales tax ___%	
Add $4.50 per item for shipping and handling	
TOTAL	

Charge my:

❑ **Visa**

❑ **MasterCard**

❑ **AmExpress**

❑ **Check enclosed, payable to M&T Books.**

CARD NO. _____

SIGNATURE _____ EXP. DATE _____

NAME _____

ADDRESS _____

CITY _____

STATE _____ ZIP _____

M&T GUARANTEE: If your are not satisfied with your order for any reason, return it to us within 25 days of receipt for a full refund. Note: Refunds on disks apply only when returned with book within guarantee period. Disks damaged in transit or defective will be promptly replaced, but cannot be exchanged for a disk from a different title.

8040

Tell us what you think and we'll send you a free M&T Books catalog

It is our goal at M&T Books to produce the best technical books available. But you can help us make our books even better by letting us know what you think about this particular title.Please take a moment to fill out this card and mail it to us. Your opinion is appreciated.

Tell us about yourself
Name_____
Company_____
Address_____
City_____
State/Zip_____

Title of this book?
_____

Where did you purchase this book?
☐ Bookstore
☐ Catalog
☐ Direct Mail
☐ Magazine Ad
☐ Postcard Pack
☐ Other

Why did you choose this book?
☐ Recommended
☐ Read book review
☐ Read ad/catalog copy
☐ Responded to a special offer
☐ M&T Books' reputation
☐ Price
☐ Nice Cover

How would you rate the overall content of this book?
☐ Excellent
☐ Good
☐ Fair
☐ Poor

Why?
_____
_____

What chapters did you find valuable?
_____
_____
_____

What did you find least useful?
_____
_____
_____

What topic(s) would you add to future editions of this book?
_____
_____
_____

What other titles would you like to see M&T Books publish?
_____
_____
_____

Which format do you prefer for the optional disk?
☐ 5.25"   ☐ 3.5"

Any other comments?
_____
_____
_____

☐ Check here for
M&T Books Catalog

M&T BOOKS